# ENVIRONMENTAL
# LAW

# ENVIRONMENTAL LAW

**Linda A. Malone**

Marshall-Wythe Foundation Professor of Law

Marshall-Wythe School of Law

College of William and Mary

## The *Emanuel Law Outlines* Series

**PUBLISHERS**

1185 Avenue of the Americas, New York, NY 10036
www.aspenpublishers.com

© 2003 Aspen Publishers, Inc.
A Wolters Kluwer Company
*www.aspenpublishers.com*

Printed in the United States of America

ISBN 0-7355-3439-X

This book is intended as a general review of a legal subject. It is not intended as a source of advice for the solution of legal matters or problems. For advice on legal matters, the reader should consult an attorney.

Siegel's, Emanuel, the judge logo, Law In A Flash and design, CrunchTime and design, Strategies & Tactics and design, and The Professor Series are registered trademarks of Aspen Publishers.

# About Aspen Publishers

Aspen Publishers, headquartered in New York City, is a leading information provider for attorneys, business professionals, and law students. Written by preeminent authorities, our products consist of analytical and practical information covering both U.S. and international topics. We publish in the full range of formats, including updated manuals, books, periodicals, CDs, and online products.

Our proprietary content is complemented by 2,500 legal databases, containing over 11 million documents, available through our Loislaw division. Aspen Publishers also offers a wide range of topical legal and business databases linked to Loislaw's primary material. Our mission is to provide accurate, timely, and authoritative content in easily accessible formats, supported by unmatched customer care.

To order any Aspen Publishers title, go to *www.aspenpublishers.com* or call 1-800-638-8437.

To reinstate your manual update service, call 1-800-638-8437.

For more information on Loislaw products, go to *www.loislaw.com* or call 1-800-364-2512.

For Customer Care issues, e-mail CustomerCare@aspenpublishers.com; call 1-800-234-1660; or fax 1-800-901-9075.

**Aspen Publishers**
**A Wolters Kluwer Company**

To Erin and Corey

# Abbreviations Used in Text

## A

**AEA** — Atomic Energy Act

**AFT** — American Farmland Trust

**ALI** — American Law Institute

**ALJ** — Administrative Law Judge

**APA** — Administrative Procedure Act

**AQMA** — Air Quality Maintenance Area under the Clean Air Act

**ASCS** — Agricultural Stabilization and Conservation Service

## B

**BACT** — best available control technology, usually referring to the standard for major sources in prevention of significant deterioration areas under the Clean Air Act (see also BAT and BADT)

**BADT** or **BADCT** — best available demonstrated control technology, usually referring to standards for new sources under the Clean Air Act or Clean Water Act (see also BAT and BACT)

**BAT** — best available control technology, usually referring to the standard for nonconventional and toxic pollutants under the Clean Water Act (see also BADT and BACT)

**BCT** — best conventional pollutant control technology applicable to conventional pollutants under the Clean Water Act

**BDAT** — best demonstrated available technology, treatment standard for hazardous waste under the Resource Conservation and Recovery Act

**BLM** — Bureau of Land Management

**BMP** — best management practice for control of nonpoint sources under the Clean Water Act

**BOD** — biochemical oxygen demand, a conventional pollutant under the Clean Water Act

**BODS** — biochemical oxygen demanding substances (see also BOD)

**BPCTCA** — best practicable control technology currently available under the Clean Water Act, also referred to as BPT

**BPJ** — best professional judgment, a standard utilized in permit issuance in the absence of national effluent limitations under the Clean Water Act

**BPT** — best practicable control technology currently available under the Clean Water Act, also referred to as BPCTCA

## C

**CAA** — Clean Air Act

**CBRA** — Coastal Barrier Resources Act

**CCA** — California Coastal Act

**CEQ** — Council on Environmental Quality, established under the National Environmental Policy Act

**CERCLA** — Comprehensive Environmental Response, Compensation, and Liability Act, also referred to as the Superfund Act

**CO** — carbon monoxide, air pollutant, and one of the criteria pollutants under the Clean Air Act

**CPSC** — Consumer Product Safety Commission

**CRP** — Conservation Reserve Program under the 1990 Farm Bill

**CV** — contingent value under the Comprehensive Environmental Response, Compensation, and Liability Act

**CWA** — Clean Water Act, or the Federal Water Pollution Control Act

**CZEG** — Coastal Zone Management Act

# D

**DER** — Department of Environmental Resources

**DMC** — *de minimis* classification under the Comprehensive Environmental Response, Compensation, and Liability Act

**DNA** — deoxyribonucleic acid

**DO** — dissolved oxygen, an indicator of water quality

**DOE** — Department of Energy

**DOI** — Department of the Interior

**DOL** — Department of Labor

**DOT** — Department of Transportation

**DRI** — development of regional impact

# E

**EA** — environmental assessment under the National Environmental Policy Act

**EAJA** — Equal Access to Justice Act

**ECARP** — Environmental Conservation Acreage Reserve Program under the 1990 Farm Bill

**EDF** — Environmental Defense Fund

**EIA** — environmental impact assessment under the National Environmental Policy Act

**EIS** — environmental impact statement under the National Environmental Policy Act

**EPA** — Environmental Protection Agency

**ESA** — Endangered Species Act

**EUP** — experimental use permit under the Federal Insecticide, Fungicide, and Rodenticide Act

# F

**FAA** — Federal Aviation Administration

**FDF** — fundamentally different factor variance under the Clean Water Act

**FEISS** — Federal Environmental Impact Statement under the National Environmental Policy Act

FEMA — Federal Emergency Management Agency

FIFRA — Federal Insecticide, Fungicide, and Rodenticide Act

FLPMA — Federal Land Policy and Management Act

FOIA — Freedom of Information Act

FONSI — finding of no significant impact under the National Environmental Policy Act

FPPA — Farmland Protection Policy Act

FSA — Food Security Act (Farm Bill)

FWPCA — Federal Water Pollution Control Act, commonly referred to as the Clean Water Act

FWS — Fish and Wildlife Service under the Endangered Species Act


## G

GACT — generally available control technology for area sources under the Clean Air Act

g/BHR-hr — grams per brake horsepower hour under the Clean Air Act

GSA — General Services Administration

GVWR — gross vehicle weight rating under the Clean Air Act


## H

HAP — hazardous air pollutant under the Clean Air Act

HC — hydrocarbon, air pollutant, and one of the criteria pollutants under the Clean Air Act until 1982

HCP — habitat conservation plan under the Endangered Species Act

HRS — Hazard Ranking System under the Comprehensive Environmental Response, Compensation, and Liability Act

HSWA — Hazardous and Solid Waste Amendments to the Resource Conservation and Recovery Act


## I

ICC — Interstate Commerce Commission

ICS — individual control strategy for a toxic pollutant under the Clean Water Act

I/M — vehicle emission inspection and maintenance under the Clean Air Act

ITC — Interagency Testing Committee under the Toxic Substances Control Act


## L

LAER — lowest achievable emissions rate for major sources in nonattainment areas under the Clean Air Act

lb/MBtu — pounds per million British thermal units, a measurement of heat energy

LDT — light-duty truck under the Clean Air Act

LEV — low emission vehicle under the Clean Air Act

LMFBR — liquid metal fast breeder reactor

LVW — loaded vehicle weight under the Clean Air Act

## M

MACT — maximum achievable control technology for hazardous air pollutants under the Clean Air Act

MSHA — Mine Safety and Health Administration

MY — model year under the Clean Air Act

## N

NAAQS — National Ambient Air Quality Standard under the Clean Air Act

NAD — non-applicability determination for preconstruction review in prevention of significant deterioration areas under the Clean Air Act

NALS — National Agricultural Land Study

NBAR — non-binding allocations of responsibility under the Comprehensive Environmental Response, Compensation, and Liability Act

NCP — National Contingency Plan under the Comprehensive Environmental Response, Compensation, and Liability Act

ND — non-detectable value of a water pollutant

NEPA — National Environmental Policy Act

NFIP — National Flood Insurance Program

NFMA — National Forest Management Act

NGPRP — Northern Great Plains Resources Program

NIH — National Institute of Health

NMHC — non-methane hydrocarbon, air pollutant regulated under the Clean Air Act

NMOG — non-methane organic gas, air pollutant regulated under the Clean Air Act

$NO_x$ — nitrogen oxide, air pollutant

$NO_2$ — nitrogen dioxide, air pollutant, and one of the criteria pollutants under the Clean Air Act

NPDES — National Pollutant Discharge Elimination System under the Clean Water Act

NPL — National Priorities List under the Comprehensive Environmental Response, Compensation, and Liability Act

NRDC — Natural Resources Defense Council

NSPS — new source performance standard under the Clean Air Act and Clean Water Act

NWF — National Wildlife Federation

NWP 26 — Nationwide Permit Number 26 under the Clean Water Act

## O

$O_3$ — ozone, air pollutant, and one of the criteria pollutants under the Clean Air Act

OCPSF — organic chemicals, plastics, and synthetic fibers, an industrial classification under the Clean Water Act

**OCRM** — Office of Ocean and Coastal Resource Management under the Coastal Zone Management Act

**OCS** — outer continental shelf

**OCSLA** — Outer Continental Shelf Lands Act

**OMB** — Office of Management and Budget

**OPA** — Oil Pollution Act

**OSHA** — Occupational Safety and Health Administration

**P**

**PCBs** — polychlorinated biphenyls, regulated under the Toxic Substances Control Act and other environmental statutes

**PDR** — purchase of development rights

**pH** — quantitative measure of the acidity of water and a conventional water pollutant under the Clean Water Act

**PM** — particulate matter, air pollutant (see also PM-10 and TSP)

**PM-10** — particulate matter of 10 micrometers or less, the particulate standard which replaced in 1987 the National Ambient Air Quality Standard for total suspended particulates

**POM** — polycyclic organic matter, air pollutant regulated under the Clean Air Act

**POTW** — publicly owned treatment works under the Clean Water Act

**lb/MBtu** — pounds per million British thermal units, a measurement of heat energy

**ppb** — parts per billion

**ppm** — parts per million

**PRA** — Paperwork Reduction Act

**PRP** — potentially responsible party under the Comprehensive Environmental Response, Compensation, and Liability Act

**PSD** — prevention of significant deterioration under the Clean Air Act

**PSES** — pretreatment standard for existing sources under the Clean Water Act

**PSI** — pounds per square inch

**R**

**RA** — regional administrator of the Environmental Protection Agency

**RACT** — reasonably achievable control technology for existing sources in nonattainment areas under the Clean Air Act

**RCA** — Soil and Water Resources Conservation Act

**RCRA** — Resource Conservation and Recovery Act

**RDT** — rural density transfer

**RHA** — Rivers and Harbors Act

**RVP** — Reid vapor pressure

# S

**SARA** — Superfund Amendments and Reauthorization Act

**SDWA** — Safe Drinking Water Act

**SIP** — state implementation plan under the Clean Air Act

**SOx** — sulfur oxides, air pollutant

**SO₂** — sulfur dioxide, air pollutant, and one of the criteria pollutants under the Clean Air Act

**SS** — suspended solids, a conventional water pollutant under the Clean Water Act

# T

**TCDD** — 2, 3, 7, 8-tetrachlorodibenzo-p-dioxin (dioxin), toxic byproduct covered by the Comprehensive Environmental Response, Compensation, and Liability Act

**TCP** — 2, 4, 5-trichlorophenol, toxic byproduct covered by the Comprehensive Environmental Response, Compensation, and Liability Act

**TDR** — transferable development rights

**TMDL** — total maximum daily load set as part of state water quality standards under the Clean Water Act

**TOSCA or TSCA** — Toxic Substances Control Act

**TSDFs** — treatment, storage, and disposal facilities under the Resource Conservation and Recovery Act

**TSP** — total suspended particulates, air pollutant (see also PM-10 and particulates)

**TSS** — total suspended solids, a conventional water pollutant under the Clean Water Act (see also SS)

**TVA** — Tennessee Valley Authority

# U

**UCA** — Uniform Contribution Act

**UCAJTA** — Uniform Contribution Among Joint Tortfeasors Act

**UCFA** — Uniform Comparative Fault Act

**USDA** — United States Department of Agriculture

**USLE** — universal soil loss equation

# V

**VOC** — volatile organic compound, air pollutant which is precursor to ozone

# W

**WEE** — wind erosion equation

**WQA** — Water Quality Act of 1987, amending the Clean Water Act

**WQM** — water quality management under the Clean Water Act

**WQS** — water quality standard under the Clean Water Act

# Summary of Contents

# Table of Contents

CHAPTER 1

## APPROACHES AND METHODOLOGIES

CHAPTER 2

# COMMON LAW THEORIES AND ENVIRONMENTAL LITIGATION

CHAPTER 3

# THE JUDICIAL ROLE IN ENVIRONMENTAL LITIGATION AND THE ADMINISTRATIVE PROCESS

CHAPTER 4

# CONSTITUTIONAL LIMITS ON ENVIRONMENTAL REGULATION

CHAPTER 5

# NATIONAL ENVIRONMENTAL POLICY ACT (NEPA)

CHAPTER 6

# THE CLEAN AIR ACT (CAA)

CHAPTER 7

# THE FEDERAL WATER POLLUTION CONTROL ACT (FWPCA)

## CHAPTER 8

# SAFE DRINKING WATER ACT (SDWA)

CHAPTER 9
# CONTROL OF TOXIC SUBSTANCES

CHAPTER 10

# LAND USE

CHAPTER 11

# INTERNATIONAL ENVIRONMENTAL LAW

# Preface

Thank you for buying this book.

Here are some of its special features:

- **Casebook Correlation Chart** — This chart, located just after this Preface, correlates each section of the Outline with the pages covering the same topic in the leading environmental law casebooks.

- **Capsule Summary** — This is a summary of the key concepts of environmental law, specifically designed for use in the last week or so before your final exam.

- **Quiz Yourself** — At the end of every chapter there are short-answer questions and answers.

- **Exam Tips** — These tips alert you to issues most often appearing on exams, and factual patterns commonly used to test those issues.

This book is useful both throughout the semester and for exam preparation. Here are a few suggestions for using it:

1. During the semester, use the book in preparing each night for the next day's class. To do this, first read your casebook. Then, use the *Casebook Correlation Chart* to get an idea of what part of the Outline to read. Reading the Outline will give you a sense of how the cases in your casebook fit into the overall structure of the subject. You may want to use a highlighter to mark key portions of the Outline.
2. If you mark your outline for the course, use this book to give you a preliminary structure, and to supply black-letter principles. The Capsule Summary is helpful for this purpose.
3. When studying for exams, read the Capsule Summary to get an overview. This will probably take about one day.
4. Either during exam study or earlier in the semester, do some or all of the Quiz Yourself short-answer questions. When you do these questions: (1) record your short "answer" on the small blank line provided after the question, but also (2) try to write out a "mini essay" on a separate piece of paper.
5. Three or four days before the exam, review the Exam Tips appearing at the end of each chapter. These Tips can help you spot the issues in the short-answer questions. Follow up from the Tips to the main Outline's discussion of the topic.
6. The night before the exam: (1) do some Quiz Yourself questions to review the most likely sections to be tested; and (2) re-scan the Exam Tips (spending about two to three hours).

Even if you never practice as an environmental lawyer, the knowledge you have acquired in this field is fundamental to today's law practice. Environmental law now pervades almost every area of the law — including corporate law, real estate law, bankruptcy, and securities law.

Good luck in your Environmental Law course. If you'd like any other publications of Aspen Publishers, you can find them at your bookstore or at *www.aspenpublishers.com.*

*Linda Malone*
*William and Mary Law School*

July 2003

# Casebook Correlation Chart

Note: general sections of the outline are omitted for this chart.
NC = not directly covered by this casebook.

| Emanuel's Environmental Law Outline (by chapter and section heading) | Anderson, Glicksman, Mandelker & Tarlock: *Environmental Protection* (3d ed. 1999) | Findley & Farber: *Cases and Materials on Environmental Law* (5th ed. 1999) | Percival, Miller, Schroeder & Leape: *Environmental Regulation* (4th ed. 2003) | Plater, Abrams, Goldfarb & Graham: *Environmental Law and Policy* (2d ed. 1998) | Tabb & Malone: *Environmental Law* (2d ed. 1997) |
|---|---|---|---|---|---|
| CHAPTER 1 APPROACHES AND METHODOLOGIES | | | | | |
| I. Methods of Environmental Regulation | NC | NC | 111-139 | 587-610 | NC |
| II. Economic Considerations | 70-94 | 42-62, 728-740 | 24-35 | 97-124 | 6-21 |
| III. Ethical Considerations | 58-70 | 62-77, 740-744 | 9-23 | 6-16 | 21-45 |
| CHAPTER 2 COMMON LAW THEORIES AND ENVIRONMENTAL LITIGATION | | | | | |
| I. Nuisance as a Common Law Action | 13-19 | 267-275, 290-302 | 61-85 | 158-187 | 73-90 |
| II. Damages at Common Law | 13-19 | 708-726 | NC | 197-232 | 49-73 |
| III. Other Common Law Causes of Action | 13-19 | NC | 85-88 | 187-197 | NC |
| IV. Causation | 773-796 | | 75-78 | | 51-53, 56-57 |
| V. Procedural Issues | NC | | NC | | NC |
| CHAPTER 3 THE JUDICIAL ROLE IN ENVIRONMENTAL LITIGATION AND THE ADMINISTRATIVE PROCESS | | | | | |
| I. Subject Matter Jurisdiction in the Federal Courts | 594-613 | 118-123 | NC | NC | NC |
| II. Standing | 97-135 | 80-118 | 973-996, 1007-1018 | 398-414 | 181-220 |
| III. Reviewability of Administrative Decisions | 97-171 | 118-134 | 95-96 | 381-391, 427-430 | NC |
| IV. Remedies | 1027-1048, 1085-1140 | 567-703 | NC | 382-383, 914-915, 928-934 | NC |

| Emanuel's Environmental Law Outline (by chapter and section heading) | Anderson, Glicksman, Mandelker & Tarlock: *Environmental Protection* (3d ed. 1999) | Findley & Farber: *Cases and Materials on Environmental Law* (5th ed. 1999) | Percival, Miller, Schroeder & Leape: *Environmental Regulation* (4th ed. 2003) | Plater, Abrams, Goldfarb & Graham: *Environmental Law and Policy* (2d ed. 1998) | Tabb & Malone: *Environmental Law* (2d ed. 1997) |
|---|---|---|---|---|---|
| **CHAPTER 4** **CONSTITUTIONAL LIMITS ON ENVIRONMENTAL REGULATION** | | | | | |
| I. Introduction | NC | 202-223 | 100-104 | 323-344 | 91 |
| II. The Reach of the Commerce Clause | 594-598 | 214-217, 223-250 | 106-111, 587-604, 866-887 | 344-356 | 91-112 |
| III. Limitations Under the Takings Clause | 346-347, 355-362, 729-731 | 744-763 | 719-781 | 1035-1102 | 126-179 |
| IV. Limitations on Federal Law Under the Tenth Amendment | NC | 210-223 | 104-108 | 356-370 | 112-126 NC |
| **CHAPTER 5** **NATIONAL ENVIRONMENTAL POLICY ACT (NEPA)** | | | | | |
| I. General Information | 191-199 | 134-137 | 783-792 | 611-618 | 235-239 |
| II. The Environmental Impact Statement (EIS) | 199-309 | 138-200 | 792-850 | 639-653 | 240-344 |
| III. Substantive Review Under NEPA | 265-269 | NC | 830 | 649-651 | 343-344 |
| IV. International Application of NEPA | NC | NC | | 616 | 279-286 |
| V. State Environmental Policy Acts | 309-311 | NC | NC | NC | NC |
| VI. Criticisms of NEPA | 311-318 | 200-201 | | 615 | NC |
| **CHAPTER 6** **THE CLEAN AIR ACT (CAA)** | | | | | |
| I. Air Pollution Regulation Prior to 1970 | 374-376 | | 87-89, 494-498 | | 347-349 |
| II. Key Statutory Provisions of the CAA | 379-387 | NC | 499-500, 554-555 | 442-446 | 347-350 |
| III. Air Quality Standards | 388-437 | NC | 501-521 | 446-458 | 350-368 |
| IV. Air Quality Control Regions and State Implementation Plans | 437-458 | 344-368 | 521-532 | 458-483 | 368-389 |
| V. Nonattainment Areas | 463-507 | 360-368 | 496, 536 | 483-493 | 380-389 |
| VI. Prevention of Significant Deterioration (PSD) Areas | 507-531 | 355-359 | 496 | 493-495 | 389-415 |
| VII. Visibility Protection | 521-531 | 820 | NC | NC | 415-427 |
| VIII. Interstate and International Air Pollution | 531-551 | 278-282, 399-403 | 141, 541-552 | 493-501 | 439-445 |
| IX. Nationwide Emission Limitations | 458-463, 531 | 303-315 | 542-549, 554-558 | 446-449 | 445-486 |
| X. Permit Program | 541-549, 564-573 | 387-404 | 532-536 | 473-483, 746-754 | 427-439, 486-493 |
| XI. Enforcement | 387 | NC | 944 | 905-906, 912-916, 928, 940-942 | 493-522 |

| Emanuel's Environmental Law Outline (by chapter and section heading) | Anderson, Glicksman, Mandelker & Tarlock: *Environmental Protection* (3d ed. 1999) | Findley & Farber: *Cases and Materials on Environmental Law* (5th ed. 1999) | Percival, Miller, Schroeder & Leape: *Environmental Regulation* (4th ed. 2003) | Plater, Abrams, Goldfarb & Graham: *Environmental Law and Policy* (2d ed. 1998) | Tabb & Malone: *Environmental Law* (2d ed. 1997) |
|---|---|---|---|---|---|
| **CHAPTER 7** **THE FEDERAL WATER POLLUTION CONTROL ACT (FWPCA)** | | | | | |
| I. Regulatory Framework | 585-594 | 315-318 | 579-580, 587-604 | 502-552 | 523-542 |
| II. Key Statutory Provisions of the CWA | 590-594 | | 581-587 | | 523-528 |
| III. National Pollutant Discharge Elimination System (NPDES) Program | 591-594, 613-620, 631-634 | 315-319 | 579, 582, 585, 604-605, 610-611, 620, 637, 648, 662, 695 | 508-510, 516-533 | NC |
| IV. Pretreatment Program for Indirect Discharges | 735-739 | 342-343 | 583, 632-636 | 525-526 | 564-568 |
| V. Water Quality Standards | 668-714 | 368-377 | 578, 639-640 | 533-545 | 584-623 |
| VI. Permits | 613-615 | 315-319 | 604-605, 610-611 | 516-545 | 535-536 |
| VII. Enforcement | 1073-1126 | 317-318, 341 | 582-583, 585, 933, 943 | 881-885, 908-919, 931-942 | 576-583 |
| VIII. Nonpoint Source Pollution | 613-631 | NC | 575-576, 694-699 | 513-515, 545-549 | 631-635 |
| IX. Wetlands | 602-613, 719-733 | 764-777 | 593-602, 673-693 | 368-369, 1151-1162 | 641-700 |
| **CHAPTER 8** **SAFE DRINKING WATER ACT (SDWA)** | | | | | |
| I. Purpose | 862-870 | 343 | 427-443 | 526-527 | NC |
| II. Protection Methods | 862-870 | 343 | 428-431 | 361, 795, 796 | NC |
| **CHAPTER 9** **CONTROL OF TOXIC SUBSTANCES** | | | | | |
| I. Risk Assessment and Management | 745-837 | 405-473 | 343-470 | 124-156 | NC |
| II. The Resource Conservation and Recovery Act (RCRA) | 892-945 | 515-554, 600-612 | 174-201, 220-223 | 764-802 | 701-747 |
| III. Comprehensive Environmental Response, Compensation, and Liability Act (CERCLA) | 957-1071 | 613-675 | 223-272 | 803-866, 945-949 | 749-866 |
| IV. Toxic Substances Control Act (TSCA) | 840-862 | 496-513 | 407-425 | 593-600, 730-743 | 867-906 |
| V. Federal Insecticide, Fungicide, and Rodenticide Act (FIFRA) | 862 | 474-496 | 86-87, 101-102, 386-387, 1097, 1099, 1100 | 717-730 | 907-946 |

| Emanuel's Environmental Law Outline (by chapter and section heading) | Anderson, Glicksman, Mandelker & Tarlock: *Environmental Protection* (3d ed. 1999) | Findley & Farber: *Cases and Materials on Environmental Law* (5th ed. 1999) | Percival, Miller, Schroeder & Leape: *Environmental Regulation* (4th ed. 2003) | Plater, Abrams, Goldfarb & Graham: *Environmental Law and Policy* (2d ed. 1998) | Tabb & Malone: *Environmental Law* (2d ed. 1997) |
|---|---|---|---|---|---|
| **CHAPTER 10** **LAND USE** | | | | | |
| I. Coastal Zone Management | NC | 792-806 | 580-581, 705, 709-710 | 1135-1142 | 951-972 |
| II. Soil Conservation | NC | NC | 708-709 | 1121-1130 | 972-988 |
| III. Farmland Preservation | NC | NC | 707-708, 718-719 | 181-185 | 988-1016 |
| IV. Special Management Techniques | NC | NC | | 1163-1170 | 1017-1032 |
| V. The Endangered Species Act (ESA) | 325-355 | 820-837 | 842-843, 858-865, 887-920 | 367-368, 672-709 | 1032-1053 |
| **CHAPTER 11** **INTERNATIONAL ENVIRONMENTAL LAW** | | | | | |
| I. Emergence of International Environmental Law | NC | 22-37 | 1033-1037 | 1207-1231 | NC |
| II. Transboundary Pollution | 549-551 | 266-267 | 1036-1037 | 1183-1198 | 439-445 |
| III. Ozone Depletion and Global Warming | 551-564 | 20-21, 23, 25, 34-37 | 1046-1048 | 560-572, 1229 | NC |
| IV. Wildlife Preservation | NC | 23-24 | 51-57, 922 | 1199-1203 | NC |
| V. Hazardous Waste, Radioactive Pollution, and Environmental Emergencies | NC | 23 | 1098-1108 | 1174-1198 | NC |
| VI. Antarctica | NC | NC | NC | NC | 279-286 |
| VII. Deforestation | NC | 25 | NC | NC | NC |
| VIII. Desertification/Land Degradation | NC | 25-26 | NC | NC | NC |
| IX. Marine Environment | NC | 22-23 | 579-580, 1081-1086 | 1199-1203 | NC |
| X. International Trade and Environment | NC | 253-266 | 1075-1100 | 1225 | NC |
| XI. Military Activities and the Environment | NC | 22 | NC | NC | NC |

# Capsule Summary

This Capsule Summary is intended for review at the end of the semester. Reading it is not a substitute for mastering the material in the main outline. The order of topics is occasionally somewhat different from that in the main outline; that's because this Capsule Summary is meant to be a separate outline for night-before-the exam review, not just be a summary of the main outline.

CHAPTER I

# APPROACHES AND METHODOLOGIES

## I. METHODS OF ENVIRONMENTAL REGULATION

There are *three main approaches* to providing protection for the environment.

**A. Imposed controls:** The government can protect the environment by *dictating amounts or methods* of controlling pollution. The controls may be based on:

1. the existing technology's ability to control the pollution (*technology-based standards*, such as BAT limitations), or, [2]

2. the environment's ability to assimilate the pollution (ambient *environmental quality standards*, such as NAAQSs). [2]

**B. Market incentives:** The government may use market forces to induce private organizations to reduce pollution to the levels that they find economically desirable.

1. **Effluent fees:** The most direct method is to *tax the polluter* based on the amount of pollution it creates. [2]

2. **Marketable pollution rights:** Marketable pollution rights create a system in which each facility is allocated an allowable amount of pollution and is *permitted to sell* its surplus by "emissions trading." [2-3]

   a. **Netting:** Netting allows a firm to avoid the most stringent emissions limits by *reducing emissions from another source* within the same plant as if a "bubble" were placed over the entire plant.

   b. **Offsets:** Offsetting allows a firm to *obtain emission credits* from sources in the same area, through internal or external trades, to offset its new emissions.

   c. **Bubbles:** By placing an imaginary *bubble over a multi-source plant*, in effect, emission credits are created by some sources within the plant and used by others.

   d. **Banking:** Banking provides a mechanism for firms to *save emission credits* for future use.

3. **Subsidies:** The converse of taxing a polluter is to give a *subsidy* to the facilities that produce the least pollution. [3]

C. **Information disclosure:** A third approach to protecting the environment is the requirement that *information* be produced about *the effects* of an action. The publication of information about the facility's actions may influence the facility to choose a less harmful alternative. [3]

## II. ECONOMIC CONSIDERATIONS

Both the government and individual profit-seeking facilities take economic considerations into account when determining the level of pollution to set.

A. **Externalities:** Externalities are effects from an activity that are not directly reflected in the costs of production. [3]

B. **Economic analysis**

1. **Cost-benefit:** A cost-benefit analysis compares the cost of an action or regulation to the benefit it produces. [3]

2. **Cost-effectiveness:** A cost effectiveness analysis compares the cost of two options as well as how effective each will be. [3]

3. **Cost-oblivious:** The cost oblivious model describes the situation in which protection is so important that regulation is mandated without regard to the cost of implementation. [3]

## III. ETHICAL CONSIDERATIONS

Aside from economic considerations, there are ethical issues which often conflict with economic considerations. For example:

A. **Protecting nature**. [3]

B. **Protecting future generations**. [3]

C. **Environmental justice:** The secondary effects of environmental regulation, especially those that *disproportionately affect the poor or minorities* by redirecting the cost of protection or the place-ment of facilities. [4]

1. **Problems with siting locally undesirable land uses (LULUs):** There is a concern that sites for such uses are placed most often in low income and minority neighborhoods. These sites are problematic in part because *benefits are received by a large population* but the *costs are imposed on by a small group*. [4]

2. **Compensation proposals:** One solution to such disparate effects and the resulting opposition to LULU siting is to *compensate the community* in which the proposed site will be located. [4]

   a. **Different types of proposals:** Compensation may serve as either a *remedy for damages*, as a mitigating factor, or as a *reward and incentive* for the community's acceptance.

   b. **Justifications for proposals:** Proponents argue for the positive effects of compensation, in that it *reduces community opposition, promotes efficiency, and results in equity.*

    c. **Equitable concerns:** Positive compensation effects must be weighed against questions of fairness including *whether it is moral to pay a community to assume health and safety risks, how "voluntary" a poor community's acceptance of compensation is, and the lack of representation* for future generations.

3. **Equal protection:** In one recent case, community members protested a landfill site adjacent to a minority neighborhood, and challenged its placement on equal protection grounds. The court allowed the siting, holding that the plaintiffs failed to prove a discriminatory intent in the decision-making process. *East Bibb Twiggs Nhd. Assoc. v. Macon-Bibb County Planning & Zoning Comm.*, 706 F. Supp. 880 (M.D. Ga.), *aff'd*, 888 F.2d 1573 (11th Cir. 1989). [4-5]

CHAPTER 2

# COMMON LAW THEORIES AND ENVIRONMENTAL LITIGATION

## I. NUISANCE AS A COMMON LAW ACTION

The primary theory of recovery for environmental damage at common law was the nuisance cause of action.

A. **Types of actions**

1. **Private nuisance:** A private nuisance exists when one's conduct, whether negligent or intentional, *unreasonably* interferes with the *use and enjoyment of another's property.* A private nuisance is a suit filed by private citizens who have individual claims. [7]

2. **Public nuisance:** A public nuisance exists when one's conduct *unreasonably* interferes with a right common to the public. A public nuisance action is *filed by the government* in representation of the public. An individual can only file a public nuisance claim if that individual can show *"special" damage* that is more severe and distinct from the public harm. [8]

B. **Availability of equitable relief:** The availability of injunctive relief depends upon whether the economic effects of an injunction are *required to protect* some important interest and whether the nuisance is *prospective in nature.* [8]

1. **Balancing test:** The court must balance the *competing interests* and *hardships* of the parties in determining whether to award injunctive relief. [8]

2. **Prospective nuisances:** A party seeking an injunction of a prospective nuisance must show a *sufficiently serious and immediate threat of irreparable injury.* [8]

C. **Standing in nuisance actions:** An individual must show *special damage* in order to sue to abate a public nuisance. Special damage is damage *distinct from* and *more severe* than that suffered by other members of the public. [8]

D. **Preemption of nuisance claims by federal environmental protection statutes:** The Supreme Court has determined when there is preemption of a nuisance cause of action by federal environmental statutes in several key cases. [8-9]

## II. DAMAGES AT COMMON LAW

Common law damages may undercompensate for injuries to natural resources because of the difficulty of quantifying such damage.

**A. Cost of restoration damages:** Both courts and legislatures at the state and federal level have expanded damages to include the *cost of restoring and rehabilitating* an injured environment to its preexisting condition. [9]

**B. Alternative damage theories**

1. **Increased risk of disease:** A plaintiff may recover for his or her increased or enhanced risk of disease by establishing that the disease is medically *reasonably certain to follow* from the plaintiff's present injury. [9]

2. **Fear of the increased risk of disease:** A plaintiff may recover for *emotional distress* suffered from *fear of contracting a disease* by showing that such distress is a *foreseeable* or natural consequence of the present injury. Emotional distress cannot be too remote or tenuous. [10]

3. **Medical monitoring:** A plaintiff may recover the costs of *periodic medical examinations* to detect and diagnose the onset of disease. [10]

   a. **Rationale:** The medical monitoring cause of action developed because an individual exposed to a toxic substance would not have to be tested periodically but for the exposure. [10]

   b. **Elements:** [10]

      i. *Significant exposure*;

      ii. *Increased risk*;

      iii. *Necessary exams*; and

      iv. *Available procedures*: Early detection of disease is possible because medical procedures exist.

**C. Prejudgment interest:** Courts will award prejudgment interest if the *claim is liquidated* (ascertainable in amount) and the *date of injury is determinable*. Courts are generally reluctant to award prejudgment interest in tort claims unless the nature of the harm to real or personal property is *susceptible to valuation with reasonable certainty prior to trial*. [10-11]

**D. Temporary vs. permanent damages in nuisance actions**

1. **Temporary nuisance and damages:** A nuisance is temporary if *alteration or abatement* of the activity constituting the nuisance is possible. Temporary damages include the *reasonable cost of repair* and any special damages. [11]

2. **Permanent nuisance and damages:** A nuisance is permanent if the cause of injury is *fixed*, and the property will always remain *subject to that injury*. Permanent damages are the *diminished fair market value* of the property. *McAlister v. Atlantic Richfield Co.* [11]

**E. Punitive damages:** Punitive damages may be *available under common law or by statute*. Punitive damages have generally been held to be constitutional by the Supreme Court. Some environmental statutes contain limits on punitive damages. [11]

**F. Economic losses:** The traditional rule is that *no recovery exists* in negligence for economic losses absent physical harm to person or property. Some courts have departed from this rule. [11]

# III. OTHER COMMON LAW CAUSES OF ACTION

Besides nuisance law, other remedies under common law exist to ensure the protection of the environment and to compensate victims of pollution. [11-12]

**A. Trespass:** A trespass involves an ***unlawful interference*** with one's property. A trespass in an environmental context may occur when a person's or company's ***actions have resulted in pollutants entering onto another's property***. [12]

**B. Negligence:** In some cases, environmental pollution may have been caused by a ***failure to use the care necessary*** under the given circumstances. [12]

**C. Strict liability:** A person or company can be liable for environmental damage ***regardless of negligence or fault***.

    **1. Ultrahazardous activity:** A party may be held strictly liable if engaging in an "ultrahazardous" or "abnormally dangerous" activity, such as toxic waste disposal. [12]

    **2. Product liability:** A manufacturer or seller may be held strictly liable for damages or injuries caused by the use of a product. In most cases, a plaintiff must prove either that there is a ***defect in the design*** of the product, or that the ***manufacturer failed to warn*** of the risks involved in the use of the product. [12]

# IV. CAUSATION

All private common law actions require the plaintiff to show that the defendant's actions were the ***proximate cause*** of the injury or damage. The plaintiff has the burden of proving by a preponderance of evidence that the pollution caused by the defendant caused the injury or damage. There has also been debate about the level of scrutiny scientific evidence should receive. In answer, the Supreme Court held that ***scientific evidence need not be known with certainty***, but must be supported by appropriate validation; the trial judge has the power to screen such evidence for both relevance and reliability. *Daubert v. Merrell-Dow Pharmaceuticals, Inc.* [12]

# V. PROCEDURAL ISSUES

Some procedural issues exist that may put restraints on an environmental tort action.

**A. Statute of limitations:** Statutes of limitations place a ***limit on the time*** in which a person can file a tort action. [12-13]

    **Problem:** For many toxic pollutants, there are ***long latency periods*** that exist from the time the person is exposed to the pollutant to the occurrence of the disease. As a result, a number of state statutes begin to ***run upon discovery*** rather than exposure.

**B. Splitting the causes of action:** Most jurisdictions require that all claims arising from a common set of facts be brought in ***one action***. Plaintiffs are not allowed to divide or split their claims by suing for some damages in one suit and other damages in a latter suit both arising from the same facts. [13]

C. **Class action suits:** Problems may result from overly broad class action settlements, which **could preclude** legitimate causes of action that arise later in time. [13]

CHAPTER 3

# THE JUDICIAL ROLE IN ENVIRONMENTAL LITIGATION AND THE ADMINISTRATIVE PROCESS

## I. SUBJECT MATTER JURISDICTION IN THE FEDERAL COURTS

In order for a court to review an agency action, it must have **subject matter jurisdiction**. There are three main sources of federal jurisdiction over environmental issues.

A. **Judicial review provisions:** Most federal environmental statutes provide for **judicial review** of agency action and regulation. [16]

B. **Citizen suit provisions:** Citizen suit provisions allow **private individuals** to sue agencies to compel non-discretionary decisionmaking and to sue violators to compel compliance with environmental requirements. [16]

C. **Federal question:** Federal question provisions of 28 U.S.C. §1331 grant jurisdiction to federal courts to hear disputes arising from the ''Constitution, laws, or treaties'' of the United States. [16]

## II. STANDING

The doctrine of standing ensures that a suit in federal court is brought by the **appropriate individual**: one who has a personal stake in the outcome. The standing doctrine has its source in the **''Case or Controversies''** requirement of Article III of the Constitution. An individual must meet certain criteria to obtain standing in federal court in environmental cases. [17]

A. **Injury in fact:** Many key cases in the development of the injury in fact requirement for standing have involved environmental litigation. After years of broad recognition of standing, the Supreme Court recently has **limited** the availability of standing in environmental cases, making it harder for environmental plaintiffs to bring suit to redress harm to the environment. [17]

1. **Sierra Club v. Morton:** An individual must allege that she **used the environment in question**. *Sierra Club v. Morton*, 405 U.S. 727 (1972). **Aesthetic harm** will satisfy the injury in fact requirement. *Id.* [17]

2. **Lujan v. National Wildlife Federation:** An individual's allegation of use of a particular environment **must be specific**. *Lujan v. National Wildlife Federation*, 497 U.S. 871 (1990). [17]

3. **Lujan v. Defenders of Wildlife:** An environmental plaintiff's injury must be **sufficiently imminent** to constitute injury in fact. *Lujan v. Defenders of Wildlife*, 504 U.S. 555 (1992). [17]

4. *Friends of the Earth v. Laidlaw:* A plaintiff must be able to show an **ongoing violation**, and there must be a possibility of **future violations**. *Friends of the Earth, Inc. v. Laidlaw Environmental Services (TOC), Inc.*, 528 U.S. 167 (2000). [17]

5. **Special injury in fact issues**

   a. **Procedural injury:** The Supreme Court is divided as to whether procedural injury under an environmental statute is sufficient to satisfy the injury in fact requirement. [18]

   b. **Prospective harm:** The Supreme Court has found that **future harm** of radiation was **sufficiently concrete** to meet the injury in fact requirement, although the case involved other, more immediate environmental harm as well. *Duke Power Co. v. Carolina Envtl. Study Group, Inc.*, 438 U.S. 59 (1978). [18]

   c. **Representational standing:** The Supreme Court has held that an **organization may sue** on behalf of its members if: [18]

      ■ some members would have **standing**;

      ■ the interest that it seeks to protect is **related** to the organization's purposes; and

      ■ individual members **do not need to participate**. *Hunt v. Adv. Comm'n*, 432 U.S. 333 (1977).

   d. **Informational standing:** An organization may have standing if an agency's action **deprives the organization** of information essential to the organization and its activities and programs. [18]

   e. **Animal standing:** An organization **may not** obtain standing in cases in which animals are **privately-owned** and no public right of use exists. [18-19]

B. **Zone of interest:** For suits brought under §702 of the Administrative Procedure Act, a plaintiff must also establish that the type of harm alleged is within the **"zone of interests" protected under the violated statute**. Ordinarily, the test is easily satisfied. [19]

C. **Causation:** An individual must establish that the **injury is "fairly traceable"** to the challenged conduct. Mere bystanders or those with remote or attenuated links to harm will not satisfy the causation prong of standing. Generally, an individual must show a **"substantial likelihood"** that the defendant's acts caused his harm. [20]

D. **Redressability:** An individual must show that the judicial relief he seeks will serve some **useful purpose** if he prevails on the merits. [20]

# III. REVIEWABILITY OF ADMINISTRATIVE DECISIONS

Reviewability depends on whether an issue is **suitable for judicial resolution**. The principal agency responsible for environmental decisionmaking is the Environmental Protection Agency.

A. **Environmental Protection Agency:** The EPA is responsible for the implementation of most of the major federal environmental statutes. Most environmental statutes give EPA the power to promulgate regulations implementing statutes and governing issuance of permits and enforcement. [20-21]

1.  **Structure of EPA:** EPA is headed by an Administrator appointed by the President. The *regional offices* primarily are responsible for the issuance of permits and enforcing compliance within their regions. [21]

2.  **Other agencies:** Other federal administrative agencies implement and enforce environmental regulations as well. These agencies include: the Corps of Engineers, Department of the Interior, Department of Energy, Food and Drug Administration, and the Occupational Safety and Health Administration. [21]

B.  **General rule of reviewability:** The Administrative Procedure Act §701 provides that agency actions are *reviewable except in two instances*.

1.  **Statute exception:** Agency actions are unreviewable if a *statute prohibits review*. [21]

2.  **Discretion exception:** Agency actions are unreviewable if *"committed to agency discretion by law."* 5 U.S.C. §701(a)(l)-(2). The discretion exception is very narrow and *only applies* in cases in which statutes are phrased in such *broad language* that virtually no law exists for the courts to apply in reviewing an agency's decision. [21]

3.  **"Final action" requirement:** In addition, the action challenged *must be a final agency action* in order to be reviewed. [21]

C.  **Standards of review:** The standards of review depend on the applicability of APA §706(2) and the *nature of the issue* reviewed in the case: whether legal, factual, or procedural. [21]

1.  **Legal issues:** *Courts generally defer* to an administrative agency's interpretation of law. Several reasons support this deference: [21-22]

■ the agency has *more experience* in applying the statute;

■ Congress gave the agency *primary responsibility* for executing the law;

■ individuals may *rely* on the agency's interpretation of the law without litigation; and

■ policy choices should be made by the political branches of government.

2.  **Factual issues:** The standards of review depend upon the type of agency proceeding.

a.  **Adjudicatory proceedings and formal rulemaking:** The *"substantial evidence"* test is the standard of review. 5 U.S.C. §706(2)(E). The court must uphold the agency's action unless no substantial evidence exists in the record to support the agency's decision. *Overton Park v. Volpe*, 401 U.S. 402 (1971). [22]

b.  **Informal rulemaking and non-adjudicatory proceedings:** The *"arbitrary and capricious"* test is the standard of review. 5 U.S.C. §706(2)(A). A court must consider whether the agency considered *all relevant factors* and whether the agency clearly *erred* in its judgment; the standard is a narrow one. [22]

**Note:** Formal rulemaking by an agency is very rare. When an agency makes a decision of general applicability, it is generally done through informal rulemaking. Determination of the rights or responsibilities of a particular party is an adjudication. Any other type of decision by an agency falls within *Overton Park* and is governed by the arbitrary and capricious standard of review. [22]

3. **Procedural issues:** Whether an agency has followed the procedures required by the APA is a question of law subject to *de novo review* by a court. However, courts do not have the general authority to require additional procedures beyond those required by statute (specifically the APA), the Constitution, or agency rules, but additional procedures may be imposed in *compelling circumstances*. *Vermont Yankee v. Natural Resources*, 435 U.S. 519 (1978). [22]

## IV. REMEDIES

A. **Injunctive relief:** Injunctive relief *may be mandated or discretionary* depending upon the goals of the environmental statutes at issue.

1. **Mandated injunctions:** Injunctive relief is mandated *if necessary to effectuate Congressional goals* in an environmental statute. *Tennessee Valley Auth. v. Hill*, 437 U.S. 153 (1978). [23]

2. **Discretionary injunctions:** In most environmental cases, however, courts retain their *traditional discretion to balance* the equities in determining whether an injunction should issue. *Weinberger v. Romero-Barcelo*, 456 U.S. 305 (1982). [23]

B. **Attorneys' fees:** There are two major issues regarding attorneys' fees in environmental cases: when should an attorney receive fees and how much should an attorney receive. [23]

1. **Prevailing party rule:** Most environmental statutes require a party to be a *"prevailing or substantially prevailing party"* to recover attorneys' fees. [23]

a. **American rule:** The prevailing party rule is in accord with the historical fee-shifting "American Rule," which states that the costs of litigation must be *borne by each party*. Congress may create exceptions to the American Rule. [23-24]

b. ***Ruckelshaus v. Sierra Club*:** The Court has held that a *party must show some success* on the merits before an attorney is eligible for a fee award under the Clean Air Act. *Ruckelshaus v. Sierra Club*, 463 U.S. 680 (1983). The prevailing party rule applies under the Clean Air Act even though the "prevailing or substantially prevailing party" language does not appear in the statute. [24]

2. **Reasonable fees rule:** Courts presume that a *"lodestar" figure* is a reasonable fee. [24]

a. **Calculation of lodestar:** The lodestar is calculated by multiplying the number of hours worked by a reasonable hourly rate for each attorney involved.

b. **Adjustment of lodestar:** The *courts may not adjust* the lodestar figure for the contingency of losing a case or risk of nonpayment.

CHAPTER 4

# CONSTITUTIONAL LIMITS ON ENVIRONMENTAL REGULATION

## I. INTRODUCTION

The Constitution of the United States limits the government's power to enact environmental protection.

A. **Federalism:** The United States is a federalist system: a dual-governing system between the federal and state governments. [27]

B. **Federal government has limited powers:** The United States Constitution limits the federal government to those powers specifically granted in the Constitution. The *Commerce Clause*, the *basis for most federal environmental regulation*, grants Congress the power to regulate interstate commerce. U.S. Const., art. I, §8. The *states retain the general authority to enact environmental regulations* pertaining to the safety, health, and welfare of their citizens. [27-28]

C. **Sources of constitutional limits on state actions**

  1. **The Commerce Clause:** Federal regulation under the Commerce Clause may preempt state regulation (a) if the federal regulation leaves *no room for the state regulation*, (b) if there is a *dominant federal interest*, or (c) if the *state regulation conflicts* with the federal regulation. [28]

  2. **The Takings Clause:** The Fifth Amendment provides the federal government shall not take private property for public use *"without just compensation."* U.S. Const., amend. V. This prohibition is applicable to state and local governments under the Fourteenth Amendment. [28]

## II. THE REACH OF THE COMMERCE CLAUSE

Most congressional regulation of environmental protection is predicated on the nexus to interstate commerce.

A. **Role of the federal courts:** The Supreme Court has *limited state legislation* and *actions* affecting interstate commerce even when Congress has not acted. [28]

B. **The negative implication of the Commerce Clause:** Most state laws can have some impact on the interstate market. If such laws *interfere or burden the interstate market*, courts may use the ''negative implication'' of the Commerce Clause to strike down such laws. [28]

  1. **The *Pike* balancing test:** In *Pike v. Bruce Church, Inc.*, 397 U.S. 137 (1970), the Supreme Court established a *three-part test* to evaluate whether a state statute is precluded by the Commerce Clause.

    a. **Legitimate purpose:** The state statute must have a *legitimate local purpose* as the public interest. [29]

    b. **Balancing of interests:** The *interest protected must clearly outweigh its effects* on interstate commerce. Most courts require that the burden on interstate commerce be merely incidental in order for the state law to pass this second prong of the *Pike* test. [29]

    c. **No alternatives:** Finally, there must be no *other alternative available* that has a lesser impact on interstate activities. [29]

  2. **Interstate shipment of waste and the ''Not In My Backyard'' syndrome:** The *Pike* test is still used to determine when a state or local government can prevent the disposal or shipment of hazardous waste in its boundaries. [29]

    a. *Per se* **discrimination under** *City of Philadelphia v. New Jersey:* In *City of Philadelphia*, 437 U.S. 617 (1978), the Supreme Court struck down a New Jersey statute prohibiting the import of most waste into the state. The law was enacted by the state in response to the extensive use of New Jersey landfills by cities in Pennsylvania and New York. [29]

    **i.**   **Protectionism is *per se* invalid:** The Court found that the statute protected the state's economy at the expense of other states. The Court held that such a ***"protectionist measure" discriminates*** against articles of interstate commerce *per se*, and thus the Court found it unnecessary to determine whether the purpose of the statute was to protect its limited land resources to favor its local economy. [29]

    **ii.**   **Quarantine laws distinguished:** The Court distinguished the New Jersey statute from a narrow class of "quarantine" laws aimed at preventing unreasonable health hazards (i.e., diseased livestock or contaminated foods). Such laws ban the importation of materials that are hazardous to health at the moment of transportation. Although these laws are openly discriminatory against interstate commerce, they nevertheless pass constitutional scrutiny because they are directed at protecting public health and safety. [29]

    **iii.**   **Defining *per se* discrimination under *Fort Gratiot*:** Statutes that ***prohibit private landfill*** operators from accepting waste originating ***outside the county in which their facilities are located*** are *per se* discriminatory and violate the Commerce Clause, even though in-state as well as out-of-state waste is restricted in its movement. *Fort Gratiot Sanitary Landfill, Inc. v. Michigan Dep't of Natural Resources*, 504 U.S. 353 (1992). [29]

    **iv.**   **Fees and disposal surcharges:** A state violates the Commerce Clause if it imposes ***disposal fees*** for ***out-of-state*** hazardous wastes at commercial facilities within the states when no fee is applied to such waste generated ***within*** the state. *Chemical Waste v. Hunt*, 504 U.S. 334 (1992). Larger ***surcharges*** on out-of-state waste may be similarly invalid. [30]

**b.**   **Balancing interstate burdens and environmental goals:** The *Pike* balancing test applies if the state statute does not *per se* discriminate against interstate commerce under *City of Philadelphia*. [30]

    **i.**   ***Minnesota v. Clover Leaf Creamery Co.*,** 449 U.S. 456, *reh'g denied*, 450 U.S. 1027 (1981): Supreme Court upheld Minnesota statute allowing milk to be sold only in cardboard containers with the stated purpose being the promotion of conservation and the reduction of solid waste disposal problems. The Court found the statute was an ***"even-handed"*** regulation applying to both in-state and out-of-state businesses. [30]

    **ii.**   **Environmental purpose must outweigh protectionist effect:** Even if environmental or health reasons justify an ordinance, it ***cannot discriminate*** against interstate commerce if ***less-discriminatory alternatives are available***. *C & A Carbone v. Clarkstown*, 114 S. Ct. 1677 (1994). [30]

**c.**   **Market participant doctrine:** When a state acts as a market participant and not solely as a regulatory actor, the state is ***not*** barred from discriminating against interstate commerce. [30]

**C.**   **The interstate commerce nexus:** Congress's power under the Commerce Clause is very broad. The Supreme Court has held that the commerce power not only extends to the use of channels or means of interstate commerce, but also to ***any activity that may affect*** such commerce. [30-31]

## III. LIMITATIONS UNDER THE TAKINGS CLAUSE

The Fifth Amendment provides that the federal government shall not take private property for public use "without just compensation." U.S. Const. amend. V.

A. **Applicability**

1. **Applicable to state governments:** This restriction is made applicable to state and local governments through the *Fourteenth Amendment*. [32]

2. **Not limited to the physical seizure of property:** In addition to physical invasions of property, the takings clause *also applies to private property* which is over-regulated by the government. [32]

B. **Legitimate state interest:** In imposing environmental regulations which regulate land use, the state must have a *"legitimate state interest"* (i.e., preserving landmarks, protecting the environment). *Agins v. City of Tiburon*, 447 U.S. 255 (1980). [32]

1. **Environmental preservation as the state's interest:** Regulation of a private owner's use of his property to protect the environment is regarded as a *public interest*. [32]

2. **Means-end fit:** There must also be a *close fit* between the *means chosen by the state*, such as the type of regulation to be used, and the *state's objective* in passing the regulation. [32]

a. *Nollan v. California Coastal Commission:* In *Nollan*, 483 U.S. 825 (1987), the Supreme Court stated that a regulation does not effect a taking if it *"substantially advance[s] legitimate state interests"* and *"does not den[y] an owner economically viable use* of his land." [32]

b. **"Rough proportionality test" of *Dolan*:** In *Dolan v. City of Tigard*, 114 S. Ct. 2309 (1994), the Supreme Court held that conditions placed on development permits must be *"roughly proportional"* to the effects the applicant's proposed land use will have on the community. [32-33]

C. **Temporary taking:** A temporary taking occurs when a regulation is *promulgated but later removed*. When suit is filed against the government for a temporary taking, just compensation is the damages for the losses resulting from loss of property use from the time that the interference occurs to the time in which the regulation is amended, withdrawn, or compensation is paid for the complete loss from the taking. [33]

D. **The "nuisance" exception:** Early Supreme Court decisions suggested that a regulation *preventing harm that is a nuisance* to the public, is not a taking. [33]

1. **Pollution regulations:** "Nuisance exception" for regulations prohibiting manufacturing in residential areas because it prevents air pollution. [33]

2. **Alcoholic beverage restrictions:** Restrictions on the selling and production of intoxicating beverages on private property upheld as nuisance to the community. [33]

3. **Securing a public benefit:** However, when the government passes a regulation to *secure a public* benefit, rather than preventing a public harm, the regulation may be seen as a *taking*. [34]

4. **Denial of all economic value of land and the nuisance exception:** In general, when a regulation has deprived a private land owner of all the economically viable use of his land, *per se* a

taking has occurred. It is *not sufficient*, however, to constitute a taking if the owner has *only lost a particular use* of his land. [34]

## IV. LIMITATIONS ON FEDERAL LAW UNDER THE TENTH AMENDMENT

In *New York v. United States*, 505 U.S. 144 (1992), the Supreme Court struck down a provision of the Low-Level Radioactive Waste Policy Amendments Act of 1985. The provision required states that lack disposal capacity for low-level radioactive wastes generated within their borders to take title to those wastes after January 1, 1996. The provision was found to *violate the Tenth Amendment* because it allowed the states *no alternative* to carrying out the federal policy. [34]

CHAPTER 5

# NATIONAL ENVIRONMENTAL POLICY ACT (NEPA)

## I. GENERAL INFORMATION

The National Environmental Policy Act (NEPA) is an environmental statute that emphasizes *information rather than regulation*. It requires the publication of information about the environmental effects of and alternatives to potential government actions. NEPA does not dictate environmental standards or controls. [37]

**A. History:** NEPA was enacted in order to require federal agencies to consider the *quality of the human environment* in their decisionmaking. [37-38]

**B. Purpose:** NEPA establishes policy, sets goals, and provides means for carrying out the policy. 40 C.F.R. §1500.1. Its emphasis is on information: both the documentation of environmental statistics and the *dissemination* of the documentation. [38]

    **1. NEPA requires agencies to take environmental factors into account:** NEPA requires federal agencies to consider the effects of their actions on the environment by preparing a detailed *Environmental Impact Statement (EIS)*. The agency, however, does not have to elevate environmental concerns over other considerations. Where environmental consequences have been considered, no more is required by NEPA. [38]

    **2. NEPA requires agencies to consider alternatives:** Included in the EIS must be a discussion of the *alternative proposals* to the government action and the environmental impact of each. Consideration of alternatives is required even if an EIS does not have to be prepared. [38]

    **3. Provide information to the public:** The main purpose of the EIS is to *inform the public as well as the decision-makers* about the proposed action and the alternatives to such action. [38]

**C. Establishment of the Council on Environmental Quality:** NEPA established the Council on Environmental Quality (CEQ) to assist the President with environmental concerns. NEPA §105, 42 U.S.C. §4342. [38]

    **1. Authority of the CEQ Guidelines:** Although the list of its functions and duties is expansive, the main responsibility of CEQ is to *issue guidelines* explaining to government agencies what they must do to follow NEPA's mandate. [39]

a. **Decisions of Council entitled to substantial deference:** Courts owe ***substantial deference*** to the CEQ Guidelines interpretation of NEPA. *Andrus v. Sierra Club*, 442 U.S. 347 (1979). [39]

b. **No enforcement authority:** The CEQ has ***no power to alter or stop*** a federal agency's actions under NEPA. [39]

# II. THE ENVIRONMENTAL IMPACT STATEMENT (EIS)

## A. Process

1. **Exemptions from EIS obligation:** An agency is excused from NEPA compliance (a) if the Act's requirements ***conflict with other statutory obligations***, (b) if Congress grants the agency an ***express statutory exemption***, or (c) if the terms of another applicable statute require duties that are ***"functionally equivalent"*** to NEPA's duties. [39]

2. **Environmental Assessment:** The Environmental Assessment (EA) is a short document which ***outlines the proposal and its possible environmental impact***. It aids the agency in determining whether a full EIS is necessary. [39]

3. **Finding of No Significant Impact:** With the aid of the EA, the agency decides whether to do an EIS. If it decides not to, it issues a ***"Finding of No Significant Impact"*** or FONSI. A FONSI may not be issued for activities that have a potential for disturbing the environment. In such a case, an EIS must be prepared in order to fully assess the possible environmental consequences. [39]

4. **Notice of Intent and scoping:** If an agency determines that an EIS is necessary, it will publish a "Notice of Intent" to prepare the EIS. The next step in the EIS process is "scoping," when the agency ***defines the topics and issues*** involved in the proposal. [39]

5. **Draft EIS:** Once a draft of the EIS has been completed, it ***must be circulated*** for comment from the public and other agencies. The agency has some discretion as to whether to hold public hearings to discuss the draft. [40]

6. **Final EIS:** After responding to comments and incorporating the answers into the EIS, the final EIS is completed. [40]

7. **EPA review of EIS:** The EPA evaluates both the adequacy of the EIS and the environmental impact of the proposed action, although it does not have the power to veto other federal agencies' decisions following the submission of the EIS. [40]

8. **Record of decision:** The final decision of the agency must be set forth with a justification for the action and the ***reasons why the alternatives were rejected***. [40]

9. **Judicial review:** Compliance with NEPA is ***subject to judicial review*** even though NEPA lacks a "citizen suit" provision. [40]

   a. **Standard of review:** The decision not to prepare a supplemental EIS is reviewed under the ***"arbitrary and capricious"*** standard. It is presumed that the same standard of review applies to the decision whether to prepare an EIS. [40]

**b. Scope:** Courts may review the decision *whether to prepare* an EIS and the *adequacy* of an EA or EIS, as well as the *procedures by which such decisions are made*. The usual remedy for a NEPA violation is injunctive relief. [40]

**B. Threshold issue:** When must an EIS be prepared? Environmental Impact Statements are only required for *"proposals for legislation and other major Federal actions significantly affecting the quality of the human environment."* NEPA §102(2)(C). [40]

1. **Proposals for legislation or action:** An EIS need only be prepared when an agency *has actually made a proposal*, not when it is merely contemplating some action. [40]

2. **Federal inaction:** Federal *inaction* requires an EIS only when the agency has some decision-making obligation. [40-41]

3. **Federal:** Only federal actions are affected by EIS requirements. State and local governmental actions, as well as private actions, are not subject to NEPA. If there is a *sufficient amount of federal involvement* in a private action, the EIS requirement may be triggered. [41]

4. **Major/significantly affecting:** According to the CEQ guidelines, "major" before Federal action reinforces but in practice has no meaning independent of the "significantly affecting" requirement. [41]

   **a. Context and intensity:** The CEQ Guidelines interpret this phrase to require *consideration of the effects in terms of context* (society as a whole, regionally, locality, etc.) and intensity (severity of the impact). 40 C.F.R. §1508.27. [41]

   **b. Controversial:** These CEQ Guidelines require an EIS for action likely to be highly controversial. [41]

   **c. Balancing test:** Some courts have applied a two-part test, requiring an agency to *consider the extent* to which the action will cause adverse environmental effects in excess of those created by existing uses in the area; and the *absolute quantitative adverse environmental effects* of the action itself. [41]

   **d. Effects:** "Effects" is synonymous with *impacts* and includes *ecological, aesthetic, historic, cultural, economic, social, or health effects, whether direct or indirect*. 40 C.F.R. §1508.8. However, psychological harm from fear of an adverse effect is too attenuated to be considered by the agency. [41]

5. **Quality of human environment:** The human environment means the natural and physical environment and its relationship with the people of that environment. *Economic and social effects are not enough in and of themselves* to require an EIS. 40 C.F.R. §1508.14. A significant impact on the physical environment must be demonstrated. [41]

**C. Scope:** The scope of an EIS can be a complex question. This is especially true when it is unclear whether a federal action is a small, discrete project or a series of actions that should be studied as a whole. [41]

1. **Single project/segmentation:** An EIS may be prepared for a *single project or segment* rather than the more comprehensive if the segment or project has independent utility. [42]

2. **Comprehensive EIS:** Conversely, a comprehensive EIS is required for proposals which *must be considered in a broader context* than their own completion because they are *dependent upon other actions*. [42]

   **a. Programmatic actions:** A single EIS is necessary when the proposals for federal actions are *so closely related* as to constitute a single course of action. [42]

   **b. Cumulative actions:** When the agency has several proposals that may have a cumulative effect on the environment, an EIS covering them all is necessary. [42]

   **c. Connected actions:** ''Connected actions'' must also be considered together in a single EIS. 40 C.F.R. §1508.25(a). [42]

**D. Adequacy of the Environmental Impact Statement:** Generally, the EIS must include the *environmental effects* of the proposed action, *alternatives* to the proposed actions, and the *alternatives' own effects*. [42]

   **1. Consideration of alternatives:** The agency must consider alternatives to the proposal and the environmental impact of those alternatives, *even if no EIS is required*. NEPA §102(2)(E), 42 U.S.C. §4332(2)(E). [42]

   **a. Council on Environmental Quality Guidelines:** The CEQ Guidelines suggest there are three types of alternatives: (1) the *no action* alternative; (2) *reasonable alternatives* to the proposed action; and (3) *mitigation measures* for the proposed action. [42]

   **b. Primary and secondary alternatives:** A primary alternative is a course of action *entirely different* from the proposal. A secondary alternative is one that *goes forward* with the proposal, but *in a different way*. [42]

   **c. Determination of reasonable alternatives:** Generally, courts are reluctant to require an agency to consider primary alternatives to the proposed action. NEPA does, however, require *consideration of alternatives* that meet only a *portion* of the stated goals of the project. [42-43]

   **i. Rule of reason:** Although an agency need not consider speculative or experimental technologies, it is *required to consider all reasonable alternatives*, whether or not the alternatives are within the authority of that agency. [43]

   **2. Mitigation:** Mitigation of the environmental impact *must be* considered in the EIS. [43]

   **a. Council on Environmental Quality Guidelines:** Mitigation is *required* to be discussed in the scope of the EIS, as part of the alternatives, and in the final decision of the agency. [43]

   **b. Review:** Although the agency is required to consider mitigation and include such discussion in the EIS, it is *not obligated to implement* any of the mitigation measures. [43]

   **c. Mitigation is construed liberally:** Mitigation does not necessarily have to affect the particular action in question, but can rather be a *separate action to offset the environmental impact*. [43]

   **3. Lack of available information:** When relevant evidence or scientific data is inadequate or lacking, the agency is required to *publicly note this lack of information*, or include it if it is essential and the costs of obtaining it are not exorbitant. [43]

   **4. ''Worst case'' analysis:** The CEQ guidelines *no longer require* an EIS to include a worst case analysis, an assessment of potentially catastrophic consequences of low probability. However, NEPA has been interpreted by courts to *require a probability analysis* even when information about the project and environment is unavailable or too costly to obtain. [43]

5. **Supplemental EIS:** An agency may be required to file an additional supplement to either its draft or final EIS if it *makes substantial changes* in its proposed action relevant to the environmental concerns; or significant new circumstances or information arise that are relevant to the environment. 40 C.F.R. §1502.9(c). [44]

# III. SUBSTANTIVE REVIEW UNDER NEPA

A. **Standard of review of the substantive decision:** The role of the reviewing court is *limited to insuring that the agency actually considered* environmental matters — not to substitute its judgment for the agency's on the merits. Moreover, a reviewing court *cannot elevate* environmental considerations over other legitimate factors when determining agency compliance with NEPA. [44]

B. **Consideration of all relevant factors:** Agency decisions under NEPA are reviewed under the *arbitrary and capricious* standard. This narrow standard of substantive review requires *full consideration of all relevant factors*. If an agency has failed to give adequate consideration to environmental factors, not only will its EA or EIS be procedurally defective under NEPA, but also its substantive decision to proceed may be attached as deficient under the APA. [44-45]

# IV. INTERNATIONAL APPLICATION OF NEPA

NEPA is generally not considered to be applicable to federal actions abroad or those that have significant extraterritorial effects.

A. **Exceptions:** The presumption against extraterritorial application of NEPA has been held *not* to apply when the conduct takes place primarily within the United States and the effects are felt in Antarctica, a continent without a sovereign. *EDF v. Massey*, 986 F.2d 528 (D.C. Cir. 1993). [45]

B. **International application by Executive Order:** Executive Order 12114, however, imposes somewhat similar requirements to NEPA on federal actions that have significant environmental effects abroad. The coverage of the order is more limited than NEPA and *private citizens may not sue* to compel compliance. [45]

# V. STATE ENVIRONMENTAL POLICY ACTS

A majority of states have enacted their own state environmental policy acts (SEPAs) that require some form of *environmental study for state government actions*. [45]

# VI. CRITICISMS OF NEPA

NEPA has met with *mixed reviews* ranging from concerns about the actual use of the EIS in the decision-making process to support for the EIS motivating the public to get involved. Critics and supporters agree that the EIS process delays the proposed actions. [45]

CHAPTER 6

# THE CLEAN AIR ACT (CAA)

## I. AIR POLLUTION REGULATION PRIOR TO 1970

There have been four phases of air pollution regulation: (1) Before 1955, air pollution regulation was *completely in the control of state and local* governments. (2) In 1955, Congress enacted the Air Pollution Control Act, which gave *research and technical assistance* to the states, with states maintaining control over regulation. (3) The Air Quality Control Act of 1967 created a *federal regulatory program* based on ambient air quality standards, but states still retained the responsibility for promulgating such standards. (4) In 1970, Congress enacted the Clean Air Act (CAA), which *expanded the federal role* in the air regulation of air pollution. [49]

## II. KEY STATUTORY PROVISIONS OF THE CAA

Understanding the scope and structure of the Clean Air Act requires a careful reading of the underlying statutes. [49]

## III. AIR QUALITY STANDARDS

The fundamental goal of the CAA is the nationwide attainment and maintenance of *National Ambient Air Quality Standards (NAAQSs)*. [50]

A. **Regulatory controls and pollutant sources:** The CAA utilizes two types of regulatory controls: (1) *health-based standards* representing the ''safe'' level of a pollutant in the ambient air; and (2) *technology-based standards* representing the amount of pollutant reduction within an industry's economic and technological capabilities. The CAA applies these regulatory controls to *stationary* and *mobile* pollutant sources. [50-51]

B. **Types of NAAQSs:** EPA is required to establish ''primary'' and ''secondary'' NAAQSs for ''criteria pollutants.'' [51]

   1. **Primary NAAQSs:** The *acceptable concentration* of a pollutant in the ambient air that will protect the public health. [51]

   2. **Secondary NAAQSs:** Set at a level to *protect the public welfare*. [51]

   3. **Criteria pollutants:** A pollutant that the EPA has determined *endangers the public health or welfare* and that is *produced by numerous and diverse sources*. [51]

C. **Promulgation of NAAQSs:** EPA's duty to list a pollutant as a criteria pollutant becomes *non-discretionary* if EPA makes a determination that (a) the pollutant *endangers public health or welfare*, or (b) the pollutant results from *numerous or diverse mobile or stationary sources*. Within 12 months of including a pollutant on a criteria pollutant list, the EPA must issue and *submit for public comment* air quality criteria and proposed primary and secondary NAAQSs. EPA *may not* consider economic and technological feasibility in setting air quality standards because the Act is technology-forcing. [51]

D. **Review of NAAQSs:** EPA's duty to review NAAQS every five years is *non-discretionary*. [51]

# IV. AIR QUALITY CONTROL REGIONS AND STATE IMPLEMENTATION PLANS

**A. Air quality control regions:** The entire nation is divided into air quality regions. Each state is required to designate every area in the state as attainment, nonattainment, or unclassifiable as to each criteria pollutant within one year of EPA's promulgation or revision of an NAAQS: (1) an ***attainment area*** meets the primary or secondary NAAQS for a criteria pollutant; (2) a ***nonattainment area*** fails to meet the primary or secondary NAAQS for a criteria pollutant; and (3) an ***unclassifiable area's*** compliance with the primary or secondary NAAQS for a criteria pollutant cannot be determined with current information. [52]

**B. General SIP requirements:** Once EPA has promulgated or revised an NAAQS, the states and EPA begin the SIP process. Every SIP must be promulgated ***"after reasonable notice and public hearings"*** in accordance with state administrative procedures and must contain certain provisions. Examples of SIP requirements include: (1) ***enforceable emissions limitations***; (2) ***methods*** for compiling air quality data for the state; (3) ***boundaries*** of the SIP; (4) an ***enforcement*** program; (5) ***provisions to control*** interstate and international pollution; (6) measures to ensure adequate personnel, funding, and authority; and (7) ***requirements for sources to monitor and report*** their emissions. [52]

**C. SIP evaluation procedures**

   **1. State preparation of SIP:** After an NAAQS is promulgated or revised, a state has ***three years*** from the promulgation of the NAAQS to prepare or revise its SIP for an attainment area. ***For a nonattainment area,*** the three year period ***begins on the date of the designation*** of an area as nonattainment. [52]

   **2. EPA determination of completeness:** After a state submits its SIP, EPA has ***six months*** to determine whether the SIP is complete. [53]

   **3. EPA consideration of cost and feasibility in review of SIP:** EPA has 12 months from its completeness determination to decide if the SIP meets the requirements of the CAA. EPA may only consider the factors listed in §110(a)(2), an exclusive list ***that does not include economic and technological feasibility***, and upon review, it may approve, disapprove, partially approve, or conditionally approve an SIP. [53]

   **4. State's obligations upon conditional approval:** A state may create an SIP, which is more ***stringent*** than necessary to meet the NAAQS. Should an SIP receive a conditional approval, a state has one year to meet EPA's conditions or the SIP is deemed disapproved. [53]

   **5. Variances:** States may adopt variance provisions which allow individual sources to seek relief from stringent SIP provisions if they feel the SIP requirements are ***economically or technologically infeasible***. [53]

   **6. Compliance orders:** EPA may issue a ***"delayed compliance order"*** to sources who fail to meet SIP requirements. Considering factors such as cost and feasibility, these orders may specify a later date than established in the SIP for a source to come into compliance with the relevant SIP requirements provided that the extension is less than one year. Courts have the authority to issue ***injunctions*** requiring sources to comply with the SIP. This power is broader than EPA's, in that courts have discretion to grant sources extensions of more than one year to come into compliance. [53]

7. **Conformity criteria:** Conformity criteria are criteria that indicate that a plan or project conforms to an SIP's purpose of achievement of NAAQSs and does not cause or contribute to a new violation. In *EDF v. Browner*, the court held that EPA had to issue conformity criteria for all geographic areas covered by SIPs, *including attainment and unclassifiable areas*. [53]

D. **Sanctions:** Sanctions for a state's failure to comply with SIP requirements differ according to whether an area is an attainment or nonattainment area. [53]

1. **Federal implementation plans (FIPs):** FIPs apply to both attainment and nonattainment areas. Deficiencies that trigger the FIP sanction include: *failure to submit a complete SIP, partial approval or disapproval* of an SIP, or disapproval after *not meeting the conditions* of a conditional approval. [54]

2. **Other sanctions in attainment areas:** EPA may impose other discretionary sanctions for any deficiency or the failure to implement any SIP requirement. [54]

3. **Other sanctions in nonattainment areas:** Must impose either the *highway funding cutoff* or the *offset requirement* as a sanction for any deficiency or the failure to implement any SIP requirement, unless the state corrects the deficiency within 18 months. EPA must impose both sanctions if the state did not act in good faith. [54]

# V. NONATTAINMENT AREAS

Special SIP provisions are required for nonattainment areas such as a *preconstruction review process for new and modified sources*. The CAA also designates attainment deadlines for nonattainment areas. [54]

A. **SIP requirements:** SIP provisions for *pre-1990 NAAQSs* must include *graduated control programs* for ozone, carbon monoxide, and particulates, but they *need not have any special control measures* for sulfur dioxide, nitrogen dioxide, or lead. For *post-1990 NAAQSs*, states must include several special provisions in their SIPs such as: (1) a requirement that sources in nonattainment areas must use *reasonably available control technology* (RACT); (2) *automatic contingency measures* that take effect if any deadlines are missed; (3) *preconstruction review* for new major and modified sources. [54]

B. **Nonattainment preconstruction review**

1. **Threshold for nonattainment preconstruction review:** A *major stationary source* constructed or modified in a nonattainment area must obtain a preconstruction permit. [55]

a. **Major stationary source defined:** A source is "major" if it *emits or may potentially emit 100 tons per year* of any pollutant for which an area is designated as nonattainment. The Supreme Court has upheld the use of the plant-wide bubble in determining whether a source is "major." [55]

b. **"Constructed" or "modified" defined:** A modification results when a *significant increase* in emissions of a pollutant occurs, and the emission is a pollutant for which the area is designated nonattainment and for which the source is major. [55]

2. **Substantive nonattainment review requirements:** Sources must use the *lowest achievable emission rate* (LAER) and meet the offset requirement for nonattainment pollutants. [55]

**a. LAER:** The lowest achievable emission rate must be the ***more stringent of:*** (1) the most ***stringent emission limitation in an SIP*** for the class or category of source; or (2) the most ***stringent emission limitation achieved by the class or category*** of source. The LAER must be at least as stringent as the applicable new source performance standard. [55]

**b. Offsets:** A major source can offset its emissions by obtaining emissions reductions from a source in the same nonattainment area. A source can offset its emission with a source in another nonattainment area if: (1) the ***other area's nonattainment classification*** is ***equal or higher***; and (2) the other area's ***emission contributes to the violation of an NAAQS*** in the source's area. EPA allows states to ''bank'' offsets (unused emissions reductions), and if a source voluntarily reduces emissions, the state may give it an emissions reduction credit (ERC). [55]

    **i. Problems in implementing offsets:** An offset program raises a variety of concerns:

        **(1) Need same pollutants:** For an offset to be effective, the ***reduction must be in the same*** pollutant. [56]

        **(2) Paper reductions:** An offset achieves only a ''paper reduction'' if a source already operating with emissions below legal limit is ***allowed to offset the difference between their actual emission and the legal limit***. [56]

        **(3) Marketability:** For an offset system to work, a market must be developed to allow buyers and sellers to ***interact efficiently***. [56]

        **(4) Initial allocations:** Most systems allow for allocation of offset credits by ***allowing sources to sell*** their pre-existing legal authorized emission levels. Other schemes would allow for no initial allocation of emission rights, but would auction off these rights. [56]

        **(5) Future concerns:** The fear of future governmental regulations may hamper the market for credits. [56]

        **(6) Ethical concerns:** The idea of selling a ''right to pollute'' raises significant ethical concerns. [56]

**C. Other requirements:** A source must also satisfy other requirements before a preconstruction permit will be issued: (1) the party seeking the permit ***may not be operating another source*** in the state which violates CAA; (2) EPA must determine that the state has ***adequately implemented its SIP*** for nonattainment areas; (3) the benefits from construction or modification of a source must ***substantially outweigh*** the social and environmental costs. [56]

**D. Attainment deadlines:** For ***pre-1990 NAAQSs***, the time allowed for attainment for nonattainment areas, and the strength of control measures required, ***increases*** with the severity of pollution. The time periods range from five to twenty years. ***Post-1990 primary and secondary NAAQSs*** are to be attained as ***expeditiously as practicable***; however, primary NAAQSs must be attained no later than five years from the nonattainment designation with the possibility of a five year extension. Upon failure to meet these deadlines, a state has one year to revise its SIP and five years to achieve attainment. [57]

# VI. PREVENTION OF SIGNIFICANT DETERIORATION (PSD) AREAS

**A. Generally:** In the 1977 Amendments to the CAA, Congress included a PSD section that addressed the protection of areas with air quality better than required by an NAAQS. A PSD area is one *classified as attainment or unclassifiable*. All SIPs must contain measures necessary to prevent the degradation of air quality in these areas through a preconstruction review process. [57-58]

**B. Threshold for preconstruction review:** A *"major emitting facility"* must obtain a PSD preconstruction permit if constructed or modified in a PSD area. [58]

    **1. Major emitting facility defined:** A "major emitting facility" *emits or has the potential to emit* (1) *100 tons per year of any pollutant* and is in one of the listed categories, or (2) *250 tons per year of any pollutant*. A facility's potential is determined by the plant's full design capacity with federally enforceable pollution control equipment in operation. [58]

    **2. Modification defined:** A modification results when a *significant increase* in the emission of any regulated pollutant occurs, or when *new pollutants are emitted*. Some emissions are exempt as *de minimis*. The use of the *plant-wide bubble*, which is authorized in determining whether a modification has occurred, reduces the possibility that a source will have to undergo review. [58]

**C. Substantive PSD review requirements:** PSD review includes: (1) *control technology review*, which requires that a facility use the "best available control technology" for every regulated pollutant; and (2) *air quality impact review*, which requires that a facility demonstrate that its emissions of sulfur dioxide, nitrogen dioxide, and particulates will not violate any NAAQSs or any allowable increment over the "baseline concentration" for an area. The baseline concentration is the existing ambient pollution level in a PSD area at the time of the first application for a PSD permit. [58-59]

**D. Exemptions from PSD review:** A facility is not required to engage in preconstruction review if (1) it *emits pollutants* in *de minimis* amounts, or (2) it *emits pollutants* for which the area is designated *nonattainment*. [59]

# VII. VISIBILITY PROTECTION

**A. Generally:** The CAA contains provisions specifically aimed at protecting visibility in certain areas. Once the Secretary of the Interior determines which areas need visibility protection, a state in which an area is located or which may contribute to visibility impairment must incorporate special provisions in its SIP such as: (1) the use of *best available retrofit technology* (BART); (2) a long-term goal of achieving *"reasonable further progress"* toward alleviating visibility impairment. [59]

# VIII. INTERSTATE AND INTERNATIONAL AIR POLLUTION

**A. Expansion of transboundary air pollution controls:** In the 1990 Amendments to the CAA, Congress expanded EPA's obligation in the area of transboundary air pollution by providing *stronger controls*. These include: (1) a *sulfur trading program* designed to address the acid rain problem; (2) *interstate SIP requirements* to control sources which hamper the achievement of NAAQS goals; (3) special requirements for interstate transport regions; (4) provisions for the designation of *ozone transport regions*; and (5) special rules in *multistate ozone nonattainment areas*. [60]

B.  **Acid rain title:** Traditional solutions to the acid rain problem, such as scrubbers and low sulfur coal, have not been entirely effective, so the 1990 Amendments created new programs to address the problem. [60]

   1.  **The market-based allowance system:** A market-based emission allowance system for sulfur limits the number of ''sulfur allowances'' issued by allowing one ton of sulfur to be emitted per year by the holder. The program is implemented in two phases: (1) Phase I addresses the *largest and dirtiest* power plants; and (2) Phase II encompasses *all utility plants*. The Act also allows for *sulfur allowances* to be freely bought and sold through *free market mechanisms* as well as by *sale by EPA*. [60-61]

   2.  **Nitrogen oxide:** Sources which are subject to the sulfur allowance program are also required to reduce nitrogen oxide emissions. [59]

C.  **International air pollution:** The problem of migrating pollution is addressed by the CAA and by international agreement. [61]

   1.  **CAA §155:** If EPA determines, based on reports from a ''duly constituted international agency,'' that emissions from U.S. sources are *causing or contributing* to serious pollution problems in another country, or if requested by the Secretary of State, EPA may require the source's state to modify its SIP. [61]

   2.  **Montreal Protocols:** The Montreal Protocols are an international agreement to limit the production and use of chemicals which harm the ozone layer, with provisions that several chloroflurocarbons be phased out of use. The Montreal Protocols were incorporated into the CAA by the 1990 Amendments. [61]

# IX. NATIONWIDE EMISSION LIMITATIONS

A.  **New source performance standards (NSPSs):** NSPSs cover (1) pollutants that *do not meet the size thresholds* of PSD and nonattainment areas, and (2) pollutants *other than criteria pollutants.* [61]

   1.  **Promulgation of category list and standards:** EPA must promulgate lists of categories of sources that *cause or contribute greatly* to air pollution and that endanger public health or welfare. [61-62]

      a.  **Standards of performance:** One year from the inclusion of a category in the category list, EPA must propose a ''standard of performance'' for *''new sources within the category.''* The emission standards for new sources are *technology-forcing* and are set at a level which reflects the emissions limitation that is achievable through the application of the best system of emission reduction which has been adequately demonstrated. [62]

      b.  **Threshold for the application of NSPSs:** A ''new'' source is one that is constructed or modified after the publication of the standard of performance. A ''modification'' is any *change, physical or in operation, of a stationary source that results in an increase in emissions* of a particular pollutant or a new pollutant. A ''stationary source'' is ''any building, structure, facility, or installation which emits or may emit air pollution.'' The ''bubble'' concept may apply to a facility subject to NSPS to determine if there has been an increase in emissions. Although NSPSs apply only to "new sources," the states are also required to develop programs to apply NSPS to existing sources. [62]

**B. Hazardous air pollutants (HAPs):** Prior to the 1990 Amendments to the CAA, HAPs were regulated by health-based standards. In 1990, Congress abandoned this system and adopted a scheme of ***technology-based, nationwide standards***. Congress created a list of 189 pollutants as HAPs to which EPA may add and individuals may petition to modify. [63]

1. **Source categories:** EPA must publish and revise every eight years, a list of categories and subcategories of major and area sources. A "major" source is any ***stationary source or group of stationary sources that emits or has the potential to emit 10 tons per year*** or more of any hazardous air pollutant or ***25 tons per year or more of any combination*** of hazardous air pollutants. A source is an ***"area source"*** if stationary and not major. [63]

2. **Emission standards for major sources**

   a. **Technology-based MACT standards:** These standards must require the ***"maximum degree of reduction in emissions"*** that EPA determines is achievable after considering costs and technological feasibility. For new sources, emission standards must require controls ***at least as stringent*** as the emission control "achieved in practice by the best controlled similar source." Emission standards for existing sources may be less stringent provided that they require at least ***the average emission limitation*** achieved by the best 12 percent of existing sources in the same category, or if there are fewer than 30 sources, the level of the best 5. Area sources are required to meet the ***generally available control technology*** (GACT) standard. The "MACT Hammer Clause" requires states to issue permits on a case-by-case basis if the EPA does not meet the deadline for promulgating MACT standards. [63-64]

   b. **Residual risk standards:** These are additional standards implemented to provide an ample margin of safety to protect public health if, after eight years of MACT standards, the EPA determines that the ***public health is still at risk***. Except for carcinogens, EPA has discretion in its decision whether to promulgate residual risk standards. [64]

   c. **Compliance:** Compliance is determined based on the ***source's classification*** as a new or existing source and whether the ***standard is a technologically-based MACT or a health-based*** residual risk standard. [64]

      i. **New sources:** After the effective date of the hazardous emission standard (MACT or residual risk), no major source subject standard may be constructed or reconstructed unless EPA or a state under a Title V program determines that it ***will be in compliance***. [64]

      ii. **Existing sources:** Residual risk standards are effective from the date of promulgation, but an existing source has 90 days to come into compliance. EPA has three years from promulgating a new MACT to bring existing sources into compliance. [64]

      iii. **Modification of existing sources:** The modification of an existing source accelerated the deadlines for compliance of an existing source with MACT standards. [65]

**C. Motor vehicle emission standards:** As the primary source of hydrocarbons, carbon monoxide, and nitrogen oxides, motor vehicles are extensively regulated by the CAA as "mobile sources." [65]

1. **Emission limits:** The CAA establishes *technology-forcing* federal standards for limiting automobile emissions. CAA preempts any state (with the exception of California) from establishing a separate standard. Federal standards are imposed based upon the *class of the mobile source*. The EPA is authorized to recall vehicles that fail to meet emission levels, and auto manufacturers must also provide warranties of the effectiveness of their control measures. Due to the severe problem of mobile-source pollution in California, the CAA allows California to establish limits more stringent than the federal requirements. [65]

2. **Automotive fuels:** The composition of fuel has a significant impact on automobile emissions. The CAA allows the EPA to regulate the composition of these fuels. These include: (1) a requirement that no gasoline may contain *lead or lead-additives*; (2) for some areas that fail to meet NAAQS ozone limits, the 1990 Amendments require the use of *reformulated fuels* designed to reduce the emission of organic volatiles which can form ozone and other toxic emissions; and (3) for some areas which fail to meet NAAQS limits for carbon monoxide, the 1990 Amendments require the use of *oxygenated fuels*. [65-66]

3. **Clean alternative fuels:** The 1990 Amendments created new programs to encourage the use of ''alternative fuels'' such as ethanol, natural gas, and electricity. The *clean fleet program* applies more stringent standards to single operators using a group of ten or more vehicles that are capable of being fueled at a central location in an ozone or carbon monoxide nonattainment area. Beginning in 1996, the CAA requires a minimum of 150,000 clean fuel vehicles to be sold in California, and by 1999, at least 300,000. [66]

# X. PERMIT PROGRAM

A. **History:** Unlike the Clean Water Act, which required all emission sources to obtain a federal NPDES permit, the CAA, when originally drafted, had *no provisions for a permit program*. The 1990 Amendments in Title V require all *''major sources'' and other sources* under the CAA to have a permit. [66]

B. **State permit programs:** States *must submit permit programs* to EPA for approval, which EPA may reject if they fail to meet the standards of the CAA. The public has opportunities to participate in the permitting process. EPA must act on a permit program within one year of submission. Once a permit program is in place, permits must be issued within three years. A state may be subject to sanctions for any failure in the permit program process. [66]

1. **Elements of a state permit program:** All state permit programs must include: (1) *public access*; (2) *public participation*; (3) *minimal conditions*; (4) *modification provisions*; (5) *a standardized permit application*; (6) *permit fees*. [67]

2. **EPA review of state permit issuance:** EPA *may object* to a permit issuance if it *does not comply* with the CAA. If the state ignores EPA's objection, *EPA may assume control* over permit issuance in that state. [67]

3. **Public participation:** Any person has the opportunity *to comment* on permits, to *seek review* of permits in state courts, and to *compel the state to take final action* on a permit application. Any person may also petition EPA regarding state permits and seek judicial review of EPA's action. [67]

C.  **Sources:** "Major source" is defined in a variety of ways by Title V. These include: (1) *major source* for HAP; (2) major *stationary source*; (3) *nonattainment* major source; (4) *affected source*; (5) *EPA-designated* sources; (6) other sources *subject to permit under nonattainment programs*, the PSD program, or new sources subject to NSPS. [67-68]

D.  **Benefits of permits:** Permits help in *enforcing* the provisions of CAA, and must have *specific conditions*. [68]

   1.  **Enforcement benefits:** Permits *simplify monitoring* and *review* and allow for increased monitoring by state agencies and reporting by sources. [68]

   2.  **Environmental group benefits:** Environmental groups like the permit system because it *allows for public participation* in the permitting process. [68]

   3.  **Source benefits:** Sources like the permit system because *compliance with a permit* is generally deemed to be in *compliance with the CAA*. This type of protection is known as a "permit shield," and it protects a source operating in compliance with its permit from prosecution under sections of the CAA. [68]

# XI.  ENFORCEMENT

A.  **EPA enforcement:** EPA's primary method of enforcement under the CAA is to *bring a civil suit* for injunctive relief or penalties. Administrative penalties and criminal sanctions are also available. EPA must take several preliminary steps prior to enforcement under any mechanism. These include: (1) *a notice of noncompliance* to the violator; (2) a *30-day waiting period* after notice before EPA can act on certain violations; and (3) *a conference* with the violator regarding the violation. [68]

   1.  **Civil judicial enforcement:** EPA must seek enforcement against violators who are *owners or operators* of an "affected source, a major emitting facility, or a major stationary source," but has discretion with respect to other parties. EPA may seek injunctive relief or civil penalties. [68-69]

   2.  **Criminal sanctions:** There are *five* separate criminal offenses under the CAA. Each offense is a *felony* carrying penalties of fines and imprisonment. [69]

   3.  **Other options:** EPA's other enforcement options include: (1) *administrative compliance* orders; (2) administrative *penalties*; (3) and *noncompliance penalties*. [69]

   4.  **Enforcement issues:** Appropriate issues in an enforcement proceeding include: (1) whether the *source was in compliance*; (2) whether the requirement *applies to the particular source*; and (3) limited procedural issues. A source may raise the economic or technological infeasibility of a requirement in conferences about compliance orders and in enforcement proceedings. Infeasibility may also be raised during the penalty stage of a noncompliance proceeding to aid in fashioning a remedy. [69]

B.  **Citizen suits:** Any person may bring a citizen suit against a source to enforce any emission standard or permit limitation provided that the person or group satisfies the constitutional requirements for *standing* and provided that the citizen has given *60-days notice* to EPA, the state, and the violator before bringing the suit. If the EPA is already pursuing an action against the violator, the citizen's action will be precluded. The federal district courts have jurisdiction. The CAA allows citizen suits not only for continuing violations, but for *wholly past* violations as long as the past violation occurred more than once. Costs and civil penalties are available in addition to injunctive relief. Citizen suits may be brought against the EPA to *compel* the EPA to perform a *non-discretionary duty* and to compel agency action "unreasonable delayed." [69-70]

C. **Petitions for review:** A person or group may petition for review of the actions of EPA in promulgating or acting upon any national, local, or regional standard or regulation. A person may also challenge rulemaking procedural determinations if he objected to the procedural error during the public comment period with reasonable specificity. Lastly, a person may petition for review *EPA's failure to act*. A petition for review must be filed within 60 days of publication of EPA's action in the Federal Register. [70-71]

D. **PSD enforcement:** The type of PSD program (whether it is state or federal) controls the type of enforcement action. [71]

E. **Criminal sanctions:** A party who knowingly violates the CAA may be subject to criminal penalties. A person may also be subject to criminal sanctions if they *"negligently"* or *"knowingly"* release hazardous air pollutants that place another person in *"imminent danger of death or serious bodily injury."* [71]

CHAPTER 7

# THE FEDERAL WATER POLLUTION CONTROL ACT (FWPCA)

# I. REGULATORY FRAMEWORK

The Federal Water Pollution Control Act of 1972 (FWPCA) is also commonly referred to as the Clean Water Act (CWA). The basic framework of the statute is a system of *nationally uniform, technology-based standards* imposed on individual sources through a permit system. The requirements of the Act vary depending upon the type of discharger and the type of pollutant. [76]

A. **Goals of FWPCA:** The original goals of the Act were to make the nation's waters *fishable and swimmable* by 1983, and eliminate the discharge of pollutants into navigable waters by 1985. [76]

B. **Programs:** The Act consists of three major programs that deal with point sources of pollution, nonpoint sources, and oil spills. [76]

    1. **Point sources:** The point source is "any *discernible, confined and discrete conveyance* . . . from which pollutants are . . . discharged." Several programs are aimed at preventing or controlling the pollution caused by these sources. [76]

        a. **Direct discharges and the NPDES program:** The National Pollutant Discharge Elimination System grants *permits that control the amount and concentration* of pollutants that are discharged directly into navigable waters by industrial and municipal facilities. Permits may be issued by the state or by EPA. Permits last for five years. [76]

            i. **Private:** All private industrial facilities discharging pollutants into U.S. waters may only discharge *subject to stringent technology-based standards*. [76]

    ii.  **Publicly Owned Treatment Works (POTWs):** POTWs, otherwise known as municipal sewage treatment plants, are subject to different discharge standards than private facilities. [76]

  **b. Indirect discharge and pretreatment program:** Indirect dischargers allow their waste to enter the municipal sewage treatment system to be treated there. The FWPCA imposes some ''pretreatment'' requirements on these dischargers. [77]

  **c. Dredge and fill program:** A *separate national permit system* exists for construction activities that result in dredging or filling of wetlands. [77]

**2. Nonpoint sources:** Pollution from runoff or from a nondiscrete source, also called areawide pollution, requires *different methods of control*. The Act addresses nonpoint source pollution but these provisions have failed to control the significant amount of nonpoint source pollution that is produced. [77]

**3. Oil spill program:** The FWPCA contains a separate section pertaining solely to the spills of oil and other hazardous substances into navigable waterways. It applies *exclusively to oil* and only to *navigable waterways*. [77]

## II. KEY STATUTORY PROVISIONS OF THE CLEAN WATER ACT

Understanding the scope and structure of the CWA requires a careful reading of its underlying statutes. [77-78]

## III. NATIONAL POLLUTANT DISCHARGE ELIMINATION SYSTEM (NPDES) PROGRAM

NPDES permits are granted to control the amounts of pollutants discharged from industrial and municipal facilities. The limits on the quantities discharged will be based on either the pollution control technology available or ambient water quality standards. [78]

**A. Direct discharges and technology-based limitations:** In a technology-based limitation, the present or future status of the environment is not a factor: facilities are to use the *"best" technology* to control the amount of pollution discharged. [78]

**1. Existing sources:** Existing sources of pollution are required to use *technology-based limitations*, although typically from an add-on standpoint. Requirements to change an already functioning industrial process are unusual. [78]

**2. New sources:** New sources may be required to *modify the process itself*—to place pollution control mechanisms within the design of the facility. This is potentially more stringent than existing source requirements. [78]

**3. Publicly Owned Treatment Works (POTWs) standards:** The standards for these facilities are somewhat less stringent than other sources. [78]

  **a. Primary treatment:** Primary treatment involves collection of sewage into tanks so that solid matter settles and the POTW can *use chemicals to remove organic matter*. [78]

**b. Secondary treatment:** Secondary treatment involves the *further removal of organic matter* through physical, chemical, or biological treatment methods. Certain biological treatment methods are deemed the equivalent of secondary treatment under the Act. [78-79]

**4. Standards:** Point-source standards are the core of the FWPCA, and include *best practicable control technology* (BPT), *best available control technology* (BAT), and *best conventional control technology* (BCT). [79]

    **a. BPT:** The best practicable control technology is the *average of the best technology* in use at the time an effluent limitation is set. [79]

    **b. BAT and BCT:** In the 1977 Amendments to the FWPCA, the second phase of regulation prescribed different standards for different categories of pollutants. [79]

        **i. Conventional pollutants:** Point sources discharging pollutants such as biochemical oxygen demanding (BOD), suspended solids, and pH must achieve the *best conventional control technology* (BCT) as to these pollutants by the deadline. [79]

        **ii. Nonconventional pollutants:** Point sources discharging pollutants that are not conventional or toxic *must achieve BAT* by the deadline. [79]

        **iii. Toxic pollutants:** Point sources discharging ordinary toxics *must achieve BAT* by the deadline. [79]

    **c. Setting effluent limitations:** EPA may set BPT and BAT on a *classwide basis* through regulation, and is not required to set the standards on a case-by-case basis through permits. [79]

    **d. Factors in setting limitations:** Generally, EPA may consider factors set forth in the statute in setting effluent limitations. [79]

        **i. Receiving water quality:** EPA *may not consider* the quality of receiving water because of the clear Congressional intent to adopt technology-based standards and to avoid the scientific uncertainty involved in making water quality determinations. [79-80]

        **ii. Cost:** The role of cost in setting effluent limitations differs depending on the standard being set. [80]

            **(1) BPT:** Cost is a *comparison factor*. EPA must compare the cost of the technology with the effluent reduction benefits. [80]

            **(2) BCT:** Cost is a *double comparison factor*. EPA must engage in a two-step analysis: (1) determine the industry cost-effectiveness ratio, and (2) compare that ratio to the cost-effectiveness ratio for equivalent POTW limitations. [80]

            **(3) BAT:** Cost is a *consideration factor*. [80]

**5. Variances and exceptions from federal standards:** The types of variances allowed depend upon the technological standard involved. [81]

    **a. BPT:** By regulation, EPA has provided for variances from BPT for individual plants. This variance is known as the *fundamentally different factor* (FDF) variance, and the Supreme Court has required its use. [81]

b. **BCT for conventional pollutants:** The *FDF variance is allowed* under §301(n). An innovative technology variance is also allowed. [81]

c. **BAT for nonconventional pollutants:** Variances include the *FDF* variance, the *economic inability* variance, the *water quality* variance, and the *innovative technology* variance. [81]

d. **BAT for toxic pollutants:** The FDF variance is available, but *no economic inability* variance will be allowed as to toxic pollutants. [81]

e. **New source standards:** No variances are allowed. [81]

f. **POTWs standards:** Certain municipalities may qualify for a POTW variance that waives discharges into marine waters. [81]

g. **Scope of FDF variance:** *Economic inability* to meet technology costs is *not grounds* for granting an FDF variance. [82]

h. **Deadlines for FDF variances:** A source *must apply* for an FDF variance within 180 days of EPA's promulgation of a standard. EPA must approve or deny the variance within 180 days. [82]

i. **Upset defense:** EPA has recognized that even in the best controlled atmosphere, pollution limits may be exceeded for reasons beyond the control of the facilities. The upset defense was inserted in all federally issued permits for this occurrence (state permits are not required to contain the provision). To assert this affirmative defense, the facility must show: [82]

   ■ that it had *installed the appropriate technology*;

   ■ that the facility with the technology was being *properly operated*;

   ■ that the excess in limit was *beyond the control* of the facility; and

   ■ that the facility *notified the government* within 24 hours.

# IV. PRETREATMENT PROGRAM FOR INDIRECT DISCHARGES

Many industrial facilities discharge into sewer systems of POTWs and not directly into navigable waters. These *"indirect"* dischargers must comply with the *"pretreatment"* program of §307(b). There is no national permit program for indirect dischargers as there is with direct dischargers. Indirect dischargers only comply with such pretreatment standards as are promulgated and standards are set only for pollutants that interfere with or pass through POTWs. Thus, the statutory scheme imposes very different requirements on point source discharges depending upon the type of discharger—direct private discharger, POTW discharger, or indirect discharger. Indirect dischargers are treated differently from direct dischargers because indirect discharges will be treated twice—once by the indirect discharger and once by the POTW. [83]

A. **Pretreatment standards:** There are basically three types of pretreatment standards. [83]

   1. **General pretreatment standard:** The general pretreatment standard is *applicable to all indirect dischargers*, and prohibits facilities from discharging waste that will *cause or contribute to the POTW violating* its permit or the sewage sludge standards. [83]

   2. **Categorical standards:** Categorical technology-based limitations for existing and new sources are imposed on an *industry-by-industry basis*. Pursuant to a consent decree, EPA pro-

mulgates the categorical restrictions for classes and categories of industrial sources equivalent to technological standards for new and existing direct dischargers. Restrictions apply to those pollutants that would *otherwise pass through or interfere with a POTW*, and are based in part on the *economic and technological capacity of the industry as a whole*. [83]

The Water Quality Act of 1987 amended §307 to provide an innovative technology extension similar to that for direct dischargers.

3. **Locally imposed standards:** Local limits may *be developed on an industry or pollutant basis* and be included in a municipal ordinance, or developed for a specific facility and included within the municipal contract or permit for that facility. In addition, POTWs with previous problems of interference and pass through which are likely to recur must develop *specific local limits to implement the prohibition* on interference and pass through of pollutants. [83]

B. **Sewage sludge standards:** Sewage treatment by POTWs produces sewage sludge. Sludge can be used as fertilizer unless it is contaminated with metals or other toxic pollutants. In 1977 an amendment authorized POTWs to grant *"removal credits"* to dischargers of toxic pollutants to reduce categorical standards for such pollutants by the level of treatment achieved by the POTW, in order to avoid duplicative treatment by the indirect discharger and the POTW. Removal credit is *precluded if it would prevent sludge use or disposal* in accordance with sludge management guidelines. EPA is required to promulgate standards for POTWs because most toxic metals discharged into POTWs end up in the POTWs' sewage sludge. [84]

# V. WATER QUALITY STANDARDS

In addition to federal effluent standards, each state retains the authority to promulgate its own standards regulating water quality. [84]

A. **State water quality standards:** States go through several steps in promulgating and revising water quality standards. [84]

1. **Designate uses:** A state must *designate the use* of each body of water within the state. The use *need not be an existing use*. EPA may not review use designations because of the resistance to perceived federal interference in land use. By regulation, however, existing uses and the water quality necessary to meet them *may not be downgraded* by the state. [84]

2. **Determine criteria:** A state then determines criteria, or the *maximum concentration* of a pollutant that can be allowed without jeopardizing the designated use. Recommended national criteria have presumptive applicability. [84]

3. **Determine total maximum daily load:** A state next determines the *total maximum daily load* (TMDL), or the total amount of a pollutant from point sources and nonpoint sources that will not cause the water to exceed the criteria. States may allocate the TMDL among various dischargers as it sees fit, which can be a difficult process. [84]

4. **Translate into permit limitation:** Finally, the state translates an individual plant's share of the TMDL into a *numerical limitation in the source's permit*. [84]

B. **Antidegradation policy:** States may not lower existing uses and the water quality necessary for them. A state may lower the use of certain high quality water to a fishable and swimmable level if *necessary to accommodate important social or economic development*. A state may not lower the use of outstanding national resources such as waters in national and state parks or of other exceptional importance. [84-85]

C.  **Problems with system:** Various problems have prevented the state water quality standards system from being effective. [85]

D.  **Toxic hot spots:** Areas that consistently *fail to meet water quality standards* due to toxic pollution are known as toxic hot spots. The FWPCA requires states to identify those areas and the facilities involved in those areas, and to develop "individual control strategies" to ensure that these areas come into compliance. [85]

E.  **Compliance with downstream water quality standards:** One significant issue is whether EPA or a state must consider the water quality standards of downstream state in issuing a permit. In *Arkansas v. Oklahoma*, 503 U.S. 91 (1992), the Court upheld an EPA regulation that required compliance with downstream water quality standards, but held that a permit could be denied only if discharges would cause an *"actual detectable violation"* of a downstream state's water quality standards. [85]

F.  **Compliance with minimum flow requirements:** In *PUD No. 1 of Jefferson County v. Washington Department of Ecology*, 114 S. Ct. 1900 (1994), a local utility challenged the state's inclusion in a dam's NPDES permit of a minimum flow requirement to maintain its water quality standard to ensure a habitat for fish downstream. The Court upheld applicability of this requirement as part of the §401 certification because *compliance with state water quality standards is required* for §401 certification. [85]

# VI.  PERMITS

The Clean Water Act permit system is the National Pollutant Discharge Elimination System (NPDES). Permits may be issued by the state or by EPA. Permits last for five years. The purpose of a permit is to *identify and limit* the most harmful pollutants while leaving the vast number of other pollutants to disclosure requirements. Therefore, polluters may discharge pollutants not specifically listed in the permit(s) as long as they report the other pollutants. [85]

A.  **State-issued permits:** A state may issue permits if it has an EPA-approved permit program.

1.  **Approval and review of permits:** Permit procedures are governed by *state law*, and subject to review in state courts. [85]

2.  **EPA veto:** EPA may veto a state-issued permit if the permit is *outside the guidelines* and requirements of the Act. [86]

B.  **EPA-issued permits:** EPA has permitting authority in states without an approved program.

1.  **Approval and review of permits:** Each federal permit involves a *full adjudication* of the issues. [86]

2.  **State certification:** Each source must provide state certification that the *discharges of the source will comply* with the Act as a condition to EPA permit issuance. [86]

# VII. ENFORCEMENT

Enforcement of FWPCA provisions is similar to the enforcement scheme under the Clean Air Act. [86]

**A. EPA enforcement:** EPA may issue a *compliance order*, may institute a *civil action*, or may pursue *criminal sanctions* against an alleged violator. [86]

1. **Compliance orders:** The order must state the violation with *reasonable specificity* and must give the alleged violator *reasonable time to comply* with the order. [86]

2. **Civil actions:** EPA should bring suit in the federal district court ''for the district in which the defendant is located or resides or is doing business.'' Relief available includes *temporary or permanent injunctions or civil penalties*. [86]

3. **Criminal liability:** EPA may seek criminal penalties against a violator who *negligently or knowingly violated an Act provision.* The criminal enforcement provisions of the CWA list four categories of criminal conduct: negligent violations, knowing violations, knowing endangerment, and false statements. Convictions carry fines and imprisonment terms. [86-87]

4. **Other enforcement options** [87]

   a. **Administrative penalties:** These penalties are classified as *per violation* penalties and per day penalties.

   b. **EPA inspection:** EPA may require sources to *maintain records* and *institute monitoring* mechanisms. EPA may visit sources and inspect these records and monitoring equipment.

**B. Citizen suits:** *Any person with standing* may sue any alleged violator of an effluent limitation or an order issued by a state or EPA. A citizen suit may not be brought to enforce state regulations that mandate stricter standards than required by the CWA. A citizen may also bring suit to *compel the EPA to perform a non-discretionary duty*. [87]

1. **Procedural requirements:** A citizen must *give notice* to EPA, the state, and the alleged violator 60 days prior to commencing suit. If suing a discharger, the citizen must bring suit in the *federal district court* for the district in which the *source is located*. [87]

2. **Available relief:** A citizen may seek *injunctive relief or civil penalties*. A court may award costs to the prevailing party. [87]

3. **Jurisdiction:** A citizen must allege an *ongoing or repeated* violation of the Act for subject matter jurisdiction to exist under the citizen suit provision; no suit exists for a ''wholly past'' violation. [87-88]

**C. Petitions for review:** Any interested person may seek judicial review of certain listed actions of EPA. [88]

1. **Procedural requirements:** The person should sue in the United States Court of Appeals for the circuit in which the interested party resides or does business. The person must bring suit within 120 days of EPA's action unless new grounds arise after the notice period has expired. [88]

2. **Available relief:** The court may award the costs of litigation to the prevailing party. [88]

## VIII. NONPOINT SOURCE POLLUTION

nonpoint source pollution is usually *runoff, or pollution not channeled* through a discrete conveyance. The Act addresses nonpoint source pollution but these provisions have failed to control the significant amount of nonpoint source pollution that is produced. [88]

A. **Act provisions:** The FWPCA provisions dealing with nonpoint source pollution involve federal funding of state programs.

    1. **Section 208:** This section provides for a *federal funding* mechanism to fund state programs developed to control nonpoint source pollution. Most states' programs attempt to control runoff through land use controls, an intrusive and expensive method of control. [88]

    2. **Section 319:** States are required to develop nonpoint source pollution *management programs* by 1988 with federal funding. [88]

        a. **Identification of problem:** Each state must *identify the waters threatened* by nonpoint source pollution. [88]

        b. **Promulgation of program:** Each state must *develop a state management program* that identifies "best management practices," sets up implementation programs, and establishes a schedule of milestones. [89]

B. **Failure of provisions:** The programs under §§208 and 319 have failed to control nonpoint source pollution.

    1. **No adequate funding:** Both programs were designed to be funded by the federal government, yet Congress did not adequately fund these programs. States were also left to spend what money was provided without any oversight. [88]

    2. **No sanctions:** If a state failed to implement programs to control nonpoint source pollution, *EPA had no authority* to develop a plan for the state, unlike the sanction of a federal implementation plan under the Clean Air Act. [88]

    3. **Difficult to control:** Developing programs to control nonpoint source pollution is a difficult task because the most effective way of controlling such pollution is through *regional programs*. Yet, states do not organize their affairs on a regional basis, but on a state-wide or local basis. [88]

    4. **No meaningful enforcement:** EPA cannot use its enforcement authority to compel control over nonpoint source pollution and citizen suits are unavailable. [89]

## IX. WETLANDS

The Clean Water Act does not specifically address wetlands protection, but EPA and the Army Corps of Engineers have utilized the §404 permit process to provide some protection for wetlands. [89]

A. **Definition of wetlands:** Both the Corps and the EPA utilize the definition of wetlands as "those areas that are *inundated or saturated* by surface or ground water at a *frequency and duration sufficient to support . . . a prevalence of vegetation* typically adapted for life in saturated soil conditions." 30 C.F.R. §328.3(b). [89]

**B. Section 404 jurisdiction:** A §404 permit must be issued for the "***discharge of dredged or fill material*** into the navigable waters at specified disposal sites." FWPCA §404(a). [89]

1.  **Discharge:** *Redepositing* of materials may constitute a discharge. [89]

2.  **Dredged and fill materials:** Dredged material is *excavated or dredged from the waters* of the United States. EPA and the Corps have different definitions of fill material. [89]

3.  **Navigable waters:** The Corps and EPA broadly define navigable waters under §404 to include *wetlands adjacent to the waters* of the United States. The Supreme Court has upheld this interpretation. [89]

**C. Exemptions from permit requirement:** Certain activities are exempt from the permit requirement for discharges of dredged or fill material. [90]

1.  **Exemptions:** The exemptions include discharges from (1) ***normal farming activities***, (2) ***maintenance or reconstruction of dams***, (3) ***construction or maintenance of farm ponds*** or irrigation and drainage ditches, (4) construction of temporary sedimentation basins, (5) construction of ***farm roads, forest roads, or roads for mining*** operations, and (6) ***activities covered by nonpoint source pollution programs***. [90]

2.  **No exemption:** Any of the discharges exempted under §404(f)(1) will be subject to the permit requirement if the purpose of the activity is to convert the waters to a new use. [90]

**D. Permit requirements:** Each §404 permit must meet certain substantive guidelines promulgated. [90]

1.  **Substantive requirements:** A permit will issue if: *no practicable alternative* exists to the proposed project; *no significant adverse impacts* on aquatic resources will result; *all reasonable mitigation measures* are employed; and the proposed project will *not violate any statute*. [90]

2.  **Practicable alternatives analysis:** If an activity is not water dependent, a practicable alternative is presumed available unless the applicant demonstrates otherwise. [90]

3.  **Role of EPA:** EPA has the power to *veto* a §404 permit. [90]

4.  **General permits:** The Corps may issue a general permit as an alternative to a §404 permit on a state, regional, or nationwide basis for categories of activities that are similar in nature if: each activity alone causes minimal adverse environmental effects, and the cumulative impacts on the environment are also minimal. [91]

**E. The takings issue in wetlands regulation:** The Fifth Amendment prohibits the federal government from taking private property without just compensation. There have been many cases asserting that imposition of *governmental restrictions* on wetlands development constitutes a *regulatory taking* of the property without compensation. Of these cases, only a few before the late 1980s had succeeded on the taking claim. [91]

1.  **The effect of the navigational servitude:** In *Kaiser Aetna v. United States*, 444 U.S. 164 (1979), an artificially created pond was developed into a marina and connected to a bay through dredging and filling. The Supreme Court held that *public access to the pond constituted a taking* because the pond was not a waterway traditionally subject to the navigational servitude and public access would deprive the owners of an essential property right, the right to exclude others. [91]

2. **Wetlands regulation under §404:** In contrast, taking challenges to §404 permit denials have utilized the more traditional taking analysis. Traditional taking clause analysis focuses on whether the *regulation substantially advances a legitimate state interest and whether the landowner is deprived of all or almost all of the property.* Before the 1987 trilogy of Supreme Court takings cases, takings challenges to permit denials were rarely successful. [91-92]

CHAPTER 8

# SAFE DRINKING WATER ACT (SDWA)

## I. PURPOSE

The Safe Drinking Water Act of 1972 (SDWA) is designed to *assure the safety of public water* supplies for human consumption. Protection of underground sources of drinking water from toxic contaminants is of special concern. [95]

## II. PROTECTION METHODS

The SDWA uses various methods to protect drinking water.

A. **National Drinking Water Regulations:** National Drinking Water Regulations are *health-based standards* promulgated by the EPA that regulate public water systems and that specify and limit contaminants in drinking water through *maximum contaminant levels* (MCLs) and treatment techniques. The goal of these regulations is to protect public health and welfare to the extent feasible through *"the use of the best technology . . . available."* This best available technology (BAT) standard is limited only by additional health risk considerations that a BAT may introduce into the drinking water supply and by cost-benefit considerations. BAT is not often feasible for smaller public water systems; therefore the EPA is charged with identifying variance technologies for use by those smaller public water systems that are unable to implement the best technologies and treatment standards. [95]

1. **National Primary Drinking Water Standards (NPDWSs):** NPDWSs are used to protect the public health by *regulating the level of physical, chemical, biological, or radiological substances or matter in the drinking water* of "public water systems." A "public water system" is "a system for the provision to the public of water for human consumption *through pipes or other constructed conveyances*, if such system has at least 15 service connections or regularly serves at least 25 individuals." NPDWSs are enforceable standards and *require compliance* by public water systems with MCLs or treatment techniques for those contaminants that raise public health concerns and require regulation. In addition to those contaminants that the EPA may deem necessary to regulate, the SDWA requires specific regulation for arsenic, sulfate, and radon.

   A state may have primary enforcement responsibility for public water systems provided that it has adopted drinking water regulations that are at least as stringent as federal standards. [95-96]

2. **National Secondary Drinking Water Standards (NSDWSs):** NSDWSs are *nonenforceable aesthetic standards* established by the EPA to protect public welfare. Secondary drinking water

regulations may apply to the *odor, appearance, or other aesthetic quality* of drinking water that may adversely affect the public welfare. [96]

3. **Public information and notice:** As of the 1996 Amendments to the SDWA, each person served by a public water system is required to be informed of any *conditions affecting their drinking water that may have an impact on public health*. Owners and operators of public water systems are required to give notice of any failure to comply with an MCL, any failure to perform a requirement, the existence of a variance or exemption, the existence of a concentration of any unregulated contaminant for which the EPA has required public notice.

In addition to requiring public notice, the SDWA also requires annual reports by the EPA, or the state, as the primary enforcement agency, informing the public of violations within the state. Lastly, by August 1998, the EPA, in consultation with public water systems are required to produce consumer reports informing the public about their water systems and the regulations that apply to it. [96]

4. **Enforcement:** Whenever the EPA determines that a public water system does not comply with an applicable requirement such as an MCL, the EPA must issue an *administrative order* requiring the public water system to comply with the regulation, or the EPA must *commence a civil enforcement action*. In states which have primary enforcement responsibility, the EPA must first notify the state and provide it with *advice and technical assistance* to help bring the public water system into compliance. If 30 days after notification, the state has not commenced enforcement action, the EPA must either initiate a civil action against the public water system or it may issue an administrative order requiring compliance.

Though secondary drinking water regulations are not enforceable by the EPA, the SDWA requires the EPA to notify a state when it determines that a public water system within the state is violating a secondary regulation and such noncompliance is due to the state's failure to take ''reasonable action'' to assure compliance. [96]

B. **Protection of underground sources of drinking water:** This category of regulation is aimed at maintaining the *purity* of drinking water at its source. [96]

1. **Wellhead protection:** All states must have programs to protect ''wellhead protection areas'' from potentially dangerous contaminants. A ''wellhead protection area'' consists of the *surface and subsurface area surrounding a well* that supplies a public water system and through which contaminants are reasonably likely to move toward and reach such a water well or wellfield. Each state program must have at a minimum: a protection area, a protection program, a contingency plan, and a requirement that all potential sources of contamination must be considered. [97]

2. **Sole source aquifer demonstration program:** This is a grant program that *reimburses* states for 50 percent of their costs in developing and implementing state programs to identify and preserve critical aquifer protection areas. The objective of this program is to *maintain the quality of groundwater in a manner reasonably expected to protect human health*, the environment, and groundwater resources. [97]

3. **Underground injection control program:** The purpose of this program is to *regulate deep well injection* of wastes into ''dry'' wells in order to assure that underground injection will not endanger drinking water sources. The extent of regulation depends upon which of five regulatory categories the well encompasses. Excluded from the program are aquifers that are not and

will not be suitable for water supply purposes and aquifers that are "mineral, hydrocarbon or geothermal energy producing," or are capable of becoming commercially mineral or hydrocarbon energy producing. [97]

CHAPTER 9

# CONTROL OF TOXIC SUBSTANCES

## I. RISK ASSESSMENT AND MANAGEMENT

**A. Generally:** Risks include: (1) *private risks* which are either of natural origin or man-made, and are produced in relatively discrete units, with local impacts more or less subject to personal control; and (2) *public risks* which are man-made threats to human health or safety that are centrally or mass produced, broadly distributed, and largely outside the risk bearer's direct understanding and control. Public risks carry unique problems such as long latency periods, diffuse impact, diffuse cost, and discounting of risk. [99-100]

**B. Process of risk assessment and risk management:** Policy-making for environmental contaminants and hazards involves two steps. *Risk assessment* is the use of a base of scientific research to define the probability of some harm coming to an individual or a population as a result of exposure to a substance or situation. This phase is solely concerned with generating data, and it is supposed to be value neutral. *Risk management* is the public process of determining and applying values and of deciding what to do where the risk has been determined to exist by the risk assessment phase. Theoretically, these are two independent processes. [100]

**C. Risk assessment concerns**

    **1. Inexact science:** The types of choices which scientists make during this process can influence the outcome. These choices include the type of *statistical models* used to manipulate data and the *types of tools used to translate data*. [100]

    **2. Increasing neutrality in risk assessment:** The way scientists and experts present their data and the assumptions on which the data is based *can affect the neutrality* of the risk assessment. [101-102]

**D. Problems with risk management**

    **1. Identifying societal attitudes regarding risk:** Policymakers are faced with the inherent difficulties of ascertaining society's level of risk aversion. [102]

    **2. Costs of risk management:** Society must determine how it wishes to *weigh* the cost of prevention against the cost of unmitigated risk. [102]

    **3. Decision by experts:** Delegating risk management to scientists or other experts may be problematic because their views *do not always adequately represent* the sentiments of society. [102]

**E. Risk management and the judiciary:** The courts' role in risk management has not been the balancing of interests, but rather procedural reviews of agency decisions such as: (1) *when* risk management should occur; (2) *what factors* should be considered by the agency; (3) and the *adequacy* of the agency's consideration. [102-103]

# II. THE RESOURCE CONSERVATION AND RECOVERY ACT (RCRA)

**A. Generally:** RCRA provides a comprehensive regulatory structure for *managing both hazardous and non-hazardous solid wastes* and has health-oriented goals of conservation, reducing waste disposal, and minimizing threats to human health and the environment. The Act creates *four separate programs* governing hazardous waste, non-hazardous waste, underground storage tanks, and used oil. Understanding the Resource Conservation and Recovery Act (RCRA) requires a careful reading of the underlying statutes. [103-104]

**B. Cradle-to-grave program:** This management system requires waste materials to be *classified*, written manifests to *track waste shipments from generation until disposal*, and *certification* of disposal facilities for hazardous wastes through a permit system. [105]

**C. Identification of hazardous wastes:** For hazardous materials to be subject to regulation they *must first fall under the definition of solid waste* before the question of whether the material is actually hazardous may be explored. [105]

    **1. Solid wastes:** The solid waste definition for RCRA is *extremely broad.* For the most part, it includes *discarded* semi-solids, liquids, and contained gases. EPA has defined "discarded material" as any material which is either: (1) abandoned; (2) recycled; or (3) considered inherently wastelike. EPA has also promulgated regulations that further divide the RCRA definition of solid waste into *three groups*: (1) garbage, refuse, or sludge; (2) solid, liquid, semi-solid, or contained gaseous material; or (3) other substances. Materials in the first category are always subject to RCRA; materials in the third category are always excluded. [105-107]

    **2. Determining which wastes are hazardous:** RCRA requires EPA to develop criteria for identifying hazardous wastes in one of two ways: (1) by *"listing"* a waste as hazardous or (2) by determining a waste hazardous because of certain *"characteristics."* Hazardous wastes are defined as solid waste that (a) causes or significantly *contributes to an increase in mortality or reversible illness*; and (b) poses a *substantial hazard* to human health or the environment when improperly handled. [107]

        **a. Listed hazardous waste:** This is the simplest way EPA can designate a waste as hazardous. The criteria includes: (1) a waste exhibits ignitability, corrosivity, reactivity, or toxicity; (2) a waste may be considered "acutely toxic"; and (3) a waste contains certain toxic constituents and is capable of posing substantial harm. [107]

        **b. Characteristic hazardous waste:** This is the more common way EPA determines if a waste is hazardous. A material cannot be deemed hazardous unless the characteristic in question can be *measured by an available standardized test* method that is reasonably feasible or unless the characteristic can be reasonably detected through general knowledge of the waste. A material may also be deemed hazardous if it exhibits (1) ignitability; (2) corrosivity; (3) reactivity; or (4) toxicity. Toxicity is determined by a complicated "toxicity characteristic leaching procedure" (TCLP). [107-108]

        **c. Mixtures and "derived from" wastes:** EPA regulations define hazardous wastes to include certain mixtures of *hazardous and non-hazardous* materials. [108-109]

        **d. Exclusions:** EPA regulations exclude certain extremely common materials from classification as hazardous wastes such as *household wastes and mining/oil production wastes*. [109]

D. **Requirements for generators, transporters, and treatment, storage, and disposal facilities:** RCRA imposes *specific requirements* on generators and transporters of hazardous waste as well as on those who treat, store, and dispose of hazardous waste. These special requirements include *obtaining EPA identification numbers and permits*. [110]

E. **Land disposal of hazardous wastes, "land ban":** In 1984, Congress passed the Hazardous and Solid Waste Amendments (HSWA), which *prohibits all land disposal* of hazardous wastes except when substances are *treated satisfactorily or a petition is granted*. The satisfactory treatment exception requires waste to be treated with the "best demonstrated technology" (BDAT). Petitions may be granted only after a petitioner shows that their methodology meets health and safety requirements and that there will be *"no migration"* from the hazardous waste disposal site for "as long as the wastes remain hazardous." [111]

   1. **Special provisions for groundwater contamination:** The 1984 Amendments placed a *total ban* on the placement of liquid hazardous wastes into landfills in order to protect groundwater supplies. The amendments also require groundwater monitoring. [111-112]

F. **Export of hazardous wastes:** RCRA requires *informed consent* before export of hazardous wastes may take place. [112]

G. **Regulation of non-hazardous wastes:** Facilities receiving non-hazardous wastes are known as "sanitary landfills." EPA has also imposed *more detailed requirements on certain landfills* known as Municipal Solid Waste Landfills. RCRA completely bans the dumping of any kind of solid waste anywhere other than at sanitary landfills. [112]

H. **Judicial Review:** Section 7006 of RCRA authorizes judicial review of EPA regulations and EPA's denial or issuance of permits. Section 7002(a)(2) is a citizen suit provision against EPA for failing to perform non-discretionary duties. [112]

I. **EPA's power of remedial action:** Section 7003 of RCRA provides the government with a *means of responding* to existing contamination problems. The relief provided by §7003 is equitable and frequently takes the form of an injunction. This section may be applied to inactive sites as well as active ones. [112-113]

J. **Government enforcement:** RCRA gives the federal government a wide range of enforcement provisions to ensure compliance with the hazardous waste management provisions of the Act. EPA is authorized to *assess civil penalties* for past or current violations, *issue compliance orders, revoke permits,* or seek temporary or permanent *injunctive relief*. RCRA also contains *criminal provisions* for knowing violations of the Act. Criminal liability may apply to both *corporations* and their responsible officials. [114-115]

K. **Citizen suits:** RCRA permits an individual to commence an action in federal district court to enforce RCRA's waste disposal requirements if the citizen can show that someone is creating an *"imminent and substantial endangerment."* Prevailing parties can obtain *injunctive relief, civil penalty awards, litigation costs,* and expert *witness fees,* and reasonable attorneys' fees. Citizens suits are *barred if EPA* or a delegated state *has already commenced and is diligently pursuing* an enforcement action. Since government agencies have primary enforcement responsibility, an individual must notify the state, the EPA, and the violator *60 days* prior to filing suit. [115-116]

   1. **Suits against federal agencies:** An individual may also bring a citizen suit against federal agencies for both "coercive" fines imposed to induce compliance and "punitive" fines imposed to punish past violations. Sovereign immunity is waived in these instances. [116]

**2. Past cleanup costs:** The Supreme Court has held that ***RCRA precludes recovery*** of past cleanup costs. A suit must allege a continuing danger at the time of a suit. [116]

# III. COMPREHENSIVE ENVIRONMENTAL RESPONSE, COMPENSATION, AND LIABILITY ACT (CERCLA)

**A. Generally:** CERCLA is essentially a tort-like, backward-looking statute designed to clean up hazardous waste sites and respond to hazardous spills and releases of toxic waste into the environment. CERCLA is ***remedial*** rather than regulatory, and thus it focuses on remediation of ***past*** activities. The Act creates the "Superfund," which the government may use to finance governmental response activities, to pay claims arising from private party response activities, and to compensate federal and state governments for damage to natural resources. Section 1107(a) attaches liability only if there is a ***release*** or ***threatened release***. Notification to the National Response Center is required under §103(a) for the release of a reportable quantity of a hazardous substance. Understanding CERCLA requires a careful reading of the underlying statutes. [117-118]

**B. Scope of liability**

**1. Cost recovery actions:** Congress created a bifurcated method for cleaning up hazardous waste sites by providing both ***government and private parties*** with authority to respond to hazardous releases at abandoned and inactive waste disposal sites. Whereas the federal government may turn to the Superfund in responding to hazardous waste disposal problems, private parties may maintain claims to recover costs of cleanup from parties responsible for the harm. [118-120]

**2. Strict and joint and several liability:** CERCLA imposes both ***strict liability and joint and several liability***; consequently, a person responsible for a small fraction of the waste at a site could conceivably be liable for 100 percent of the cleanup costs. However, courts have held that damages should be apportioned if the harm is divisible. [120]

**3. Liable classes under CERCLA:** Four classes of persons are liable for cleanup costs: (1) ***current owners or operators*** of a facility subject to cleanup; (2) ***past owners or operators*** of a such facility at any time in the past when hazardous substances were disposed of; (3) ***generators***, or any person who ***"arranged for"*** the treatment or disposal of a hazardous substance at the facility; and (4) ***transporters, or persons who transported*** hazardous substances to the facility. [120]

**a. "Arranged for":** Courts have interpreted this phrase very broadly. [120]

**b. Owner/operator:** An owner or operator generally ***participates in the management of a facility or has the authority to control the facility***. [121]

**c. Parent corporation:** The Supreme Court has held that parent companies may be held liable under direct or derivative liability. *United States v. Bestfoods*, 524 U.S. 51 (1998). [122]

**d. Successor liability:** The First Circuit applied the ***"mere continuation"*** test to determine if liability was appropriate. *United States v. Davis*, 261 F.3d 1 (1st Cir. 2001). Two district courts have applied the federal ***"substantial continuation"*** test. [122]

**e. Individual liability:** Individuals acting in a corporate capacity may be held liable under the ***"responsible corporate officer"*** doctrine. [122-123]

**4. Resource Conservation and Recovery Act §7003 compared to CERCLA §§106(a) and 107(a):** RCRA §7003 is broader than CERCLA; however CERCLA provides the government with several powerful tools not available under the RCRA. For example, CERCLA allows EPA to issue **abatement orders** to any class of persons, and CERCLA is **more easily triggered** due to its more lax standard for what constitutes an infraction. However, CERCLA does not provide these tools to citizens seeking abatement of potential harms from hazardous substances. [123]

5.  **Hazardous substances:**  The "hazardous waste" definition in CERCLA incorporates by reference hazardous or toxic substances under RCRA, the Clean Water Act, the Clean Air Act, and the Toxic Substances Control Act. CERCLA **also covers "pollutants or contaminants"** that "may present an imminent and substantial endangerment" to health of the environment. The Act specifically **excludes petroleum and natural gas** from CERCLA coverage; however the exclusion does not apply to petroleum products or contaminants. [123]

6.  **Disposal:**  Liability under §107(a) also **requires a showing that the hazardous substances** were **"disposed of."** Sales and transfers of a useful product are not considered disposal. [123-124]

7.  **Retroactivity:**  CERCLA applies retroactively to **acts committed before the effective date** (December 11, 1980) of the statute. [124]

8.  **Burden of proof regarding consistency with NCP:**  One of the elements for a cost recovery action is that the costs incurred cleaning up the site be **consistent with the National Contingency Plan (NCP)**, a plan designed to establish procedures and standards for preparing for and responding to releases of hazardous substances. [124]

9.  **National Priorities List:**  CERCLA authorizes EPA to create a list of the **worst hazardous waste sites** in the country. These sites are placed on the National Priorities List (NPL). EPA employs a Hazard Ranking System (HRS) for determining which waste sites should be placed on the NPL. The EPA can use Superfund resources for undertaking a **remedial action only** at sites on the NPL. [125]

10. **EPA's enforcement options:**  When EPA determines that an actual or threatened release of hazardous substances presents an **"imminent and substantial endangerment"** to health or the environment, the EPA may issue an **abatement order**. If the abatement order is ignored, EPA may: (1) **bring action** in federal court to hold the violator in contempt or impose fines; (2) **take over cleanup** without pre-enforcement judicial review; or (3) **seek punitive damages**. [125]

11. **Jury trial:**  Parties have a constitutional right to a jury trial if the relief sought is characterized as a legal action pursuant to common law or statute, but the right to a jury trial is not recognized for equitable claims. [125-126]

12. **Attorneys' fees:**  Courts are split over whether the prevailing party in a private cost recovery suit under CERCLA may be awarded attorneys' fees. Under the **American Rule**, a successful plaintiff cannot receive litigation costs absent the showing of bad faith litigation or a statutory authorization. Under CERCLA, attorneys' fees are expressly authorized for government response actions and citizen suits, but are not expressly provided for in private cost recovery actions. [126]

C.  **Defenses:** CERCLA liberalizes the causation requirement by dispensing of the traditional concept of limiting accountability to the harms directly traceable to the offending conduct. This reflects a **scientific rationale** that waste sites often contain chemicals and substances from numerous generators which have commingled, thus making a specific causal link virtually impossible. CERCLA shifts the **burden to the defendant** to prove that its waste was not responsible for the harm. The moderated causation requirement also reflects the ***public interest*** in an effort to impose liability more readily and effectively on the actors responsible. Joint and several liability exists if the harm is indivisible, but since the harm is almost always indivisible at Superfund sites, joint and several liability is almost always applied. [127]

1. **Affirmative defenses:** The three narrow affirmative defenses are that the hazardous substance release was: (1) caused *solely* by an act of God; (2) caused *solely* by an act of War; or (3) attributed *solely* to a third party. [127]

2. **Innocent landowner defense:** One important manifestation of the third-party defense is the innocent landowner defense which allows a landowner to escape liability by showing that the ***harm was caused "solely" by a third party***. Partial fault by the landowner invalidates the defense. The defense also requires that the defendant had no contractual relationship with the third party connected to the harms caused by the third party. This "contractual relationship" can include real estate transactions. [127-128]

3. **Lender liability:** CERCLA *excludes* from the definition of owner/operator those institutions that ***hold the property as a security interest***, such as a bank. This exclusion ***does not apply if the lender "participated in management"*** rather than simply held the property on paper. [128-129]

4. **Bankruptcy:** Courts are split as to whether a CERCLA claim that arises before a debtor files bankruptcy is discharged. The dispute is over whether a CERCLA action becomes a claim when the waste is released or when the person asserting the claim has reason to know of the potential claim. [129]

D. **Settlement:** CERCLA *encourages* settlement where ***practicable and in the public interest***; however, the ultimate decision regarding settlement rests with EPA. [129]

1. **Incentives to settle:** For the government, settlement through ***consent decrees*** offers an attractive vehicle to economize limited administrative resources while expeditiously cleaning up hazardous waste sites. For ***potentially responsible parties*** (PRPs), CERCLA contains several provisions that give PRPs tremendous incentives to forego litigation such as: (1) settling parties are ***shielded from contribution claims***; (2) ***non-settlors*** are effectively ***penalized*** by bearing the risk of disproportionate liability; (3) ***non-settlors*** must face ***strict liability*** with narrow defenses; and (4) non-settlors face joint and several liability irrespective of fault. [129-130]

2. **Three types of settlement:** Three distinct types of settlements are provided for in CERCLA: (1) ***agreements for the cleanup*** of a hazardous waste site; (2) ***de minimis settlement*** with small volume generators; and (3) cost recovery settlements. [130]

3. **Contribution:** Under the 1986 Amendments to CERCLA, any ***PRP has the right to seek contribution*** from other PRPs during or following an action under §§106 or 107. To facilitate the negotiating process, EPA has the discretion to allocate 100 percent of the response costs among PRPs prior to cleanup by assessing non-binding allocations of responsibility (NBAR) which later serve as a useful framework for allocating cleanup costs among themselves and to develop settlement offers. [130-131]

4. **Judicial review of consent decrees:** The standard of review for a consent decree is whether the proposed decree is ***fair, reasonable, and faithful*** to the objectives of the governing statute. A consent decree will not be approved where the agreement is illegal, a product of collusion, inequitable, or contrary to the public good. [131-132]

E.  **Natural resource damages:** In addition to authorizing recovery of response costs from dealing with contaminated sites, CERCLA also establishes *liability for damages* to natural resources. Overall, the requirements for recovering damages under this second scheme are *much tougher* to meet than the requirements for recovering damages for cleanup costs. Liability includes "damages for *injury to, destruction of, or loss* of natural resources, including the reasonable costs of assessing such injury, destruction, or loss resulting from such a release." CERCLA authorizes "trustees to bring natural resource damage claims on behalf of state and federal governments and Indian tribes." CERCLA does not provide for private recovery of natural resource damages. A *government is not required to possess title* to the affected resource in order to seek damages, but it must show that it substantially controls, regulates, or manages the resource. The government cannot recover natural resource damages for harms to private property. [132]

F.  **Brownfields Economic Redevelopment Initiative:** The EPA has announced a series of programs to encourage and empower states, localities, and other agents of economic redevelopment to prevent, assess, clean up, and reuse contaminated community property. Brownfields are abandoned, idle, or under-used industrial and commercial facilities that the EPA hopes to remediate and reuse through the Brownfields Action Agenda, announced January 1995. [133-134]

# IV.  TOXIC SUBSTANCES CONTROL ACT (TSCA)

A.  **Goals:** The principle goals of TSCA are to (1) *gather information* regarding chemical toxicity, use and exposure, and (2) *to utilize that data to protect human health and the environment* from unreasonable risks. [134]

1.  **Information gathering:** The Act provides EPA with a variety of means to generate information on chemical substances which allows the agency to ascertain gaps in coverage. These tools include: (1) *required testing* by manufacturers; (2) *pre-manufacture notification* (PMN); (3) *imposing reporting and record-keeping duties* on industry and mandating chemical inventories. [134]

B.  **Two-tier evaluation system:** The Act permits EPA to *require* health and environmental *effects testing* of chemicals by and at the expense of their manufacturers and processors. Second, it empowers EPA to *regulate substantively the manufacturing* and processing of those chemicals. [134]

1.  **Required testing:** EPA may require testing where (1) the manufacture, distribution, processing, use, or disposal of a particular chemical substance *"may present an unreasonable risk"* of injury to human health or the environment; or (2) where there has been substantial human exposure to chemical substances or where chemicals may reasonably be anticipated to enter the environment in *substantial quantities*. Voluntary testing agreements are not allowed. [135]

2.  **Implementation of regulations:** The data acquired under required testing provides EPA with the necessary information to determine whether to regulate. EPA has broader testing authority than regulatory authority, thus in regulating, it must do so using the *"least burdensome"* means. EPA must consider economic consequences to industry in addition to considering the human health and the environment when deciding to regulate. [136]

a.  **Judicial review:** Unlike most environmental statutes, the standard of review of EPA regulations under TSCA is *far less deferential* than the "arbitrary and capricious" standard used under the Administrative Procedure Act. [136]

3. **Interagency Testing Committee (ITC):** The ITC is a committee of representatives from specified agencies and federally funded institutions. The ITC's principle charge is to provide EPA with a *list* of no more than the *50 most dangerous chemicals* for priority consideration for testing. [136-137].

C. **Enforcement:** TSCA contains a wide range of both civil and criminal remedies including penalties, attorneys' fees, and emergency enforcement. [137]

D. **Miscellaneous provisions:** In addition to regulating toxics generally, the Act also contains provisions specifically dealing with *asbestos, PCBs, and radon*.

1. **Asbestos:** Title II, a 1986 Amendment to TSCA, establishes four principle goals to combat the asbestos problem: (1) *inspection* of school buildings; (2) *development of asbestos management plans* by local agencies; (3) determination and implementation of appropriate response actions; and (4) *training and accreditation* of asbestos contractors and laboratories. [137]

2. **PCBs:** TSCA sets forth a detailed scheme to dispose of polychlorinated biphenyls (PCBs), to *phase out manufacture, processing, and distribution* of PCBs, and to *limit the use* of PCBs. Congress provided an exemption to this regulation for "totally enclosed" use of PCBs. [137-138]

3. **Radon:** Title III, a 1988 Amendment to TSCA, deals with indoor radon pollution by establishing provisions aimed at *providing information to the public* so that detection and mitigation steps can be taken. [138]

4. **Regulation of biotechnology:** EPA has declared its authority to *regulate substances created through genetic engineering* and biotechnology under FIFRA and TSCA. [138]

5. **Coordination with other federal agencies and laws:** TSCA provides for *coordination of actions* between the EPA and other federal agencies with respect to the health risks presented by chemical substances. [138-139]

# V. FEDERAL INSECTICIDE, FUNGICIDE, AND RODENTICIDE ACT (FIFRA)

A. **Regulatory framework:** The cornerstone of the regulatory framework *requires registration* with the EPA of pesticide products in the United States, coupled with *provisions for review, cancellation, and suspension* of registration in certain circumstances. [139]

1. **Registration:** This process requires an agency determination that the *pesticide will not present unreasonable adverse* risks to human health or the environment when used appropriately. FIFRA allows EPA to disclose some testing information about a pesticide that has been submitted by an applicant. The Act provides for trade secret protections such as data protection and compensation. [139-140]

2. **Experimental use permits:** FIFRA provides for the issuance of experimental use permits (EUPs) by EPA to *allow for testing* of unregistered chemicals or for the application of registered pesticides for an approved use. [140]

3. **Local regulation:** FIFRA does not contain any express language preempting local regulation; however, it *precludes states from imposing labeling or packaging requirements different* from the Act. [140]

4. **Reregistration:** Pesticides registered *prior to 1984* are *required to reregister* under the now more stringent standards. [140]

5. **Pesticide contamination of groundwater:** FIFRA *does not regulate* pesticide contamination of groundwater. [140]

6. **Export of pesticides:** The Act provides an *exemption* for pesticides produced solely for export to a foreign country; the rationale being that other countries can apply their own requirements tailored to their needs. However, the foreign purchaser must sign a statement acknowledging restrictions on resale and distribution in the United States. [140-141]

B. **Cancellation and suspension:** These measures are the *most critical* mechanisms designed to ensure that the public and the environment continue to be protected from dangerous pesticides. The trigger for an agency to *initiate proceedings for the removal* of a product from the market mirrors the type of cost-benefit analysis involved in the original registration process. [141]

1. **Cancellation:** Cancellation *bans* a pesticide from shipment or use in interstate commerce. Cancellation proceedings may be initiated whenever it "*appears* to the [EPA] that a pesticide . . . generally causes unreasonable adverse effects on the environment." 7 U.S.C. §136d(b). [141]

2. **Suspension:** Suspension may be used to *remove* a pesticide more swiftly from the market than cancellation. Absent an emergency, EPA may not issue a suspension order until it has (1) notified registrants of the pesticide of the cancellation of the registration and the plan to issue a suspension based on a finding of "imminent hazard"; and (2) given registrants an opportunity for an expedited hearing on whether an imminent hazard exists. Emergency suspension orders do not require these preliminary steps and are issued as a last resort. [142]

3. **Existing stocks:** When a cancellation or suspension order is issued, FIFRA allows EPA to allow *continued sale and use* of existing stocks of pesticides as long as doing so is *not inconsistent with the purpose of the Act* and has no unreasonable adverse effects on the environment. FIFRA requires EPA to indemnify registrants and applicants holding unused stocks of suspended and canceled pesticides. [142-143]

4. **Economic consequences:** Before suspending a pesticide, EPA *must consider* "the economic, social, and environmental costs and benefits of the use of [the] pesticide." [143]

C. **Pesticides and the Federal Food, Drug and Cosmetic Act (FFDCA):** The Delaney Clause of the FFDCA provides that *no food additive shall be deemed safe if it induces cancer*. [143]

D. **Pesticides and the Clean Water Act:** FIFRA and CWA are complementary, but FIFRA was not designed to take local and specific conditions into account. [143]

CHAPTER 10

# LAND USE

# I. COASTAL ZONE MANAGEMENT

A. **Coastal Zone Management Act (CZMA):** Passed by Congress in 1972, the Coastal Zone Management Act declared a *national interest in land use decisions* previously viewed as local in nature. [149]

1. **Purpose:** The purpose of CZMA is to *preserve the unique values* of coastal lands and waters by encouraging the states to devise land and water use plans for coastal protection. The Act provides funds to states that develop programs consistent with the Act's standards. In addition, federal agencies, permittees, and licensees must show that their proposed developments on the outer continental shelf are consistent with the state's management program. [149]

2. **Definition of coastal zones:** The CZMA defines coastal zones as "the *coastal waters* (including the lands therein and thereunder) and the *adjacent shorelands* (including the waters therein and thereunder), strongly influenced by each other and in proximity to the shorelines of the several coastal states, [which] includes islands, transitional and intertidal areas, salt marshes, wetlands, and beaches." A coastal zone's *seaward boundary* is limited to the *extent of state ownership and title*, and a zone extends inland "to the extent necessary to control shorelands . . . and to control those geographical areas which are likely to be affected by or vulnerable to sea level rise." The definition is intentionally vague, giving states great discretion in setting their own jurisdiction. [149]

   a. **Exclusions from definition:** Excluded from the definition of coastal zones is *land held in trust by or solely subject to the discretion* of the federal government. [149]

3. **Funding of state management programs:** In order to receive federal grants under CZMA, a state must coordinate its coastal zone program with other state and local plans applicable to areas within the coastal zone, establish an effective mechanism for continuing consultation and coordination between the designated management agency and other agencies within the coastal zone, and obtain approval from the Assistant Administrator of the Office of Ocean and Coastal Resource Management (OCRM) after complying with the requirements of the management process. A state must also *satisfy certain technical requirements* such as identifying the boundaries of the coastal zone, providing definitions of certain terms, identifying control mechanisms, and setting up guidelines. In addition, in order to receive grants for the management and administration of its program, a state must satisfy additional requirements. [150-151]

4. **Methods of regulation:** *States may choose* the method of regulation of their programs. These include:

   a. State *establishment of criteria and standards* subject to administrative review and enforcement compliance; [151]

   b. Direct state *land and water use planning and regulation*; [151]

   c. State administrative *review for consistency* with the power to approve or disapprove after public notice and an opportunity for hearings. [151]

5. **Federal participation and consistency review:** *Certain categories* of activity "affecting any land or water use or natural resource of the coastal zone" trigger review of federal actions for consistency with state CZMA plans. These include: activities conducted or supported by a federal agency, federal development projects, federal licensed and permitted activities, and federal assistance to state and local governments. The most controversial consistency determinations have involved oil and gas lease activities in the outer continental shelf. A Presidential exemption is authorized if the activity is in the paramount interest of the United States. [151]

B. **Coastal Zone Enhancement Grants (CZEG):** Created by the 1990 Amendments to the CZMA, the Coastal Zone Enhancement Grant Program *provides grants* to coastal states for the purpose of *attaining any one or more of the coastal zone enhancement objectives.* If a state fails to implement a CZEG program then it is subject to grant withholding under CZMA or the Clean Water Act. [152]

1. **CZEG objectives:** The CZEG program is aimed at the: [152]

   a. *protection* of existing coastal wetlands or creation of new coastal wetlands;

   b. *minimization or elimination* of development in natural hazard areas;

   c. *increased public access* to coastal areas having recreational, historical, aesthetic, ecological, or cultural value;

   d. *reduction of marine debris* through increased management of contributing uses and activities;

   e. *development and adoption of procedures to control impacts* created by coastal growth and development;

   f. *preparation and implementation of special area management plans* for important coastal areas;

   g. *planned use* of ocean resources; and

   h. *adoption of enforceable procedures and policies* regarding the siting of coastal energy and government facilities.

2. **nonpoint source pollution control measures:** Every state and federally approved program must develop a program to implement coastal land use management measures for controlling nonpoint source pollution. [153]

C. **The Coastal Barrier Resources Act (CBRA):** Enacted in 1982, the Coastal Barrier Resources Act was the first environmental law that coordinated federal fiscal policy with environmental preservation. The purposes of CBRA were to *minimize danger to human life* from poorly located coastal development, to *end federal expenditures for such developments*, and to *preserve the natural resources of the coastal barriers*. It accomplishes these purposes by restricting new federal assistance or expenditures, including financial assistance for construction or purchases of structures, roads, bridges, facilities, etc. within coastal barrier areas. Thus, the cost of development must be borne by the developer and consumer of coastal barrier property. [153]

D. **Floodplain regulation:** Substantial regulation of land use, development, construction practices, and insurance coverage in *areas prone to flooding* exists at the federal, state, and local levels. [153]

1. **National Flood Insurance Program (NFIP):** Since flood insurance is not widely available through the private insurance market, participation in the federal flood insurance scheme is a *practical necessity* for owners of the many residences and businesses erected in floodplain areas. NFIP has become a source of leverage for the federal government to exert pressure on state and local government land use measures. [153-154]

   a. **Who is regulated?** NFIP regulates property owners in flood-prone communities who *agree to meet federal requirements* for reducing potential flood damage. The regulatory measure is the *"100 year floodplain,"* any area that hydrologists determine will flood once in every 100 years on average. The NFIP is administered by the Federal Insurance Administration and the Federal Emergency Management Agency (FEMA). [154]

b. **Liability of the federal government:** The United States government is *not liable* for damages arising from floods or the administration of the NFIP; this applies to claims of property damage and personal injury. [154]

c. **Disaster Relief Act of 1974:** The Disaster Relief Act *provides financial assistance* to state and local governments, individuals, and businesses in the event of a Presidentially declared ''emergency'' or ''major disaster.'' [154]

d. **Executive Order 11988 — practical alternatives:** This executive order requires federal agencies *to avoid direct or indirect support of floodplain development* when there is a ''practicable'' alternative. [154]

E. **Takings in coastal and floodplain regulation:** The Supreme Court has taken a narrow view of what constitutes a ''regulatory taking.'' A taking may be found, however, if a landowner is deprived of *all economically feasible use* of ''the parcel as a whole,'' even if the taking is only temporary. [154-155]

F. **Public trust doctrine:** This doctrine *protects public access* to water resources. It generally requires that the resources cannot be sold and must be maintained for uses that serve the public. This doctrine has been expanded to include the preservation of tidelands in their natural state for recreational and ecological value. [155]

# II. SOIL CONSERVATION

Agriculture is the primary contributor to soil loss and nonpoint source water pollution.

A. **Soil loss and nonpoint source pollution:** Soil loss per acre is estimated by one of two methods, the *universal soil loss equation* (USLE) or the *wind erosion equation* (WEE), both of which estimate the average annual tonnage of soil lost from each soil type. These losses are compared to *loss tolerances* (T-values) which reflect the amount of annual loss that can be sustained without adversely affecting the productivity of the land. In addition to affecting productivity, *soil erosion and water runoff are major contributors to nonpoint source pollution*. It harms air and water quality and also impacts toxic contamination from nutrients and pesticides contained in the soil. [155-156]

B. **Federal programs designed to control soil erosion:** There are more than 27 programs under 8 different agencies designed to control soil erosion. All of these programs are *voluntary* and provide technical assistance and cost-sharing for conservation measures. [156]

1. **1985 Farm Bill:** The basic purpose of programs under the Farm Bill is to *ensure cross-compliance* between conservation programs and the price and income support programs of the USDA. When introduced, the bill contained conservation provisions that were new to agricultural programs such as sodbuster, swampbuster, conservation compliance, and conservation reserve programs. Although compliance with these programs is voluntary, a producer will receive no USDA program payments unless the producer is in compliance with the conservation provisions. [156]

2. **1990 Farm Bill:** This bill, known as the Conservation Program Improvements Act, was a congressional reauthorization of the 1985 Farm Bill that *expanded the scope* of the conservation program. [156]

3. **1996 Farm Bill:** Known as the Federal Agriculture Improvement and Reform Act, this reauthorization of the earlier Farm Bills establishes seven years of guaranteed but annually declining program payments to producers who contract with the USDA. It also created several new, primarily voluntary conservation programs and provided for more flexibility through new definitions and more flexible guidelines. [156-157]

   a. **Sodbusting and conservation compliance:** This provision is designed to ensure that *no highly erodible land will be placed into production* of an agricultural commodity for the first time without full application of a compliance plan. There are different time lines for the implementation of conservation plans, depending on whether the highly erodible land was in production or not set aside during the period between 1981 through 1985. The provisions provide for graduated sanctions for good faith violations, restricted liability, and re-eligibility. [157]

   b. **The Environmental Conservation Acreage Reserve Program (ECARP):** Created by the 1990 Farm Bill, the ECARP's goals are to *assist owners and operators of highly erodible lands*, other fragile lands, and wetlands in conserving and improving the soil and water resources of their farms and ranches. Under the 1996 Amendments, the Secretary may designate conservation priority areas for compliance with nonpoint source pollution requirements. Assistance payments to producers are based on the significance of the resource problems and the practices that ''maximize environmental benefits for each dollar expended . . . '' [157-158]

      i. **Eligible land:** Eligible lands include highly erodible croplands, marginal pasture lands, and croplands that the Secretary determines contribute to the degradation of water quality. In order to put eligible land into the conservation program, the owner must agree by contract for a duration of 10 to 15 years to: (1) apply an approved conservation plan and (2) not to use land for agricultural purposes other than permitted by the Secretary. [158]

      ii. **Landowner assistance:** If the requirements are met, the owner of the land receives technical assistance and cost-sharing for all conservation measures required. The contracts last between 10 to 15 years. [158]

      iii. **Environmental Quality Incentives Program (EQIP):** The 1996 Farm Bill consolidated programs created under prior bills into one conservation cost-share program, the EQIP. The 1996 Act allows for a sort of self-certification of compliance. In addition, landowners who certify their compliance may revise the conservation plan so long as the landowner is maintaining the same level of conservation treatment. If a USDA employee observes a possible violation of a plan and the landowner does not take corrective action within one year, a review of compliance may be conducted. [158-159]

   c. **Swampbusting:** Under this provision, a person is totally or partially *ineligible* for USDA benefits if that person produces an agricultural commodity on wetlands converted after December 23, 1985, or who, after December 23, 1990, converts a wetland by any means so as to make possible the production of an agricultural commodity. There is a provision for graduated sanctions in case of a good faith violation in the conversion of a wetland. [159]

      i. **Exemptions:** There are a number of exemptions for land converted from wetlands before December 23, 1985 or for production of an agricultural commodity on a wetland using normal farming or ranching techniques. In addition, the Secretary may grant an exemption if the action has a minimal effect on the wetland, or if the wetland values and functions are mitigated by the restoration of another converted wetland in accordance with a restoration plan. [159]

    **d. Wind erosion:** The 1996 Farm Bill creates a wind erosion estimation pilot project to review wind erosion factors. [159]

## III. FARMLAND PRESERVATION

**A. Introduction:** Concern about irreversible conversion of agricultural land to non-agricultural uses in the 1970s led to a wave of farmland preservation measures. These measures are aimed at *reducing the attractiveness of farming areas for development*. [160]

**B. National Agricultural Lands Study (NALS):** This study set forth the idea of the *"impermanence syndrome,"* an effect of development and the threat it poses on farmers that eventually leads to the sale of farmland for development. [160]

**C. The Farmland Protection Policy Act (FPPA):** Adopted in 1981, the FPPA's purpose is to preserve the United States' ability ''to *produce food and fiber in sufficient quantities* to meet domestic needs and the demands of our export markets.'' The Act is applicable to federal agencies and depends on a balancing of national interests and the importance of farmland protection. There is no private enforcement provision. [160]

**D. Right-to-farm laws:** These laws are essentially a codification of the common law and *provide protection to agricultural operators* that were in place before neighboring residential development. There are four model right-to-farm laws on which most right-to-farm laws have been based: [160]

    **1. New York model:** Prohibits local laws that unreasonably restrict agricultural operations. [160]

    **2. North Carolina model:** Prohibits nuisance lawsuits that occur as a result of changed locality conditions if the agricultural facility has been in operation for at least one year before the changed conditions. This is the most frequently utilized model. [160]

    **3. Tennessee model:** Applies to feedlots, dairy facilities, and egg production facilities and protects the facility from state and local regulations and from nuisance lawsuits by persons if the facility has been in operation for at least one year prior to the complaining person's ownership of the land. [160]

    **4. Washington model:** An agricultural facility is *presumed reasonable* if it is operated in accordance with good agricultural practices and was established prior to the surrounding nonagricultural uses. [161]

**E. Agricultural zoning:** Zoning is one of the most popular types of farmland preservation. [161]

    **1. Exclusive zoning:** Exclusive zoning *prohibits nonagricultural use* of land within the district. The main advantage of this type of zoning is that it insures that there will be no conflict between residential and agricultural uses in those areas where non-farm dwellings are prohibited. The disadvantage is the higher administrative costs due to the extensive restrictions and the requirement for review of farm dwellings. In addition, this type of zoning is more difficult to pass because it prohibits residential development. [161]

2. **Nonexclusive zoning:** Preservation is accomplished through the *limiting of density of residential development* by establishing agricultural use as one of the permitted uses within the district. There are four types of this zoning: [161]

   a. **Conditional use zoning:** where *non-farm dwellings* are a conditional or special use for which a permit must be obtained; [161]

   b. **Large-lot zones:** where a minimum lot size is set in an area in which non-farm development is permitted. The lot size usually corresponds to the usual size of a farm in the area. This is the most common form of nonexclusive zoning; [161]

   c. **Fixed area-based allocation zoning:** where there is a direct linear relationship between the size of the tract and the number of dwelling units permitted on the tract; and [161]

   d. **Sliding-scale area-based allocation zoning:** where the number of dwelling units permitted does not increase in direct linear proportion to the size of the parcel. [161]

F. **Agricultural districting:** Districting programs provide incentives to farmers to join in the voluntary creation of districts to resist pressure development. Membership entitles farmers to an array of benefits that vary from state to state. Formation of a district is initiated by one or more farmers and approved by an authorized governmental agency. [161]

# IV. SPECIAL MANAGEMENT TECHNIQUES

Some states have state or regional agencies that have supervisory authority over the local governments with regard to land use planning and controls. The *Model Land Development Code (1975)* authorizes the designation of areas of critical concern in which the state may establish general principles for guiding development. *Regional programs* ordinarily govern regions contained entirely within a state but may also govern an interstate region. In a program for the *purchase of development rights (PDRs)*, a state or local planning board purchases the development rights and holds them indefinitely (land banking). In a program for *transferable development rights (TDRs)*, the rights are purchased by private buyers to be transferred for use in another area. TDRs can be used to allow building at a higher density than ordinarily allowable under the applicable zoning guidelines. [162]

# V. THE ENDANGERED SPECIES ACT (ESA)

A. **Purpose:** Congress enacted ESA in 1973 to conserve *both endangered and threatened species* and also to protect the ecosystems upon which those species depend. ESA has become one of the most controversial limitations on land development. [162]

B. **Listing a species:** Section 4 provides the Secretary of the Interior with the authority to determine whether any species is endangered or threatened.

   1. **Endangered species:** The following factors are considered in determining if a species is endangered: (1) degree of habitat destruction; (2) overutilization; (3) disease or predation; (4) *failure of existing regulatory mechanism* to protect; and (5) other factors affecting continued existence. [163]

   2. **Threatened species:** A species is considered threatened if it is *likely to become endangered* in the foreseeable future. [163]

3. **Critical habitat:** Whenever a species is listed as endangered, the Secretary is required to *specify the range over* which the species is endangered and *designate areas of critical habitat.* [163]

4. **Fish and Wildlife Service:** The Secretary receives recommendations from the Fish and Wildlife Service whose role is to assess technical and scientific data against relevant listing criteria. [163]

C. **Limits on federal agency action — §7:** Section 7 of ESA prohibits a federal agency from engaging in any action (including any federally funded projects) that is *likely to jeopardize the continued existence of endangered or threatened species or that destroys or adversely affects the critical habitat of such species.* Any federal agency proposing an action with such a potential must consult with the Fish and Wildlife Service before carrying out the action. Section 7 covers direct and indirect threats. A violation of the Act occurs if either set of guidelines, procedural or substantive, are not followed. [163-164]

D. **Limits on private development — §9:** Section 9 has the greatest impact on private land development activities by making it *unlawful for any person* to "take" an endangered or threatened species. [164]

1. **"Person" defined:** "Person" is defined *very broadly* under the Act and includes individuals, private entities, governmental bodies and their subdivisions, political subdivisions, or any other entity subject to the jurisdiction of the United States whether foreign or domestic. [164]

2. **"Taking" defined:** "Taking" means to "harass, harm, pursue, hunt, shoot, wound, kill, trap, capture, or collect, or attempt to engage in any such conduct." [164]

3. **"Harm" defined:** "Harm" is also defined very broadly and *includes direct and indirect* methods of killing or injuring. Habitat modification that eventually leads to death or injury, such as through impairing essential behavioral patterns, is included in the definition. There has been much debate over the extent that habitat modification can be considered "harm." [164-165]

4. **"Harass" defined:** The regulations define "harass" to mean "an intentional or negligent act or omission which creates the likelihood of injury to wildlife," and *includes annoying* an animal to the extent that *normal behavioral patterns are disrupted.* [165]

5. **Exceptions:** Section 10(a) provides for issuance of permits for *scientific studies* and *incidental takings.* A taking is considered incidental if the "taking is incidental to, and not the purpose or, the carrying out of an otherwise lawful activity." No incidental taking permit may be issued unless the permit applicant submits a *habitat conservation plan.* In reviewing the plan, courts consider issues such as whether the taking will appreciably reduce survival likelihood and any measures taken to "minimize and mitigate possible adverse effects." The "No Surprises" rule provides for exceptions to rules and standards governing permit issuance. [165-166]

E. **Enforcement:** ESA provides four avenues for enforcing §9 prohibitions. These include: *civil penalties, criminal charges, Attorney General injunctions*, or *citizen suits.* Private citizens may bring suit in federal court for injunctive relief, and environmental groups have standing to bring suit on behalf of their members. However, no citizen suit may be brought to compel the Secretary to enforce prohibitions of the Act if the Secretary has already commenced an investigation. [166]

CHAPTER **11**

# INTERNATIONAL ENVIRONMENTAL LAW

## I. EMERGENCE OF INTERNATIONAL ENVIRONMENTAL LAW

The principles of modern international environmental law began to emerge in 1972 during the Stockholm Conference, and recently culminated in the 1992 "Earth Summit" in Rio de Janeiro. Many international organizations, including the United Nations (UN), have played a fundamental role in its development. [170]

**A. Stockholm Conference:** The Stockholm Conference, sponsored by the United Nations, was the *first global environmental conference*. It was attended by 113 parties, who adopted two major documents: the Stockholm Declaration on the Human Environment, and Action Plan for the Human Environment. [172]

    **1. Stockholm Declaration on the Human Environment:** The Stockholm Declaration *established a global approach* to environmental problems. Its most important provisions state the principles that humans have a *"fundamental right to . . . an environment of a quality that permits a life of dignity and well-being (Principle 1)";* states have the right to exploit their own resources, but must ensure that activities *within their jurisdiction do not cause damage* to areas outside of that jurisdiction (Principle 21); and noted that states should develop international law regarding liability and compensation for pollution victims (Principle 22). [172]

    **2. Action Plan for the Human Environment:** In the Action Plan, the parties adopted 109 resolutions *aimed to assist states* in assessing environmental problems and providing solutions. [172]

**B. United Nations Environment Program (UNEP):** UNEP was established in 1973 partly as a result of the Stockholm Conference. It is a *subsidiary organ* of the U.N. and *coordinates its environmental activities*. UNEP has a Governing Council, a Secretariat in Kenya, and an Environment Fund. Functions of UNEP include gathering information on environmental problems, recommending possible solutions, and funding programs. It has played a lead role in the formulation of international environmental law, and has sponsored major global agreements. [172-173]

**C. World Charter for Nature:** The World Charter for Nature was drafted in 1982 by the World Conservation Union (IUCN). Its preamble and 24 articles set forth global environmental principles that *focus on the value of nature, the importance of integrating nature with economic planning,* and suggest ways that states can implement these goals. [173]

**D. Draft Articles on State Responsibility:** The International Law Commission (ILC) has drafted various articles that *focus on state liability with regard to transboundary pollution* and other environmental damage. Article 1 states that "every international wrongful act of a state entails the international responsibility of that state." Article 19(3)(d) lists among international crimes "a serious breach of an international obligation . . . for the safeguarding and preservation of the human environment . . . " Articles 29 to 31 describe situations that preclude the liability of a state for an otherwise wrongful act: (1) an act made with consent by the affected state, (2) an act legally made in response to a wrongful act by the affected state, and (3) an act due to extraordinary events that made it materially impossible for the state to act in conformity with its obligations. [173-174]

**E. Restatement (Third) on Foreign Relations Law in the United States:** The American Law Institute has drafted a Restatement on Foreign Relations which provides in §601 that a *state is obligated* *to take measures to ensure that activities under its control conform to general international principles* regarding transboundary pollution, and are not conducted so as to cause significant injury to another state. It also states that a state is legally responsible for such an injury. [174]

**F. The 1992 Rio Earth Summit:** The United Nations Conference on Environment and Development (UNCED), or Earth Summit, was held in Rio de Janeiro, Brazil, and was the largest global conference on the environment. The Earth Summit produced *five major documents*: the Convention on Biological Diversity, the Climate Change Convention, the Declaration of Principles on Forest Conservation, and the Rio Declaration and Agenda 21. [174]

    **1. The Rio Declaration:** The Rio Declaration, the modern equivalent of the Stockholm Declaration, contains 27 non-binding principles, endorsed by the Conference and U.N. General Assembly. It reflects a compromise between developed and developing nations, and *specifically includes the "right to development."* Principle 2 provides that states have a right to exploit their resources pursuant to environmental and developmental policies, a revision of Principle 21 of the Stockholm Declaration. Other key provisions relate to notification of environmental disasters, environmental impact assessments, and liability for transboundary pollution and compensation to its victims. [174]

    **2. Agenda 21:** This 800-page document contains a plan of action for sustainable development and environmental preservation. It includes a *set of priority actions and means to accomplish them*. A Commission for Sustainable Development is established to monitor and review implementation of Agenda 21. [175]

# II. TRANSBOUNDARY POLLUTION

**A. General rule:** Generally, *no state may use or permit the use* of its territory in a manner that is *injurious to another state* or its persons or property. [175]

    **1. *Trail Smelter Case:*** This landmark case, brought by the United States against Canada, established two fundamental principles of liability under international law for transboundary pollution: (1) a state *must show damage and causation*, and (2) a state has a *duty to prevent*, and may be responsible for pollution by private parties within its jurisdiction. The Tribunal held that Canada was legally responsible for harm caused to U.S. forests in Washington state by a smelter near Trail, Canada. [175-176]

    **2. *Corfu Channel Case:*** The *Corfu Channel Case* was brought in the International Court of Justice (ICJ) by the United Kingdom against Albania for damages to British warships by mines in the Straits of Corfu. The court held against Albania and established the principles that *every state has an obligation not to knowingly allow its territory to be used contrary to the rights of other states*, and a duty to notify other states of imminent danger. [176]

    **3. *Lake Lanoux Arbitration:*** This case was brought by France against Spain, and established the principle that a *downstream state does not have the right to veto an upstream state's use of water*, but the upstream state must consider counterproposals of the downstream state. [176]

    **4. *Nuclear Test Cases:*** These cases, brought in the ICJ by Australia and New Zealand against France, left the legality of nuclear testing unresolved on the merits. However, the ICJ did preliminary enjoin France from testing while it heard the dispute. [176]

B. **Possible theories of liability for transboundary pollution under international law:** Such theories include: (1) *strict liability* for ultrahazardous activities, (2) *liability for negligent or intentional acts* ("abuse of rights"), and (3) *liability for pollution that exceeds an amount a state's neighbors can reasonably endure* ("good neighborliness"). [176]

   1. **Specific treaties focusing on transboundary pollution:** Treaties in this area take a variety of approaches, including agreeing to try to reach agreement ("framework conventions"), establishing substantive standards, "freezing" pollution at current levels, providing for notification and consultation, and authorizing an international organization to establish rules. [176-177]

   2. **Example:** *The acid rain treaties:* Various agreements have been drafted that address the problem of acid rain. The Convention on Long-Range Transboundary Air Pollution of 1979 went into effect in 1983, and had 33 parties, including the U.S., by December of 1991. Its purpose is to "limit and, as far as possible, gradually reduce and prevent air pollution including long-range transboundary air pollution." The Convention provides for research, exchange of information, and an Interim Executive body to monitor pollution in Europe. The Convention does not contain specific ceilings and timetables. Two Protocols to the Convention have been adopted by some of the parties, establishing standards for reduction of sulfur and nitrogen oxides. [177]

# III. OZONE DEPLETION AND GLOBAL WARMING

A. **Protection of the ozone layer:** The ozone layer protects the earth by filtering out harmful ultraviolet radiation from the sun. It is currently being depleted primarily by chloroflourocarbons (CFCs) from air conditioning, aerosols, styrofoam, and refrigerators. Two major treaties address this problem. [177]

   1. **The Vienna Convention for the Protection of the Ozone Layer 1985:** The 1985 Vienna Convention is a *framework convention* that focuses upon *information exchange* and *cooperation* among states for research with a goal to protect human health and the environment from the adverse affects of a diminished ozone layer. [177]

   2. **Montreal Protocol on Substances that Deplete the Ozone Layer:** This Protocol to the Vienna Convention was adopted in 1987, and amended in 1990. It sets forth *timetables* for a 50 percent reduction in use of CFCs by 1999. The 1990 Amendments establish an escalated timetable for reduction in use of CFCs, placing a total ban by the year 2000. The Amendments also establish a fund to assist developing countries in the transition to technology free of CFCs. [177-178]

B. **Protection of the climate:** Another serious global environmental problem is climate change due to the greenhouse effect, which results when certain gases in the air trap infrared radiation near the earth's surface, thus elevating global temperatures. [178]

   1. **United Nations resolutions on climate change:** In 1989, the U.N. passed two resolutions that formally recognized climate change as a global concern to be given high priority. They emphasize the *need for governmental efforts* to prevent climate change, and reviewed possible elements for an international climate change convention. [178]

   2. **United Nations Framework Convention on Climate Change:** This Convention was signed at the 1992 Earth Summit, and *emphasizes the global concern about climate change* caused by

greenhouse gases. Its objective is to stabilize gas concentrations in the atmosphere, with an implicit goal of returning to 1990 levels of emissions by 2000. The parties do not agree to specific goals or deadlines. However, they do commit to periodic national inventories of emissions; mitigation programs; development of technology to control emissions; consider climate change in decision-making processes; and cooperate in the exchange of information, education, and public awareness. Developed countries also agree to use the best available scientific technology, and assist developing countries with financing their obligations under the agreement. [178]

## IV. WILDLIFE PRESERVATION

### A. Provisions under the Stockholm Declaration and the World Charter for Nature

1. **Stockholm Declaration:** Principle 4 of the Declaration states that plants and animals are a world heritage, and that man has a *responsibility to safeguard nature and also consider conservation* when planning economic development. [179]

2. **World Charter for Nature:** Principle 2 of the Charter stresses the need to *safeguard habitats* to protect global genetic viability, and *maintain animal populations* to ensure their survival. In Principle 3, the Charter states that all areas of the earth are subject to conservation. [179]

### B. International Convention for the Regulation of Whaling: This Convention, adopted in 1946, established the International Whaling Commission, and *intended to regulate the fishing industry*. It is increasingly being directed to conservation of whales. Under the Convention, an annual schedule of whaling regulations is published, which the Commission may modify. In 1990, the Commission set a ten-year moratorium on whaling. Any member may opt-out of its obligations under the Convention by objecting. [179]

### C. Convention on International Trade in Endangered Species of Wild Fauna and Flora (CITES): This Convention has over 100 parties, and *sets up a system of import and export permits and regulations* to protect endangered species from overexploitation. The Convention establishes a Secretariat at UNEP to prepare scientific studies and coordinate national recordkeeping required by the Convention. The state parties are required to meet every two years to modify the Convention if necessary. The permits required under the Convention are nationally administered, and keyed to categories of endangered species. No permit may be issued for a species, or a recognizable part or derivative thereof, that is threatened with extinction. [179]

### D. United Nations Convention on Biological Diversity: This Convention was signed at the 1992 Earth Summit. Its objectives include *conserving biological diversity* and the sustainable *use* of biological resources, and *equitable sharing* of the benefits of genetic resources. The parties to the Convention are committed to developing and implementing national strategies to protect biological diversity. The Convention establishes a Conference of the Parties to review implementation and adopt protocols or amendments, a Secretariat to arrange meetings and prepare reports, and a technical body to provide scientific advice to the Conference. [180]

## V. HAZARDOUS WASTE, RADIOACTIVE POLLUTION, AND ENVIRONMENTAL EMERGENCIES

### A. Early conventions on civil liability for nuclear damage: These conventions include the Paris Convention of Third Party Liability in the Field of Nuclear Energy of 1960, the Brussels Conven-

tion Supplementary to the Paris Convention, the Vienna Convention on Civil Liability for Nuclear Damage of 1963, and the Joint Protocol Relating to the Application of the Vienna Convention and the Paris Convention of 1988. [180]

B. **The Chernobyl accident and resulting conventions:** In 1986, an explosion occurred at the Chernobyl nuclear power plant in the Soviet Union. The accident raised questions about the *adequacy of international law* to address this type of emergency. Two conventions were negotiated as a result of the accident: the Convention on Early Notification of a Nuclear Accident, and the Convention on Assistance in the Case of a Nuclear Accident or Radiological Emergency, both signed in 1986. The Convention on Early Notification provides for *notification "forthwith" and information* regarding a nuclear accident which may have a transboundary effect. The Convention on Assistance provides for cooperation between states in the event of a transboundary radiological release. It focuses upon efforts prior to and after nuclear accidents. The International Atomic Energy Agency (IAEA) has a central role under this Convention to *coordinate* emergency response. [180-181]

C. **Basel Convention on the Control of Transboundary Movements of Hazardous Wastes and Their Disposal:** The Basel Convention regulates international trade in hazardous wastes, with an objective to *limit* such trade. Under the agreement, a party *may not export* hazardous waste to another party without consent of that party and proof that it has adequate facilities to dispose of the waste. The Convention contains labeling standards, and prohibits trade with nonparties. [181]

# VI. ANTARCTICA

Antarctica comprises about ten percent of the earth's land and water mass and is the *only continent* that has not been exploited for commercial purposes. There are five principle mechanisms that protect the Antarctic environment: [181]

A. **Antarctica Treaty of 1959:** This Treaty was the first to protect the Antarctic environment. It *assured continued scientific research and suspended the states' right to claim "sectors"* of the continent. The Antarctic Treaty Consultative Parties (ATCPs) include 38 states, 12 original signatories, and 26 other states who have signed the treaty and conducted substantial scientific activity in Antarctica. Key environmental provisions prohibit nuclear explosions and disposal of radioactive waste, and require the ATCPs to meet annually to consult and formulate, if necessary, measures to preserve or conserve living resources in Antarctica. [181-182]

B. **Convention for the Conservation of Antarctic Seals:** This 1972 Convention establishes a *regulatory system* for the hunting of seals, which had almost disappeared from excessive hunting. Some species are completely protected. [182]

C. **Convention on the Conservation of Antarctic Marine Living Resources:** This Convention, signed in 1980, establishes a system for *conservation of marine resources* within the entire Antarctic marine ecosystem extending to the boundaries of the Antarctic Ocean, called the Antarctic Convergence. The Convention permits a "rational use" of resources within the context of its conservation goals. [182]

D. **Agreed Measures for the Conservation of Antarctic Fauna and Flora:** These Measures, adopted by the ATCPs in 1964, declares the Antarctic Treaty Area a "Special Conservation Area," and establishes a *regulatory permit system* for harming wildlife in the area. It also requires that states take steps to minimize habitat interference and water pollution. Areas of scientific interest are designated "Specially Protected Areas," and are subject to special regulatory protections. [182]

E. **The 1991 Madrid Protocol:** The Madrid Protocol provides the *most comprehensive* protection of the Antarctic environment. Article 3 establishes the basic environmental principle that protection of the Antarctic environment "shall be the fundamental consideration[] in the planning and conduct of all activities in the Antarctic Treaty Area." The Protocol provides standards by which to assess the environmental impact of all human activities in the Treaty area, requires that adverse impacts on the environment be limited, and provides for "regular and effective monitoring" to assess environmental impacts. Its annexes provide procedures for environmental impact assessment and waste disposal, and also address conservation of wild flora and fauna, prevention of marine pollution, and area protection and management. Most significantly, Article 7 of the Protocol effectively bans mining on Antarctica for at least 50 years, when the agreement first becomes open for review by Conference of the Parties. [182-183]

# VII. DEFORESTATION

Deforestation involves the unsustainable use of forests and their genetic resources. Of primary concern today is the *destruction of tropical rainforests*. [183]

A. **Consequences:** A fundamental cause of deforestation is thought to be *poverty*. Local impacts include floods, droughts, siltation of rivers, destruction of breeding areas, and the threat to the survival of millions of forest dwellers worldwide. Globally, deforestation is considered the *primary loss of biodiversity* and a major contributor to global warming through the greenhouse effect. [183]

B. **The 1984 International Tropical Timber Agreement:** This Agreement accounts for 95 percent of the international timber trade and is the only global agreement regulating tropical timber. It is administered by the International Tropical Timber Organization, and includes 46 party states. The Agreement is *based on free trade principles*, and is unlikely to be modified for environmental reasons alone. [183]

C. **The Rio Forest Principles:** The Non-Legally Binding Authoritative Statement of Principles for a Global Consensus on the Management, Conservation, and Sustainable Development of All Types of Forests, or Rio Forest Principles, were proposed by the United States at the 1992 Earth Summit after meeting resistance from developing countries to a more binding forestry agreement. In the Rio Forest Principles, the parties *agree to promote international cooperation on forestry, but do not commit to any specific actions*. [183]

D. **Debt-for-nature swaps:** First introduced in 1987 by NGOs, debt-for-nature swaps involve the *purchase of foreign debt* in exchange for domestic forest reserves or other environmental projects. Countries such as Bolivia and Ecuador have participated in swaps, and many others are currently considering them. [183-184]

   1. **Public vs. private debt-for-natures swaps:** The first swaps were "private," meaning at least one of the parties was private. A "second generation" of swaps has emerged, called "public swaps." These occur between sovereign states and account for a greater amount of debt reduction than private swaps. There are three types of public swaps: (1) *government debt purchases*, (2) *government grants* to environmental groups, and (3) *debt forgiveness*. [184]

# VIII. DESERTIFICATION/LAND DEGRADATION

Desertification is identified in Agenda 21 as a key global environmental problem that is *critically linked* to the goal of achieving sustainable development in all countries. It affects about one sixth of the population and one quarter of the total land area of the world. Land that is severely degraded may be permanently lost. [184]

A. **Definition:** The U.N. has defined desertification as land degradation in arid, semi-arid, and dry sub-humid areas (including irrigated cropland) resulting mainly from adverse human impact. [184]

B. **The Lome IV Convention:** This Convention was signed in 1989 between the European Community and the African, Caribbean, and Pacific states, and specifically *calls for national, regional, and international action to preserve resources* and protect ecosystems against desertification and drought. [185]

C. **Past U.N. efforts to combat desertification:** The U.N. Conference on Desertification (UNCOD), held at UNEP in Nairobi in 1977, was the first world conference to set out a plan for initiating and sustaining a cooperative effort to combat desertification. It *focused on technical and economic reforms*, and attempted to integrate national, regional, and international efforts within and outside the U.N., with little progress. [185]

D. **Current U.N. efforts:** Chapter 12 of Agenda 21 includes six program areas addressing desertification that states agree to focus upon, including developing *information and monitoring systems and integrating comprehensive anti-desertification programs* into national development plans. [185]

E. **Treaty envisioned:** Agenda 21 requires the UN General Assembly to establish a committee to oversee the creation of an international convention addressing land degradation and drought. [185]

# IX. MARINE ENVIRONMENT

A. **Generally:** States must ensure, in exercising their sovereign rights to exploit their resources, "that activities within their jurisdiction or control *do not cause damage* to the environment of other states or of areas beyond the limit of national jurisdiction." (Stockholm Declaration). [185]

B. **Third United Nations Conference on the Law of the Sea:** States are required to take *all measures necessary to prevent pollution* of the marine environment from any source. [186]

C. **Vessel-source pollution:** States are required to establish *international guidelines* governing vessel-source pollution through international organizations. Flag states are required to adopt laws and regulations for the prevention of pollution of the marine environment from ships flying their flag or of their registry. Coastal states may adopt laws and regulations for the prevention, reduction, and control of marine pollution from foreign vessels within their territorial sea but may not hamper innocent passage. States may regulate vessel-source pollution in their EEZs through an international organization or diplomatic conference. A state also may make a request to the appropriate international organization for additional coastal state regulation of vessel-source pollution in the EEZ if international rules provide inadequate protection. [186]

D. **Pollution from land-based sources:** All states must adopt laws or regulations to prevent pollution of the marine environment from land-based sources. [187]

E. **Ocean dumping:** States are required to adopt laws and regulations to prevent pollution of the marine environment by the dumping of *sewage, sludge, and other waste materials* into the ocean. These laws must be *comparable to global standards*. Dumping in the coastal zones of states requires consent and also is regulated under the Dumping Convention. [187]

CAPSULE SUMMARY

**F. Pollution from seabed activities subject to national jurisdiction:** States are required to adopt all laws and regulations necessary to prevent pollution of the marine environment arising from, or in connection with, their exploration and exploitation of the seabed and subsoil. [187]

**G. Pollution from deep seabed mining:** The LOS Convention authorizes the Authority to adopt *appropriate rules and regulations* to prevent pollution of the marine environment from deep seabed activities. [187]

**H. Pollution from or through the atmosphere:** All states are required to adopt laws and regulations to prevent pollution of the marine environment from or through the atmosphere. [187]

**I. Protection of fragile ecosystems:** States are obligated to take measures necessary to protect and preserve *rare or fragile ecosystems* as well as the habitat of *depleted, threatened, or endangered species and other forms of marine life*. [187]

**J. Liability:** A state which fails to fulfill its obligations to protect and preserve the marine environment is liable in accordance with international law. [187-188]

**K. Enforcement:** Flag states, coastal states, and port states may all enforce rules and regulations relating to the marine environments depending on the *source* of pollution, the *location* of the violation, and the *degree of harm* to the environment. A state is obligated to compensate the flag state for any injury or loss attributable to unlawful or excessive measures taken against a foreign ship. [188]

**L. Notification and cooperative action:** As soon as a state is aware that injury to the marine environment has occurred or is imminent, it must notify immediately the *appropriate global or regional international organizations* and *all states likely to be affected*. [189]

**M. Government noncommercial ships:** Ships that are used by governments for noncommercial purposes are *not subject* to the international rules, standards, and enforcement procedures discussed above. [189]

# X. INTERNATIONAL TRADE AND ENVIRONMENT

There is a growing recognition that trade and the environment are inextricably linked. Thus, the effects of environmental policy on trade, and environmental implications of trade are emerging as issues of international concern. [189]

**A. The GATT:** The General Agreement on Tariffs and Trade (GATT) *codifies most of the rules* governing international trade. It was established in 1948 and is periodically reviewed by the parties. GATT rules are based primarily on concepts *promoting free trade*, and environmental regulations are frequently viewed as a type of non-tariff barrier, to be forbidden under GATT. There is *no mention* in GATT of environmental protection as a justification for limiting trade. However, *states may legitimately restrain trade* under Article XX if "necessary to protect human, animal or plant life or health" and impose measures "relating to the conservation of natural resources." The Uruguay Round of GATT talks was begun in 1985 and is the first round to link international trade and the environment, with the participants signing a pledge that they agree to undertake a dialogue on the "interlinkages between environmental and trade policies." In 1971, GATT established a Group on Environment Measures and Trade, which first became active in 1991 following a GATT debate on environment and trade. The Group will initially examine trade provisions in existing multilateral environmental agreements, national regulations likely to have an international effect, and trade effects of packaging and labeling requirements aimed at protecting the environment. [189]

**B.** **Conflicting views of traditional free trade theorists and environmentally oriented economists:** GATT negotiators have *difficulty coming to agreement* about the role of the environment in international trade because economists' views in this area conflict. Environmentally oriented economists argue that goods in the international market that do not reflect the environmental costs of production distort the trade process, giving an unfair advantage to those who degrade the environment, termed "ecological dumping." However, under the GATT, this kind of advantage is not recognized as unfair, and the practice is not forbidden. [189-190]

**C.** **The Tuna/Dolphin Decision:** This 1991 decision by a GATT panel was the result of a formal complaint by Mexico against the United States claiming that a United States embargo on Mexican yellowfin tuna was protectionist and a violation of GATT. The United States had imposed the trade sanction to compel Mexico to bring down its kill rate of dolphin in the harvesting of yellowfin tuna to United States standards. The United States argued that it was treating the Mexican product no less favorably than products of national origin, and also invoked the exemption for the protection of natural resources and animals. The panel found that the *import ban* by the United States *violated GATT*, stating that a *product may only be regulated according to its properties*, and the natural resources exemption can only be used to protect living or natural resources in the jurisdiction of the party invoking the exemption. [190]

**D.** **The Global Environment Facility (GEF):** The GEF was established by the World Bank in 1991 as a pilot program to *provide financial assistance to developing countries* to help them implement programs addressing global environmental problems including: ozone layer protection, limiting greenhouse gas emissions, protection of biodiversity, and protection of international waters. The 1992 Biodiversity Treaty and the Montreal Protocol both contain the GEF as a funding mechanism. Contributions to the fund are currently voluntary. It is administered by the World Bank, UNEP, and UNDP. [190]

**E.** **North America Free Trade Agreement (NAFTA):** NAFTA is a unique trade agreement for its *incorporation of environmental protections*. The preamble states that trade must be consistent with environmental protection and conservation. The agreement calls for "harmonization" of the parties' domestic standards with international environmental standards, while preserving in certain circumstances each country's ability to maintain domestic environmental standards which exceed prevailing international standards. Disputes over environmental standards may be resolved by an arbitral panel, with the burden under NAFTA on the party challenging the environmental measure. Although NAFTA by its terms is generally to be given priority over conflicting international agreements, exceptions are made for several major international environmental treaties. A separately negotiated environmental agreement focuses on cleanup of the Mexico/U.S. border area and establishment of a Commission on Environmental Cooperation to ensure enforcement of environmental standards by the parties. [190]

> In *Public Citizen v. U.S. Trade Representative*, 5 F.3d 549 (D.C. Cir. 1993), the D.C. Circuit Court of Appeals held that an environmental impact statement did not have to be prepared for NAFTA because it was not "final agency action" under the Administrative Procedure Act and NEPA itself does not create a private right of action. [190-191]

# XI. MILITARY ACTIVITIES AND THE ENVIRONMENT

The international community is increasingly willing to condemn an aggressor and impose liability for environmental crimes committed during military activities. Liability may arise under a number of international agreements or customary law. [191]

A. **Protocol I to the 1949 Geneva Conventions Relating to the Protection of the International Armed Conflicts:** This Protocol prohibits warfare methods which ''are intended, or may be expected, to cause widespread, long-term and severe damage to the natural environment.'' It also states that ''care shall be taken in warfare to protect the natural environment against . . . damage,'' and that, ''[a]ttacks against the natural environment by way of reprisals are prohibited.'' The Protocol's status as customary law is controversial. [191]

B. **Environmental Modification Convention of 1977 (ENMOD):** ENMOD was drafted during the Vietnam War *in response to concern about the military's use in Vietnam of chemicals* that change the ''dynamics, composition, or structure'' of the environment. ENMOD prohibits member states from using environmental modification techniques that have ''widespread, long-lasting, or severe'' effects as a means to harm another state. [191]

C. **General customary laws of war:** Customary laws of war require proportionality and necessity of all methods of warfare. It has been argued that the body of law that restricts the use of certain weapons *prohibits any method of war that causes unnecessary suffering*. It is not clear whether general norms of international environmental law are suspended during armed conflict. [191]

## CHAPTER 1

# APPROACHES AND METHODOLOGIES

## *ChapterScope*

This chapter provides a brief introduction to the law of environmental protection in the United States. A multi-faceted approach to environmental problems is often required, because environmental laws can have wide-ranging effects. The important concepts in this chapter are:

- **Regulation:** Many of the larger government regulatory schemes use a combination of the *three primary methods of environmental regulation* to most effectively reach the goals set forth by legislation.

  - The government may *impose controls* on pollution using *technological or quality controls*.

  - The government encourages private organizations to reduce or control pollution through *market-based incentives*.

  - The *publication of environmental effects* may encourage a facility to consider alternatives.

- **Economic impact:** Regulation-setting requires consideration of the economic impact of the proposed regulation.

  - **Externalities:** Regulations may impose costs on a facility to equal the externalities, the negative environmental *effects from an activity not directly reflected in the production costs*.

  - **Economic analyses:** It is important to conduct economic analyses to determine the *economic efficiency* of the proposed regulation.

- **Environmental ethics:** Not all values are economically quantifiable, so there must be consideration of the *ethical issues* underlying proposed environmental regulation. Such issues include the *uniqueness of natural resources* and the assumption of health and safety risks.

## I. METHODS OF ENVIRONMENTAL REGULATION

A. **Introduction:** There are *three main approaches* to providing protection for the environment: (1) controls imposed by the government; (2) market incentives structured to induce the private sector to behave in a more environmentally protective way; and (3) information requirements designed to educate the actors and the public about environmental consequences of proposed actions.

B. **Imposed controls:** The government can protect the environment by *dictating amounts or methods of controlling pollution*. The controls may be based on the existing technology's ability to control the pollution (technology-based standards) or the environment's ability to assimilate the pollution (ambient environmental quality standards).

   1. **Technology-based regulation:** Technology-based regulation *specifies the amount and/or method of controlling pollution* by reference to that which the available technology can control. The regulation is promulgated after studies of the technology, its availability, and its cost; the effect or lack of effect on the environment is not normally a factor.

**Example:** The "Best Available Technology" (BAT) limitation in the Clean Water Act is a control standard based on available technology. For further details, see *infra*, p. 79.

2. **Environmental quality-based regulation:** Regulation based on the environmental quality aims at a *certain level* of environmental quality and sets pollution controls to achieve that end. Factors in determining regulation may include the *effects on human welfare* as well as on the ecosystem.

**Example:** The National Ambient Air Quality Standards (NAAQSs) in the Clean Air Act are set with reference to a goal level of ambient air quality. See *infra*, p. 50.

C. **Market incentives:** The government may use market forces to *induce private organizations to reduce* pollution to the levels that they find economically desirable.

1. **Effluent fees:** The most direct method is to *tax the polluter* based on the amount of pollution it creates. Polluting then becomes another cost of production to the industry and will be factored into the amount and method of production.

2. **Marketable pollution rights:** Marketable pollution rights create a system in which each facility is *allocated an allowable amount* of pollution and is *permitted to sell* its surplus by *"emissions trading."* Under the Clean Air Act, for example, firms engaged in emissions trading are generally large emitters operating with permits written under state implementation plans (SIPs). These permits fix allowable maximum emission limits for each of the criteria pollutants from each source. The central device for emissions trading is the recognition of credit for reducing pollution below the permitted levels previously established by the Clean Air Act, allowing the exchange of surplus emission rights, both externally (between firms) and internally (within a single firm).

   a. **Netting:** Netting allows a firm to avoid the most stringent emissions limits by *reducing emissions from another source* within the same plant as if a "bubble" were placed over the entire plant. It reduces the net emissions increase to a level below that which is considered significant.

   b. **Offsets:** Offsetting allows a firm to *obtain emission credits from sources in the same area*, through internal or external trades, to offset its new emissions. This approach permits some economic growth to continue in areas that do not meet air quality deadlines.

   **Example:** A Virginia SIP was approved which required the Virginia Highway Department to decrease usage of a certain type of asphalt, thereby reducing hydrocarbon pollution by more than enough to offset expected pollution from a proposed refinery. *Citizens Against the Refinery's Effects, Inc. v. EPA*, 643 F.2d 183 (4th Cir. 1981).

   c. **Bubbles:** By placing an imaginary bubble over a multi-source plant, levels of emission controls applied to different sources in a bubble *may be adjusted to reduce control costs* so long as the aggregate limit is not exceeded. In effect, emission credits are created by some sources within the plant and used by others.

   **Example:** The Supreme Court has allowed the EPA to apply the bubble concept broadly in satisfying the requirements for nonattainment areas under the Clean Air Act, by defining a "stationary source" as "all of the pollutant-emitting activities which belong to the same industrial grouping, are located on one or more contiguous or adjacent properties, and are under the control of the same person or persons.'' *Chevron U.S.A., Inc. v. Natural Resources Defense Council*, 467 U.S. 837, *reh'g denied*, 468 U.S. 1227 (1984).

    **d. Banking:** Banking provides a mechanism for firms to *save emission credits for future use.*

    **3. Subsidies:** The converse of taxing a polluter is to *give a subsidy to the facilities that produce the least* pollution. This approach has essentially the same economic effect as a tax.

**D. Information disclosure:** A third approach to protecting the environment is the requirement that *information be produced about the effects* of an action. This regulation does not set controls or directly induce facilities to control the amount of pollution. The publication of information about the facility's actions, however, may influence the facility to choose a less harmful alternative.

## II. ECONOMIC CONSIDERATIONS

Both the government and individual profit-seeking facilities take economic considerations into account when determining the level of pollution to set.

**A. Externalities:** Externalities are effects from an activity that are *not directly reflected in the costs* of production. Regulation can impose costs on the facilities that equal the negative externalities created by production (*e.g.,* damage to the atmosphere from emissions) and in effect *force* the facility to consider the pollution as a cost of production.

**B. Economic analysis:** A central theory of law and economics is that every proposed action or regulation can be *evaluated in terms of economic impact.*

    **1. Cost-benefit:** A cost-benefit analysis compares the cost of an action or regulation to the *benefit it produces.* If the benefit exceeds the cost, the action is economically efficient.

    **2. Cost-effectiveness:** A cost-effectiveness analysis compares the *cost of two options* as well as *how effective each will be*. The option that can achieve the most for the least cost is economically more efficient.

    **3. Cost-oblivious:** Rather than a decision-making analysis, the cost-oblivious model describes the situation in which *protection is so important* that regulation is *mandated without regard to the cost* of implementation. Regulation protecting human health from carcinogens is often cited as an example of this approach.

## III. ETHICAL CONSIDERATIONS

Aside from economic considerations, there are ethical issues which often conflict with economic considerations. Underlying most ethical considerations is the premise that *some values*, such as protection of human health and unique natural resources, *cannot be adequately quantified* in monetary values. For example:

**A. Protecting nature:** The importance of nature *relative to the human species and technological progress.*

**B. Protecting future generations:** The cost to the present of *protecting* future generations.

C. **Environmental justice:** The secondary effects of environmental regulation, especially those that disproportionately affect the poor or minorities by *redirecting the cost of protection or the placement of facilities.*

1. **Problems with siting locally undesirable land uses (LULUs):** Locally undesirable land uses include public benefits such as highways, waste disposal landfills, and nuclear storage facilities. There is a concern that sites for such uses are placed most often in low income and minority neighborhoods. These sites are problematic in part because *benefits are received by a large population* but the costs *are imposed on a small group.*

2. **Compensation proposals:** One solution to such disparate effects and the resulting opposition to LULU siting is to *compensate* the *community* in which the proposed site will be located.

   a. **Different types of proposals:** Compensation may serve as either a *remedy* for damages suffered by the community, as a *mitigating factor* to prevent possible community harm, or as a *reward and incentive* for the community's acceptance.

   b. **Justifications for proposals:** Proponents argue for the positive effects of compensation, in that it *reduces community opposition, promotes efficiency* by forcing developers to internalize community costs, and *results in equity* by reducing the impact of a community bearing the disproportionate burden of the site.

   c. **Equitable concerns:** Positive compensation effects must be weighed against questions of *fairness* including *whether it is moral* to pay a community to assume health and safety risks, *how "voluntary"* a poor community's acceptance of compensation is when no other funds exist, and the *lack of representation* for future generations.

3. **Equal protection:** In one recent case, community members protested a landfill site adjacent to a minority neighborhood, and challenged its placement on equal protection grounds. The court allowed the siting, holding that the plaintiffs failed to prove a *discriminatory intent* in the decision-making process. *East Bibb Twiggs Nhd. Assoc. v. Macon-Bibb County Planning & Zoning Comm.*, 706 F. Supp. 880 (M.D. Ga.), *aff'd*, 888 F.2d 1573 (11th Cir. 1989).

---

# *Quiz Yourself on* *APPROACHES AND METHODOLOGIES*

1. The state of Ember is overflowing with garbage, so the state legislators are considering sites for a new landfill. Two sites are submitted for review: near the affluent city of Silverspoon and near the low-income city of Hardknocks. Both communities are outraged. Neither feels that discriminatory intent led to the choice of sites, but both have concerns beyond the displeasure of a nearby landfill. Silverspoon fears the loss of property value which would accompany placement of a landfill near their expensive homes, and is not interested in any form of compensation offered as an incentive to accept the site. Hardknocks would accept the compensation to improve their school system, but fears the loss of the Bengal Ant habitat, which happens to be the very area of the proposed site. Ember legislators

know they must conduct an economic analysis of each site before selecting the "winner." If Ember determines that one site is more economically efficient than the other, is that the end of the debate? _____

2. WePollute, Inc., a large manufacturing plant located in the state of Ember, is currently bringing their pollution levels to the level allowed under state regulations. Clean Living, Inc. is a smaller plant nearby whose pollution levels are significantly below state regulations. Ember has provided a subsidy in the past to Clean Living for producing such little pollution. Ember officials recently have threatened to shut down WePollute if they do not come into compliance. Should WePollute voluntarily go out of business? _____

---

## Answers

1. **No.** Ember also must consider the ethical implications for the landfill placement, which may conflict with their cost-effectiveness findings. Compensation for Silverspoon would have to come in the form of damages for any corresponding loss of property values. Ember likely will not consider this economically efficient, so it will remove Site Silverspoon from consideration. This puts the burden on Hardknocks. Ember should consider whether this is truly a fair proposal since Hardknocks cannot afford to turn away funding. Additionally, Ember must address the Bengal Ant habitat. Studies will have to be done to determine the likelihood of relocating the habitat and preserving the species elsewhere. These ethical considerations may encourage Ember to reconsider the economics of simply paying damages to Silverspoon residents.

2. **No.** Ember must control the pollution levels emitted within its state, and has created market incentives to encourage private companies such as WePollute to reduce their pollution levels. WePollute has a variety of options, including netting within their plant or purchasing marketable pollution rights from Clean Living. WePollute also could reevalute its production costs to include the costs of pollution control or reduce its pollution and seek a subsidy similar to Clean Living's.

---

 ***Exam Tips*** *on*
***APPROACHES AND METHODOLOGIES***

Here are things to remember about the methods of regulation and the economic and ethical considerations of environmental laws:

☛ Determine which of the three main approaches the government is using to protect the environment:

   ☞ Remember that the government can *impose controls* dictating amounts or methods of controlling pollution through *available technology* or by aiming for *environmental quality levels*.

   ☞ Look for *market-based incentives* encouraging private organizations to control pollution.

   *Example*: WePollute, a multi-source plant, has complied with state pollution regulations through the *bubble* concept of applying emission credits from one plant source to a different, noncompliant source within the same plant. If WePollute runs into further trouble meeting the pollution levels, they could approach Clean Living, Inc. about *emissions trading* and the purchase of Clean Living's marketable pollution rights.

☞ Consider the effect of a state's *information disclosure* requirement on a facility's polluting activities and whether that would force the facility to consider alternatives.

☛ Remember that *economic considerations* as well as *ethical issues* must be taken into account when proposing environmental regulations.

☞ Don't forget that a state should do a *cost-benefit, cost-effectiveness, or cost-oblivious analysis* when setting pollution levels, BUT

☞ Look for the ethical issues implicated as well. Consider the *fairness* of the proposal, possible *compensation* for LULU, as well as issues involving the *protection of future generations* and *natural resources*.

## CHAPTER 2

# COMMON LAW THEORIES AND ENVIRONMENTAL LITIGATION

## *ChapterScope*

Prior to the 1970s, environmental regulation was primarily the province of state and federal common law. While subsequent legislation has largely preempted earlier schemes of environmental protection, many of these remedies are still available under certain circumstances, and help in developing a broader understanding of the balance between economic and environmental concerns. This chapter provides an overview of these causes of actions and remedies:

- ■ **Nuisance claims:** This claim, which may be *private or public*, remains the primary common law theory of environment protection and regulation. Relevant issues include *availability of equitable relief*, *standing*, and *federal preemption*.

- ■ **Common law damages:** While courts strive to strike a balance between competing environmental and economic concerns, and evaluate the role of evolving scientific knowledge, the difficulty of quantifying environmental damages has led to the development of *alternative damage theories* and the inclusion of *cost of restoration damages*.

- ■ **Other common law claims:** There are alternative common law approaches to environmental regulation, including *trespass*, *negligence*, and *strict liability*.

- ■ **Causation:** The plaintiff must demonstrate *proximate cause* to prevail in environmental litigation.

  - ■ **Burden of proof:** The defendant's actions must be the proximate cause of the damage or injury to plaintiff, which must be shown through a *preponderance of the evidence*.

  - ■ **Scientific evidence:** *Daubert* does *not require certainty*, but the trial judge may screen the evidence for *relevance and reliability*.

- ■ **Procedural issues:** Accommodating environmental concerns can be difficult in a system generally designed for individual causes of action. Some restraints may involve *statute of limitations*, *splitting action*, and *class action suits*.

## I. NUISANCE AS A COMMON LAW ACTION

The primary theory of recovery for environmental damage at common law was the *nuisance* cause of action. Relevant nuisance issues include the *availability* of equitable relief, *standing* to abate a public nuisance, and the relationship between nuisance law and federal environmental statutes.

**A. Types of actions:** Nuisance claims can be either private or public.

    **1. Private nuisance:** A private nuisance is defined as *an invasion of a person's interest in the use and enjoyment of his/her property*. A private nuisance exists when one's conduct, whether negligent or intentional, *unreasonably* interferes with the use and enjoyment of another's property. See *Madison v. Ducktown Sulphur, Copper & Iron Co.,* 113 Tenn. 331, 83 S.W. 658 (Tenn. 1904).

2. **Public nuisance:**  A public nuisance exists when one's conduct *unreasonably* interferes with a right common to the public. See *Missouri v. Illinois,* 200 U.S. 496 (1906), and *Georgia v. Tennessee Copper Co.,* 240 U.S. 650 (1916). A key distinction between the two types of nuisances is a public nuisance action is *filed by the government* in representation of the public, whereas a private nuisance is a suit filed by private citizens who have individual claims. An individual can only file a public nuisance claim if that individual can show *"special" damage* that is more severe and distinct from the public harm.

B. **Availability of equitable relief:**  The availability of injunctive relief depends upon whether the economic effects of an injunction are *required to protect* some important interest and whether the nuisance is *prospective in nature.*

1. **Balancing test:**  The court must balance the *competing interests* and *hardships* of the parties in determining whether to award injunctive relief. *Boomer v. Atlantic Cement Co.,* 26 N.Y.2d 219, 257 N.E.2d 870 (N.Y. 1970).

   **Example:**  In *Boomer,* the court balanced the interests of the defendant, the cement plant, with those of the plaintiffs, whose property was injured by the dirt, smoke, and vibration of the cement plant. The court awarded an injunction against continued operation unless the cement plant paid permanent damages to the plaintiffs.

   **Example:**  In *Spur Indus., Inc. v. Del E. Webb Dev. Co.,* 108 Ariz. 178, 494 P.2d 700 (Ariz. 1972), the court awarded injunctive relief against a cattle feedlot operation on the condition that the residential developer pay the reasonable costs of moving or shutting down the business. This novel award was due to the fact that the developer had "come to the nuisance," yet the people living in the development were suffering widespread harm which could most economically be remedied by relocation or termination of the feed lot.

2. **Prospective nuisances:**  A party seeking an injunction of a prospective nuisance must show a *sufficiently serious and immediate threat of irreparable injury.* Some courts have liberalized this standard in cases in which the potential harm is devastating. See *Village of Wilsonville v. SCA Servs., Inc.,* 86 Ill. 2d 1, 426 N.E.2d 824 (Ill. 1981).

   **Example:**  In *Village of Wilsonville,* the court applied a dangerous probability of harm standard because the hazardous chemical waste disposal site operated by the defendant presented an imminent and substantial threat to public health. This threat was substantial due to the location of the site above a mine, the occurrence of subsidence, and the permeability of the soil.

C. **Standing in nuisance actions:**  An individual must show *special damage* in order to sue to abate a public nuisance. Special damage is damage *distinct from* and *more severe* than that suffered by other members of the public. See RESTATEMENT (SECOND) OF TORTS §821C(1) (1977); *Philadelphia Elec. Co. v. Hercules, Inc.,* 762 F.2d 303 (3d Cir.), *cert. denied,* 474 U.S. 980 (1985).

D. **Preemption of nuisance claims by federal environmental protection statutes:**  The Supreme Court has determined when there is preemption of a nuisance cause of action by federal environmental statutes in several key cases.

1. *Illinois v. Milwaukee:*  In 1972, the Court recognized a nuisance action under federal common law but noted that a *federal regulatory scheme may preempt* federal common law nuisance.

*Illinois v. Milwaukee (Milwaukee I)*, 406 U.S. 91 (1972). A few years later, the Court determined that the comprehensive federal water pollution statute preempted federal common law nuisance claims for water pollution. *Milwaukee v. Illinois (Milwaukee II)*, 451 U.S. 304 (1981).

2. ***International Paper Co. v. Ouellette:*** The Court held that the Clean Water Act ***precluded an action*** by Vermont landowners against a New York plant under Vermont common law, but recognized an action against the plant under New York nuisance law. *International Paper Co. v. Ouellette*, 479 U.S. 481 (1987).

3. ***Arkansas v. Oklahoma:*** Despite the preemption of federal common law and state common law of an affected state for water and (most probably) air pollution, a source may still have ***some obligations to comply*** with the law of other states affected by its pollution. For example, in *Arkansas v. Oklahoma*, the Court found that EPA had to condition the authority under the Clean Water Act permits issued by EPA upon compliance with applicable water quality standards of affected downstream states. *Arkansas v. Oklahoma*, 503 U.S. 91 (1992). See additional discussion *infra*, p. 85.

# II. DAMAGES AT COMMON LAW

Common law damages may undercompensate for injuries to natural resources because of the difficulty of quantifying such damage. Legislatures and courts have devised various methods of addressing this inadequacy of traditional damages.

A. **Cost of restoration damages:** Both courts and legislatures at the state and federal level have ***expanded*** damages to include the ***cost of restoring and rehabilitating*** an injured environment to its preexisting condition. See, *e.g., Commonwealth of Puerto Rico v. The SS Zoe Colocotroni*, 628 F.2d 652 (1st Cir. 1980) (discussing Puerto Rico's antipollution statute), *cert. denied*, 450 U.S. 912 (1981); *Board of County Comm'rs of the County of Weld v. Slovek*, 723 P.2d 1309 (Colo. 1986) (awarding restoration costs); *Osburne v. Hurst*, 947 P.2d 1356 (Alaska 1997) (allowing property owners to argue for restoration costs greater than the diminution in value of the land).

B. **Alternative damage theories:** There are ***three alternative damage theories*** developed at common law in the toxic torts context.

1. **Increased risk of disease:** A plaintiff may recover for his or her increased or enhanced risk of cancer or other disease by establishing that the disease is medically ***reasonably certain to follow*** from the plaintiff's present injury. A mere possibility that the disease will develop is insufficient to allow recovery for these damages. *Sterling v. Velsicol Chem. Corp.*, 855 F.2d 1188 (6th Cir. 1988). *Sterling* was subsequently modified in *American & Foreign Insurance Co. v. General Electric Co.*, 45 F.3d 135 (6th Cir. 1995) to have courts factor in a reliability assessment in considering the admissibility of scientific evidence.

   **Example:** In *Sterling*, the court determined that the plaintiffs had not established their enhanced risk of cancer with reasonable medical certainty. The court found that a 25- to 30-percent chance that the disease would develop was too speculative and represented only a mere possibility, not medical certainty.

   **Example:** One court has determined that a greater than 50-percent chance of contracting a disease establishes sufficient medical certainty. *Jackson v. Johns-Manville Sales Corp.*, 781 F.2d 394 (5th Cir.), *cert. denied*, 478 U.S. 1022 (1986).

2. **Fear of the increased risk of disease:** A plaintiff may recover for *emotional distress* suffered from *fear of contracting cancer or another disease* by showing that such distress is a *foreseeable or natural consequence* of the present injury. Emotional distress *cannot be too remote or tenuous.* *Sterling v. Velsicol Chem. Corp.*, 855 F.2d 1188 (6th Cir. 1988). In negligence actions, a plaintiff may only recover for fear of disease after proving that future disease from exposure is more likely than not, except when the toxic exposure is caused by conduct amounting to ''oppression, fraud or malice.'' *Potter v. Firestone Tire & Rubber Co.*, 6 Cal. 4th 965, 863 P.2d 795 (Cal. 1993).

   **Example:** In *Sterling*, the plaintiffs lived near a landfill from which hazardous chemicals had leaked and contaminated the water supply. The plaintiffs recovered damages for their fear of contracting cancer because their fear was a present injury caused by their ingestion of Velsicol's chemicals.

3. **Medical monitoring:** A plaintiff may recover the costs of *periodic medical examinations* to detect and diagnose the onset of disease. *Mauro v. Raymark Indus., Inc.*, 116 N.J. 126, 561 A.2d 257 (N.J. 1989).

   a. **Rationale:** The medical monitoring cause of action developed because an individual exposed to a toxic substance would not have to be tested periodically *but for the exposure.* *Mauro v. Raymark Indus., Inc.*, 116 N.J. 126, 561 A.2d 257 (N.J. 1989).

   b. **Elements:** The medical monitoring cause of action contains four elements:

      i. **Significant exposure:** The *negligent actions* of the defendant exposed the plaintiff to a hazardous substance in a significant manner;

      ii. **Increased risk:** Because of the exposure, plaintiff's chances of contracting a serious disease are *increased significantly;*

      iii. **Necessary exams:** Because of the enhanced risk of disease, the plaintiff needs periodic medical examinations; and

      iv. **Available procedures:** Early detection of disease is possible because medical procedures exist. *In re Paoli R.R. Yard PCB Litig.*, 916 F.2d 829, 852 (3d Cir. 1990), *cert. denied, General Electric Co. v. Knight*, 499 U.S. 961 (1991). Subsequently, the court in *In re Paoli R.R. Yard PCB Litig. (Paoli II)*, 35 F.3d 717 (3d Cir. 1994) stated that although some Pennsylvania courts had raised questions as to whether they might accept claims for medical monitoring, the court would not change its conclusion reached in *Paoli I*, namely that Pennsylvania law recognizes a claim for medical monitoring. The court ruled that absent a clear statement or persuasive evidence to the contrary, claims for medical monitoring are recognized.

C. **Prejudgment interest:** Courts will award prejudgment interest if the *claim is liquidated* (ascertainable in amount) and the *date of injury is determinable*. *Hutchinson Utils. Comm'n v. Curtiss-Wright Corp.*, 775 F.2d 231 (8th Cir. 1985). Courts are generally reluctant to award prejudgment interest in tort claims, unless the nature of the harm to real or personal property is *susceptible to valuation with reasonable certainty prior to trial. Brockelsby v. United States*, 767 F.2d 1288 (9th Cir. 1985), *cert. denied, Jeppesen & Co. v. Brockelsby*, 474 U.S. 1101 (1986).

**Example:** In *Brockelsby*, the court awarded interest in a case in which the damages to an aircraft were sufficiently certain because of the availability of reasonably ascertainable market prices.

**D. Temporary vs. permanent damages in nuisance actions:** The determination of whether a nuisance is a temporary or permanent one will determine the formula for calculating damages.

    **1. Temporary nuisance and damages:** A nuisance is temporary if *alteration or abatement* of the activity constituting the nuisance is *possible*. Temporary damages include the *reasonable cost of repair* and any special damages. *Miller v. Cudahy Co.*, 858 F.2d 1449 (10th Cir. 1988), *cert. denied*, 492 U.S. 926 (1989); *Morsey v. Chevron USA, Inc.*, 94 F.3d 1470 (10th Cir. 1996).

    **Example:** In *Miller*, the defendant's salt mining operations caused pollution of the underground aquifer under plaintiffs' farms such that they could not use the aquifer for irrigation. The court found evidence existed that the damages to the aquifer were remediable if the defendant abated its pollution, and thus the nuisance was temporary.

    **2. Permanent nuisance and damages:** A nuisance is permanent if the ''*cause of injury is fixed*, and . . . the property will always remain subject to that injury.'' Permanent damages are the diminished fair *market value* of the property. *McAlister v. Atlantic Richfield Co.*, 233 Kan. 252, 262, 662 F.2d 1203, 1211 (Kan. 1983).

    **Example:** In *McAlister*, the plaintiff's well water was polluted by the defendants' oil fields, and the plaintiff estimated the water would not be fit to drink for 150 to 400 years. The court found a permanent nuisance because no evidence existed that the pollution was abatable, especially because the defendant had stopped its oil operations forty years earlier.

**E. Punitive damages:** Punitive damages *may be available* under common law or by statute. Punitive damages have generally been held to be constitutional by the Supreme Court in several cases. See *Honda Motor Co. v. Oberg*, 114 S. Ct. 2331 (1994); *TXO Prod. Corp. v. Alliance Resources Corp.*, 509 U.S. 443 (1993). Some environmental statutes contain limits on punitive damages. See, *e.g.*, CERCLA §107(c)(3), 42 U.S.C. §9607(c)(3), *infra*, p. 125.

    **Example:** In *BMW v. Gore*, 116 S. Ct. 1589 (1996), a purchaser sued BMW for failing to disclose that the car had been damaged and repainted prior to delivery. The Supreme Court held that the two million dollars in punitive damages (already reduced from four million) was *grossly excessive* and *exceeded the constitutional limit*. The Court stated that in assessing the award, the analysis must be limited to conduct that occurred solely within a state's border. In addition, since the harm was purely economic, there was no evidence that BMW had acted in bad faith and the award was 500 times the actual harm, the punitive damages were clearly excessive. The Court also stated that it would be impossible to provide a mathematical calculation to determine in every case whether an award is constitutional or unconstitutional.

**F. Economic losses:** The traditional rule is that *no recovery exists in negligence* for economic losses absent physical harm to person or property. Some courts have departed from this rule. See, *e.g.*, *Pruitt v. Allied Chem. Corp.*, 523 F. Supp. 975 (E.D. Va. 1981) (allowing boat, bait, and tackle shops, and marina owners who lost money because of the pollution of the Chesapeake Bay to recover their indirect economic losses).

# III. OTHER COMMON LAW CAUSES OF ACTION

Besides nuisance law, other remedies under common law exist to ensure the protection of the environment and to compensate victims of pollution. These causes of action, nuisance included, are often the only means of recovery for the private plaintiff.

A. **Trespass:** A trespass involves an ***unlawful interference*** with one's property. A trespass in an environmental context may occur when a person's or company's actions have ***resulted in pollutants entering onto another's property***.

B. **Negligence:** In some cases, environmental pollution may have been caused by a ***failure to use the care necessary*** under the given circumstances. In order to establish negligence, the plaintiff must prove that the defendant failed to use such care as a reasonable and prudent person would use under similar circumstances. *Adams v. Star Enterprise*, 51 F.3d 417 (4th Cir. 1995).

C. **Strict liability:** A person or company can be liable for environmental damage ***regardless of negligence or fault***. These cases generally arise in two situations.

   1. **Ultrahazardous activity:** A party may be held strictly liable if engaging in an "ultrahazardous" or "abnormally dangerous" activity, such as toxic waste disposal.

   2. **Product liability:** A manufacturer or seller may be held strictly liable for damages or injuries caused by the use of a product. In most cases, a plaintiff must prove either that there is a ***defect in the design*** of the product, or that the ***manufacturer failed to warn*** of the risks involved in the use of the product.

# IV. CAUSATION

All private common law actions require the plaintiff to show that the defendant's actions were the proximate cause of the injury or damage. The plaintiff has the burden of proving by a preponderance of evidence that the ***pollution caused by the defendant caused the injury or damage***. Recently, at least one court has discussed the possibility of admitting inferential, epidemiological evidence (statistics concerning the occurrence of a disease within a general group) as one factor of causation proof. *Landrigan v. Celotex*, 127 N.J. 404, 605 A.2d 1079 (N.J. 1992). There has also been debate about the level of scrutiny that scientific evidence should receive. In answer, the Supreme Court held that ***scientific evidence need not be known with certainty***, but must be supported by appropriate validation; the trial judge has the power to screen such evidence for both ***relevance*** and ***reliability***. *Daubert v. Merrell-Dow Pharmaceuticals, Inc.*, 509 U.S. 579 (1993). See also *Blum v. Merrell-Dow Pharmaceuticals, Inc.* 705 A.2d 1314 (Pa. Super. Ct. 1998) (scientific evidence must be shown to meet the standard for relevance and reliability before being admitted); *General Electric Co. v. Joiner*, 118 S. Ct. 512 (1997) (holding that judges may reject scientific evidence because of discrepancies found through independent review and decisions will only be reviewed with the "abuse of discretion" standard even if outcome-determinative).

# V. PROCEDURAL ISSUES

Some procedural issues exist that may put restraints on an environmental tort action.

A. **Statute of limitations:** Statutes of limitations place a limit on the ***time*** in which a person can file a tort action.

**Problem:** For many toxic pollutants, there are *long latency periods* that exist from the time the person is exposed to the pollutant until the occurrence of the disease. The statute of limitations creates an obstacle for a tort action if the statute has run by the time the injured person discovers the disease. As a result, a number of state statutes begin to run upon *discovery rather than exposure*.

B. **Splitting the causes of action:** Most jurisdictions require that all claims arising from a common set of facts be brought in *one action*. Plaintiffs are not allowed to divide or split their claims by suing for some damages in one suit and other damages in a latter suit, both arising from the same facts.

   **Problem:** Not being able to split causes of action may present problems in cases where a plaintiff first sues for exposure to a toxic pollutant and later develops a disease caused by the same exposure. The injured party *may later be barred* from bringing an action for damages when the actual disease develops.

C. **Class action suits:** Problems may result from overly broad class action settlements, which *could preclude legitimate causes of action* that arise later in time. The New Jersey Supreme Court avoided one such pitfall by refusing to allow a settlement that settled all future claims, including personal injury claims, when the class suit dealt only with negligence and trespass. *Shults v. Champion Int'l Corp.*, 821 F. Supp. 520 (E.D. Tenn. 1993). See *Amchem Products Inc. v. Windsor*, 117 S. Ct. 2231 (1997) (holding that a class could not be formed in asbestos litigation because of commonality of exposure, the more demanding predominance criterion must be met).

---

## *Quiz Yourself* on
## *COMMON LAW THEORIES AND ENVIRONMENTAL LITIGATION*

3. Clean Living, Inc. would like to expand its main plant operations in the city of Glohing. It has never had a pollution problem, and the plant enjoys a good reputation among the citizens of Glohing. In fact, Clean Living is a major employer in Glohing and it provides significant funds to Glohing schools and charities. Expansion of the plant would likely bring additional monies into Glohing. The problem is that Farmer Logg owns all the land just behind the plant, part of which falls within the proposed expansion site. Farmer Logg does not want to sell, and he is quite worried that the plant's expanded operations will adversely affect his groundwater, soil, and crop health on that part of his farm. Clean Living's studies show that Farmer Logg's fears may be legitimate, but they are confident that Logg will either sell or they can contain the leakage. Farmer Logg decides to seek an injunction against Clean Living's proposed expansion. Since the studies seem to confirm Farmer Logg's fears, will the court automatically grant the injunction? _____

4. Same facts as above. Is an injunction Farmer Logg's only remedy? _____

---

## *Answers*

3. **No.** The court will have to balance the potential boon to Glohing's economy with the hardships Farmer Logg will potentially suffer. The court also likely will consider Clean Living's past record of successfully containing any pollutants. Rather than grant the injunction, the court may determine that it would be more beneficial for Clean Living to pay Farmer Logg a reasonable amount for his land or for them to pay him some amount to protect against possible damage. Remember that Farmer Logg would have to show that a threat of irreparable injury was serious and immediate.

4. **No.** Farmer Logg could wait for Clean Living to go ahead with the expansion. If the company is successful in containing any pollution, Farmer Logg has nothing to worry about. If, however, his fears are realized, then he can sue claiming nuisance, trespass, or possibly strict liability. Farmer Logg could first sue on a private nuisance claim. If he is successful, the court would likely find that the nuisance was a temporary one, thus awarding Farmer Logg reasonable cost of repair and any special damages. If the expansion physically intrudes onto Farmer Logg's property, he could sue on a trespass claim. He might also be successful in arguing that the pollutants are trespassing on his property. Finally, if Farmer Logg could demonstrate that Clean Living's pollutants/activities are ''ultrahazardous,'' then he could prevail on a strict liability claim. The court may also be willing to award Farmer Logg damages for fear of increased risk of disease if the pollutants on his property are shown to potentially cause a disease such as cancer.

---

*Exam Tips on*
### COMMON LAW THEORIES AND ENVIRONMENTAL LITIGATION

Here is what to look for on exams addressing common law claims, recoveries, and procedures:

☛ You may be asked to evaluate a potential-litigation fact pattern for applicable common law theories and available remedies. Remember that *nuisance causes of action* are the most common. It may be easier to organize your answer by addressing the following questions:

   ☞ Does the plaintiff have *standing* to sue?

   ☞ Is this nuisance claim *public* or *private*?

      ☞ For exam purposes, the claim will usually be private. Don't forget that a private individual bringing a public claim requires a showing of *''special'' damage*.

   ☞ Is *equitable relief* available?

      ☞ Remember that the court will have to do a *balancing test* and that the plaintiff usually has to show *immediate threat of irreparable injury*.

   ☞ If this is a state claim, is there federal *preemption*?

   *Example*: W.M. Chemicals is seeking a new location for its main chemicals plant. East Tort, Kansas is a potential site, but the location is in the middle of a growing residential development.

The residents fear the chemicals will seep into their water supply and they are seeking an injunction against the proposed plant's relocation to East Tort. If the injunction is not granted, the residents could later file a trespassing claim if the finished plant directly intruded onto their properties.

☛ Don't forget ***alternative causes of action*** if nuisance is not appropriate from the facts. If nuisance is appropriate, and you have time, you could mention these other means of recovery and why they are not the best choice based on the facts in your exam.

☛ Be certain to fully address ***causation*** and any existing procedural issues.

   ☞ The defendant had to be the ***proximate cause*** of the injury or damage.

   ☞ Your fact pattern may include injuries that are ***scientifically uncertain***. You likely will not have the time (or the need) to go into an in-depth *Daubert* analysis, but you would be remiss not to cite this case.

   *Example*: Citizens of West Moot, Indiana want to sue W.M. Chemicals, which has its main plant just outside of town. The group claims that miscarriages are on the rise within their community because of the chemicals the plant emits. A few scientific reports support the citizens' contention, but there is nothing conclusive. The citizens will have to prove through a preponderance of the evidence that the chemicals from W.M. Chemicals are the proximate cause of the increase in miscarriages. Scientific certainty is not necessary, but the trial judge will submit the scientific reports to *Daubert* analysis to determine their relevance and reliability.

   ☞ ***Procedural issues*** are rarely tested, but be on the lookout for problems arising from a statute of limitations, claim-splitting, or a class action suit.

☛ Finally, you will want to address ***damages***. Remember that ***cost of restoration damages*** are available at both federal and state levels and ***economic losses*** are not recoverable.

   ☞ Evaluate whether a nuisance claim is ***temporary or permanent*** and whether ***punitive damages*** would be appropriate.

   ☞ Consider the award of ***prejudgment interest***.

   ☞ If the recovery is for a toxic tort, remember to address ***risk of disease*** and ***medical monitoring*** costs.

## CHAPTER 3

# THE JUDICIAL ROLE IN ENVIRONMENTAL LITIGATION AND THE ADMINISTRATIVE PROCESS

## *ChapterScope*

Translating broad environmental policies into specific practices often can be a difficult and contentious process. Federal and state court systems play a significant role in defining the scope and applicability of various environmental regulatory schemes, both for those enforcing the laws and those whose activities are affected by the laws. Here are the key concepts in this chapter:

■ **Subject matter jurisdiction:** A federal court must have subject matter jurisdiction to review an agency action. Jurisdiction is granted through *judicial review provisions*, *citizen suit provisions*, and the broader *"federal question"* jurisdiction of 28 U.S.C. §1331.

■ **Standing:** Determination of standing is often controversial because of the criteria an individual must meet to obtain it.

■ A plaintiff in an environmental suit must be able to show that an *injury in fact* exists.

■ The injury must be *fairly traceable* to the challenged conduct.

■ A prevailing plaintiff must show that the governing statutes provide *redressability*.

■ **Reviewability of administrative decisions:** There are procedural and substantive requirements for the review of agency decisions and actions.

■ Reviewability and standards of review are governed by the Administrative Procedures Act.

■ **Remedies:** Available remedies may include *injunctive relief* and *attorneys' fees*.

## I. SUBJECT MATTER JURISDICTION IN THE FEDERAL COURTS

In order for a court to review an agency action, it must have subject matter jurisdiction. There are three main sources of federal jurisdiction over environmental issues: judicial review provisions in federal statutes, citizen suit provisions in federal statutes, and "federal question" jurisdiction under Title 28.

**A. Judicial review provisions:** Most federal environmental statutes *provide for judicial review* of agency action and regulation.

**B. Citizen suit provisions:** Citizen suit provisions allow private *individuals to sue* agencies to compel non-discretionary decisionmaking and to sue violators to compel compliance with environmental requirements.

**C. Federal question:** Federal question provisions of 28 U.S.C. §1331 grant jurisdiction to federal courts to hear disputes arising from the "Constitution, laws, or treaties" of the United States.

# II. STANDING

The doctrine of standing ensures that a suit in federal court is brought ***by the appropriate individual***: one who has a ***personal stake*** in the outcome. The standing doctrine has its source in the ''Case or Controversies'' requirement of Article III of the Constitution. An individual must meet certain criteria to obtain standing in federal court in environmental cases.

A. **Injury in fact:** Many key cases in the development of the injury in fact requirement for standing have involved environmental litigation. After years of broad recognition of standing, the Supreme Court recently has ***limited*** the availability of standing in environmental cases, making it harder for environmental plaintiffs to bring suit to redress harm to the environment.

   1. ***Sierra Club v. Morton***: An individual must allege that she ***used the area affected by agency action in question***. *Sierra Club v. Morton*, 405 U.S. 727 (1972). ***Aesthetic harm*** will satisfy the injury in fact requirement. *Id.*

      **Example:** In *Morton*, the Supreme Court held that Sierra Club failed to establish injury in fact based solely on its long-standing interest in preserving the environment. The Court required an allegation that Sierra Club's members had used the area in question for recreational purposes, and that they would be injured if the project were built.

   2. ***Lujan v. National Wildlife Federation***: An individual's allegation of use of a particular environment ***must be specific***. *Lujan v. National Wildlife Federation*, 497 U.S. 871 (1990).

      **Example:** In *National Wildlife Federation*, the Court held that allegations that the National Wildlife Federation's members had used land in the vicinity of the particular tracts at issue were insufficient to constitute injury in fact. The Court required that the members allege more specific claims of proximity to or actual use of the particular tracts allegedly harmed.

   3. ***Lujan v. Defenders of Wildlife***: An environmental plaintiff's injury must be ***sufficiently imminent*** to constitute injury in fact. *Lujan v. Defenders of Wildlife*, 504 U.S. 555 (1992).

      **Example:** In *Defenders of Wildlife*, the Court denied standing to a plaintiff who professed an intent to return to the area in question, but without any specific plans to do so. The Court also held that the animal nexus and vocational nexus theories asserted by the plaintiff were too speculative to support injury in fact.

   4. ***Friends of the Earth, Inc. v. Laidlaw Environmental Services (TOC), Inc.***: A plaintiff must be able to show that the defendant's violation was ongoing at the time of the complaint, and there must be a possibility of future violations. *Friends of the Earth, Inc. v. Laidlaw Environmental Services (TOC), Inc.*, 528 U.S. 167 (2000).

      **Example:** In *Laidlaw*, the Court held that plaintiffs had sufficient standing because of reasonable concerns about the effects of ongoing and illegal discharges into a local river, and because of conditional statements from plaintiffs that they would use the river in question for recreation if not for the discharges. The Court held that this evidence represented ''dispositively more than the mere 'general averments' and 'conclusory allegations' found inadequate in *National Wildlife Federation*.''

   5. **Special injury in fact issues:** Other injury in fact issues include procedural injury, prospective harm, representational standing, informational standing, and animal standing.

a. **Procedural injury:** The Supreme Court is divided as to whether procedural injury under an environmental statute is sufficient to satisfy the injury in fact requirement. *Lujan v. Defenders of Wildlife*, 504 U.S. 555 (1992).

   i. **Justice Scalia:** An individual can enforce procedural rights only if the procedure is *designed to protect some threatened concrete interest* that is the ultimate basis of standing. In other words, an individual must still demonstrate the *type of harm* traditionally considered to be injury in fact under Article III, just as for any other type of injury.

   ii. **Justices Kennedy and Souter:** Congress is able to identify an injury and relate it to a class of persons so that some procedural injuries alone *might be sufficiently concrete* to constitute injury in fact. They noted that these minimum requirements were not met by the Endangered Species Act at issue in *Defenders of Wildlife*.

   iii. **Justices Blackmun and O'Connor:** In some cases, a procedural duty is *so enmeshed* with the prevention of a substantive, concrete harm that a plaintiff may demonstrate a *sufficient likelihood* of injury merely by showing a breach of that procedural duty.

b. **Prospective harm:** The Supreme Court has found that *future harm* of radiation was *sufficiently concrete* to meet the injury in fact requirement, although the case involved other, more immediate environmental harm as well. *Duke Power Co. v. Carolina Envtl. Study Group, Inc.*, 438 U.S. 59 (1978).

   **Example:** In *Duke Power Co.*, the plaintiffs lived near construction sites for nuclear power plants. These plaintiffs alleged that if a nuclear accident were to occur, they would suffer environmental and aesthetic harm.

c. **Representational standing:** The Supreme Court has held that an *organization may sue on behalf* of its members if:

   i. some members would have *standing;*

   ii. the interest that it seeks to protect is *related* to the organization's purposes; and

   iii. individual members *do not need to participate. Hunt v. Washington Apple Adv. Comm'n*, 432 U.S. 333 (1977).

d. **Informational standing:** An organization may have standing if an agency's action *deprives the organization of information* essential to the organization and its activities and programs. See *Foundation on Economic Trends v. Watkins*, 731 F. Supp. 530 (D.D.C. 1990).

   **Example:** In *Foundation on Economic Trends*, the plaintiff was a public interest organization. The organization alleged informational injury due to a federal agency's failure to comply with documentation requirements of the National Environmental Policy Act (NEPA). The court found injury because NEPA's central purpose is to inform the public and the organization specifically identified the affected environment as the global atmosphere. For a full discussion of NEPA, see *infra*, p. 37.

e. **Animal standing:** An organization *may not* obtain standing in cases in which animals are *privately owned and no public right of use* exists. See *International Primate Protection League v. Tulane Educational Fund*, 895 F.2d 1056 (5th Cir. 1990), *rev'd on other grounds*, 500 U.S. 72 (1991).

**Example:**  In *International Primate Protection League*, the plaintiff preservation organization suffered no injury due to the euthanization of monkeys used for medical research. No injury occurred because the monkeys were privately owned laboratory animals.

**Example:**  A public right of use may more easily be established for feral animals such as whales. *Japan Whaling Ass'n v. American Cetacean Soc'y*, 478 U.S. 221 (1986) (an individual who watches and studies whales suffers injury in fact due to whale harvesting).

**B. Zone of interest:**  For suits brought under §702 of the Administrative Procedure Act, a plaintiff also must establish that the type of harm alleged is within the "zone of interests" ***protected under the violated statute***. Ordinarily, the test is easily satisfied.

1. ***Clarke v. Securities Indus. Ass'n***:  In *Clarke v. Securities Indus. Ass'n*, 479 U.S. 388 (1987), the Court concluded that a plaintiff can sue unless the plaintiff's interest is so marginally related to the relevant statute that Congress did not ***intend*** to permit such a suit.

2. ***Bennett v. Spear***:  In *Bennett v. Spear*, 63 F.3d 915 (9th Cir. 1997), *reversed*, 520 U.S. 154 (1997), irrigation districts and ranchers sued the Fish and Wildlife Service alleging that the Service's Biological Opinion (determining that a large reclamation project might jeopardize two endangered species of fish and indicating that minimum water levels be maintained as an alternative) violated §7 of the Endangered Species Act and the requirement in §4(b)(2) that economic impact be considered for designations of critical habitat. They also claimed the Service's actions violated the Administrative Procedure Act. The Ninth Circuit Court of Appeals dismissed the case for ***lack of standing***, holding that only plaintiffs ***seeking to preserve species*** have an interest which falls within the zone of interests of the ESA.

   a. **Supreme Court's holding:**  The Court first held that the prudential zone of interests test was not a limitation on standing under the broad citizen suit provision of the ESA, even for plaintiffs seeking to ***restrict*** rather than expand the environmental protections of the Act. The only standing requirements for an ESA citizen suit which must be met are those for Article III standing: ***injury-in-fact, causation***, and ***redressability***. The reduction in available water was a sufficient showing of injury-in-fact at the pleading stage. Although the Secretary of the Interior did not have to accept the conclusions of the Service's opinion, the significance of the opinion in the ESA process made the injury ***"fairly traceable"*** to the opinion and redressable by setting aside the opinion.

   b. **Significance:**  The ESA citizen suit, however, only authorizes suits against persons "in violation of" the Act or against the Secretary to compel performance of a non-discretionary duty. The plaintiff's challenge under §7 to the opinion's jeopardy and water level determinations did not fall within either of those categories. An alleged error in administration of the Act, according to the Court, is ***not a "violation" of the Act***. The claim that the opinion failed to consider economic impact in making an implicit determination of critical habitat as required by §4(b)(2) was, however, a suit to ***compel a non-discretionary duty***. The claims under §7 could be determined by the particular statutory provision at issue (requiring economic considerations) rather than by the overall purpose of the Act (preserving species), so that the plaintiff's economic interests were sufficient for standing. Although the ultimate decision on the project would be made by the Secretary and not the Service, the opinion altered the "legal regime" sufficiently to constitute "final agency action" for purposes of the APA.

C. **Causation:** An individual must establish that the injury is *"fairly traceable"* to the challenged conduct. Mere bystanders or those with remote or attenuated links to harm will not satisfy the causation prong of standing. Generally, an individual must show a *"substantial likelihood"* that the defendant's acts caused his harm. *Public Interest Research Group of New Jersey v. Powell Duffryn Terminals*, 913 F.2d 64 (3d Cir. 1990), *cert. denied*, 498 U.S. 1109 (1991). The Court did find causation, however, in one of its earlier environmental cases involving an attenuated chain of causation. See *United States v. Students Challenging Regulatory Agency Procedures (SCRAP I)*, 412 U.S. 669 (1973).

**Example:** In *Powell Duffryn Terminals*, an environmental organization alleged a plant had violated the permit requirements of the Clean Water Act. The organization did not satisfy the causation requirement for standing because the group merely alleged a statutory violation. To obtain standing, the organization needed to allege that the plant's unlawful discharge of pollutants harmed the organization's members.

**Example:** In *SCRAP I*, students challenged an Interstate Commerce Commission order that approved a railroad freight surcharge. The students alleged that the rate increase would discourage recycling by promoting the use of new raw materials over the use of scrap materials. The lack of recycling would lead to a depletion of natural resources and more waste materials being discarded in the national parks. The students alleged that they used the parks and would thus be injured by the rate increase. The Court found causation.

D. **Redressability:** An individual must show that the judicial relief he seeks will serve some *useful* purpose if he prevails on the merits.

**Example:** In *Defenders of Wildlife*, the Court determined that the redressability element was not met because even if the district court ordered revision of the consultation regulation, the regulation would not necessarily bind the agencies funding the harmful projects. *Lujan v. Defenders of Wildlife*, 504 U.S. 555 (1992).

**Example:** In *Powell Duffryn Terminals*, the Court found the redressability element satisfied because if the court imposed civil penalties under the Clean Water Act, the plant would be deterred from future violations. In *Friends of the Earth, Inc. v. Laidlaw Environmental Services (TOC), Inc.*, 528 U.S. 167 (2000), the Court found that civil penalties imposed under the Clean Water Act were an appropriate form of redress not only for preventing future violations but also for abating continuing or existing violations.

## III. REVIEWABILITY OF ADMINISTRATIVE DECISIONS

Reviewability depends on whether an issue is suitable for judicial resolution. The principal agency responsible for environmental decisionmaking is the Environmental Protection Agency.

A. **Environmental Protection Agency:** Created in 1970, the Environmental Protection Agency (EPA) is responsible for the implementation of most of the major federal environmental statutes.

Most environmental statutes give EPA the power to promulgate regulations implementing the relevant statutes to issue permits, and compel enforcement.

1. **Structure of EPA:** EPA is headed by an Administrator appointed by the President. The main office is located in Washington, D.C. The ***regional offices***, located across the country, ***primarily are responsible*** for the issuance of permits and enforcing compliance within their regions.

2. **Other agencies:** Other federal administrative agencies implement and enforce environmental regulations as well. These agencies include: the Corps of Engineers, Department of the Interior, Department of Energy, Food and Drug Administration, and the Occupational Safety and Health Administration.

B. **General rule of reviewability:** The Administrative Procedure Act §701 provides that agency actions are reviewable except in two instances.

1. **Statute exception:** Agency actions are unreviewable if a ***statute prohibits review.***

2. **Discretion exception:** Agency actions are unreviewable if "***committed to agency discretion by law.***" 5 U.S.C. §701(a)(l)-(2). The discretion exception is very narrow and ***only applies*** in cases in which ***statutes are phrased in such broad language*** that virtually no law exists for the courts to apply in reviewing an agency's decision. *Citizens to Preserve Overton Park, Inc. v. Volpe*, 401 U.S. 402 (1971).

3. **"Final action" requirement:** In addition, the action challenged ***must be a final agency action*** in order to be reviewed.

   **Example:** The Trade Representative's preparation of NAFTA was not a final agency action, and thus the failure to prepare an EIS under NEPA was not reviewable. *Public Citizen v. United States Trade Representative*, 5 F.3d 549 (D.C. Cir. 1993), *cert. denied*, 114 S. Ct. 685 (1994).

C. **Standards of review:** The standards of review ***depend on the nature of the issue*** reviewed in the case: whether legal, factual or procedural. Section 706(2) of the APA provides:

> To the extent necessary to decision and when presented, the reviewing court shall decide all relevant questions of law, interpret constitutional and statutory provisions, and determine the meaning of applicability of the terms of an agency action. The reviewing court shall —
>
> (1) compel agency action unlawfully withheld or unreasonably delayed; and
> (2) hold unlawful and set aside agency action, findings, and conclusions found to be —
>    (A) arbitrary, capricious, an abuse of discretion, or otherwise not in accordance with law;
>    (B) contrary to constitutional right, power, privilege, or immunity;
>    (C) in excess of statutory jurisdiction, authority, or limitations, or short of statutory right;
>    (D) without observance of procedure required by law;
>    (E) unsupported by substantial evidence in a case subject to sections 556 and 557 of this title or otherwise reviewed on the record of an agency hearing provided by statute; or
>    (F) unwarranted by the facts to the extent that the facts are subject to trial *de novo* by the reviewing court.
>
> In making the foregoing determinations, the court shall review the whole record or those parts of it cited by a party, and due account shall be taken of the rule of prejudicial error. 5 U.S.C. §706.

1. **Legal issues:** Courts generally ***defer*** to an administrative agency's interpretation of law. Several reasons support this deference:

■ the agency has *more experience* in applying the statute;

■ Congress gave the agency *primary responsibility* for executing the law;

■ individuals *may rely* on the agency's interpretation of the law without litigation; and

■ policy choices should be made by the political branches of government. See *Chevron U.S.A., Inc. v. Natural Resources Defense Council, Inc.,* 467 U.S. 837, *reh'g denied,* 468 U.S. 1227 (1984).

2. **Factual issues:** The standard of review depends upon the *type* of agency proceeding.

   a. **Adjudicatory proceedings and formal rulemaking:** The *"substantial evidence"* test is the standard of review. 5 U.S.C. §706(2)(E). The court must uphold the agency's action unless no substantial evidence exists in the record to support the agency's decision. *Citizens to Preserve Overton Park, Inc. v. Volpe,* 401 U.S. 402 (1971).

   b. **Informal rulemaking and non-adjudicatory proceedings:** The *"arbitrary and capricious"* test is the standard of review. 5 U.S.C. §706(2)(A). A court must consider whether the agency considered *all* relevant factors and whether the agency clearly *erred* in its judgment; the standard is a narrow one. *Citizens to Preserve Overton Park, Inc. v. Volpe,* 401 U.S. 402 (1971). In *Overton Park,* the Supreme Court held that the agency decision to put a highway through a park was a reviewable decision governed by the arbitrary and capricious standard of review. Some courts in environmental cases have applied the arbitrary and capricious test in an intensive manner, focusing on whether the agency gave full consideration to all relevant factors; this application is known as the "hard look" approach. See *Greater Boston T.V. Corp. v. FCC,* 444 F.2d 841, 851 (D.C. Cir. 1970), *cert. denied,* 403 U.S. 923 (1971).

   **Note:** Formal rulemaking by an agency is very rare. When an agency makes a decision of general applicability (*e.g.,* issuance of an air pollution standard), it is generally done through informal rulemaking. Determination of the rights or responsibilities of a particular party (*e.g.,* issuance or refusal of a permit) is an adjudication. Any other type of decision by an agency (such as putting a road through a park) falls within *Overton Park* and is governed by the arbitrary and capricious standard of review. Of course, the line between rules and adjudications blurs when a precise and limited number of parties is affected by an agency decision.

3. **Procedural issues:** Whether an agency has followed the procedures required by the APA is a question of law subject to *de novo review* by a court. However, courts do not have the general authority to require *additional* procedures beyond those required by statute (specifically the APA), the Constitution, or agency rules; but additional procedures *may be imposed in compelling circumstances*. *Vermont Yankee Nuclear Power Corp. v. Natural Resources Defense Council, Inc.,* 435 U.S. 519 (1978). The *Vermont Yankee* opinion rejected some courts' prior practice of "hybrid rulemaking," in which a court would look at the subject matter, decide whether the notice and comment procedures were adequate, and impose additional procedures beyond those required under the Administrative Procedure Act. It is not clear if *Vermont Yankee* precludes federal courts from ever requiring anything more procedurally than the APA or if courts may still impose procedural requirements on agencies when the APA does not specifically detail what procedures are required.

# IV. REMEDIES

Remedial issues in environmental cases include the propriety of injunctive relief and the availability of attorneys' fees.

**A. Injunctive relief:** Injunctive relief may be ***mandatory or discretionary*** depending on the goals of the environmental statutes at issue.

**1. Mandated injunctions:** Injunctive relief is mandatory ***if necessary to effectuate congressional goals*** in an environmental statute. *Tennessee Valley Auth. v. Hill*, 437 U.S. 153 (1978). It is very unusual for a court to find that its traditional equitable discretion has been thus limited.

**Example:** In *Hill*, the Court upheld an injunction against the completion of an expensive and substantially completed dam project because of the adverse impacts on the snail darter fish, an endangered species. The Court determined that the Endangered Species Act clearly had as its goal the preservation of endangered species, and that Congress had determined that no other relief could effectuate that goal.

**Example:** The Ninth Circuit has held that the National Defense Authorization Act (NDAA) does not provide for alternative methods for achieving its aims other than injunctive relief. See *Friends of the Earth v. Department of Navy*, 841 F.2d 927 (9th Cir. 1988). In *Friends of the Earth*, the court determined that the NDAA mandated enjoining construction until the Navy acquired the proper permits. In *Friends of the Earth v. United States Navy (Friends II)*, 850 F.2d 599 (9th Cir. 1988), the court held the Shorelines Management Act permit to have been issued for purposes of NDAA when the decision of the Shorelines Hearings Board became final. Even though the permit would still be subject to judicial review and would not be effective until the state court proceedings were complete, the court dissolved the early injunction.

**2. Discretionary injunctions:** In most environmental cases, however, courts retain their ***traditional discretion to balance*** the equities in determining whether an injunction should issue. *Weinberger v. Romero-Barcelo*, 456 U.S. 305 (1982).

**Example:** In *Romero-Barcelo*, the Navy had dropped bombs off the Puerto Rican coast without a permit as required under the Federal Water Pollution Control Act (FWPCA). The Court viewed the goal of the FWPCA as the protection of the nation's waters, not the permit process in itself. Despite the undisputed violation, the Court asserted its equitable discretion as to the granting of injunctive relief and refused an injunction.

**Example:** The Court followed the *Romero-Barcelo* analysis in *Amoco Production Co. v. Village of Gambell*, 480 U.S. 531 (1987). At issue in *Gambell* was a grant of oil and gas leases that involved special procedures to protect the environment. The Court held that injunctive relief required a showing that actual environmental harm was likely to occur, not a mere showing that the defendant failed to follow statutory procedures.

**B. Attorneys' fees:** There are two major issues regarding attorneys' fees in environmental cases: when should an attorney receive fees and how much should an attorney receive.

**1. Prevailing party rule:** Most environmental statutes require a party to be a ***"prevailing or substantially prevailing party"*** to recover attorneys' fees. See, *e.g.*, FWPCA §505(d), 33 U.S.C. §1365(d).

    **a. American Rule:** The prevailing party rule is in accord with the historical fee-shifting "American Rule," which states that the costs of litigation must be borne ***by each party***. The

Supreme Court has recognized that Congress may create exceptions to the American Rule. *Alyeska Pipeline Serv. Co. v. Wilderness Soc'y*, 421 U.S. 240 (1975).

   **b.** ***Ruckelshaus v. Sierra Club***: The Court has held that a party must show ***some success on the merits*** before an attorney is eligible for a fee award under the Clean Air Act. *Ruckelshaus v. Sierra Club*, 463 U.S. 680 (1983). The prevailing party rule applies under the Clean Air Act even though the "prevailing or substantially prevailing party" language does not appear in the statute. See CAA §307(f), 42 U.S.C. §7607(f) (stating that a court may award fees "whenever it determines that such award is appropriate").

**2. Reasonable fees rule:** Federal courts presume that a "lodestar" figure is a ***reasonable fee***. *Pennsylvania v. Delaware Valley Citizens' Council for Clean Air (Delaware Valley I)*, 478 U.S. 546 (1986).

   **a. Calculation of lodestar:** The lodestar is calculated by multiplying the number of hours worked by a reasonable hourly rate for each attorney involved. The attorney's ***performance and skill*** are reflected in the lodestar amount. *Delaware Valley I*, 478 U.S. at 553-554.

   **b. Adjustment of lodestar:** The courts ***may not adjust*** the lodestar figure for the contingency of losing a case or risk of nonpayment. See *Pennsylvania v. Delaware Valley Citizens' Council for Clean Air (Delaware Valley II)*, 483 U.S. 711 (1987).

   **Example:** In a citizens' suit under the Resource Conservation and Recovery Act (RCRA) and the Clean Water Act, a court may not impose a 25-percent enhancement of an attorney fee award to compensate the attorney for the risk of nonpayment. *City of Burlington v. Dague*, 505 U.S. 557 (1992).

---

## *Quiz Yourself on*
## THE JUDICIAL ROLE IN ENVIRONMENTAL LITIGATION AND THE ADMINISTRATIVE PROCESS

**5.** Cubi Lohs, a successful entrepreneur, has gotten permission from the Environmental Preservation Agency (EPA) to build her new plant in the state of Cardonskee along a wide creek that runs down from a public forest area into a main river. The EPA has determined that the plant will not unreasonably adversely affect the creek environment. The plant will, however, cut off public access to that area. Joe D. Camper loves to hike in the forest and along the creek, because he enjoys the native plant-life and fish. Serene Arich is the president of Ember state's Flora, Fauna, & Fish Fan Club. Both Joe and Serene are quite perturbed by Lohs's proposed site. Assume that the EPA's statute provides subject matter jurisdiction and ignore standard of review issues. Who has standing to sue? _____

**6.** Law Ren is suing the EPA, claiming a recent decision was arbitrary and capricious. She asserts that the EPA did not address her written report before making their decision, and she argues that addressing her concerns would have altered the final outcome. Should the EPA have considered Ms. Ren's report? _____

---

## Answers

5. **Joe D. Camper and the Flora, Fauna, & Fish Fan Club probably have standing, while Serene Arich probably would not.** Joe D. Camper has a personal stake in the outcome of his suit to stop the development along the creek. He should be able to demonstrate injury-in-fact under *Sierra Club v. Morton*, because he uses the affected environment when he regularly hikes. He meets the sufficiently imminent test of *Lujan v. Defenders of Wildlife* because he will be injured as soon as Cubi Lohs ends public access along the creek. He also will be able to satisfy the causation requirement because his injury will be fairly traceable to the plant's existence. The Flora, Fauna, & Fish Fan Club likely has standing under representational standing if they can produce a member who enjoys using the Cardonskee creek area. Once they find such a member, their interest is related enough to pass muster. They also will be able to meet the causation requirement because the potential injury to the local flora, fauna, and fish would be fairly traceable to the plant. Serene Arich probably does not have standing to sue since she is a citizen of the state of Ember and does not regularly visit the state of Cardonskee. Being president of a club with related interests is too attenuated a tie. She would not personally suffer an injury if the EPA's decision was upheld.

6. **Yes.** The court will apply the arbitrary and capricious standard of review, which means they will consider whether the EPA addressed all relevant factors and whether the agency erred in its decisionmaking. The fact that Law Ren's report was overlooked, however, is not determinative. Courts generally defer to agency legal interpretations and the arbitrary and capricious standard is a narrow one. The EPA would likely be able to offer an acceptable explanation for the overlooked report and the decision would be upheld.

---

 *Exam Tips on*
## THE JUDICIAL ROLE IN ENVIRONMENTAL LITIGATION AND THE ADMINISTRATIVE PROCESS

If your exam fact pattern involves the federal courts and an agency action, such as an EPA decision, you need to address the issues introduced in this chapter.

☛ The federal courts cannot review an agency action unless ***subject matter jurisdiction*** has been established through judicial review provisions, citizen suit provisions, or if there is a federal question.

☞ Exams rarely include ***"federal question" jurisdiction***, so check your hypothetical for the agency's statute. If your professor wants you to evaluate subject matter jurisdiction, you will likely be given a statute with language providing for ***judicial review*** or ***citizen suits***.

☛ Once jurisdiction has been established, make sure your plaintiff has ***standing*** to sue. This requires an evaluation of several criteria:

☞ Professors love to test on *injury in fact* because it can be a controversial issue. Make certain your plaintiff's injury is *not speculative*, her *proximity and use* to the environment at issue is sufficient, and the damage is *ongoing*.

☞ Even if you see that your plaintiff has an injury in fact, be sure to address the opposing argument.

*Example*: Members of the Leaf Society of Southern California learn of an EPA decision that could someday adversely affect leaves native to a park in New Hampshire. The group sues to protect the park, claiming their group meetings involve the leaves in question. The Leaf Society does not have standing because they do not actually use the park, the injury is not sufficiently imminent, and there is no ongoing damage.

☛ If it is not immediately obvious that your plaintiff has standing, see if she has standing using *special injury in fact* considerations.

*Example*: The Leaf Society members could obtain *representational standing* if someone who uses the New Hampshire park is a member of the Leaf Society of Southern California. The group is seeking to protect *an interest related to their organization* — leaves. Finally, no one individual needs to participate.

☛ Once you have established injury in fact, turn to establishing that the injury is *fairly traceable to the challenged conduct* and that there is *relief available* under the agency's statutes if your plaintiff prevails.

☞ Causation will probably be tested more often than redressability.

☛ When considering the reviewability of an agency decision, look to the Administrative Procedures Act. This material is more often tested in an Administrative Law course, but your professor may want you to demonstrate that you are at least aware of the different standards of review.

☞ Read your hypothetical carefully to determine the *type — formal or informal —* of agency proceeding.

☞ The *substantial evidence* test applies to formal and adjudicatory proceedings.

☞ *Arbitrary and capricious* applies to informal proceedings. The majority of agency actions will be subject to this standard of review, so if you are tested on reviewability, this standard will be your best bet. Remember that the standard is a narrow one.

☛ Courts traditionally have equitable discretion, so you will rarely find a hypothetical looking for *mandatory injunctive* relief as its answer. Focus more on the traditional balancing tests that courts perform with *discretionary injunctions*.

☛ Professors do not often test on the award of attorneys' fees, but remember that the *American Rule* usually applies and that a *"lodestar" figure* is a reasonable fee.

## CHAPTER 4

# CONSTITUTIONAL LIMITS ON ENVIRONMENTAL REGULATION

## *ChapterScope* ────────────────────────────

In addition to striking a balance between environmental and economic concerns, environmental laws must be sensitive to the requirements of the Constitution of the United States. While much of environmental law is governed by federal statute and administered by the EPA, states and their agencies are intimately involved in the day-to-day administration of environmental protection. This complex federal interplay, along with the Fifth Amendment's restrictions on government takings of private property, necessitates a brief examination of how the Constitution shapes our environmental law. This chapter considers:

- ■ **Specified powers:** There is a basic constitutional framework that sets forth the powers of our federal system, and the limitations of those powers.

- ■ **Reach of Commerce Clause:** This clause, Art. 1, §8, is the basis for most federal environmental regulation and restricts state legislation if it interferes with *interstate commerce*.

    - ■ *Pike* **balancing test:** Courts use a *three-part test* to determine the validity of a state statute, including when a state tries to limit or preclude passage of waste in its boundaries.

    - ■ *Per se discrimination* is invalid, but the *market participant doctrine* allows a state to favor its citizens over interstate economic interests.

- ■ **Limitations under Takings Clause:** This clause, Amend. V, limits the federal *government's ability to take* private property, which is *not limited* to the physical seizure of property.

    - ■ This limitation applies to *all levels* of government, not just the federal.

    - ■ States may impose environmental regulations that affect private property if there is a *legitimate state interest* and a close *means-end fit*.

## I. INTRODUCTION

The Constitution of the United States imposes limitations on the government's power to enact environmental protection.

- **A. Nature of federalism:** Before examining the constitutional limits imposed by the federal government on state actions in regard to environmental regulation, it is imperative to keep in mind that the governmental structure of the United States is a federalist system; that is, a dual-governing system between the federal and state governments.

- **B. Federal government has specified powers:** Under the U.S. Constitution, the power of the federal government *is limited* to those powers specifically granted in the Constitution.

1. **State powers:** In contrast, ***states have general authority***, under the exercise of the police power, to enact environmental regulations pertaining to the safety, health, and welfare of their citizens.

2. **Commerce Clause:** The clause that is the basis for most federal environmental regulation is the Commerce Clause. The Commerce Clause grants Congress the power to regulate interstate commerce. U.S. CONST, art. I, §8.

C. **Sources of constitutional limits on state actions:** Federal environmental regulation must be derived from specific powers under the U.S. Constitution.

1. **The Commerce Clause:** Under Article I, §8 of the Constitution, Congress has the power to "regulate Commerce with foreign Nations, among the several states, and with Indian tribes." Federal regulation under the Commerce Clause may preempt state regulation.

   a. **Factors to be considered in preemption cases:** The Supreme Court has set forth various factors to be considered in preemption cases.

      i. **No room for state regulation:** The federal regulations may be ***so detailed and comprehensive*** that they leave no room for the state to regulate.

      ii. **Dominant federal interest:** The regulations or statute may involve a field in which the ***federal interest is so dominant*** that state law is precluded.

      iii. **State statute cannot conflict with federal regulation:** Even where Congress has not fully foreclosed state regulation, a ***state law is void*** if it conflicts or interferes with federal regulation under the Supremacy Clause. U.S. CONST. art. VI, cl. 2.

   b. **No structured framework:** The Supreme Court has not established a unified framework of analysis for preemption cases. Instead, the Court applies each of these tests on a ***case-by-case basis*** to determine preemption.

2. **The Takings Clause:** The Fifth Amendment provides the federal government shall not take private property for public use "without just compensation." U.S. CONST. amend. V. This prohibition is applicable to state and local governments under the Fourteenth Amendment.

# II. THE REACH OF THE COMMERCE CLAUSE

Most congressional regulation of environmental protection is predicated on the nexus to interstate commerce.

A. **Role of the federal courts:** Although the Commerce Clause is a grant of power to Congress and not to the federal courts, since the early 19th century the Supreme Court has ***limited state legislation*** and ***actions*** affecting interstate commerce even when Congress has not acted.

B. **The negative implication of the Commerce Clause:** Most state laws can have some impact on the interstate market. If such laws ***interfere or burden*** the interstate market, courts may use the "negative implication" of the Commerce Clause to strike down such laws.

1. **The *Pike* balancing test:** In *Pike v. Bruce Church, Inc.,* 397 U.S. 137 (1970), the Supreme Court established a ***three-part test*** to evaluate whether a state statute is precluded by the Commerce Clause.

a. **Legitimate purpose:** The state statute must have a *legitimate local purpose* as the public interest.

b. **Balancing of interests:** The state interest sought to be protected must *clearly outweigh its detrimental effects* on interstate commerce. Most courts require that the burden on interstate commerce be merely incidental in order for the state law to pass this second prong of the *Pike* test.

c. **No alternatives:** No other alternatives are available to the state that *may have a lesser impact* on interstate activities.

2. **Interstate shipment of waste and the ''Not In My Backyard'' syndrome:** The *Pike* test is still used to determine when a state or local government can *prevent* the disposal or shipment of hazardous waste in its boundaries. Many measures have been passed by state and local governments designed to limit or preclude the passage of waste across state lines.

a. *Per se* **discrimination under** *City of Philadelphia v. New Jersey***:** In *City of Philadelphia,* 437 U.S. 617 (1978), the Supreme Court struck down a New Jersey statute prohibiting the import of most waste into the state. The law was enacted by the state in response to the extensive use of New Jersey landfills by cities in Pennsylvania and New York.

   i. **Protectionism is** *per se* **invalid:** The Court found that the statute protected the state's economy at the expense of other states. The majority held, in a 7-2 vote, that such a *''protectionist measure'' discriminates* against articles of interstate commerce *per se,* and thus the Court found it unnecessary to determine whether the purpose of the statute was to protect its limited land resources to favor its local economy.

   ii. **Quarantine laws distinguished:** The Court distinguished the New Jersey ban on importation of waste from a narrow class of ''quarantine'' laws aimed at preventing unreasonable health hazards (*i.e.,* diseased livestock or contaminated foods). Such laws ban the importation of materials that are hazardous to health at the *moment of transportation*. Although these laws are openly discriminatory against interstate commerce, they nevertheless pass constitutional scrutiny because they are directed at protecting public health and safety.

   **Example:** The Supreme Court upheld a state law prohibiting the interstate transportation of dead animals to prevent the spread of disease. *Clanson v. Indiana,* 306 U.S. 439 (1939).

   **Example:** State law banning the shipping of non-native baitfish is valid. Non-native baitfish can be contaminated with parasites, and the introduction of certain species of fish can damage the fragile aquatic ecosystem. The Court found that these reasons constituted a legitimate purpose and that no other alternatives existed which would have less discriminatory impact on interstate commerce. *Maine v. Taylor,* 477 U.S. 131 (1986).

   iii. **Defining** *per se* **discrimination under** *Fort Gratiot***:** Statutes that *prohibit private landfill operators from accepting waste originating outside the county* in which their facilities are located are *per se* discriminatory and violate the Commerce Clause, even though in-state as well as out-of-state waste is restricted in its movement. *Fort Gratiot Sanitary Landfill, Inc. v. Michigan Dep't of Natural Resources,* 504 U.S. 353 (1992).

iv. **Fees and disposal surcharges:** A state cannot impose disposal fees for *out-of-state* hazardous wastes at commercial facilities within the state when there is no fee applied to such waste generated *within* the state. Such differential treatment is in violation of the Commerce Clause. *Chemical Waste Management, Inc. v. Hunt*, 504 U.S. 334 (1992). Similarly, ordinances that require a larger surcharge on out-of-state waste than in-state waste may be invalid.

**Example:** the Supreme Court struck down a state ordinance imposing a surcharge on out-of-state waste that is three times greater than the surcharge on in-state waste. There is no clear nexus between the costs incurred to dispose of the out-of-state waste and the surcharge charged for that disposal. The underlying rationale of the ordinance is economic protectionism and is thus invalid under the Commerce Clause. See *Oregon Waste Systems, Inc. v. Department of Envtl. Quality of the State of Oregon*, 511 U.S. 93 (1994).

b. **Balancing interstate burdens and environmental goals:** If a state statute does not *per se* discriminate against interstate commerce under *City of Philadelphia*, the *Pike* balancing test applies.

i. *Minnesota v. Clover Leaf Creamery Co.*, 449 U.S. 456, *reh'g denied*, 450 U.S. 1027 (1981): The Supreme Court upheld a statute in which the stated purpose was to *promote conservation and to reduce solid waste disposal problems*. The state of Minnesota passed a law banning the sale of milk in plastic, nonreturnable, nonrefillable containers, but permitting the sale in cardboard containers. Out-of-state milk sellers challenged the statute claiming that it was an economic protectionism measure designed to shift business to Minnesota dairy and pulpwood industries. The Court found that the statute did not violate the Commerce Clause because it was an *"even-handed"* regulation which applied to both in- and out-of-state businesses. The law imposed only an incidental effect on interstate commerce and the environmental interests of the statute clearly outweighed any burdens on commerce across state lines.

ii. **Environmental purpose must outweigh protectionist effect:** Even if an ordinance is justified by environmental or health reasons, it *cannot discriminate* against interstate commerce if other *less-discriminatory alternatives are available*. *C & A Carbone, Inc. v. Town of Clarkstown, N.Y.*, 114 S. Ct. 1677 (1994). In this case, the town passed a local flow control ordinance requiring that all non-recyclable solid waste processed or handled within the town be deposited at a local town operator for processing of the waste. The town justified the ordinance as a way to steer solid waste away from out-of-town disposal sites that may be harmful to the environment. The Supreme Court held that the ordinance was a protectionist measure favoring the local town operator and depriving out-of-state disposal businesses access to the local market by preventing everyone except the local operator from performing the initial processing of the waste. The town could have dealt with the alleged environment and health concerns through less discriminatory alternatives, such as uniform safety regulations that would prevent competitors from cutting corners on environmental safety, or by providing a subsidy to the local facility to ensure long term operation.

c. **Market participant doctrine:** When a state acts as a market participant by participating in proprietary activities, and not solely as a regulatory actor, the state is *not* barred from discriminating against interstate commerce. Thus, a state acting as a market participant may favor its citizens over interstate economic interests.

i. ***Hughes v. Alexandria Scrap Corp.,*** 426 U.S. 794 (1976): In an effort to free its scrap yards of ''scrapped'' cars (hulks), Maryland passed a law that allowed the state to purchase hulks from out-of-state scrap processors for above the market rates, thus favoring in-state processors and reducing the number of hulks in the state's scrap yards. A Virginia processor challenged the law under the Commerce Clause. The Supreme Court held that the Commerce Clause was ***not applicable*** in cases where the state acts as a market participant. The Court based its opinion on the fact that Maryland was not regulating the flow of hulks, but had ''entered the market itself'' to bid up the price of the scrapped cars. The Commerce Clause does not prevent a state from participating in the market and favoring its own citizens over others.

ii. ***Reeves, Inc. v. Stake,*** 447 U.S. 429 (1980): In *Reeves*, the Court relied on *Hughes* to uphold a South Dakota policy of selling cement produced by a state-owned plant to its citizens in preference to out-of-state customers during a cement shortage. The Court described the state policy as ***fitting within*** the market participant exception to Commerce Clause restrictions, finding no constitutional limitation on states ''to operate freely in the free market.'' 447 U.S. at 436.

C. **The interstate commerce nexus:** The Supreme Court has held that the commerce power not only extends to the use of channels or means of interstate commerce, but also to ***any activity that may affect such commerce***. A recent decision, however, suggests that the Court is becoming less expansive in defining the reach of the clause.

1. ***Hodel v. Virginia Surface Mining and Reclamation Ass'n, Inc.***: *Hodel*, 452 U.S. 264 (1981), involved a challenge to the Surface Mining and Reclamation Act enacted under the authority of the Commerce Clause. The Act establishes a detailed plan of land use restrictions on strip-mining. The challenged restriction in the case involved a requirement that some land be restored to its original state after the strip-mining. The mining association claimed that the goal of the Act was not to regulate the effects of mining on interstate commerce, but to regulate the use of private lands within each state.

   The Court held that strip-mining affects interstate commerce, noting that mining often results in water pollution. It was irrelevant that the restrictions affected the essentially intrastate activity of mining, because ***Congress had intended the Act to protect interstate commerce*** from the adverse effects of activities and pollutants (*i.e.*, water and land pollution). See also *Hodel v. Indiana*, 452 U.S. 314 (1981).

2. **Significance:** The holding in *Hodel* indicates that Congress's power under the Commerce Clause is very broad. If Congress can rationally conclude that the effects of an activity, ***taken as a whole***, may cross state lines, the federal statute will be upheld.

3. ***Lopez v. United States***: In *Lopez v. United States*, 115 S. Ct. 1624 (1995), the Supreme Court took a much less generous approach to what findings will satisfy the interstate commerce requirement. In finding that the Gun-Free School Zones Act of 1990, which forbids any person from knowing possession of a firearm in a school zone, exceeded Congress's Commerce Clause authority because possession of a gun in a local school zone had nothing to do with commerce nor was it part of larger regulation of economic activity. Compare the discussion of the Commerce Clause in wetlands regulation on p. 31, *infra*.

4. ***Solid Waste Agency of Northern Cook County v. U.S. Army Corps of Engineers***: In *SWANCC*, 531 U.S. 159 (2001), the U.S. Army Corps of Engineers denied a Clean Water Act

§404 permit to fill wetlands under their Migratory Bird Rule, a regulation that brought intrastate waters under Corps jurisdiction if they were used or could be used by certain species of migratory birds. The Supreme Court found that isolated, intrastate waters without any significant nexus to navigable waters were not intended by Congress to fall under the jurisdiction of the Corps under the Clean Water Act.

# III. LIMITATIONS UNDER THE TAKINGS CLAUSE

The Fifth Amendment provides that the federal government shall not take private property for public use ''without just compensation.'' U.S. CONST. amend. V.

**A. Applicability:** The Takings Clause of the Fifth Amendment is applicable to *all levels* of government: federal, state and local.

1. **Applicable to state governments:** This restriction is made applicable to state and local governments through the *Fourteenth Amendment*. See *Penn. Cent. Transp. Co. v. New York*, 438 U.S. 104, 107, *reh'g denied,* 439 U.S. 883 (1978).

2. **Not limited to the physical seizure of property:** A physical invasion of property is *per se* a taking. *Loretto v. Teleprompter Manhattan CATV Corp.*, 458 U.S. 419 (1982). The takings clause is *not limited* to the physical taking of property or seizure of title. In the *Pennsylvania Coal* decision, Justice Holmes said only that when a regulation goes ''too far'' it is taking. Therefore, the question often raised in takings cases is what extent is too far? *Pennsylvania Coal Co. v. Mahon*, 260 U.S. 393 (1922). The actual extent of over-regulation to constitute a taking is uncertain.

**B. Legitimate state interest:** In imposing environmental regulations which affect land use, the state acting pursuant to its police powers must have a *''legitimate state interest''* (*i.e.*, preserving landmarks, protecting the environment). *Agins v. City of Tiburon*, 447 U.S. 255 (1980).

1. **Environmental preservation as the state's interest:** Regulation of a private owner's use of his property to protect the environment is regarded as a *public interest*. *Penn Cent. Transp. Co. v. City of New York*, 438 U.S. 104, *reh'g denied*, 439 U.S. 883 (1978) (finding that a New York landmark preservation law did not constitute a taking of plaintiff's property).

2. **Means-end fit:** There must also be a *close fit* between the means chosen by the state, such as the type of regulation to be used, and the state's objective in passing the regulation.

   a. *Nollan v. California Coastal Commission*: In *Nollan*, 483 U.S. 825 (1987), the Supreme Court stated that a regulation does not effect a taking if it ''substantially advance[s] legitimate state interests'' and ''does not den[y] an owner economically viable use of his land.'' According to the court, the state agency's conditioning of a permit to rebuild a beach house on granting the agency a public easement parallel to the ocean was *not sufficiently related to the agency's declared purposes* of preventing congestion, and improving the public's visual and ''psychological'' access to the beach to warrant the condition imposed.

   b. **''Rough Proportionality Test'' of *Dolan***: In *Dolan v. City of Tigard*, 114 S. Ct. 2309 (1994), the Supreme Court clarified the closeness of the means-end fit and held that conditions placed on development permits must be *''roughly proportional''* to the effects the applicant's proposed land use will have on the community. Florence Dolan filed an application with the City of Tigard, Oregon, seeking permission to replace her hardware store with a much larger facility and to pave a 39-space parking lot. Dolan's application was submitted to the City Planning Commission. The Commission granted approval of Dolan's application on several conditions, including that Dolan was to dedicate a portion of her land falling within the floodplain for improvement of the city storm drainage system; and that Dolan was required to dedicate to the city a 15-foot-wide strip of land adjacent to the floodplain to permit the continued development of Tigard's pedestrian/bicycle pathway system and allow for additional public greenway. The Court found that Tigard's dedication requirements could not pass the rough proportionality test. The Court stated that until the city made "some effort to quantify its findings in support of the dedication," Dolan could not be forced to give up her land without receiving just compensation. The Court indicated that more evidence of congestion was necessary to justify the pathway and that floodplain problems did not substantiate the need for a *public* greenway.

C. **Temporary taking:** A temporary taking occurs when a regulation is *promulgated but later removed*. The Supreme Court has held that when suit is filed against the government for a temporary taking, just compensation is the damages for the losses resulting from loss of property use from the time that the interference occurs to the time in which the regulation is amended, withdrawn, or compensation is paid for the complete loss from the taking. See *First English Evangelical Lutheran Church of Glendale v. Los Angeles County*, 482 U.S. 304 (1987).

**Example:** *Palazzolo v. State ex rel. Tavares*: In *Palazzolo*, 746 A.2d 707 (R.I. 2000), the Supreme Court held that a regulatory takings claim is not necessarily defeated simply because the regulation existed before petitioner acquired the land. The Court pointed out that one of the main purposes of the Takings Clause was to enable citizens to obtain compensation for manifestly unreasonable and onerous state actions, and that such actions do not become more reasonable merely through passage of time or transfer of ownership. The Court also held that restrictions on review would penalize new owners for the failure of prior owners to protest the state action, and would penalize prior owners by restricting transferability of the land.

**Example:** *Tahoe Sierra Preservation Council, Inc. v. Tahoe Regional Planning Agency*. In *Tahoe*, 70 U.S.L.W. 4260 (Apr. 23, 2002), the Supreme Court concluded that a temporary moratorium on development — even one that denies all economically viable use — is not a *per se* or categorical taking. A temporary moratorium, by its very nature, restores the value of the property once the restriction is lifted, and the Court noted that regulatory takings are still to be assessed under the factors set out in *Penn Central*.

D. **The "nuisance" exception:** Several early Supreme Court cases suggested that when a regulation is passed *to prevent harm* in the nature of a nuisance to the public, there is *no taking*. Thus, anything that could be perceived as a private or public nuisance potentially fell within this so-called "nuisance exception" to the takings clause. See *Keystone Bituminous Coal Association v. DeBenedictis*, 480 U.S. 470 (1987).

1. **Pollution regulations:** Regulations prohibiting manufacturing on property in residential areas to prevent air pollution were held to come under the "nuisance" exception. See *Hadacheck v. Sebastian*, 239 U.S. 394 (1915).

2. **Alcoholic beverage restrictions:** Certain restrictions on the production and selling of intoxicating beverages on private property that may be viewed as nuisance to the community were similarly upheld. See *Mugler v. Kansas*, 123 U.S. 623 (1887).

3. **Securing a public benefit:** However, when the government passes a regulation to **secure a public benefit**, rather than **preventing a public harm**, the regulation may be seen as a taking. The distinction is often a difficult one to draw. For example, a regulation that limited the use of private property on wetlands to hunting and fishing and required a permit for all other uses was held not to be a taking because it prevented harm for a change in the ''natural character'' of the property. See *Just v. Marinette County*, 56 Wis. 2d 7, 201 N.W.2d 761 (Wis. 1972).

4. **Denial of all economic value of land and the nuisance exception:** The Supreme Court has held that when a regulation has deprived a private land owner of all the economically viable use of his land, *per se* a taking has occurred. *Lucas v. South Carolina Coastal Council*, 505 U.S. 1003 (1992). The *Lucas* decision did not address what will constitute a taking if the owner has only lost a **particular** use of his land or part of its value. *Lucas*, 505 U.S. at 1030. In *Lucas*, Justice Scalia limited the nuisance exception in cases of a **total taking** to nuisances as defined under state nuisance and property law. The Court did not decide the scope of the exception in partial takings cases. See also *M & J Coal Co. v. United States*, 47 F.3d 1148, *cert. denied*, 116 S. Ct. 53 (1995) (holding that a mining company's acquisition of rights by deed did not allow the right to mine in such a way as to endanger public health and safety, and that no taking occurred because the mining company never had such a right in the first place).

## IV. LIMITATIONS ON FEDERAL LAW UNDER THE TENTH AMENDMENT

In *New York v. United States*, 505 U.S. 144 (1992), the Supreme Court struck down a provision of the Low-Level Radioactive Waste Policy Amendments Act of 1985. The provision required states that lack disposal capacity for low-level radioactive wastes generated within their borders to take title to those wastes after January 1, 1996. The provision was found to **violate the Tenth Amendment** because it allowed the states **no alternative** to carrying out the federal policy.

## *Quiz Yourself on* CONSTITUTIONAL LIMITS ON ENVIRONMENTAL REGULATION

7. May a state ever validly burden or interfere with interstate commerce? _____

8. The state of Ember has miraculously decreased its garbage output over the last decade. This has left it in the enviable position of having presently unneeded landfill space. The bordering state of Overflo has sadly increased its garbage output over the last decade, and they have no more landfill space. Overflo legislators have been bugging Ember legislators about letting them truck their trash into Ember, but Ember wants to remain Overflo garbage–free. The Ember legislators decide to contract

with various garbage companies throughout their state and only allow those companies to dump in the Ember landfills. Overflo claims this violates the Commerce Clause because it discriminates against their garbage companies. May Ember do this? _____

9. If a state statute does not facially discriminate against interstate commerce, will it be upheld? _____

10. Joe Dee recently purchased a two-acre wetlands area so that he can have his buddies over for weekends of debauchery. For the first couple of months, things went swimmingly as his friends came over, drank his homemade wine, and went splashing through the wetlands. Soon though, he had too many ''friends'' coming over and Joe realized he couldn't afford the payments on the land if he didn't start charging money for the weekend follies. He no longer served his homemade wine for free, but charged for it by the jug. That didn't slow the drinkers down and more than one buddy ended up wading too far into the waters and the fire department had to rescue them. Joe also wanted to start charging for wading and fishing on his land. He asked the city what he needed to do to begin this, and was shocked when they told him to cease these activities. Joe demanded compensation from the city when he was no longer able to make money from his weekend buddies. Joe claimed he was the victim of a ''taking'' without just compensation because he could not use his private property as he wanted. Is this a taking? _____

---

## Answers

7. **Yes.** A state may burden or interfere with interstate commerce if the burden is minimal and the state has a legitimate interest it is seeking to protect. A legitimate interest, for example, includes protecting the state's clean water supply through imposing regulations and controls on detergents containing phosphate. The controls burdened interstate commerce because the detergent sales in other states were affected. When the detergent manufacturer sued, the court concluded that the burden was less important than the state's interest in maintaining a clean water supply. See *Proctor & Gamble v. Chicago*, 509 F.2d 69 (7th Cir. 1975).

8. **Yes.** Ember is acting as a market participant rather than a regulator and contracting for garbage disposal is a legitimate act. Overflo's garbage companies are not regulated against, they simply were not chosen for the contracts.

9. **Not necessarily.** If the statute is not *per se* discrimination, then the court will apply the *Pike* three-part balancing test. If the state's interest does not sufficiently outweigh the burden or there were other alternatives, then the court will not uphold the statute.

10. **No.** The city is allowed to protect its citizens through certain regulations that would be considered ''takings'' except for the nuisance exceptions. The city is justified in limiting or eliminating Joe's ability to produce and sell his homemade wine on his land, especially when it led to the near-death experiences of several drunk ''customers.'' The city also is allowed to limit or eliminate Joe's ability to allow all activities on his land if these activities could be damaging to the natural environment of the wetlands. Joe's land still has economic viability, so there is no *per se* taking either.

*Exam Tips on*
## CONSTITUTIONAL LIMITS ON ENVIRONMENTAL REGULATION

The information from this chapter will be especially important when evaluating a hypothetical that includes facts involving state regulations that may affect other states' actors.

☛ When evaluating a state environmental statute, consider whether federal regulations might preempt it:

☞ *Preemption* occurs when federal regulations in the same area are *detailed and comprehensive*, the federal interest is *dominant*, or the state law *conflicts*.

☛ Apply the *Pike* balancing test if the state statute *interferes or burdens* the interstate market, but do not forget that the clause *could* reach *any activity* affecting commerce.

☛ Exam short-answer questions often include a question involving state regulation of hazardous waste disposal or shipment within the state.

*Example*: The state of Ember wants to pass legislation limiting hazardous waste disposal within its boundaries, because legislators fear their state is becoming the "dumping ground" for all the coastal states. Ember cannot outright prohibit other states' waste because that would be *per se* discrimination under *City of Philadelphia*. Ember could, however, pass safety regulations ensuring the environmental health of its citizens, but which are equally applicable to in-state and out-of-state actors.

☞ Don't forget the state action must protect a *legitimate state interest*, outweigh the *detrimental effect* on interstate commerce, and *no other alternatives* are available.

☞ A quick way to demonstrate your understanding of the material is to apply the facts of your exam hypothetical to each of the three requirements and conclude with your determination of the legitimacy of the state statute.

☛ Remember that a government taking is *not limited* to physical seizure, and it applies to *all levels* of government.

☞ There may be a taking if it protects a *legitimate state interest*.

*Example*: A state may "take" to protect a landmark. Some private property owners may even seek landmark designation, so that the state will take and the property will be protected.

☞ When you are considering whether a taking has occurred, argue both sides: that the taking may not be just, because there was not a close enough *means-end fit* OR that the taking was just, because the state's objective and the type of regulation were satisfactory. Remember to address the *rough proportionality test* of *Dolan*.

☞ If the facts outline a private or public *nuisance*, remember that there is an exception which allows the taking.

## CHAPTER 5

# NATIONAL ENVIRONMENTAL POLICY ACT (NEPA)

## *ChapterScope* ───────────────────────

The National Environmental Policy Act is an environmental statute that emphasizes information rather than regulation. NEPA governs certain classes of government action, and requires the publication of information on anticipated environmental effects of, and possible alternatives to, the proposed action. We examine the following concepts of NEPA in this chapter:

■ **Purpose of NEPA:** NEPA forced federal agencies, for the first time in history, to consider the *environmental impact* of their regulations and present alternatives to the proposed governmental actions. This *information* was then presented to the public and to decision-makers.

   ■ There have been *criticisms* of NEPA and its actual usefulness.

   ■ **Council on Environmental Quality:** NEPA established the CEQ to *assist the President* with environmental concerns. CEQ mainly *issues guidelines* to interpret NEPA's requirements, and courts owe *substantial deference* to these guidelines.

■ **Environmental Impact Statement (EIS):** This is the *primary document generated* under NEPA, and it only applies to *federal* actions. Agencies must make a *threshold finding* of whether the EIS must be prepared, determine the *scope and adequacy* of the EIS, and make a *summary of existing credible scientific evidence* relating to potential environmental impacts.

   ■ NEPA generally is not considered applicable to *international* federal actions.

   ■ States may enact their own version of NEPA — state environmental policy acts (SEPAs).

■ **Substantive review:** The court may *not substitute its judgment* for that of the agency, but it must determine that the agency did, in fact, *actually consider* the environmental issues and make *full consideration* of all relevant factors.

▬▬▬▬▬▬▬▬▬▬▬▬▬▬▬▬▬▬▬▬▬▬▬▬▬▬▬▬▬▬▬▬▬▬▬▬▬▬▬▬

## I. GENERAL INFORMATION

The National Environmental Policy Act (NEPA) is an environmental statute that emphasizes *information* rather than regulation. It requires the publication of information about the environmental effects of and *alternatives* to potential government actions. The broad policy goals of NEPA are in §101, 42 U.S.C. §4331. NEPA does not dictate environmental standards or controls.

A. **History:** NEPA, Pub. L. No. 91-190, 83 Stat. 852 (1970) (codified as amended at 42 U.S.C. §§4321-4370(d)), was enacted in 1969 in order to *require* federal agencies to consider the *quality* of the human environment in their decisionmaking. It is widely considered to be the first act of the modern environmental legislation.

   1. **Federal agencies prior to NEPA:** Prior to 1970 many federal agencies claimed to have *no authority* to consider the environment in their actions.

    **a. Attitudes of the agencies:** This disregard for the environment was premised on the assumption that environmental concerns were *beyond the mission* of the agency.

    **b. Impact on the environment:** Often the primary mission of the agency resulted in *detrimental effects* to the quality of the environment.

  **2. Changes within the federal agencies after NEPA:** The "action forcing" provisions of NEPA created an *explicit mandate* for all federal agencies requiring a specific analysis and procedures to take into consideration environmental factors.

**B. Purpose:** NEPA establishes policy, sets goals, and provides the means for carrying out the policy. 40 C.F.R. §1500.1. Its emphasis is on information: both the *documentation* of environmental statistics and the *dissemination* of the documentation.

  **1. NEPA requires agencies to take environmental factors into account:** NEPA requires federal agencies to consider the effects of their actions on the environment by preparing a detailed *Environmental Impact Statement (EIS)*. See *infra*, p. 39. The agency, however, does not have to elevate environmental concerns over other considerations. The agency need only consider the environmental *consequences* of its actions. Once the agency has made a decision, the court may only interject to ensure that environmental consequences were indeed considered, and not to change the decision made by the agency. Where environmental consequences have been considered, no more is required by NEPA. *Strycher's Bay Neighborhood Council, Inc. v. Karlen*, 100 S. Ct. 497 (1980).

  **2. NEPA requires agencies to consider alternatives:** Included in the EIS must be a discussion of the *alternative proposals* to the government action and the *environmental impact* of each. Consideration of alternatives is required even if an EIS *does not* have to be prepared. See *infra*, p. 42.

  **3. Provide information to the public:** The main purpose of the EIS is to *inform the public as well as the decision-makers* about the proposed action and the alternatives to such action.

**C. Establishment of the Council on Environmental Quality:** NEPA established the Council on Environmental Quality (CEQ) to *assist the President* with environmental concerns. NEPA §105, 42 U.S.C. §4342.

  **1. Duties and functions:** Under NEPA §204 (42 U.S.C. §4344), the duties and functions of the CEQ are to:

    **a.** aid the President in preparing the Environmental Quality Report;

    **b.** gather information on the conditions and trends in the quality of the environment;

    **c.** review the activities of the federal government in light of the purposes of NEPA and make recommendations on them;

    **d.** develop and recommend to the President national environmental policies;

    **e.** conduct investigations, studies, surveys, research, and analyses relating to the ecological systems;

    **f.** document and define changes to the natural environment and interpret their underlying causes;

    **g.** report at least once a year to the President on the state of the environment; and

   **h.** make studies and reports as the President may wish.

  **2. Authority of the CEQ Guidelines:** Although the list of functions in NEPA is expansive, the actual role of the CEQ is less so. The main responsibility of the CEQ is to *issue guidelines* to interpret NEPA's requirements.

    **a. Issue guidelines:** The CEQ publishes guidelines that explain to government agencies what they must do to follow NEPA's mandate.

    **b. Decisions of Council entitled to substantial deference:** Courts owe *substantial deference* to the CEQ Guidelines interpretation of NEPA. *Andrus v. Sierra Club,* 442 U.S. 347 (1979).

    **c. No enforcement authority:** The CEQ Guidelines have no power to *alter or stop* a federal agency's actions under NEPA.

# II. THE ENVIRONMENTAL IMPACT STATEMENT (EIS)

### A. Process

  **1. Exemptions from EIS obligation:** Certain situations exist in which the obligations under NEPA *cannot or need not be met* by an agency.

    **a. Conflicts with statutory obligations:** If an agency's obligations under another statute make it *impossible to fully comply* with the NEPA obligations, NEPA must give way. *Flint Ridge Dev. Co. v. Scenic Rivers Ass'n of Oklahoma,* 426 U.S. 776, 791, *reh'g denied,* 429 U.S. 875 (1976).

    **b. Express statutory exemption:** Congress can *exempt* an agency from having to comply with NEPA duties. See, *e.g.*, 33 U.S.C. §1371(c)(l) (exempting the EPA from having to prepare an EIS for the Clean Water Act).

    **c. "Functional equivalence" of NEPA:** When the terms of another applicable statute require duties that are *"functionally equivalent"* to NEPA's duties, the agency may be excused. *Western Nebraska Resources Council v. EPA*, 943 F.2d 867, 871 (8th Cir. 1991).

  **2. Environmental Assessment:** The Environmental Assessment (EA) is a short document which *outlines the proposal and its possible environmental impact*. It aids the agency in determining whether a full EIS is necessary. 40 C.F.R. §1508.9.

  **3. Finding of No Significant Impact:** With the aid of the EA, the agency decides whether to do an EIS. If it decides not to, it issues a "Finding of No Significant Impact" or FONSI. An issuance of a FONSI is *usually the last NEPA action* on a project. A FONSI *may not* be issued for activities which have a potential for disturbing the environment. In such a case, an EIS must be prepared in order to fully assess the possible environmental consequences. *Sierra Club v. Peterson*, 717 F.2d 1409 (D.C. Cir. 1983).

  **4. Notice of Intent and scoping:** If an agency determines that an EIS is necessary, it will *publish a "Notice of Intent"* to prepare the EIS. The next step in the EIS process is "scoping," when the agency *defines the topics and issues* involved in the proposal. 40 C.F.R. §§1501.7 and 1508.25.

5. **Draft EIS:** Once a draft of the EIS has been completed, it must be ***circulated for comment*** from the public and other agencies. The agency has some discretion as to whether to hold public hearings to discuss the draft.

6. **Final EIS:** After responding to comments and incorporating the answers into the EIS, the final EIS is completed.

7. **EPA review of EIS:** Under §309(a), 42 U.S.C. §7609(a), the EPA is authorized to review EISs prepared by other federal agencies. The EPA evaluates both the adequacy of the EIS and the environmental impact of the proposed action. The EPA does not have the power to change decisions made by other agencies following the submission of the EIS.

8. **Record of decision:** The final decision of the agency must be set forth with a ***justification*** for the action and the ***reasons why*** the alternatives were rejected.

9. **Judicial review:** Compliance with NEPA is subject to judicial review ***even though*** NEPA lacks a "citizen suit" provision.

   a. **Source of jurisdiction:** NEPA cases come to the federal court system under federal question jurisdiction. The courts have taken an ***active role*** in ensuring NEPA compliance. See *Calvert Cliffs' Coordinating Comm., Inc. v. Atomic Energy Comm'n*, 449 F.2d 1109 (D.C. Cir. 1971). In *Calvert Cliffs*, the court held the agency to strict compliance with the procedural requirements of NEPA.

   b. **Standard of review:** The Supreme Court has held that the decision ***not to prepare*** a supplemental EIS is reviewed under the ***"arbitrary and capricious"*** standard. *Marsh v. Oregon Natural Resources Council*, 490 U.S. 360 (1989). It is presumed that the same standard of review applies to the decision whether to prepare an EIS.

   c. **Scope:** Courts may review an agency's decision on ***whether to prepare*** an EIS, the ***adequacy*** of an EIA or EIS, as well as ***the procedures*** by which such decisions are made. The usual remedy for a NEPA violation is injunctive relief.

B. **Threshold issue — when must an EIS be prepared?** The threshold question in deciding whether an EIS is needed is determined by §102(2)(C). Environmental Impact Statements are ***only required*** for "proposals for legislation and other major Federal actions significantly affecting the quality of the human environment."

   1. **Proposals for legislation or action:** When do an agency's actions reach a point that there is a "proposal?" The Supreme Court has ruled that an EIS need only be prepared when an agency has ***actually made a proposal***, not when it is merely contemplating some action. *Kleppe v. Sierra Club*, 427 U.S. 390 (1976); see also 40 C.F.R. Section 1508.23. Compare *Scientists' Institute for Public Information v. AEC*, 481 F.2d 1079 (D.C. Cir. 1973), which used a balancing test similar to that in the CEQ Guidelines (late enough for meaningful analysis, early enough to make a difference) to determine whether agency action has progressed to the point at which environmental consequences should be assessed. The regulatory definition of "proposal" makes it clear that there may be a de facto proposal even if not characterized by the agency as a proposal.

   2. **Federal inaction:** Federal ***inaction*** requires an EIS only when the agency has some decision-making obligation. *Defenders of Wildlife v. Andrus*, 627 F.2d 1238 (D.C. Cir. 1980) (holding that Department of Interior's decision not to stop a state plan to kill wolves is not subject to

NEPA; although it had the authority to stop the hunt, it had no obligation to decide whether or not the hunt should take place. The courts have been reluctant to require an EIS for an agency's failure to act).

3. **Federal:** Only federal actions are affected by EIS requirements. State and local governmental actions, as well as private actions, are *not subject to NEPA*. If there is a sufficient amount of federal involvement in a private action, the EIS requirement may be triggered. See also 40 C.F.R. §1508.18.

   **Example:** When the federal government leases land for the construction of a power plant, an EIS may be required; when the federal government merely gives a right of way over navigable water for the construction of a power line, an EIS is not required. See, *e.g, Winnebago Tribe of Nebraska v. Ray*, 621 F.2d 269 (8th Cir. 1980), *cert. denied*, 449 U.S. 836 (1980).

4. **Major/significantly affecting:** According to the CEQ Guidelines, ''major'' *reinforces but in* practice *has no meaning independent* of ''significantly affecting.'' Determining when an action significantly affects the environment has been the most contentious issue under NEPA.

   a. **Context and intensity:** The CEQ Guidelines interpret this phrase *to require consideration of the effects in terms of context* (society as a whole, regionally, locally, etc.) *and intensity* (severity of the impact). 40 C.F.R. §1508.27.

   b. **Controversial:** These CEQ Guidelines require an EIS for action *likely to be highly controversial.*

   c. **Balancing test:** Some courts have applied a two-part test, requiring an agency to consider:

      i. the *extent to which the action will cause adverse environmental* effects in excess of those created by existing uses in the area; and

      ii. the *absolute quantitative adverse environmental effects* of the action itself. See *Hanly v. Kleindienst*, 471 F.2d 823 (2d Cir. 1972), *cert. denied*, 412 U.S. 908 (1973).

   d. **Effects:** ''Effects'' is synonymous with impacts and includes ecological, aesthetic, historic, cultural, economic, social, or health effects, *whether direct or indirect*. 40 C.F.R. §1508.8. However, psychological harm from fear of an adverse effect, such as the fear of a nuclear power accident, was held by the Supreme Court to be too attenuated to be considered by the agency. See *Metropolitan Edison Co. v. People Against Nuclear Energy*, 460 U.S. 766 (1983).

5. **Quality of human environment:** The human environment means the natural and physical environment and its relationship with the people of that environment. Economic and social effects are *not enough* in and of themselves to require an EIS. 40 C.F.R. §1508.14. A significant impact on the physical environment must be demonstrated.

   **Example:** The possible introduction of weapons, drugs, and crime into a neighborhood as a result of government action does not require an EIS because the changes are not physical but socioeconomic. *Olmsted Citizens for a Better Community v. United States*, 793 F.2d 201 (8th Cir. 1986).

C. **Scope:** The scope of an EIS can be a complex question. This is especially true when it is unclear whether a federal action is a small, discrete project or a series of actions that should be studied as a whole.

1. **Single project/segmentation:** An EIS may be prepared for a *single project or segment* rather than the more comprehensive action if the segment or project has independent utility. See *Daly v. Volpe*, 514 F.2d 1106 (9th Cir. 1975); *South Carolina v. O'Leary*, 64 F.3d 892 (4th Cir. 1995).

2. **Comprehensive EIS:** Conversely a comprehensive EIS is required for proposals which must be considered in a *broader context* than their own completion because they are dependent upon other actions.

   a. **Programmatic actions:** A single EIS is necessary when proposals for federal actions are *so closely related* as to constitute a single course of action.

   b. **Cumulative actions:** When the agency has several proposals which may have a *cumulative effect* on the environment, an EIS covering them all is necessary. See *Kleppe v. Sierra Club*, 427 U.S. 390 (1976).

   c. **Connected actions:** The CEQ and supporting case law require *"connected actions" to be considered together* in a single EIS. 40 C.F.R. §1508.25(a); see also *Thomas v. Peterson*, 753 F.2d 754 (9th Cir. 1985).

      **Example:** A Navy plan to build a battleship at a port and a plan to build housing at the port were not connected because neither was a necessary precondition to the other. *Hudson River Sloop Clearwater, Inc. v. Department of Navy*, 836 F.2d 760 (2d Cir. 1988).

      **Example:** Proposal for a fish hatchery and a diversion of a river were connected because the water was diverted just for the hatchery and the hatchery depended on the diversion to exist. *Morgan v. Walter*, 728 F. Supp. 1483 (D. Idaho 1989).

D. **Adequacy of the Environmental Impact Statement:** Generally, the EIS *must include* the environmental effects of the proposed action and alternatives to the proposed actions, and the alternatives' own effects.

   1. **Consideration of alternatives:** The agency must consider alternatives to the proposal and the environmental impact of those alternatives, *even if no EIS is required*. NEPA §102(2)(E), 42 U.S.C. §4332(2)(E).

      a. **Council on Environmental Quality Guidelines:** The CEQ has stated that the EIS must include *all reasonable alternatives*, including:

         i.   those that would eliminate the need for this action;

         ii.  those that would mitigate any environmental impact; and

         iii. the lack of any action in this case.

         The CEQ Guidelines suggest there are three types of alternatives: (1) the *no action* alternative; (2) *reasonable alternatives* to the proposed action; and (3) *mitigation measures* for the proposed action.

      b. **Primary and secondary alternatives:** A primary alternative is a course of action entirely different from the proposal. A secondary alternative is one that goes forward with the proposal, but in a different way.

      c. **Determination of reasonable alternatives:** Agencies and interest groups often clash when deciding what is a reasonable alternative.

    **i.** **No requirement to consider primary alternative:** Courts are reluctant to require an agency to *redefine the goal* of its proposal when considering the alternatives. *Citizens of Burlington, Inc. v. Busey*, 938 F.2d 190 (D.C. Cir.), *cert. denied*, 502 U.S. 994 (1991).

        **Example:** Department of Defense was not required to consider alternate weapons systems when preparing an EIS on an MX missile proposal because that would be outside of the Congressional mandate for the project. *Romer v. Carlucci*, 847 F.2d 445 (8th Cir. 1988).

    **ii.** **Alternatives that meet a portion of the stated goal:** NEPA requires consideration of alternatives which meet only a *portion of the stated goals* of the project, although the fact that only a part of the goals are met will be a disadvantage when weighing the alternative against the proposal. *North Buckhead Civic Ass'n v. Skinner*, 903 F.2d 1533 (11th Cir. 1990); see also 40 C.F.R. §1502.14. Courts frequently say that the analyses of alternatives is the ''heart'' of NEPA's requirements.

    **iii.** **Rule of reason:** Although an agency need not consider speculative or experimental technologies, it is required to *consider all reasonable alternatives, whether or not the alternatives are within the authority* of that agency. *NRDC v. Morton*, 458 F.2d 827 (D.C. Cir. 1972). *Morton* may have been limited by *Vermont Yankee Nuclear Power Corp. v. NRDC*, 435 U.S. 519 (1978). Although affirming *Morton*'s rule of reason, the Supreme Court suggested that at least some of the burden of presenting alternatives lies on the opponents of a project and not just the agency.

**2.** **Mitigation:** Mitigation of the environmental impact *must* be considered in the EIS.

    **a.** **Council on Environmental Quality Guidelines:** Mitigation is *required to be discussed* in the scope of the EIS, as part of the alternatives, and in the final decision of the agency.

    **b.** **Review:** Although the agency is required to consider mitigation and include such discussion in the EIS, it is *under no substantive obligation* under NEPA *to implement* any of the mitigation measures. *Robertson v. Methow Valley Citizens Council*, 490 U.S. 332 (1989).

    **c.** **Mitigation is construed liberally:** Mitigation *does not necessarily have to affect* the particular action in question, but can rather be a separate action to offset the environmental impact.

        **Example:** In a development affecting wetlands in land Parcel A, a company may mitigate by converting land Parcel B to wetlands. *Friends of the Earth v. Hintz*, 800 F.2d 822 (9th Cir. 1986).

**3.** **Lack of available information:** When relevant evidence or scientific data is inadequate or lacking, the CEQ Guidelines and the courts have required that the *agency publicly note this lack of information*, or include it if it is essential and the costs of obtaining it are not exorbitant.

**4.** **''Worst case'' analysis:** So-called ''worst case'' analysis refers to unobtainable information on adverse environmental impacts.

    **a.** **Prior regulation:** The CEQ Guidelines *formerly required an EIS to include a worst case analysis*, an assessment of potentially catastrophic consequences of low probability, and probability analysis even when information about the project and environment was unavailable or too costly to obtain.

    **b. New regulation:** In 1986, the worst case analysis requirement was changed to require a *summary of existing credible scientific evidence* relating to environmental impacts within the rule of reason. 40 C.F.R. §1502.22. A *probability analysis is not expressly required* by the regulation, but NEPA has been *interpreted by courts to require such analysis. Robertson v. Methow Valley Citizens Council*, 490 U.S. 332 (1989).

    **c. Not a codification of case law:** In *Robertson*, the Supreme Court held that worst case analysis as mandated by the prior regulation, unlike probability analysis, was not required by NEPA.

**5. Supplemental EIS:** An agency may be required to file an *additional supplement* to either its draft or final EIS if:

    **a.** it makes *substantial changes* in its proposed action relevant to the environmental concerns; or

    **b.** significant new *circumstances or information* arise that are relevant to the environment. 40 C.F.R. §1502.9(c).

    Even though a supplemental EIS is not expressly addressed in NEPA, the Court has found a supplemental EIS to be necessary at times *to support the "action-forcing" purpose* of NEPA. *Marsh v. Oregon Natural Resources Council*, 490 U.S. 360 (1989). A requirement of a supplemental EIS is supported by NEPA's concern with *preventing uninformed acts* by agencies.

# III.  SUBSTANTIVE REVIEW UNDER NEPA

What, if any, limits does NEPA put on an agency's substantive decision to proceed with a proposal? Put another way, if an agency follows all the procedures of NEPA, may it proceed with an environmentally destructive project despite clearly preferable alternatives so long as it has some rational reason for selecting the project it has selected?

**A. Standard of review of the substantive decision:** In *Strycker's Bay Neighborhood Council, Inc. v. Karlen*, 444 U.S. 223 (1980), the Supreme Court evaluated a decision by the court of appeals overturning the selection of a site by HUD for a proposed low income housing project. The Court held that once an agency had complied with its duties under NEPA, the role of the reviewing court was *limited to insuring that the agency actually considered environmental matters* — not to substitute its judgment for the agency's on the merits. The reviewing court could not "interject itself within the area of discretion of the executive as to the choice of action to be taken." 444 U.S. at 227 (quoting *Kleppe v. Sierra Club*, 427 U.S. 390, 410 n.21 (1976)). Moreover, a reviewing court *cannot elevate environmental considerations* over other legitimate factors when determining agency compliance with NEPA. The Court in *Robertson* affirmed this narrow nature of substantive overview over agency action under NEPA by characterizing the Act's policy in §101 as "precatory" and stating that the nature of NEPA is to prescribe a "process" for considering environmental values rather than to mandate any particular results.

**B. Consideration of all relevant factors:** Recall that in *Overton Park, supra*, p. 22, the Supreme Court held that an agency's decision to put a highway through a park would be reviewed under the arbitrary and capricious standard. Although this standard of substantive review is quite narrow, the Court said it *did require full consideration of all relevant factors*. NEPA makes environmental factors relevant to agency decisionmaking. If an agency has failed to give adequate consideration to environmental factors, not only will its EIA or EIS be procedurally defective under NEPA, but also its substantive decision to proceed may be attacked as deficient under the generally applicable standard of review under the APA.

# IV. INTERNATIONAL APPLICATION OF NEPA

NEPA is generally not considered to be applicable to federal actions abroad or those that have significant extraterritorial effects.

**A. Exceptions:** The presumption against extraterritorial application of NEPA has been held *not* to apply when the conduct takes place primarily within the United States and the effects are felt in Antarctica, a continent without a sovereign. *EDF v. Massey*, 986 F.2d 528 (D.C. Cir. 1993).

**B. International application by Executive Order:** Executive Order 12114, however, imposes somewhat similar requirements to those of NEPA on federal actions that have significant environmental effects abroad. The coverage of the order is more limited than NEPA and private citizens may not sue to compel compliance.

# V. STATE ENVIRONMENTAL POLICY ACTS

A majority of states have enacted their own state environmental policy acts (SEPAs) that require some form of environmental study for state government actions. The state acts vary, and some SEPAs may be more encompassing than NEPA, applying to private acts as well as governmental acts.

# VI. CRITICISMS OF NEPA

NEPA has met with *mixed reviews*. Critics argue that the agencies go through the motions of an EIS without actually using it in the decisionmaking process. Supporters counter that the requirement of documenting possible problems may direct an agency towards a less harmful alternative, or at least motivate the public to become involved. Both agree that the EIS process delays — for better or for worse — the proposed actions, sometimes forcing cancellation or alteration of the planned project.

---

## *Quiz Yourself* on
## *NATIONAL ENVIRONMENTAL POLICY ACT (NEPA)*

**11.** Ember state's Urban Housing Agency wants to drain a lake outside of Ember's largest city to create more land for affordable housing units in a suburban setting. Will the agency have to prepare an EIS under NEPA? _____

12. Is the Council on Environmental Quality the policing force for federal agency environmental decisions? _____

13. The federal Agency to Promote Walking has a mandate to get citizens all over the country walking rather than driving or riding. As part of a massive group of legislative proposals, the agency has decided to install a footbridge over the dividing river boundary between the states of Walkalot and Walkalittle in order to encourage the citizens of each state to walk across the river rather than travel by ferry. Ignoring possible exemptions, will the agency have to prepare a full EIS under NEPA? _____

14. Same facts as above, but now the agency is considering which alternatives to address in its final EIS draft. One comment suggested encouraging the local beaver population to build a dam, which could create a "natural" bridge and would not involve human construction labor and machines. Another alternative involves highly sophisticated technology which could be used to develop a bridge that would not actually touch down on either bank, but would be "suspended" in midair. A third alternative suggested was installing a walking path on the ferry so that people could enjoy a walk while they traveled across the river.

    (a) Does the agency need to address each alternative in its final EIS draft? _____

    (b) If they do not and they opt to go ahead with the footbridge, will a court uphold the action? _____

---

## Answers

11. **No.** NEPA only governs federal actions. The state agency could have to prepare an EIS if Ember has enacted a SEPA.

12. **No.** The CEQ was established to assist the President with environmental issues. Additionally, they issue guidelines for interpreting NEPA and courts apply substantial deference to these guidelines. CEQ cannot, however, "police" federal agency actions because they cannot alter or stop federal agency actions under NEPA.

13. **Yes.** There is a potential for environmental disturbance since the bridge will be affecting waterways, plant and animal life on either side of the river, and construction could cause pollution, so the agency cannot issue a FONSI.

14a. **Not all of them.** The agency does not need to address the first alternative, because a court would likely agree that a beaver-made dam is not a reasonable alternative to a footbridge. The second alternative is probably too technologically advanced for this project, and not enough information is available to make an informed decision. While the agency would not have to consider this alternative in the final EIS, it would have to disclose that not enough information was available. The third alternative will have to be addressed. It is reasonable and could mitigate any environmental impact caused by the footbridge. It is probably also cheaper and would be available sooner.

14b. **Probably not.** If the agency did not consider the third alternative in its final EIS draft, the court will likely find that the agency did not consider all the relevant factors or all the reasonable alternatives. Rather than losing the proposal altogether though, the court could just require the agency to file a supplemental EIS which addressed the third alternative.

# Exam Tips on
# NATIONAL ENVIRONMENTAL POLICY ACT (NEPA)

☛ The history and purpose of NEPA probably will not be tested, but you need to know that information just for general background purposes. You will likely see a fact pattern or question involving an EIS.

☛ Remember that you must answer the *threshold question*: Does an EIS need to be prepared for this federal governmental proposal? Answer this question in a step-by-step manner:

☞ Is this a federal action or state/local? Remember that NEPA only governs *federal* action, while SEPAs may address state actions.

☞ Did an agency actually *make a proposal* or is it still contemplating action?

☞ Was there agency *inaction* when action was required?

☞ Is the agency *exempted* from the EIS obligation? An agency is exempted under three circumstances: *conflict* with statutory obligations, *express* exemption, and when duties are the *functional equivalent* of NEPA duties.

☞ Does the *EA* propose a full EIS? If not, was a *FONSI* issued? Remember that a FONSI may not be issued if there might be environmental disturbance.

☛ Once you have determined that an EIS is necessary, address the *scope and adequacy* of the EIS.

☞ Is this for a *single project* or *broader* context? This will determine the *comprehensiveness* of the EIS.

*Example*: If a small piece of larger legislation potentially will have environmental impact, then the EIS may be done for that small piece. If a series of actions will have a series of effects on the environment, then a broader EIS must be done to address the whole series.

☞ Remember that the EIS must include *environmental effects, alternatives, and the alternatives' effects.*

☞ You may spot an issue involving the *reasonableness* of the proposed alternatives. An agency does not have to consider every alternative under the sun, but the *rule of reason* applies when determining whether an alternative is reasonable or not. Alternatives include: *no action* alternatives, *reasonable alternatives*, and *mitigation measures*.

☞ Was there *sufficient information*? If no, the agency must *disclose* that fact.

☞ Is there a *summary of existing credible scientific evidence*?

☛ Remember that a court will not substitute its own judgment for that of the agency, so ensure that any potential court holding involves only an evaluation of whether or not the agency considered all the *relevant factors* and all the *reasonable alternatives*.

## CHAPTER 6

# THE CLEAN AIR ACT (CAA)

## *ChapterScope* ───────────────────────────────

Congress enacted the Air Pollution Control Act in 1955. This Act provided some assistance to the states, which historically had control over air pollution regulation. The federal role continued to expand through the late 1960s. In 1970, Congress enacted the Clean Air Act (CAA). This chapter examines the federal role in the regulation of air pollution.

■ **Air quality standards:** National Ambient Air Quality Standards (*NAAQSs*) must be attained and maintained nationwide to fulfill the main goal of the CAA. There are certain procedures and requirements for the promulgation of these standards for *criteria pollutants*.

- ■ The EPA determines a criteria pollutant as one which *endangers the public health or welfare* and is produced by numerous and diverse sources.

■ **Air quality control regions and State Implementation Plans:** States designate air quality control *regions* and are responsible for developing State Implementation Plans (*SIPs*) to attain or maintain air quality requirements. States must designate *every area* as *attainment*, *nonattainment*, or *unclassifiable* as to each criteria pollutant.

- ■ **Nonattainment:** There are special requirements for addressing nonattainment areas, including *preconstruction permits* for major stationary sources and *lowest achievable emission rate (LAER)* for new or modified sources.

■ **Prevention of Significant Deterioration (PSD) areas:** There are special requirements, including *preconstruction permits*, for protecting areas with *better air quality* than required. This prevents states from allowing areas to deteriorate to NAAQSs.

■ **Visibility protection:** There are provisions of the CAA which are specifically designed to protect visibility in certain areas, and states must *incorporate* special provisions into their SIPs.

■ **Interstate and international air pollution:** Congress *expanded the EPA's obligations* in this area with the 1990 amendments. The obligations include *controls* over transboundary pollution, *acid rain*, *sulfur allowances*, and *international air pollution*.

■ **Nationwide emission limitations:** The EPA must promulgate three types of uniform, nationwide emission limitations:

- ■ **New Source Performance Standards (NSPSs):** These limitations cover pollutants that do not meet the *size thresholds of PSDs* and nonattainment areas and cover pollutants *other than criteria pollutants*.

- ■ **Hazardous air pollutants (HAPs) limitations:** These limitations are to provide a *safety margin* for the public health and may be read to *disregard cost* considerations or *technological feasibility*.

- ■ **Motor vehicle emission standards:** Limitations cover various classes of *mobile sources*, the composition of *fuels*, and encouragement of *alternative fuels*.

- ■ **Permit program:** All *major sources*, defined in a variety of ways in Title V of the 1990 Amendments, and other sources regulated under the CAA must have a *permit*.

  - ■ States must submit their permit programs to the EPA for *approval*.

- ■ **Enforcement:** There are various *enforcement mechanisms* available to the EPA, including civil and criminal sanctions, and there are *citizen suit provisions* enabling private enforcement of the CAA.

# I. AIR POLLUTION REGULATION PRIOR TO 1970

Before 1955, air pollution regulation was completely in the control of state and local governments, and private parties were confined to remedies under common law causes of action. In 1955, Congress enacted the Air Pollution Control Act, which gave research and technical assistance to the states, with the states maintaining control over regulation. The Air Quality Act of 1967 created a federal regulatory program based on ambient air quality standards, but the states still retained the responsibility for promulgating such standards. In 1970, Congress enacted the Clean Air Act (CAA), 42 U.S.C. §§7401-7671, which expanded the federal role in the regulation of air pollution.

# II. KEY STATUTORY PROVISIONS OF THE CAA

Understanding the scope and structure of the CAA requires a careful reading of the underlying statutes. This section provides an overview of the most significant provisions of the CAA.

- ■ **Section 101, 42 U.S.C. §7401:** Congressional findings and goals of the CAA.

- ■ **Section 107, 42 U.S.C. §7407:** Sets forth procedures and requirements for designation of Air Quality Control Regions.

- ■ **Section 108, 42 U.S.C. §7408:** Requires the Administrator to publish and occasionally revise an air pollutant list; to issue air quality criteria for listed pollutants; and to issue information on air pollution control technologies.

- ■ **Section 109, 42 U.S.C. §7409:** Sets forth procedures and requirements for promulgation of primary and secondary National Ambient Air Quality Standards (NAAQSs).

- ■ **Section 110, 42 U.S.C. §7410:** Sets forth procedures and requirements for state development of State Implementation Plans (SIPs); sets forth procedures and requirements for EPA approval of proposed SIPs.

- ■ **Section 111, 42 U.S.C. §7411:** Sets forth procedures and requirements for promulgation of nationwide New Source Performance Standards (NSPSs).

- ■ **Section 112, 42 U.S.C. §7412:** Sets forth procedures and requirements for promulgation of emission standards for hazardous air pollutants (HAPs); establishes an initial list of HAPs and sets forth procedures and requirements for revision of the list.

- ■ **Section 113, 42 U.S.C. §7413:** Establishes the range and scope of federal enforcement of the CAA.

- **Section 116, 42 U.S.C. §7416:** Permits states to adopt emissions and control standards that are more stringent than federal standards.

- **Sections 160-169B, 42 U.S.C. §§7470-7492:** Set forth requirements and procedures regarding Prevention of Significant Deterioration (PSD) and protection of visibility; PSD classifications (§162); preconstruction requirements and permits (§165); PSD enforcement (§167).

- **Sections 171-179B, 42 U.S.C. §§7501-7509:** Set forth general procedures and requirements for nonattainment areas.

- **Sections 181-185B, 42 U.S.C. §§7511-7511f:** Set forth procedures and requirements for the classification and enforcement of ozone nonattainment areas.

- **Sections 202-250, 42 U.S.C. §§7521-7590:** Set forth procedures and requirements regarding mobile sources; cover emission standards and enforcement, regulation of fuels.

- **Section 302, 42 U.S.C. §7602:** Definitions of terms used in the CAA.

- **Section 304, 42 U.S.C. §7604:** Sets forth procedures, requirements, and jurisdiction for citizen suits under the CAA.

- **Section 307, 42 U.S.C. §7607:** Sets forth standards of judicial review.

- **Sections 401-416, 42 U.S.C. §§7651-7651(o):** Set forth procedures and requirements regarding acid rain; establish the sulfur dioxide allowance program and requirements for transfer of allowances.

- **Sections 501-507, 42 U.S.C. §§7661-7661(f):** Set forth procedures and requirements for permit programs under the CAA.

- **Sections 601-618, 42 U.S.C. §§7671-7671(q):** Set forth procedures and requirements regarding stratospheric ozone depletion, including classification of substances with ozone depletion potential, controls on production and consumption of such substances.

## III.  AIR QUALITY STANDARDS

The fundamental goal of the CAA is the *nationwide* attainment and maintenance of National Ambient Air Quality Standards (NAAQSs).

A. **Regulatory controls and pollutant sources:** The CAA utilizes two types of regulatory controls and regulates two types of pollutant sources.

1. **Regulatory controls:** The regulatory controls comprise both *health-based* and *technology-based standards.*

   a. **Health-based standards:** Health-based standards represent the *"safe" level of a pollutant* in the ambient air.

   b. **Technology-based standards:** Technology-based standards represent the *amount of pollutant reduction* within an industry's economic and technological capabilities.

2. **Pollutant sources:** The CAA regulates both *stationary and mobile sources* of pollution. Permits are required only for stationary sources, and vehicle emissions are not attributed to the buildings that they serve. *Village of Oconomowoc Lake v. Dayton Hudson Corp.,* 24 F.3d 962, 963, *cert. denied,* 115 S. Ct. 322 (1994).

**B. Types of NAAQSs:** EPA is *required to establish* "primary" and "secondary" NAAQSs for "criteria" pollutants. CAA §109, 42 U.S.C. §7409.

1. **Primary NAAQSs:** The primary NAAQS is the *acceptable concentration* of a pollutant in the ambient air, measured over a designated averaging time, that will protect the public health with an "adequate margin of safety." CAA §109(b)(1), 42 U.S.C. §7409(b)(1).

2. **Secondary NAAQSs:** The secondary NAAQS is set at a level to protect the public welfare encompassing environmental and economic interests. CAA §109(b)(2), 42 U.S.C. §7409(b)(2).

3. **Criteria pollutants:** A criteria pollutant is one which the EPA has determined endangers the *public health or welfare* and which is produced by numerous and diverse sources. CAA §108(a)(1), 42 U.S.C. §7408(a)(1). The current criteria pollutants are sulfur dioxide, carbon monoxide, nitrogen dioxide, ozone, particulates, and lead. 40 C.F.R. pt. 50.

**C. Promulgation of NAAQSs:** In certain instances, EPA may be *compelled* to list a pollutant as a criteria pollutant and promulgate NAAQSs for that pollutant.

1. **Factors that make EPA's duty non-discretionary:** EPA's duty to list a pollutant as a criteria pollutant becomes *non-discretionary* if EPA makes a determination that

   a. the pollutant *endangers the public health or welfare*; and

   b. the pollutant results from *numerous or diverse mobile or stationary sources.* CAA §108(a)-(b), 42 U.S.C. §7408(a-b); *Natural Resources Defense Council, Inc. v. Train,* 411 F. Supp. 864 (S.D.N.Y.), *aff'd,* 545 F.2d 320 (2d Cir. 1976) (requiring EPA to place lead on the criteria list).

2. **Promulgation requirements:** EPA must issue and *submit for public comment* air quality criteria and proposed primary and secondary NAAQSs within twelve months of including a pollutant on a criteria pollutant list. CAA §§108(a)(2), 109(a)(2), 42 U.S.C. §§7408(a)(2), 7409(a)(2). The CAA's rulemaking provisions govern the promulgation of NAAQSs. See CAA §307(d), 42 U.S.C. §7607(d).

3. **Role of economic and technological feasibility:** EPA *may not* consider economic and technological feasibility in setting air quality standards because the Act is technology-forcing. *Lead Indus. Ass'n, Inc. v. EPA,* 647 F.2d 1130 (D.C. Cir.), *cert. denied,* 449 U.S. 1042 (1980). The Supreme Court confirmed this position in *Whitman v. American Trucking Association,* 531 U.S. 457, 121 S. Ct. 903, 149 L. Ed. 2d 1 (2001). The Court held that §109(b) unequivocally barred cost considerations in the setting of either primary or secondary NAAQSs.

**D. Review of NAAQSs:** EPA's duty to review NAAQSs every five years is *non-discretionary.* CAA §109(d)(1), 42 U.S.C. §7409(d)(1); *Environmental Defense Fund v. Thomas,* 870 F.2d 892 (2d Cir.), *cert. denied, Alabama Power Co. v. Environmental Defense Fund,* 493 U.S. 991 (1989).

# IV. AIR QUALITY CONTROL REGIONS AND STATE IMPLEMENTATION PLANS

Each state must devise a state implementation plan (SIP) to achieve the NAAQSs by the statutory deadlines and maintain them thereafter. The state accomplishes these goals by translating the NAAQSs into *specific emission limitations on individual sources*. The entire nation is divided into air quality control regions, and many SIP requirements depend on the air quality control classification.

**A. Air quality control regions:** Each state is required to designate *every area* in the state as *attainment, nonattainment, or unclassifiable* as to each criteria pollutant within one year of EPA's promulgation or revision of an NAAQS. CAA §107(d)(1)(A), 42 U.S.C. §7407(d)(1)(A). EPA must promulgate each state's designations within one year, and may have a one-year extension if insufficient information exists. CAA §107(d)(1)(B), 42 U.S.C. §7407(d)(1)(B).

   **1. Attainment areas:** An attainment area meets *the primary or secondary NAAQS* for a criteria pollutant. CAA §107(d)(1)(A)(ii), 42 U.S.C. §7407(d)(1)(A)(ii).

   **2. Nonattainment areas:** A nonattainment area *does not meet the primary or secondary NAAQS* for a criteria pollutant. CAA §107(d)(1)(A)(i), 42 U.S.C. §7407(d)(1)(A)(i).

   **3. Unclassifiable areas:** An unclassifiable area's *compliance* with the primary or secondary NAAQS for a criteria pollutant *cannot be determined* with current information. CAA §107(d)(1)(A)(iii), 42 U.S.C. §7407(d)(1)(A)(iii).

**B. General SIP requirements:** Every SIP must contain certain provisions. States must promulgate their SIPs ''after reasonable notice and public hearings'' and in accordance with state administrative procedures. CAA §110(a)(1), 42 U.S.C. §7410(a)(1). Examples of SIP requirements include

   **1.** enforceable emissions limitations and other measures necessary to attain and maintain the NAAQSs;

   **2.** methods for compiling air quality data for the state;

   **3.** boundaries of the SIP;

   **4.** an enforcement program;

   **5.** provisions to control interstate and international pollution;

   **6.** measures to ensure adequate personnel, funding, and authority; and

   **7.** requirements for sources in the state to monitor and report their emissions. CAA §110(a)(2)(A)-(F), 42 U.S.C. §7410(a)(2)(A)-(F).

**C. SIP evaluation procedures:** Once EPA has promulgated or revised an NAAQS, the states and EPA begin the SIP process.

   **1. State preparation of SIP:** After a NAAQS is promulgated or revised, a state has *three years to prepare or revise* its SIP. In an attainment area, the three-year period starts with the promulgation or revision of the NAAQS. CAA §110(a), 42 U.S.C. §7410(a). In a nonattainment area, the three-period begins on the date of the designation of an area as nonattainment. CAA §172(b), 42 U.S.C. §7502(b).

2. **EPA determination of completeness:** After a state submits its SIP, EPA has six months to determine whether the SIP is *complete*. CAA §110(k)(1), 42 U.S.C. §7410(k)(1).

3. **EPA consideration of cost and feasibility in review of SIP:** EPA has twelve months from its completeness determination to decide if the SIP *meets the requirements* of the CAA. EPA may approve, disapprove, partially approve, or conditionally approve an SIP. CAA §110(k)(2)-(4), 42 U.S.C. §7410(k)(2)-(4). In reviewing an SIP, EPA may only *consider the factors listed in §110(a)(2)*, an exclusive list which does not include economic and technological feasibility. 42 U.S.C. §7410(a)(2). A state also may set standards in the SIP which are more stringent than necessary to meet the NAAQS 42 U.S.C. §7416.

   **Example:** In reviewing a challenge to EPA approval of an SIP by an electric utility company, the Court held that the EPA could not consider technological or economic infeasibility when reviewing an SIP, and a state may create an SIP which is more stringent than necessary to meet the NAAQS. *Union Elec. Co. v. EPA*, 427 U.S. 246, *reh'g denied*, 429 U.S. 873 (1976). But if a state attempts to achieve their deadline at the end of three years, the EPA may consider technological and economic feasibility in disapproving the plan as insufficiently stringent. *Id.*

4. **State's obligations on conditional approval:** A state has one year to meet EPA's conditions or the SIP is deemed disapproved. CAA §110(k)(4), 42 U.S.C. §7410(k)(4).

5. **Variances:** States may *adopt variance* provisions which allow individual sources to seek relief from stringent SIP provisions if they feel the SIP requirements are *economically or technologically infeasible.* A grant of a variance is usually treated as a revision of the SIP, and may therefore require EPA approval for the source to avoid sanctions for violations of the CAA.

6. **Delayed compliance orders:** Under §113(a) of the CAA, the EPA may issue a "delayed compliance order" to sources who *fail to meet SIP requirements*. These orders may specify a later date than established in the SIP for a source to come into compliance with the relevant SIP requirements, considering factors such as cost and feasibility. Prior to 1990, the Administrator need only require that the source come into compliance in a "reasonable" time. However, Congress amended the CAA in 1990 and required that compliance orders grant *extensions of less than one year* from the date the order was issued. §113(a)(4), 42 U.S.C. §7413(a)(4).

7. **Court ordered compliance dates:** Under the government enforcement provisions of §113(b), 42 U.S.C. §7413(b), and the citizen suit provisions of §304(a), courts have the authority to issue injunctions requiring *sources to comply with the SIP*. This power is broader than EPA's, in that courts have *discretion to grant* sources *extensions of more than one year* to come into compliance. These extensions may be based on cost and feasibility factors. While cost and feasibility may be raised by sources as a defense in civil enforcement proceedings, most courts have held that these factors may only be considered in fashioning injunctive relief.

8. **Conformity criteria:** In *EDF v. Browner*, 40 Env't Rep. Cas. (BNA) 1730 (N.D. Cal. 1995), EDF sought to force EPA to prepare and issue "conformity criteria" (criteria that indicate a plan or project conforms to an SIP's purpose of achievement of NAAQSs and does not cause or contribute to a new violation) for attainment and unclassifiable areas after EPA had issued such criteria for nonattainment and maintenance areas. The court held that EPA had to *issue conformity criteria for all geographic areas covered by SIPs.*

D. **Sanctions:** Sanctions for a state's failure to comply with SIP requirements differ according to whether an area is an attainment or nonattainment area.

1. **Federal implementation plans (FIPs):** In both attainment and nonattainment areas, EPA has two years to promulgate an FIP for a state that *has failed to meet SIP requirements* unless the state corrects the deficiency and has its plan approved within that time period. CAA §110(c)(1), 42 U.S.C. §7410(c)(1). Deficiencies that trigger the FIP sanction include failure to submit or revise an SIP, failure to submit a complete SIP, partial approval or disapproval of an SIP, or disapproval after not meeting the conditions of a conditional approval.

2. **Other sanctions in attainment areas:** EPA may impose other *discretionary sanctions* for any deficiency or the failure to implement any SIP requirement. These sanctions include highway funding cutoffs. CAA §§110(m), 179(b), 42 U.S.C. §§7410(m), 7509(b).

3. **Other sanctions in nonattainment areas:** EPA must impose either the *highway funding cutoff* or the offset ratio as a sanction for any deficiency or the failure to implement any SIP requirement, unless the state *corrects the deficiency* within eighteen months. EPA *must impose both* sanctions if a state did not act in good faith. If the state does not correct the deficiency within six months after one sanction is imposed, EPA must impose the other sanction. CAA §179, 42 U.S.C. §7509. The offset ratio requires a new or modified source to reduce existing emissions by two pounds for every pound of new emissions it will contribute.

# V. NONATTAINMENT AREAS

Special SIP provisions are required for nonattainment areas. The most significant requirement is a *preconstruction review process* for new and modified sources in a nonattainment area. The CAA also designates attainment deadlines for nonattainment areas.

A. **SIP requirements:** Nonattainment area SIP requirements differ according to whether the area is nonattainment as to a primary NAAQS in effect in 1990 or as to a primary or secondary NAAQS promulgated or revised after 1990.

1. **Post-1990 NAAQSs:** States must include several special provisions, such as:

   ■ a requirement that sources in nonattainment areas use reasonably available control technology (RACT) "as expeditiously as practicable" and achieve "reasonable further progress toward compliance with annual incremental reductions," CAA §172(c)(1)-(2), 42 U.S.C. §7502(c)(1)-(2);

   ■ contingency measures that take effect automatically if any deadlines are missed, CAA §172(c)(9), 42 U.S.C. §172(c)(9); and

   ■ preconstruction review for new major and modified sources. CAA §172(c)(5), 42 U.S.C. §7502(c)(5).

2. **SIP provisions for pre-1990 NAAQSs:** In addition to the above requirements, *states must include* special graduated control programs for ozone, carbon monoxide, and particulates. See CAA §§181-192, 42 U.S.C. §§7511-7514a. States do not have to provide any special control measures for sulfur dioxide, nitrogen dioxide, or lead. The graduated control program classifies each nonattainment area for the *extent of noncompliance* (*e.g.*, from "marginal" to "extreme" for ozone). The more serious the noncompliance, the more stringent the control measures imposed, but the later the deadline for compliance with the NAAQS.

**B. Nonattainment preconstruction review:** Certain sources must have *permits to operate in nonattainment* areas. The most significant provisions in these permits are the lowest achievable emission rate (LAER) requirement and the offset requirement.

   **1. Threshold for nonattainment preconstruction review:** A major stationary source constructed or modified in a nonattainment area *must obtain* a preconstruction permit. CAA §172(c)(5), 42 U.S.C. §7502(c)(5).

   **a. Major stationary source:** A source is "major" *if it emits or may potentially emit 100 tons per year* of any pollutant. CAA §302(j), 42 U.S.C. §7602(j). The Supreme Court has upheld the use of the plant-wide bubble in determining whether a source is "major." *Chevron, U.S.A., Inc. v. Natural Resources Defense Council, Inc.*, 467 U.S. 837, *reh'g denied*, 468 U.S. 1227 (1984).

   Also, in *Chemical Manufacturers Assn. v. EPA*, 70 F.3d 637 (D.C. Cir. 1995), the Court of Appeals, relying on its decision in *National Mining*, see *infra*, p. 63, vacated and remanded EPA regulations that only took into account "federally enforceable" controls in limiting a source's potential to emit. This decision could impact both nonattainment new source review and PSD permit programs.

   Another court held that a landfill was not required to obtain a Clean Air Act permit because volatile organic compound emission from the facility were less than the 50 tons-per-year threshold applicable to the facility when the landfill's gas collection and flare system were taken into account. *Ogden Projects, Inc. v. New Morgan Landfill Co.*, 911 F. Supp. 863 (E.D. Pa. 1996). Relying on *Chemical Manufacturers Association*, the court decided the system, even though not federally enforceable, could be taken into account in reducing the source's "potential to emit."

   **b. Constructed or modified:** A modification results when an *increase in emissions* of a pollutant occurs, or a new pollutant is emitted. CAA §111(a)(4), 42 U.S.C. §7411(a)(4).

   **2. Substantive nonattainment review requirements:** New or modified sources must use the *lowest achievable emission rate* (LAER) and *meet the offset requirement* for nonattainment pollutants. A *de minimis* exemption exists for small increases in emissions. 45 Fed. Reg. 52,711 (1980).

   **a. LAER:** The lowest achievable emission rate is a *stringent standard*; it is the more stringent of

   ■ the most stringent emission limitation in a state's implementation plan for the class or category of source, or

   ■ the most stringent emission limitation achieved by the class or category of source. CAA §171(3), 42 U.S.C. §7501(3). LAER must be at least as stringent as the applicable new source performance standard. *Id.*

   **b. Offsets:** Generally, a major source can offset its emissions by *obtaining emissions reductions* from a source in the same nonattainment area. CAA §173(c)(1), 42 U.S.C. §7503(c)(1).

   **Example:** In *Citizens Against Refinery's Effects, Inc. v. EPA*, 643 F.2d 183 (4th Cir. 1981), the court upheld EPA's approval of a Virginia SIP provision. The provision allowed a new refinery to be built and its hydrocarbons pollution to be offset by the state reducing the asphalt used in road paving in three highway districts.

i.    **Offset ratio:** States have discretion in determining *how much* of an offset will achieve reasonable further progress, but they may not elect to simply maintain the status quo. Recall that one of the specific sanctions for failure to prepare an adequate SIP is a 2-to-1 offset ratio. The ozone graduated control program also imposes mandatory offset ratios in some of the worst nonattainment areas.

ii.   **Offsets in a different nonattainment area:** A source can offset its emissions with a source in another nonattainment area if:

■   the other area's nonattainment classification is equal or *higher*, and

■   the other area's emissions contribute *to the violation* of an NAAQS in the source's area. CAA §173(c)(1), 42 U.S.C. §7503(c)(1).

iii.  **Banking of offsets:** EPA allows states to *"bank" offsets* (unused emission reductions). 51 Fed. Reg. 43,814 (1986). If a source voluntarily reduces its emissions, the state may give it an *emission reduction credit* (ERC). *Id.*

iv.   **Problems in implementing offsets:** An offset program raises a variety of concerns:

■   *Need same pollutants:* For the offset to be effective, the reduction *must be in the same pollutant;*

■   *Paper reductions:* Some sources may already be operating with emissions below their legal limit. If these sources are allowed to offset the difference between their actual emissions and the legal limit, then this offset achieves *no real reduction* in emissions, but only a "paper reduction";

■   *Marketability:* For an offset system to work, a market must be developed to allow buyers and sellers to *interact efficiently.* One suggestion is for pollution banks, where offsets could be deposited for future use or purchase by other parties;

■   *Initial allocations:* Most systems allocate offset credits by *allowing sources to sell* their pre-existing legal authorized emission levels. This creates a valuable economic commodity with no cost to the polluters and no benefit for the government. Other schemes would allow for no initial allocation of emission rights, but would auction off these rights. This would also allow the government to control the total amount of pollution by controlling the total pollution rights auctioned off;

■   *Future concerns:* The fear of additional future governmental regulations may discourage polluters from freely selling their offsets, which would in turn hamper the market for credits;

■   *Ethical concerns:* For many, the idea of selling a "right to pollute," such as the offsets, raises significant ethical concerns.

C.  **Other requirements:** In addition to the above requirements, §173(a) also has the following requirements:

1.  **General compliance with CAA:** No nonattainment permit may be issued to a party who owns or operates another source in the state *which violates the CAA;*

2.  **SIP implementation:** No permit may be issued if the EPA determines that the state has not adequately *implemented its SIP* for nonattainment areas;

3. **Environmental cost-benefit analysis:** The permit writer is required to determine if the benefits from construction of the new or modified source *substantially outweigh* the social and environmental costs.

D. **Attainment deadlines:** In nonattainment areas, *different deadlines exist* for primary NAAQSs in effect before the 1990 Amendments and for NAAQSs promulgated or revised after the 1990 Amendments.

   1. **Deadlines for pre-1990 NAAQSs:** The time periods range from 5 to 20 years to achieve attainment. Under the graduated control program, the time allowed for attainment and the strength of control measures required *increases with the severity* of pollution in the area resulting from a particular pollutant. See CAA §§181-192, 42 U.S.C. §§7511-7514a.

   2. **Deadlines for post-1990 NAAQSs:** These deadlines differ as to primary and secondary NAAQSs.

      a. **Primary NAAQSs:** The deadline is as *expeditiously as practicable, but no later than five years* from the nonattainment designation, with a possible five-year extension. CAA §172(a)(2)(A), 42 U.S.C. §7502(a)(2)(A).

      b. **Secondary NAAQSs:** The deadline is as *expeditiously as practicable after* the nonattainment designation. CAA §172(a)(2)(B), 42 U.S.C. §7502(a)(2)(B).

      c. **Failure to meet §172 deadlines:** A state has *one year* to revise its SIP from the notice of nonattainment and has five to *ten years* to achieve attainment. CAA §179(d), 42 U.S.C. §7509(d).

E. ***Whitman v. American Trucking Assoc., Inc.,*** 531 U.S. 457 (2001): In this case, the Supreme Court held that EPA was not permitted to consider implementation costs in setting NAAQSs, as the cost factor was not relevant to providing an adequate margin to protect public health and had the potential for canceling conclusions drawn from direct health effects. The Court also found that the EPA's implementation approach for ozone standards was unlawful. Pointing out ambiguities regarding the interaction between the general requirements for nonattainment plans and the plan requirements for the pre-1997 ozone standard, the Court rejected EPA's interpretation of the statute and remanded to EPA to develop a reasonable interpretation of nonattainment implementation provisions applicable to the revised ozone NAAQSs. On remand, the D.C. Court of Appeals broadly rejected arguments that EPA had not provided adequate justification of the new standards. *American Trucking Assoc. Inc. v. EPA*, 54 ERC 1001 (Mar. 26, 2002).

# VI. PREVENTION OF SIGNIFICANT DETERIORATION (PSD) AREAS

Some areas have better air quality than that required by NAAQSs. These areas are known as *prevention of significant deterioration* (PSD) areas. All SIPs must contain measures *necessary to protect* these areas. CAA §§110(a)(2)(J), 161, 42 U.S.C. §§7410(a)(2)(J), 7471. The air quality in these areas is protected through a preconstruction review process. CAA §§160-169B, 42 U.S.C. §§7470-7492.

A. **History of PSDs:** In 1970, Congress did not address areas with air quality better than required by an NAAQS. Concerned that areas of superior air quality would be allowed to degrade to the NAAQS level, the Sierra Club brought suit in 1972 to compel the EPA to prevent serious deterioration in these areas. Sierra Club argued that the purpose the CAA as set out in §101(b), 42 U.S.C. §7401(b) was to protect and enhance the nation's air resources, and that the EPA was therefore required to create a program to protect these areas. The district court held that the EPA did have a ***non-discretionary duty to prevent significant deterioration of air*** quality in these areas. *Sierra Club v. Ruckelshaus*, 344 F. Supp. 253 (D.D.C. 1972), *aff'd, per curiam without opinion*, 2 Envtl. L. Rep. (Envtl. L. Inst.) 20656 (D.C. Cir. 1972), *aff'd*, 4 Env't Rep. Cas. (BNA) 1815 (D.C. Cir. 1972). However, before the EPA could implement such a program, Congress amended the CAA in 1977, adding a new part C which created PSD areas.

B.  **PSD area:** A PSD area is one classified as attainment or unclassifiable. CAA §161, 42 U.S.C. §7471.

C.  **Threshold for preconstruction review:** A "major emitting facility" ***must obtain a PSD preconstruction permit*** if constructed or modified in a PSD area. CAA §165(a), 42 U.S.C. §7475(a).

1.  **Major emitting facility:** A source is a "major emitting facility" if it emits or has the potential to emit (1) 100 tons per year of any pollutant and the source falls within one of the 26 listed categories or (2) 250 tons per year of any pollutant. Listed categories include fossil-fuel-fired steam electric plants, coal cleaning plants, and certain metal smelters. CAA §169(1), 42 U.S.C. §7479(1). A facility's potential is determined by the plant's ***full design capacity*** with federally enforceable pollution control equipment in operation. *Alabama Power Co. v. Costle,* 636 F.2d 323 (D.C. Cir. 1979); 40 C.F.R. §51.166(b)(4).

2.  **Construction and modifications:** Construction includes modifications. CAA §169(2)(C), 42 U.S.C. §7479(2)(C). A modification results when a ***significant increase*** in the emissions of any regulated pollutant occurs, or when ***new pollutants*** are emitted. CAA §111(a)(4), 42 U.S.C. §7411(a)(4). Some emission increases are ***exempt as de minimis.*** 40 C.F.R. §51.166(b)(23)(i). The use of the plant-wide bubble is authorized in determining whether a modification has occurred. *Alabama Power Co. v. Costle*, 636 F.2d 323 (D.C. Cir. 1979). Use of the bubble in the PSD preconstruction review context reduces the possibility that a source will have to undergo review, and often is viewed as necessary to ensuring that economic growth may continue. Source does not include small components such as "equipment" or "operation."

    **Example:** A plant in a PSD area has two smokestacks that each emit 80 tons per year of sulfur dioxide. With modification, stack A now emits 140 tons per year, and stack B emits 20 tons per year. Without the plant-wide bubble, the facility would be required to undergo preconstruction review for stack A (increase in amount of sulfur dioxide emitted from 80 tons to 140 tons). With the bubble, however, the source continues to emit a total of 160 tons per year, no increase in emissions occurs, and no preconstruction review is required. There is some disagreement within the circuit courts over whether "like-kind" replacement should trigger review. See *Puerto Rican Cement Co. v. EPA*, 889 F.2d 292 (1st Cir. 1989); *Wisconsin Elec. Power Co. (WEPCO) v. Reilly*, 893 F.2d 901 (7th Cir. 1990).

D.  **Substantive PSD review requirements:** PSD review includes control technology review and air quality impact review.

1.  **Control technology review for BACT:** The facility must utilize the ***"best available control technology"*** (BACT) for every regulated pollutant. CAA §165(a)(4), 42 U.S.C. §7475(a)(4).

BACT is a stringent standard which is determined on a case-by-case basis. CAA §169(3), 42 U.S.C. §7479(3). The source must use the most stringent technology available, unless significant, local factors make such technology too costly.

2. **Air quality impact review:** The facility must demonstrate that its emissions of sulfur dioxide, nitrogen dioxide, and particulates will not violate any NAAQS or any allowable increment. CAA §165(a)(3), 42 U.S.C. §7475(a)(3). Increments analysis involves determining the *"baseline concentration"* for an area, CAA §169(4), 42 U.S.C. §7479(4), and the *percentage of increases* in emissions *allowed* over the baseline. The baseline concentration is the existing ambient pollution level in a PSD area at the time of the first application for a PSD permit. *Alabama Power Co. v. Costle*, 636 F.2d 323 (D.C. Cir. 1979); CAA §169(4), 42 U.S.C. §7479(4). The percentage increase over the baseline ranges from quite low in Class I areas (such as national parks) to fairly substantial in Class III areas. For example, in a Class I area an annual increase of 2 micrograms of sulfur dioxide per cubic meter is permissible, while in a Class III area the permissible annual increase is 40 micrograms per cubic meter. PSD areas must never exceed the primary or secondary NAAQSs. §163(b)(4), §7473(b)(4).

E. **Exemptions from PSD review:** A facility is *not required* to engage in preconstruction review if (1) it emits pollutants in *de minimis* amounts, 40 C.F.R. §51.166(b)(23), 52.21(b)(23), or (2) it emits pollutants for which the area is designated nonattainment. 40 C.F.R. §51.166(i)(5); *Alabama Power Co. v. Costle*, 636 F.2d 323 (D.C. Cir. 1979). Sources which are located outside of a PSD's area are not required to submit to a preconstruction review, even if their emissions contribute to pollution in a PSD area. If a company believes they do not cross the threshold, they may request a nonapplicability determination (NAD).

# VII. VISIBILITY PROTECTION

Visibility is often impaired despite PSD review. The CAA contains provisions *specifically* aimed at protecting visibility in certain areas. CAA §§169A-169B, 42 U.S.C. §§7491-7492.

A. **Identification of areas:** The Secretary of the Interior is responsible for determining which mandatory Class I federal areas have visibility as an important value. CAA §169A(a)(2), 42 U.S.C. §7491(a)(2).

B. **SIP provisions:** After the determination of which areas need protection, a state in which an area is located or which may contribute to visibility impairment *must incorporate* special provisions into its SIP. CAA §169A(b)(2), 42 U.S.C. §7491(b)(2).

1. **BART:** The SIP must provide for the use of *best available retrofit technology* (BART) by major stationary sources which may impair visibility. CAA §169A(b)(2)(A), 42 U.S.C. §7491(b)(2)(A).

2. **Reasonable further progress:** The SIP must provide a long-term goal of achieving *"reasonable further progress"* toward alleviating visibility impairment. CAA §169A(b)(2)(B), 42 U.S.C. §7491(b)(2)(B).

# VIII.  INTERSTATE AND INTERNATIONAL AIR POLLUTION

Prior to 1990, petitions for relief under the CAA provisions focusing on transboundary air pollution generally were unsuccessful. In the 1990 Amendments, Congress *expanded EPA's obligations* in the area of transboundary air pollution.

A.  **Expansion of transboundary air pollution controls:** The 1990 Amendments amended §§110(a)(2) and 126 to provide stronger *controls* over transboundary pollution. CAA §§110(a)(2), 126, 42 U.S.C. §§7410(a)(2), 7426.

   1.  **Sulfur trading program:** A *sulfur trading program* was created to address the problem of *acid rain*. See *infra*.

   2.  **Interstate SIP requirements:** SIPs must now control sources which *"contribute significantly"* to nonattainment of an NAAQS or "interfere with maintenance" of NAAQS in another state. States may petition EPA to remedy an interstate pollution problem under §126(c), §7426(c).

   3.  **Interstate transport regions:** Special requirements were adopted for "interstate transport regions" where emissions from one or more states "significantly contribute" to violations of NAAQS. CAA §176A, 42 U.S.C. §7506A.

   4.  **Other changes:** The 1990 Amendments also provided for the designation of *ozone transport regions*, CAA §184, 42 U.S.C. §7511c, and Congress adopted special rules in *multistate ozone nonattainment areas*. CAA §182(j), 42 U.S.C. §7511a(j).

B.  **Acid rain title:** The 1990 Amendments created a program to address acid rain.

   1.  **The problem of acid rain:** Acid rain results when fossil-fuel burning plants emit sulfur dioxide and nitrogen dioxide. Air currents may carry these substances *hundreds of miles* before the substances return to earth as sulfuric or nitric acids in precipitation or dry deposition. Effects of acid rain may include acidification of lakes and other water sources, as well as damage to forests, man-made materials, and health. Traditional solutions to the acid rain problem, such as scrubbers and low sulfur coal, have not been entirely effective.

   2.  **The market-based allowance system:** The 1990 Amendments proposed to reduce acid rain with a market-based emission allowance system for sulfur. A limited number of "sulfur allowances" were issued, each allowing one ton of sulfur to be emitted per year by the holder. Facilities *must have an allowance for all sulfur emissions*. By the year 2000, this system will reduce sulfur dioxide emissions from utilities by 50 percent, with a nationwide cap of 8.9 million tons. CAA §403(a), 42 U.S.C. §7651b(a). This program is implemented in two phases:

      a.  **Phase I:** By 1995, the largest and dirtiest power plants must reduce sulfur dioxide emissions three to four million tons per year. CAA §404, 42 U.S.C. §7651c.

      b.  **Phase II:** By 2000, all utilities must have allowances to emit sulfur dioxide. CAA §411, 42 U.S.C. §7651j. Under Phase II, the large and dirty utilities must reduce their emissions even further, and other plants must reduce their emissions for the first time. If a utility is considered "clean," its emissions are subject to a nationwide cap with an allowance for a 20 percent growth margin. CAA §405, 42 U.S.C. §7651d.

   3.  **Sulfur allowances:** The Act also allows for sulfur allowances to be *freely bought and sold*.

a. **Free market mechanisms:** Any facility which can reduce its emissions below its allocation may sell its *excess* allowances to other facilities, who may find it more economical to purchase allowance than to reduce their emissions. These allowances may some day be traded on a stock exchange like other commodities.

b. **Sale by EPA:** The CAA also provides that 2.8 percent of the total sulfur allowances are to be withheld by EPA, which can later be *sold or auctioned* off to new or existing sources by EPA. Other parties can also submit allowances to EPA for sale. Proceeds from these sales may be returned to those facilities whose allowances were withheld on a pro rata basis.

4. **Nitrogen oxide:** Sources which are subject to the sulfur allowance program are also required to *reduce nitrogen oxide emissions*. CAA §407, 42 U.S.C. §7651(f). EPA is also required to issue ''annual allowable emission limitations'' for nitrogen oxide for some types of utility boilers, and revise NSPS for coal-fired power plants for improved means of controlling nitrogen oxides.

C. **International air pollution:** Just as air pollution does not respect state boundaries, it is equally disrespectful of national lines and may migrate from one country to another. This problem is addressed by the Clean Air Act and by international agreement.

1. **CAA §115:** If EPA determines, based on reports from a ''duly constituted international agency'' that emissions from U.S. sources are *causing or contributing to serious pollution problems* in another country, EPA may require the state where the source is located to modify its SIP to control this source, if the affected country has a reciprocal agreement with the U.S. CAA §115, 42 U.S.C. §7415. EPA must also take such action if requested by the Secretary of State.

2. **Montreal Protocols:** One of the major international air pollution problems is the deterioration of the global ozone layer in the upper atmosphere. This ozone layer protects the earth from high levels of ultraviolet radiation from the sun. It is believed that emissions of chlorofluorocarbons are a *primary cause of damage to the ozone layer*. The Montreal Protocols are an international agreement to limit the production and use of chemicals which harm the ozone layer, with provisions that several chlorofluorocarbons be phased out of use. The Montreal Protocols were specifically incorporated into the CAA by the 1990 Amendments by Title VI, which requires additional controls on chlorofluorocarbons. For a more complete discussion of the Montreal Protocol, see *infra*, p. 178.

## IX. NATIONWIDE EMISSION LIMITATIONS

The CAA charges EPA with promulgating three types of uniform, nationwide emission limitations:

- new source performance standards (NSPSs);
- hazardous air pollutants (HAPs) limitations;
- motor vehicle emission standards.

A. **New source performance standards (NSPSs):** NSPSs are necessary (1) to cover pollutants that do not meet the size *thresholds of PSD and nonattainment areas, and (2) to cover pollutants other than criteria pollutants*.

1. **Promulgation of category list and standards:** EPA must promulgate lists of categories of sources that cause or contribute greatly to air pollution ''*which may reasonably be* anticipated to endanger public health or welfare.'' CAA §111(b)(1)(A), 42 U.S.C. §7411(b)(1)(A). EPA

has one year from the inclusion of a category of sources on the list to propose a "standard of performance" for "new" sources within that category. CAA §111(b)(1)(B), 42 U.S.C. §7411(b)(1)(B).

a.  **Standards of performance:** The emission standards for new sources in listed categories are set at a level "which reflects the degree of emissions limitation achievable through the application of the best system of emission reduction which . . . has been adequately demonstrated." CAA §111(a)(1), 42 U.S.C. §7411(a)(1). This is referred to as a best available demonstrated technology (BADT).

b.  **"Adequately demonstrated":** Several courts have recognized and accepted the *technology-forcing character of NSPSs*. See *National Asphalt Pavement Ass'n v. Train*, 539 F.2d 775 (D.C. Cir. 1976); *Portland Cement Ass'n v. Ruckelshaus*, 486 F.2d 375 (D.C. Cir. 1973), *cert. denied*, 417 U.S. 921 (1974).

    **Example:** In *Portland Cement*, the court determined that the cost of a particular technology was only a factor in setting the standard, and held that a technology did not have to be routinely used to be adequately demonstrated.

    **Example:** In *National Asphalt*, the court followed the *Portland Cement* approach. The court held that "adequately demonstrated" looks to "what may fairly be projected for the . . . future," and accepted EPA's determination of a standard based on technology adopted in only four plants.

    **Example:** In *National Lime Ass'n v. EPA*, 627 F.2d 416 (D.C. Cir. 1980), however, the court was less deferential to EPA's determination and required that EPA show regularity of achievability if it relied on a few test plants.

2.  **"New" sources:** A "new" source is one that is constructed or modified *after the publication of the standard of performance*. CAA §111(a)(2), 42 U.S.C. §7411(a)(2). There is no review as such; companies simply apply for a permit.

    a.  **Definition of modification:** A "modification" is "any physical change in, or change in the method of operation of, a stationary source." A modification *must result in an increase in emissions* of a particular pollutant or in the emission of a *new pollutant*. CAA §111(a)(4), 42 U.S.C. §7411(a)(4).

    b.  **Interpretation of modification:** One court has held that a modification occurs if a source either *turns off or removes* outdated or ineffective pollution control equipment and the source's emissions substantially increase. *National-Southwire Aluminum Co. v. EPA*, 838 F.2d 835 (6th Cir.), *cert. denied*, 488 U.S. 955 (1988). Another court has upheld EPA's practice of comparing past actual emissions with *potential future emissions* (actual-to-potential method) for measuring increases in emissions. *Puerto Rican Cement Co., Inc. v. EPA*, 889 F.2d 292 (1st Cir. 1989).

    c.  **New source bubbles:** The definition of "stationary source" as any "building, structure, facility, or installation which emits or may emit any air pollution" raises a difficult question of how a group of related sources should be classified — *individually* or as a *"bubble,"* a cluster of related sources. EPA has applied a *dual definition* to its NSPS, which makes a facility subject to NSPS if either individual sources or the facility as a whole have an increase in emissions.

**d. Existing sources:** Although NSPSs apply only to "new sources," the states are also required to develop programs to apply NSPS to *existing sources*. CAA §111(d), 42 U.S.C. §7411(d). CAA §111(d) applies only to pollutants not covered under an NAAQS, which would be otherwise regulated by an SIP. Since there is a great deal of overlap between the NSPS and NAAQS pollutants, CAA §111(d) has not been widely applied by the EPA.

**B. Hazardous air pollutants (HAPs):** The 1970 CAA §122(e) authorized EPA to set *uniform emission limits* for HAPs which would provide an "ample margin of safety" to protect public health. This health-based standard could be read to *preclude considerations of cost* or technological feasibility, and possibly to require (in cases of scientific uncertainty about safety of exposure levels) the establishment of zero-risk level for emissions. This vagueness left EPA's regulations open for challenge by both industry as too harsh and environmentalists as too lax. See *NRDC v. EPA*, Control of Toxic Substances, I. Risk Assessment, *infra*, p. 103. In 1990, Congress abandoned this system and adopted a scheme of technology-based, nationwide standards.

**1. Listing of hazardous pollutants:** Congress listed 189 pollutants as HAPs in the 1990 Amendments. CAA §112(b)(1), 42 U.S.C. §7412(b)(1). EPA may add pollutants to the list, and individuals may petition EPA to modify the list by adding or deleting a substance. CAA §112(b)(2)-(3), 42 U.S.C. §7412(b)(2)-(3).

**2. Source categories:** EPA must publish a list of categories and subcategories of major and area sources and revise the list every eight years. CAA §112(c)(1), 42 U.S.C. §7412(c)(1).

**a. Major sources:** A "major" source is "any stationary source or group of stationary sources . . . that emits or has the potential to emit . . . 10 tons per year or more of any hazardous air pollutant or 25 tons per year or more of any combination of hazardous air pollutants." CAA §112(a)(1), 42 U.S.C. §7412(a)(1).

> In *National Mining Association v. EPA*, 59 F.3d 1351 (D.C. Cir. 1995), the petitioners challenged three elements of EPA's definition of "major source" for purposes of §112. The petitioners contended that: (1) EPA could only include emissions at a plant site in the same industrial source category or Standard Industrial Code classification; (2) EPA could not include fugitive emissions; and (3) EPA erred in considering only "federally enforceable" controls in assessing "potential to emit." The Court of Appeals upheld EPA's definition on the first two elements, but held that EPA had exceeded its statutory authority in refusing to consider "effective" state and local controls as well as federally enforceable controls in measuring "potential to emit."

**b. Area sources:** A source is an "area source" if stationary and not major, excluding cars. CAA §112(a)(2), 42 U.S.C. §7412(a)(2). This category was created to address small, diverse sources that substantially contribute to emission of hazardous pollution, such as dry cleaners, service stations, and wood stoves.

**3. Emission standards for major sources:** These standards include technology-based and health-based residual risk standards.

**a. Technology-based MACT standards:** These standards must *"require the maximum degree of reduction in emissions"* that EPA determines is achievable (the *MACT standard*). CAA §112(d)(2), 42 U.S.C. §7412(d)(2). In setting the standards, EPA *should consider* the costs of achieving the emission reduction and technological feasibility. *Id.* For new sources, emission standards must require controls at least as stringent as the emission control "achieved in practice by the best controlled similar source." Emission standards for existing sources may be less stringent, but this standard must require at least the ***average emission limitation*** achieved by the best 12 percent of existing sources in the same category, or if there are fewer than 30 sources, the level of best 5 sources. Area sources are required to meet the generally available control technology (GACT) standard.

If the EPA fails to promulgate MACT standards by the deadline, the CAA requires states to issue permits on a case-by-case basis, determining MACT standards for each facility. This is commonly referred to as the "MACT hammer clause." The EPA has recently taken steps to avoid the hammer clause, allowing industry and state permitting agencies more time to develop these emission standards.

**b. Residual risk standards:** After eight years, if EPA determines that the public health is still at risk, EPA must decide ***whether additional standards are necessary***. These additional standards are known as "residual risk" standards and must provide an ample margin of safety to protect public health. An even more stringent standard may be adopted if the EPA, considering factors such as cost, energy, and safety, deems it necessary to avoid adverse environmental effects. Except for carcinogens, EPA has discretion in its decision whether to promulgate residual risk standards. CAA §112(f)(2)(A), 42 U.S.C. §7412(f)(2)(A). For carcinogens, if the MACT standard still poses a lifetime excess cancer risk of one in one million or greater to the individual most exposed to the emission, the Administrator ***must*** promulgate a residual risk emission standard that will provide an ample margin of safety. CAA §112(d), 42 U.S.C. §7412(d).

**c. Compliance:** Compliance is determined by the source's classification as a ***new or existing source*** and whether the standard is a technologically-based MACT or a ***health-based residual risk*** standard. Under §112(e)(4), no judicial review is available for listing of pollutants under §112(b) or listing of sources under §112(c).

    **i. New sources:** After the effective date of the hazardous emission standard, regardless of its basis (MACT or residual risk), ***no major source may be*** constructed or reconstructed ***unless EPA or a state under a Title V program*** determines ***that it will*** be ***in compliance.*** CAA §112(i)(1), 42 U.S.C. §7412(i)(1). New sources which began construction after the proposal of the standard but prior to its promulgation may delay compliance for three years from the date of final promulgation. However, if the promulgated standard is more stringent than the proposed standard, the source must comply with the proposed standard for the three years. CAA §112(i)(2), 42 U.S.C. §7412(i)(2). If a source commences construction after a MACT standard has been promulgated, but prior to a residual risk standard is proposed, the source may delay compliance for ten years from commencing construction. CAA §112(i)(2), 42 U.S.C. §7412(i)(2).

    **ii. Existing sources:** Residual risk standards are effective from the date of promulgation, but an existing source has 90 days to come into compliance. A waiver of up to two years may be issued by EPA if it determines that extra time is necessary to install controls and that adequate measures will be taken to protect the health of all affected persons in the interim. CAA §112(f)(4), 42 U.S.C. §7412(f)(4). EPA has three years from promulgating a new MACT to bring existing sources into compliance. CAA §112(i)(3)(A), 42 U.S.C. §7412(i)(3)(A). A permit for an additional year may be granted if EPA or the state deems the extra time necessary to install controls. CAA §112(i)(3)(B), 42 U.S.C. §7412(i)(3)(B).

   **iii. Modification of existing sources:** The modification of an existing source accelerates the deadlines for compliance of an existing source with MACT standards. CAA §112(g)(2), 42 U.S.C. §7412(g)(2). Accelerated compliance may be offset if there is an *equal or greater decrease* in emissions of a more hazardous pollutant. CAA §112(g)(1)(A), 42 U.S.C. §7412(g)(1)(A).

**C. Motor vehicle emission standards:** The CAA extensively regulates motor vehicles as "mobile sources." These "mobile sources" of emissions are the *primary source of hydrocarbons, carbon monoxide, and nitrogen oxides*. Although the federal government had regulated vehicle emissions prior to 1970, the CAA set out the basic framework (which was expanded by the 1990 Amendments) which governs mobile sources. This framework consists of three elements:

  **1. Emission limits:** The CAA establishes federal limits for automobile emissions. CAA §202, 42 U.S.C. §7521. These standards are designed to have a *"technology forcing"* effect, as the standards were not achievable by the existing technology at the time they were imposed. To protect auto manufacturers from conflicting regulations from state to state, the CAA preempts any state from establishing a separate standard. CAA §209, 42 U.S.C. §7543. The exception to this is California, discussed below.

    **a. Federal standards:** CAA limits are imposed based on the class of the *mobile source* (*e.g.,* automobiles are generally considered "light duty vehicles"). The 1970 CAA required a 90 percent reduction in emissions of hydrocarbons ("HCs") and carbon monoxide ("CO") by 1975 and nitrogen oxide ("$NO_x$") by 1976. The standards were eventually met, but only after a series of extensions by Congressional Amendment and administrative waivers from the EPA. The standard for $NO_x$ was relaxed in 1977.

      The 1990 Amendments expanded the CAA to include emissions of non-methane hydrocarbons ("NMHC") and particulate matter ("PM"), while setting new standards for CO and $NO_x$. These limits were to be phased in from model years 1994 through 1996. CAA §202(g), 42 U.S.C. §7521(g). After these standards have been met, the EPA will once again review them to see if more stringent standards are still necessary. CAA §202(i), 42 U.S.C. §7521(1). The EPA is authorized to recall vehicles that fail to meet emission levels, and auto manufacturers must also provide warranties of the effectiveness of their control measures.

    **b. California:** Due to the severe problem of mobile source pollution in California, the CAA allows California to establish limits *more stringent* than the federal requirements. CAA §209(b), 42 U.S.C. §7543(b). Other states also may adopt the more stringent California standards. CAA §177, 42 U.S.C. §7507.

  **2. Automotive fuels:** The composition of fuels has a significant impact on automobile emissions. The CAA therefore allows the EPA to *regulate the composition of these fuels*. CAA §211, 42 U.S.C. §7545. These regulations cover:

    **a. Lead:** Lead was originally added to fuels to reduce engine knocks. However, it can decrease the effectiveness of catalytic converters (an emission control technology used on many automobiles) and poses a serious health threat. The 1970 CAA mandated the sale of lead free gasoline and the reduction of lead in all gasoline. Under the 1990 Amendments, *no gasoline* may contain lead or lead additives after 1995. CAA §211(n), 42 U.S.C. §7545(n).

    **b. Reformulated fuels:** For some areas which fail to meet NAAQS ozone limits, the 1990 Amendments require the use of *"reformulated fuels."* These reformulated fuels are designed to reduce the emission of organic volatiles which can form ozone and other toxic emissions. CAA §211(k), 42 U.S.C. §7545(k). Other areas may petition to "opt in" to this program.

    **c. Oxygenated fuels:** For some areas that fail to meet NAAQS limits for carbon monoxide (CO), the 1990 Amendments require the use of *"oxygenated fuels"* to decrease CO emissions. CAA §211(m), 42 U.S.C. §7545(m).

**3. Clean alternative fuels:** The 1990 Amendments created new programs to *encourage the use of "alternate fuels"* such as ethanol, natural gas, and electricity, which pollute less than gasoline.

    **a. Clean fleet program:** A fleet is any group of 10 or more vehicles used by a single operator and capable of being fueled at a central location. CAA §241(5), 42 U.S.C. §7581(5). If a fleet is operated in a nonattainment area for carbon monoxide or a nonattainment area designated extreme, severe, or serious for ozone, it may be required to meet more *stringent standards* for clean fuel vehicles. CAA §182(c)(4), 42 U.S.C. §7511a(c)(4). These standards will be phased in between 1998 and 2000.

    **Example:** If a cable company operates 50 repair vans which are stored and fueled at a central location, they may be required to convert some or all of these vans to an alternative fuel, such as natural gas.

    **b. California requirements:** The CAA requires a minimum of 150,000 clean fuel vehicles to be sold in California beginning in 1996. By 1999, at least 300,000 clean fuel vehicles must be sold. CAA §249, 42 U.S.C. §7589.

# X. PERMIT PROGRAM

The 1990 Amendments in Title V require all "major sources" and other sources regulated under the CAA to have a permit.

**A. History:** Unlike the Clean Water Act, which required all emission sources to obtain a federal NPDES permit, the CAA, when originally drafted, had no provisions for a permit program. While some programs (such as the PSD program) did require new and major sources to obtain permits, and some states did create their own permitting system, there *was no blanket requirement* that all sources receive some type of federally administered permit for their emissions. This created a variety of problems. Neither sources seeking to comply with requirements nor persons seeking to enforce requirements could clearly identify what standards by which a source was governed. Without a permit process it was also more difficult to monitor the activities of the various sources.

**B. State permit programs:** States *must submit permit programs to EPA for approval*, which the EPA may reject if they fail to meet the standards of the CAA. The public has opportunities to participate in the permitting process.

**1. Establishing a state permit program:** The 1990 Amendments to the CAA required each state to submit a permit program to EPA by November 15, 1993. CAA §502(d)(1), 42 U.S.C. §7661a(d)(1). EPA *must act on* a permit program *within one year* of submission. *Id.* A state permit program is effective upon approval by EPA. CAA §502(h), 42 U.S.C. §7661a(h). Once a permit program is in effect, permits must be issued within three years. CAA §503(c), 42 U.S.C. §7661b(c). A state may be subject to sanctions for any failure in the permit program process. CAA §502(d)(2), 42 U.S.C. §7661a(d)(2).

2. **Elements of a state permit program:** All state permit programs must contain several basic elements, listed in CAA §502(b), 42 U.S.C. §7661a(b).

   a. **Public access:** The permit program must allow public access to permits, permit applications, and monitoring and compliance reports.

   b. **Public participation:** All permit programs must allow the public to *participate* in the permit process and in any judicial review of final permit actions in State court.

   c. **Minimal conditions:** All permits must contain minimal *provisions*, including a maximum duration of five years.

   d. **Modification provisions:** All permits must *allow for changes at a source* without revision of an existing permit if the source provides advanced written notice to the EPA and the state issuing the permit.

   e. **Standardized permit application:** The application form for permits must be *standardized*.

   f. **Fees:** All permit programs must provide for a *permit fee* for *implementation and enforcement costs* of the permit program. Unless varied by the EPA, this fee must be at least $25 per ton of regulated pollution.

3. **EPA review of state permit issuance:** If a permit does not comply with the CAA, *EPA may object*. CAA §505(b)(1), 42 U.S.C. §7661d(b)(1). If the state ignores EPA's objection, EPA *may assume control* over permit issuance, and can then issue permits for sources in that state. *Id.* This is in contrast to the Clean Water Act, in which all permits are issued by EPA unless EPA grants a state permission to administer the permit program. For more discussion of the Clean Water Act permit programs, see *infra*, p. 85.

4. **Public participation:** Under state permit programs, any person has the opportunity to comment on permits, to seek review of permits in state courts, and to compel the state to take final action on a permit application. CAA §502(b)(6) and (7), 42 U.S.C. §7661a(b)(6) and (7). Any person also may petition EPA regarding state permits and seek judicial review of EPA's action. CAA §505(b)(2), 42 U.S.C. §7661d(b)(2).

C. **Sources:** ''Major source'' is defined in a variety of ways by Title V.

1. **Major source for HAP:** Any stationary source which *does or might emit* 10 tons per year of any HAP or 25 tons of any combination of HAPs is a ''major source'' under NESHAP and covered under Title V.

2. **Major stationary source:** Any stationary source which *might emit* 100 tons of any pollutant per year is a ''major source'' under CAA §302(j) and covered by Title V.

3. **Nonattainment major source:** Any stationary source in a nonattainment which *might emit* between 10 and 100 tons of any air pollutant (depending on the nonattainment classification) is considered a ''major'' source.

4. **Affected source:** Title V governs any source subject to the *sulfur trading* program.

5. **EPA designated sources:** Title V may be applied to any other source in a category designated by EPA.

6. **Other sources:** Title V also applies to any other source which is *subject to have a permit* under nonattainment programs, the PSD program, or subject to regulation under CAA §111 or §112 (new sources subject to NSPS).

D. **Permit conditions:** As discussed above, a permit *must have specific conditions*, such as enforceable emission limits, provisions for monitoring, a five year maximum length for permits, and allowances for modification with permit revision. CAA §504, 42 U.S.C. §7661c.

E. **Benefits of permits:** Permits help in enforcing the provisions of the CAA in several ways. Generally, both environmental groups and sources approve of the use of permits for different reasons.

1. **Enforcement benefits:** Permits simplify *monitoring and review* because all requirements that a source must meet are in one document. Permits also allow for increased monitoring by state agencies and reporting by sources.

2. **Environmental group benefits:** Environmental organizations like the permit system because the *public may participate* in the permitting process at several levels.

3. **Source benefits:** Sources like the permit system because compliance with a permit is generally deemed *to be compliance with the CAA*. This is known as a "permit shield" under CAA §504(f), 42 U.S.C. §7661c(f).

   a. A source operating in compliance with its permit is *automatically shielded* from prosecution for operating without a permit or failure to comply with permit requirements.

   b. A source also enjoys protection from other types of prosecution under the other sections of the CAA, but *only if the applicable standard is contained* in the permit or the issuer of the permit has determined that the standard is not applicable to that source. The failure of the state or EPA to include an applicable standard in a source's permit does not operate as a shield for enforcement of that standard, even if all other permit requirements are satisfied.

# XI.  ENFORCEMENT

The CAA is enforced by the EPA, through citizen suits and through petitions for judicial review of EPA's actions. See also Judicial Review of Agency Actions, *supra*, p. 20.

A. **EPA enforcement:** EPA's primary method of enforcement under the CAA is to bring a civil suit for injunctive relief or penalties. EPA also can elect other options, such as administrative penalties or criminal sanctions.

1. **Preliminary steps:** EPA must complete several *preliminary steps* before bringing a civil enforcement action or utilizing another enforcement mechanism.

   a. **Notice of noncompliance:** EPA must issue a notice of noncompliance to the violator. CAA §113(a)(1), 42 U.S.C. §7413(a)(1).

   b. **Order requirements:** EPA cannot act on certain violations until 30 days *after the notice* of noncompliance. CAA §113(a)(1), 42 U.S.C. §7413(a)(1). Any orders under §113 will not take effect until the violator and EPA have a conference regarding the violation. CAA §113(a)(4), 42 U.S.C. §7413(a)(4).

2. **Civil judicial enforcement:** EPA *must seek enforcement* against violators who are owners or operators of an "affected source, a major emitting facility, or a major stationary source," *but*

*has discretion* with respect to enforcement against other parties. CAA §113(b), 42 U.S.C. §7413(b). EPA may seek injunctive relief or civil penalties not exceeding more than $25,000 per day per violation. *Id.* EPA must comply with the 30-day notice requirement in actions involving the violation of an SIP or permit. CAA §113(b)(1), 42 U.S.C. §7413(b)(1).

3. **Criminal sanctions:** The Clean Air Act's criminal sanctions provision is §113(c), 42 U.S.C. §7413(c), which was substantially changed by the 1990 Amendments and now *contains five separate criminal offenses under* the Act. Each offense is a felony carrying penalties of fines and imprisonment.

   a. **Negligent release of hazardous air pollutants:** Section 113(c)(4) criminalizes the negligent release into the ambient air of hazardous pollutants if the release places another person in *imminent danger of death or serious bodily injury.*

   b. **Knowing release of hazardous air pollutants:** Section 113(c)(5) prescribes the *most severe CAA punishment* for any person who knowingly releases such hazardous materials into the ambient air and who knows at the time that he thereby places another person in imminent danger of death or serious bodily injury. The defendant is responsible only for actual awareness or actual belief possessed, though circumstantial evidence may be used.

4. **Other options:** EPA's other options include:

   ▪ *administrative compliance orders,* CAA §113(a), 42 U.S.C. §7413(a);

   ▪ administrative penalties of $25,000 per day per violation with a cap of $200,000, CAA §113(d), 42 U.S.C. §7413(d);

   ▪ noncompliance penalties, which are measured by the economic benefit a source derives from its violation of the CAA. CAA §120, 42 U.S.C. §7420.

5. **Enforcement issues:** In enforcement proceedings, a source may *only raise* certain defenses. Any issues that could be raised in a judicial review action under §307 cannot be addressed in a civil or criminal enforcement proceeding. CAA §307(b)(2), 42 U.S.C. §7607(b)(2). Courts have also focused on the role of economic and technological feasibility in enforcement proceedings.

   a. **Typical enforcement issues:** Appropriate issues in an enforcement proceeding include:

   ▪ whether the source was in *compliance*;

   ▪ whether the *requirement applies* to the particular source; and

   ▪ limited procedural issues.

   b. **Economic and technological feasibility:** A source may raise the *infeasibility of a requirement* in conferences about compliance orders and in enforcement proceedings. *Union Elec. Co. v. EPA (Union Elec. II)*, 593 F.2d 299 (8th Cir.), *cert. denied*, 444 U.S. 839 (1979). Infeasibility *is not a substantive defense* to noncompliance, but may be raised during the penalty stage to aid in fashioning a remedy. *Navistar Int'l Transp. Corp. v. EPA*, 858 F.2d 282 (6th Cir. 1988), *cert. denied*, 490 U.S. 1039 (1989).

B. **Citizen suits:** Any person may bring a citizen suit against a source to *enforce any emission standard or permit limitation*, or may sue EPA if the Administrator fails to perform a non-discretionary duty. CAA §304(a), 42 U.S.C. §7604(a). To bring a citizen suit, a person or group must satisfy the constitutional requirements for standing.

1. **Citizen suit procedures:** The federal district courts have jurisdiction over citizen suits, and an action against a source must be in the ***district in which the plant is located***. CAA §304(a)(3), 42 U.S.C. §7604(a)(3). A citizen must give 60 days notice to EPA, the state, and the violator before bringing suit. If EPA or the state is pursuing an action against the violator, a ***citizen may intervene*** but his own action will be precluded. CAA §304(b)(1), 42 U.S.C. §7604(b)(1).

   a. **Jurisdiction:** The CAA, following the 1990 Amendments, now allows citizen suits not only for continuing violations, but for ***wholly past*** violations as long as the past violation occurred more than once. *Fried v. Sungard Recovery Services, Inc.,* 916 F. Supp. 465 (E.D. Pa. 1996). Compare with *Gwaltney of Smithfield, Ltd. v. Chesapeake Bay Foundation,* 484 U.S. 49 (1987) (holding that the CWA did not allow citizen suits for wholly past violations), *infra,* p. 87.

2. **Citizen suit remedies:** Costs and civil penalties are available in addition to injunctive relief. CAA §304(d) and (g), 42 U.S.C. §7604(d) and (g). Money collected as civil penalties goes into a federal air compliance and enforcement fund, or may be applied toward beneficial mitigation projects that enhance public health or the environment. §304(g), 42 U.S.C. §17604(g).

3. **Non-discretionary duty cases:** Citizen suits are allowed to ***compel*** EPA to perform a non-discretionary duty. CAA §304(a)(2), 42 U.S.C. §7604(a)(2).

   a. **Jurisdiction:** These suits must be brought in the federal district court for the District of Columbia. §304(a)(3), 42 U.S.C. §7604(a)(3).

   b. **Example of non-discretionary duty:** EPA's duty to list a pollutant as a criteria pollutant is non-discretionary if (1) the pollutant endangers the public health or welfare, and (2) numerous and diverse sources emit the pollutant. See CAA §108(a)-(b), 42 U.S.C. §7408(a)-(b); *Natural Resources Defense Council v. Train,* 411 F. Supp. 864 (S.D.N.Y.), *aff'd,* 545 F.2d 320 (2d Cir. 1976).

4. **Unreasonably delayed action:** A person may bring a citizen suit against EPA to "compel . . . agency action ***unreasonably*** delayed." §304(a)(3), 42 U.S.C. §7604(a)(3). Jurisdiction is in the federal district court for the District of Columbia. *Id.*

C. **Petitions for review:** Certain actions by EPA are subject to judicial review under CAA §307, 42 U.S.C. §7607. Claims of economic and technological infeasibility ***cannot*** be raised during a §307(b) action. See *Union Elec. Co. v. EPA,* 427 U.S. 246, *reh'g denied,* 429 U.S. 873 (1976).

1. **Actions subject to review:** A person or group may petition for review of the actions of EPA in promulgating or acting upon any national, local, or regional standard or regulation, including primary and secondary NAAQSs and state implementation plans. §307(b)(1), 42 U.S.C. §7607(b)(1). A person also may challenge EPA's rulemaking procedural determinations if he objected to the procedural error during the public comment period with ***reasonable specificity***. CAA §307(d)(7)(B) and (8), 42 U.S.C. §7607(d)(7)(B) and (8). If no stated deadline for action exists, a person may petition EPA to take action, and then sue under §307(b)(1) if EPA fails to act. See *Oljato Chapter of Navajo Tribe v. Train,* 515 F.2d 654 (D.C. Cir. 1975).

2. **Jurisdiction:** If a standard has ***national applicability*** or a person is alleging procedural error during rulemaking, the suit should be brought in the United States Court of Appeals for the District of Columbia. CAA §307(b)(1) and (d)(8), 42 U.S.C. §7607(b)(1) and (d)(8). If the standard has local or regional applicability, suit is proper in the United States Court of Appeals for the particular locality or region. CAA §307(b)(1), 42 U.S.C. §7607(b)(1).

3. **Time limitations:** An action under §307(b) must be filed within *60 days* of publication of EPA's action in the Federal Register. CAA §307(b)(1), 42 U.S.C. §7607(b)(1). A person may bring an action after the 60-day period if *new grounds arise* after the sixtieth day. *Id.* "New grounds" exist if EPA would have abused its discretion if it had known of the information at the time of its decision. *Union Elec. Co. v. EPA*, 427 U.S. 246, *reh'g denied*, 429 U.S. 873 (1976).

4. **Interrelationship between judicial review and citizen suits:** The duty to review NAAQSs every five years is *non-discretionary* under §109(d)(1). An environmental group may sue under §304 to compel EPA to review its standard as to a pollutant and to make a decision as to its revision. If EPA determines no revision is necessary, the group may then seek judicial review of EPA's decision in the United States Court of Appeals for the District of Columbia under §307(b)(1), because it is a discretionary duty which affects the nation.

**D. PSD enforcement:** The type of PSD program controls the type of enforcement action. If a state has a PSD program in its SIP, EPA may enforce the PSD provisions under §§113 or 167, 42 U.S.C. §§7413, 7477. If the PSD program is a federal program or EPA has review power over the program, then the program is subject to judicial review under CAA §307, 42 U.S.C. §7607. Citizen suits against a source in violation of a PSD requirement are *only allowed if the source does not have a permit or has violated its permit*. CAA §304, 42 U.S.C. §7604.

**E. Criminal sanctions:** A source which violates the CAA, in *limited circumstances*, also may be subject to criminal sanctions. Under CAA §113(c), 42 U.S.C. §7413(c), a party who knowingly violates the CAA may be subject to criminal penalties including prison terms of up to five years and fines up to $500,000 for organizations for a first violation. A person also may be subject to stiff criminal sanctions if they *"negligently" or "knowingly"* release hazardous air pollutants (such as those listed in §112) which place another person in "imminent danger of death or serious bodily injury." CAA §113(c)(3)-(4), 42 U.S.C. §7413(c)(3)-(4).

---

# *Quiz Yourself on*
# *THE CLEAN AIR ACT (CAA)*

15. BubbleTime, Inc. is about to complete construction on its air-polluting, emission-spouting manufacturing plant in the state of Massashoot. The company supports air pollution because pollution helps their bubbles stay afloat longer. BubbleTime definitely does not want the hassle of complying with stringent CAA requirements. Massashoot has already filed, and received approval on, their SIP governing emissions, and BubbleTime is afraid that their company will emit too many pollutants to avoid stringent requirements. BubbleTime is not located in a PSD or nonattainment area. Is there anything BubbleTime can do to avoid the strictest classification? _____

16. Same facts as above. Does BubbleTime have to obtain a permit? Does BubbleTime want a permit? _____

17. Same facts as above. Once BubbleTime was classified as a new source, what can it seek in order to avoid numerous emission controls? _____

18. One more time, but with an addition. BubbleTime's only competitor, BubbleDate, is located in the neighboring state of Wawtoosee. BubbleTime modeled their state-of-the-art polluting plant after BubbleDate's plant. The bubble plants emit a type of pollutant that only bubble plants emit. BubbleTime's management unhappily notes that BubbleDate was classified as a major stationary source, and they were given specific emission controls. Does BubbleTime have to employ similar pollution controls since BubbleDate is located in another state? _____

19. Wee Company emits sulfur dioxide at an astonishingly high rate. They have put off compliance with the NAAQS because they were waiting for the EPA's non-discretionary review that must occur every five years. They have paid the civil penalties incurred during this time for their noncompliance. Their complaint is that they are too small to be able to afford the adjustments that must be made to bring them into compliance. They also have no idea how to make the adjustments because their company is state-of-the-art small and no technology yet exists (to their knowledge) to enable them to emit less sulfur dioxide. Will the EPA revise their NAAQS during their review because of Wee Company's concerns? _____

20. Wee Company exists in a nonattainment area. After being forced to comply with the NAAQSs, they decided to find out about offsets. They requested information from Evenweer, Inc. about their emissions of ozone. Wee Company knows that Evenweer only emits a little ozone, and Wee Company wants to use the rest of their emission credits to offset their own sulfur dioxide emissions. Can they do this? _____

---

## Answers

15. **Yes.** BubbleTime can restrict its pollution output so as to avoid being classified as a *major stationary source*. A major stationary source would emit (or potentially emit) 10 tons/year or more of any hazardous air pollutant or 25 tons/year or more of any combination of hazardous air pollutants. BubbleTime wants to be classified as an *area source*. This means that they do not emit air pollutants to the above level. Area sources do not have to comply with major source emission standards. Area sources must meet the generally available control technology (GACT) standard.

16. **Yes to both.** The 1990 Amendments included Title V, which requires any new source subject to NSPS to obtain a permit. BubbleTime would be classified as a *new source* if it did not meet the size thresholds of a PSD or nonattainment area. BubbleTime would likely want the permit, because then they would enjoy the ''permit shield,'' which implies they have complied with the CAA. Done in one fell swoop.

17. **Classification as a bubble,** a cluster of related sources. The plant's emissions will be grouped together and cannot reach a certain regulated level. If the bubble classification was taken away, each pollutant source would be regulated individually.

18. **Yes.** The EPA regulates nationwide emission limits as well as approving SIPs. BubbleTime will have to meet the MACT standard, which requires its standards to be at least as stringent as those of the best controlled similar source.

19. **No.** The EPA cannot take economic and technological feasibility into account when setting air quality standards. If Wee can pay the fines, Wee can come into compliance.

20. **No.** Offsets are only available for the same pollutant. If Evenweer also emitted sulfur dioxide, then offsets for Wee Company might work. Remember that Evenweer would also have to be in the same nonattainment area unless their emissions in a different nonattainment area contributed to the violation of NAAQSs in Wee Company's area.

---

# Exam Tips on
# THE CLEAN AIR ACT (CAA)

☛ Learn to love acronyms and use them in your answer (it saves writing time) *but* be certain of what they stand for and that you are using the correct one (otherwise your professor will have no idea what you mean and will be singularly unimpressed). Here is a list (not exhaustive) of the biggies:

   ☞ CAA: Clean Air Act

   ☞ NAAQSs: National Ambient Air Quality Standards

   ☞ SIP: State Implementation Plan

   ☞ FIP: Federal Implementation Plan

   ☞ LAER: Lowest Achievable Emission Rate

   ☞ PSD: Prevention of Significant Deterioration

   ☞ BACT: Best Available Control Technology

   ☞ NSPS: New Source Performance Standards

   ☞ HAP: Hazardous Air Pollutants

   ☞ MACT: Maximum Achievable Control Technology

☛ Remember to focus on the source of the pollution and determine whether it is *mobile* or *stationary*. There are stricter requirements for stationary sources, so exam questions are usually on these.

*Example:* Smokey Mountain, Inc. is expanding its manufacturing plant. The expansion will add 500 jobs — meaning 500 more people will be driving to work every day. The management wants to be regulated according to the additional motor vehicle emissions. Too bad! Under CAA requirements, the plant will need a permit, will be regulated as a stationary source, and the motor vehicle emissions will not be attributed to the plant. They are likely already regulated under the SIP.

☛ If your exam hypothetical has included a pollutant which is not currently mentioned in the CAA, remember that it may be *non-discretionary* for the EPA to list it as a *criteria pollutant* and promulgate *NAAQSs* for that pollutant. It would behoove you to argue both for and against addition of the new pollutant as a criteria pollutant.

☛ States submit their SIPs to the *EPA for approval*, but they can petition to revise it. Don't assume that a state must retain current air quality control regulations, so long as the state continues to meet the NAAQSs.

☛ Don't forget that the EPA *may not consider economic and technological feasibility* when promulgating national ambient air quality standards. Hypotheticals may include facts about the potentially high costs or lack of existing technology, but do not be sidetracked.

   ☞ Do, however, consider timelines: If the state has not met the deadline at the end of three years, the EPA is allowed to disapprove the plan because of too stringent financial or technology costs.

☛ Look for ways to avoid preconstruction review in your exam hypothetical. Remember *offsets* and *bubbles*.

☛ Always, always, always remember that the goal of the CAA regulations is to *protect the public health and safety!* This goal affects what pollutants the EPA will regulate and at what level, the severity of the regulation, and the effects of noncompliance. Be sure to focus your answer on what will lead to the most reasonable protection of public health.

☛ Remember what you learned about *review of agency action*, because that is one way the EPA (and thus the CAA) is enforced. The other way is through *citizen suits* by a person with standing to enforce EPA requirements or to force the EPA to perform a non-discretionary duty.

   ☞ Similarly, the EPA enforces the CAA against noncompliant actors. The primary method is through *civil suits*, but *criminal penalties* also are available.

   ☞ Determine if the EPA or a private individual is seeking to enforce the CAA against a company/manufacturer/source.

   ☞ The EPA may threaten states with *sanctions* such as highway funding cutoff for not implementing SIP requirements, so include this possibility in your answer when faced with a question regarding deadlines.

   ☞ Don't forget that *sanctions differ* for attainment and nonattainment areas, so be certain of the designation.

## CHAPTER 7

# THE FEDERAL WATER POLLUTION CONTROL ACT (FWPCA)

## *ChapterScope*

In 1972, Congress enacted the Federal Water Pollution Control Act (FWPCA). This Act also is known as the Clean Water Act (CWA). The Act imposes national, technology-based standards on individual sources to make the nation's waters fishable, swimmable, and to eliminate the discharge of pollutants into navigable waters. We examine the following concepts in this chapter:

■ **Regulatory framework:** There are three major programs addressing the individual pollutant sources:

  ■ A *point source* discharges pollutants from a specific conveyance. Direct discharges into water systems are *permit-controlled*.

  ■ A *nonpoint source* includes pollution from nonspecific areas, but regulation of these areas has produced little actual control.

  ■ Oil spills are directly addressed through the *oil spill program*.

■ **Direct dischargers:** The *National Pollutant Discharge Elimination System (NPDES)* has strict standards to govern this primary *permit* system for direct dischargers. Slightly less stringent standards govern *publicly owned treatment works (POTW)*. There are *technology standards*, *variances* available to point sources, and *effluent limitations*.

  ■ *States or the EPA* may issue the permits under the NPDES.

■ **Indirect dischargers:** The CWA established *pretreatment program standards* and *sewage sludge standards* for indirect dischargers operating through POTWs.

  ■ All indirect dischargers must comply with the *general pretreatment standard*.

  ■ Industrial sources must comply with *technology-based limitations* on an *industry-by-industry basis*.

  ■ *Locally imposed standards* govern on an *industry or pollutant basis*.

  ■ **Nonpoint source pollution:** *Federal funding of state programs* has not been altogether successful in actually controlling *runoff* or pollution not channeled through a discrete conveyance.

■ **Water quality standards:** *States* comply with federal standards and promulgate their own standards to regulate water quality. Standards include *designations of use* for bodies of water, *total maximum daily loads (TMDLs)*, and *effluent limitations*.

■ **Enforcement:** The EPA may enforce regulations through *compliance orders, civil or criminal sanctions*. A private citizen may employ the *citizen suit provision* against an *ongoing or repeated violation*. Citizen suits may not, however, be brought to enforce *state regulations*.

■ **Wetlands:** The EPA and the *Army Corps of Engineers* provide wetlands protection under the FWPCA. There is a *permit system* and *regulations* specific to wetlands.

# I. REGULATORY FRAMEWORK

The Federal Water Pollution Control Act of 1972 (FWPCA) is also commonly referred to as the Clean Water Act (CWA). The basic framework of the statute is a system of ***nationally uniform, technology-based standards*** imposed on individual sources through a permit system FWPCA §301, 33 U.S.C. §1311. The requirements of the Act vary depending on the type of discharger and the type of pollutant.

**A. Goals of FWPCA:** The original goals of the Act were to make the nation's waters ***fishable and swimmable*** by 1983, and ***eliminate the discharge of pollutants into navigable waters*** by 1985. FWPCA §101(a)(1)-(2), 33 U.S.C. §1251(a)(1)-(2).

**B. Programs:** The Act consists of three major programs which deal with point sources of pollution, nonpoint sources, and oil spills.

   **1. Point sources:** A point source is "any discernible, confined and discrete conveyance . . . from which pollutants are . . . discharged." FWPCA §502(14), 33 U.S.C. §1362(14). A "point source" under the CWA ***does not include human beings.*** *United States v. Plaza Health Laboratories, Inc.,* 3 F.3d 643 (2d Cir. 1993) (holding that a corporate officer who disposed of vials of hepatitis-contaminated blood in Hudson River was not a point source and therefore not criminally liable under the CWA), *cert. denied sub nom., United States v. Villegas,* 114 S. Ct. 2764 (1994). Several programs are aimed at preventing or controlling the pollution caused by these sources.

      **a. Direct discharges and the NPDES program:** The National Pollutant Discharge Elimination System grants permits that ***control the amount and concentration*** of pollutants that are discharged directly into streams, lakes, or the ocean by industrial and municipal facilities. FWPCA §301(a), 33 U.S.C. §1311(a). Permits may be issued by the state or by EPA. Permits last for five years. FWPCA §402(b)(1)(B), 33 U.S.C. §1342(b)(1)(B). For a discussion of the state programs, see *infra*, p. 85.

         **i. Private:** All private industrial facilities discharging pollutants into "waters of the United States" may ***only discharge subject to stringent technology-based standards***. In *Village of Oconomowoc Lake v. Dayton Hudson Corp.,* the Seventh Circuit held that a retention pond which collected rainwater runoff from a warehouse site could not be considered part of the Clean Water Act's coverage of "waters of the United States" 24 F.3d 962, 964, *cert. denied,* 115 S. Ct. 322 (1994). A point source does not have to be a pipe from an industrial complex. In *Headwaters Inc. v. Talent Irrigation District,* 243 F.3d 741 (9th Cir. 2001), an irrigation district was held liable for not obtaining a permit prior to discharging herbicide into irrigation canals, despite the fact that the herbicide label had been approved by the EPA. And in *Miccosukee Tribe of Indians v. Water Management District,* 280 F.3d 1364 (11th Cir. 2002), it was held that a pumping station discharging water with elevated levels of phosphorous from one body to another via a levee had to obtain a permit as a point source discharger.

         **ii. Publicly Owned Treatment Works (POTWs):** POTWs, otherwise known as municipal sewage treatment plants, are subject to different ***discharge standards*** than private facilities.

    **b. Indirect discharge and pretreatment program:** Indirect dischargers allow their waste to enter the municipal sewage treatment system to be treated there. The FWPCA imposes some *"pretreatment" requirements* on these dischargers. FWPCA §307(b), 33 U.S.C. §1317(b).

    **c. Dredge and fill program:** A separate national permit system exists for construction activities that result in dredging or filling of wetlands. The EPA and the Corps establish the criteria for the permits, but it is the Army Corps of Engineers that is responsible for issuing these permits. FWPCA §404, 33 U.S.C. §1344, discussed *infra*, p. 89.

**2. Nonpoint sources:** Pollution from runoff or from a nondiscrete source, also called areawide pollution, requires *different methods of control*. The Act addresses nonpoint source pollution in §§208 and 319, but in application these provisions have failed to control the significant amount of nonpoint source pollution that is produced.

**3. Oil spill program:** The FWPCA contains a separate section pertaining solely to the spills of oil and other hazardous substances into navigable waterways. FWPCA §311, 33 U.S.C. §1321. It is similar in content to CERCLA (see *infra*, p. 117) but applies *exclusively to oil and only to navigable waterways.*

# II. KEY STATUTORY PROVISIONS OF THE CWA

Understanding the scope and structure of the Clean Water Act requires a careful reading of the underlying statutes. This section provides an overview of the most significant provisions of the CWA.

- **Section 101, 33 U.S.C. §1251:** Congressional findings and goals of the CWA.

- **Section 208, 33 U.S.C. §1288:** Sets forth procedures and requirements for the designation of areas with substantial water quality control problems, establishes mechanism for federal funding of state nonpoint source pollution programs.

- **Section 301, 33 U.S.C. §1311:** Prohibits effluent discharge without a permit; establishes technological standards for dischargers.

- **Section 303, 33 U.S.C. §1313:** Sets forth procedures and requirements for the designation of water quality standards.

- **Section 304, 33 U.S.C. §1314:** Sets forth guidelines and factors to be considered in the development of technological standards.

- **Section 307, 33 U.S.C. §1317:** Sets forth procedures and requirements for the designation of toxic pollutants and the promulgation of toxic effluent standards; sets forth procedures and requirements for promulgation of pretreatment standards.

- **Section 309, 33 U.S.C. §1319:** Establishes the range and scope of federal enforcement of the CWA.

- **Section 311, 33 U.S.C. §1321:** Sets forth procedures and requirements for the designation of hazardous substances; establishes scope of liability for oil or hazardous substance discharge.

- **Section 319, 33 U.S.C. §1329:** Sets forth procedures and requirements for development of state nonpoint source pollution management programs.

■ **Section 401, 33 U.S.C. §1341:** Sets forth procedures and requirements for state certification of effluent discharge permits.

■ **Section 402, 33 U.S.C. §1342:** Sets forth procedures and requirements for issuance of permits under the National Pollution Discharge Elimination System (NPDES); sets forth procedures and requirements for the transfer of permitting authority to the states.

■ **Section 404, 33 U.S.C. §1344:** Sets forth procedures and requirements for permitting discharges of dredged or fill materials.

■ **Section 405, 33 U.S.C. §1345:** Sets forth procedures and requirements for permitting discharges of sewage sludge.

■ **Section 502, 33 U.S.C. §1362:** Definitions of terms used in the CWA.

■ **Section 505, 33 U.S.C. §1365:** Sets forth procedures, requirements, and jurisdiction for citizen suits under the CWA.

■ **Section 509, 33 U.S.C. §1369:** Sets forth standards for judicial review.

# III. NATIONAL POLLUTANT DISCHARGE ELIMINATION SYSTEM (NPDES) PROGRAM

NPDES permits are granted to control the amounts of pollutants discharged from industrial and municipal facilities. The limits on the quantities discharged will be based on either the ***pollution control technology*** available or ambient water quality standards.

A. **Direct discharges and technology-based limitations:** In a technology-based limitation, the present or future status of the environment is not a factor: facilities are to use the ***"best" technology to control the amount of pollution discharged***. The technological infeasibility of such limitations may result in adjustments in permit programs but that does not authorize the EPA administrator, who grants the permits, to exclude relevant point sources from the permit program. *NRDC v. Costle*, 568 F.2d 1369 (D.C. Cir. 1977).

1. **Existing sources:** Existing sources of pollution are required to use ***technology-based limitations***, although typically from an add-on standpoint. Requirements to change an already functioning industrial process are unusual.

2. **New sources:** New sources may be required to ***modify the process*** itself — to place pollution control mechanisms within the design of the facility. This is potentially more stringent than existing source requirements.

3. **Publicly Owned Treatment Works (POTWs) standards:** The standards for these facilities are somewhat ***less stringent*** than other sources. The Act requires that POTWs utilize secondary treatment by 1977, with an extension of the deadline to 1988 if federal funding is reduced. FWPCA §301(i), 33 U.S.C. §1311(i).

   a. **Primary treatment:** Primary treatment involves collection of sewage into tanks so that solid matter settles and the POTWs can use chemicals to remove organic matter.

   b. **Secondary treatment:** Secondary treatment involves the further removal of organic matter through physical, chemical, or biological treatment methods. Certain biological treatment methods are deemed the equivalent of secondary treatment under the Act. FWPCA §304(d)(4), 33 U.S.C. §1314(d)(4).

4. **Standards:** Point source standards are the core of the FWPCA, and *include best practicable control technology (BPT), best available control technology (BAT)*, and *best conventional control technology (BCT)*.

   a. **BPT:** The best practicable control technology is the average of the best technology in use at the time an effluent limitation is set. FWPCA §304(b)(1), 33 U.S.C. §1314(b)(1). The current deadline for achieving BPT is March 31, 1989. FWPCA §301(b)(3)(A), 33 U.S.C. §1311(b)(3)(A).

   The EPA failed to meet the 1989 deadlines, so in issuing permits states must establish a phased-compliance schedule not to exceed three years after the promulgation by EPA of new BAT, BPT, or BCT standards.

   b. **BAT and BCT:** In the 1977 Amendments to the FWPCA, the second phase of regulation prescribed *different standards for different categories* of pollutants. FWPCA §304(b)(2)-(4), 33 U.S.C. §1314(b)(2)-(4). The deadline for each category was set at March 31, 1989. FWPCA §301(b)(2)(C)-(F), 33 U.S.C. §1311(b)(2)(C)-(F).

      i. **Conventional pollutants:** Point sources discharging pollutants such as biochemical oxygen demand (BOD), suspended solids, and pH must achieve the *best conventional* control technology (BCT) as to these pollutants by the deadline. FWPCA §304(a)(4) and (b)(4), 33 U.S.C. §1314(a)(4) and (b)(4).

      ii. **Nonconventional pollutants:** Point sources discharging pollutants that are not conventional or toxic must achieve *BAT* by the deadline. FWPCA §304(b)(2), 33 U.S.C. §1314(b)(2). The BAT standard is *more stringent* than BPT as it is designed to force point sources to adopt the best *technology demonstrated* even if such technology is not widely used. FWPCA §304(b)(2), 33 U.S.C. §1314(b)(2).

      iii. **Toxic pollutants:** Point sources discharging ordinary toxics must achieve BAT by the deadline. FWPCA §304(b)(2), 33 U.S.C. §1314(b)(2).

   c. **Setting effluent limitations:** EPA *may* set BPT and BAT on a *classwide* basis through regulation, and is not required to set the standards on a case-by-case basis through permits. *E.I. du Pont de Nemours & Co. v. Train*, 430 U.S. 112 (1977).

   **Example:** In the *du Pont* case, the company contended that the statutory language as to BPT required EPA to set limits for individual point sources. The Court found that the "categories and classes of point sources" language in the BAT provision was equally applicable to BPT, and that EPA could set BPT limitations through regulation. The Court's interpretation was necessary to alleviate the potential administrative burden that setting limits by permits would cause. The Court also noted the availability of a variance from BPT, which made it more reasonable to set BPT through regulation.

   d. **Factors in setting limitations:** Generally, EPA may consider factors set forth in the statute in setting effluent limitations. See generally FWPCA §301, 33 U.S.C. §1311.

      i. **Receiving water quality:** EPA *may not consider* the quality of receiving water because of the clear congressional intent to adopt technology-based standards and *to avoid the scientific uncertainty* involved in making water quality determinations. *Weyerhau-*

*ser Co. v. Costle*, 590 F.2d 1011 (D.C. Cir. 1978). In *Weyerhauser*, pulp and paper makers challenged the validity of the BPT standard set for the paper industry and alleged that EPA should consider the fact that the plants were discharging into the Pacific Ocean. The court upheld EPA's approach.

ii.   **Cost:** The role of cost in setting effluent limitations differs depending on the standard being set.

(1) **BPT:** Cost is a *comparison* factor. EPA must compare the cost of the technology with the effluent reduction benefits. FWPCA §304(b)(1)(B), 33 U.S.C. §1314(b)(1)(B).

**Example:** In *Chemical Mfrs. Ass'n v. EPA*, 870 F.2d 177 (5th Cir. 1989), *cert. denied, PPG Industries, Inc. v. EPA*, 495 U.S. 910 (1990), the Association argued that cost should play a more significant role in setting BPT. The court disagreed, viewing BPT as the least stringent standard and requiring that costs be "wholly disproportionate" to benefits before it would grant relief.

(2) **BCT:** Cost is a *double comparison* factor. FWPCA §304(b)(4)(B), 33 U.S.C. §1314(b)(4)(B). EPA must engage in a two-step analysis: (1) determine the industry cost-effectiveness ratio, and (2) compare that ratio to the cost-effectiveness ratio for equivalent POTWs limitations. *American Paper Inst. v. EPA*, 660 F.2d 954 (4th Cir. 1981).

(3) **BAT:** Cost is a *consideration* factor. FWPCA §304(b)(2)(B), 33 U.S.C. §1314(b)(2)(B).

5.   **Chart of standards and deadlines:**

---

**Clean Water Act — '72, '77, '81, '87**
(brackets indicate superseded provisions)

A.   §301 Technology-Based Effluent Limitations for Point Sources
BPT — ['77] ['79] Mar. 31, '89
BAT by '83

in '77: Conventional Pollutants
(*e.g.,* BOD, FC, SS, Ph,
oil & grease)                     — BCT — ['84] Mar. 31, '89
Nonconventional
Pollutants                        — BAT — ['87] Mar. 31, '89
Toxic Pollutants                  — BAT — ['84] Mar. 31, '89

B.   §301 for POTWs — secondary treatment by '77 and '88 if no federal funding [BPT by '83 eliminated in '81]

§301 — must also comply with any more stringent state standards or federal standards

C.   §302 — federal water quality standards

D.   §303 — state ambient water quality standards

E.   §306 — New sources best available demonstrated technology

F.  §307 Toxics — (*e.g.*, aldrin/dieldrin, endrin, DDT, toxaphene, benzidine, PCBs) — ample margin of safety

G.  §307 — pretreatment standards for discharges into POTWs if discharge would interfere w/ POTWs or not be susceptible to treatment

---

6.  **Variances and exceptions from federal standards:** The types of variances allowed depend on the technological standard involved.

    a.  **BPT:** By regulation, EPA has provided for variances from BPT for *individual* plants. This variance is known as the *fundamentally different factor* (FDF) variance, and the Supreme Court has required its use. *E.I. du Pont de Nemours & Co. v. Train*, 430 U.S. 112 (1977). Economic inability may not be considered in granting variances, as the purpose of the standards is technology-forcing. However, fundamentally different cost factors for a particular source may be considered. *EPA v. National Crushed Stone Association*, 449 U.S. 64 (1980).

    b.  **BCT for conventional pollutants:** The FDF variance is allowed under §301(n). 33 U.S.C. §1311(n). An *innovative technology variance is also allowed*. FWPCA §301(k), 33 U.S.C. §1311(k).

    c.  **BAT for nonconventional pollutants:** Variances include the FDF variance, FWPCA §301(n), 33 U.S.C. §1311(n); the economic inability variance, FWPCA §301(c), 33 U.S.C. §1311(c); the water quality variance, FWPCA §301(g), 33 U.S.C. §1311(g); and the innovative technology variance, FWPCA §301(k), 33 U.S.C. §1311(k).

        i.  **Economic inability:** EPA may grant a variance from BAT if an individual plant's financial resources *limit its ability to comply* and if the plant will use the best technology it can afford. FWPCA §301(c), 33 U.S.C. §1311(c).

        ii. **Water quality:** EPA may grant a variance from BAT if the source discharges certain listed nonconventional pollutants and the modification *will not interfere* with maintaining the water quality. FWPCA §301(g), 33 U.S.C. §1311(g). Maintenance of water quality includes protecting the water, the animals in and surrounding the water, and the public health. FWPCA §301(g)(2)(C), 33 U.S.C. §1311(g)(2)(C).

    d.  **BAT for toxic pollutants:** The FDF variance is available, FWPCA §301(n), 33 U.S.C. §1311(n), but *no economic inability variance will be allowed* as to toxic pollutants. FWPCA §301(1), 33 U.S.C. §1311(1). In *Chemical Manufacturer's Association v. NRDC*, 470 U.S. 116, 130 (1985), the Court held that no variance would be available for any grounds that would justify statutory modification (*i.e.*, economic and water quality factors). In addition, the Court noted that an FDF variance ''does not excuse compliance with a correct requirement, but instead represents an acknowledgment that not all relevant factors were taken'' into account in determining the requirement in question; if they had been properly considered, the factors would have justified a new standard and the creation of a new subcategory for the discharger in question.

    e.  **New source standards:** No variances are allowed. *E.I. du Pont de Nemours & Co. v. Train*, 430 U.S. 112 (1977).

    f.  **POTWs standards:** Certain municipalities may qualify for a POTW variance that waives discharges into marine waters. FWPCA §301(h), 33 U.S.C. §1311(h).

g. **Scope of FDF variance:** Economic inability to meet technology costs is ***not grounds*** for granting an FDF variance. *EPA v. National Crushed Stone Ass'n*, 449 U.S. 64 (1980).

**Example:** In *National Crushed Stone*, the Court recognized the nature of the FDF variance as an adjustment that acknowledges that a ***limitation was set without reference to the full range of current practices***. The Court stated that the relationship between costs and benefits was relevant to setting a limitation, but a plant's economic situation was not grounds for granting a variance.

h. **Deadlines for FDF variances:** A source ***must apply*** for an FDF variance within 180 days of EPA's promulgation of a standard. FWPCA §301(n)(2), 33 U.S.C. §1311(n)(2). EPA must approve or deny the variance within 180 days. FWPCA §301(n)(3), 33 U.S.C. §1311(n)(3).

i. **Upset defense:** EPA has recognized that even in the best controlled atmosphere, pollution limits may be exceeded for reasons beyond the control of the facilities. The upset defense was inserted in all federally issued permits for this occurrence (state permits are not required to contain the provision). To assert this affirmative defense, the facility must show:

- that it had ***installed*** the appropriate technology;

- that the facility with the technology was being ***properly operated***;

- that the excess in limit was beyond the control of the facility; and

- that the facility ***notified the government*** within 24 hours.

j. **Chart of variances:**

| Standard | Pollutant | Variances Available |
|---|---|---|
| BPT | any type of pollutant | FDF Variance* |
| BAT | toxic | 301(n) [FDF]<br>Other statutory variances are not available due to section 301(l) |
| BCT | conventional | 301(n) [FDF]<br>301(k) [innovative technology] |
| BAT | nonconventional | 301(c) [economic inability]<br>301(n) [FDF]<br>301(g) [water quality variance for certain listed pollutants]<br>301(k) [innovative technology] |
| NSPS | any type of pollutant | no variances |

* Nonstatutory FDF variance.

# IV. PRETREATMENT PROGRAM FOR INDIRECT DISCHARGES

Many industrial facilities discharge into sewer systems of POTWs and not directly into navigable waters. These "indirect" dischargers *must comply with the "pretreatment" program* of §307(b), which requires EPA to promulgate

> pretreatment standards for introduction . . . into [POTWs] for those pollutants which are determined not to be susceptible to treatment by such treatment works or which would interfere with the operation of such treatment works . . . Pretreatment standards . . . shall be established to prevent the discharge of any pollutant through [POTWs] which pollutant interferes with, passes through, or otherwise is incompatible with such works. FWPCS §307(b)(1), 33 U.S.C. §1317(b)(1).

There is no national permit program for indirect dischargers as there is with direct dischargers. Indirect dischargers only comply with such pretreatment standards as are promulgated and standards are set only for pollutants that interfere with or pass through POTWs. Thus, the statutory scheme imposes very different requirements on point source discharges *depending upon the type of discharger* — direct private discharger, POTW discharger, or indirect discharger. Indirect dischargers are treated differently from direct dischargers because indirect discharges will be treated twice — once by the indirect discharger and once by the POTWs.

**A. Pretreatment standards:** There are basically three types of pretreatment standards.

1. **General pretreatment standard:** The general pretreatment standard is *applicable to all indirect dischargers*, and prohibits facilities from discharging waste that will *cause or contribute to the POTWs violating* its permit or the sewage sludge standards. The implementing regulations were upheld in *Arkansas Poultry Fed'n v. EPA*, 852 F.2d 324 (8th Cir. 1988).

2. **Categorical standards:** Categorical technology-based limitations for existing and new sources are imposed on an *industry-by-industry basis*. FWPCA §307(b), 33 U.S.C. §1317(b). Pursuant to a consent decree, EPA promulgates the categorical restrictions for classes and categories of industrial sources equivalent to technological standards for new and existing direct dischargers. Restrictions apply to those pollutants that would otherwise pass through or interfere with a POTW, and are based in part on the economic and technological capacity of the industry as a whole.

   > The FDF variance from categorical pretreatment standards was upheld in *Chemical Mfrs. Ass'n v. Natural Resources Defense Council*, 470 U.S. 116 (1985), *rev'g National Ass'n of Metal Finishers v. EPA*, 719 F.2d 624 (3d Cir. 1983). The Water Quality Act of 1987 amended §307 to provide an innovative technology extension similar to that for direct dischargers. FWPCA §307(e), 33 U.S.C. §1317(e).

3. **Locally imposed standards:** Local limits may be developed on an *industry or pollutant basis* and be included in a municipal ordinance, or developed for a specific facility and included within the municipal contract or permit for that facility. 40 C.F.R. §403.8(a) and (b). In addition, POTWs with previous problems of interference and pass through which are likely to recur must develop specific local limits to implement the prohibition on interference and pass through of pollutants.

**B. Sewage sludge standards:** Sewage treatment by POTWs produces sewage sludge. Sludge can be used as fertilizer unless it is contaminated with metals or other toxic pollutants. EPA has authority under §405(d), 33 U.S.C. §1345(d), for regulation of disposal of the sewage sludge that accumulates as a result of waste treatment by POTWs. In 1977 an amendment authorized POTWs to grant "removal credits" to dischargers of toxic pollutants to reduce categorical standards for such pollutants by the level of treatment achieved by the POTW, in order to avoid duplicative treatment by the indirect discharger and the POTW. Under §307(b)(1), 33 U.S.C. §1317(b)(1), removal *credit is precluded* if it would prevent sludge use or disposal in accordance with sludge management guidelines EPA is required to promulgate for POTWs under §405(d), because most toxic metals discharged into POTWs end up in the POTWs' sewage sludge. EPA's regulations for sludge management have been a constant source of litigation. See generally *Chicago Ass'n of Commerce & Indus. v. EPA,* 873 F.2d 1025 (7th Cir. 1989); *Armco, Inc. v. EPA,* 869 F.2d 975 (6th Cir. 1989).

# V.  WATER QUALITY STANDARDS

In addition to federal effluent standards, each state retains the authority to promulgate its own standards regulating water quality. FWPCA §303, 33 U.S.C. §1313.

**A. State water quality standards:** States go through several steps in promulgating and revising water quality standards.

   **1. Designate uses:** A state must *designate the use* of each body of water within the state. FWPCA §303(c)(2)(A), 33 U.S.C. §1313(c)(2)(A). The use *need not be an existing use.* EPA may not review use designations because of the resistance to perceived federal interference in land use. *Mississippi Comm'n on Natural Resources v. Costle,* 625 F.2d 1269 (5th Cir. 1980). However, under its "downgrading" policy, EPA requires states to designate uses at the "fishable/swimmable" level unless the state can demonstrate that level is unattainable due to natural or unremediable causes or that attainment of level would cause "substantial and widespread economic and social impact."

   **2. Determine criteria:** A state then determines criteria, or the *maximum concentration* of a pollutant that can be allowed without jeopardizing the designated use. FWPCA §303(c)(2)(A), 33 U.S.C. §1313(c)(2)(A). Recommended national criteria have presumptive applicability. *Mississippi Comm'n on Natural Resources v. Costle,* 625 F.2d 1269 (5th Cir. 1980).

   **3. Determine total maximum daily load:** A state next determines the *total maximum daily load* (TMDL), or the total amount of a pollutant from point sources and nonpoint sources that will not cause the water to exceed the criteria. FWPCA §303(d)(1)(C)-(D), 33 U.S.C. §1313(d)(1)(C)-(D). States may allocate the TMDL among various dischargers as it sees fit. 40 C.F.R. §130. This can be a difficult process: The EPA was forced to reconsider approval of New York's TMDL program for phosphorous discharge, as EPA had failed to show how TMDLs expressed as annual loads complied with the Act's requirement that TMDLs ensure compliance with water quality standards and account for seasonal variations in pollutant loadings. See *NRDC v. EPA,* 268 F.3d 31 (2001).

   **4. Translate into permit limitation:** Finally, the state translates an individual plant's share of the TMDL into a *numerical limitation* in the source's permit.

**B. Antidegradation policy:** Under EPA's antidegradation policy, states *may not lower existing uses* and the water quality necessary for them. A state may lower the use of certain high quality water to a fishable and swimmable level *if necessary* to accommodate important social or economic development. 40 C.F.R. §131.10(g). A state may not lower the use of outstanding national resources such as waters in national and state parks or of other exceptional importance. 40 C.F.R. §131.12(a)(3).

C. **Problems with system:** Various problems have prevented the state water quality standards system from being effective. Most importantly, very few TMDLs have been set and therefore few limitations have been included in permits.

D. **Toxic hot spots:** Areas that *consistently fail* to meet water quality standards due to toxic pollution are known as toxic hot spots. The FWPCA requires states to identify those areas and the facilities involved in those areas, and to develop ''individual control strategies'' to ensure that these areas come into compliance. FWPCA §304(1), 33 U.S.C. §1314(1).

E. **Compliance with downstream water quality standards:** One significant issue is whether EPA or a state must consider the water quality standards of a downstream state in issuing a permit. In *Arkansas v. Oklahoma*, 503 U.S. 91 (1992), the Court upheld an EPA regulation that required compliance with downstream water quality standards for EPA and state-issued permits, but held that a permit could be denied only if discharges would cause an ''actual detectable violation'' of a downstream state's water quality standards. The Court deferred to EPA's interpretation because of EPA's broad discretion in issuing permits and overseeing the permit process. The Court did not decide whether or not the Act required such compliance for either state- or EPA-issued permits.

F. **Compliance with minimum flow requirements:** In *PUD No. 1 of Jefferson County v. Washington Department of Ecology*, 114 S. Ct. 1900 (1994), a local utility challenged the state's inclusion in a dam's NPDES permit of a minimum flow requirement to maintain its water quality standard to ensure a habitat for fish downstream. The Court upheld applicability of this requirement as part of the §401 certification by a state of compliance with state water quality standards for federal permits and licenses. The Court said that use of water is part of a water quality standard for which certification may be required. It gave no guidance on what other state regulation of water use might be a condition for §401 certification.

# VI. PERMITS

The Clean Water Act permit system is the National Pollutant Discharge Elimination System (NPDES). Permits may be issued by the state or by EPA. Permits last for five years. FWPCA §402(b)(1)(B), 33 U.S.C. §1342(b)(1)(B). The purpose of a permit is to *identify and limit* the *most harmful pollutants* while leaving the vast number of other pollutants to disclosure requirements. Therefore, polluters may discharge pollutants not specifically listed in the permit(s) as long as they report the other pollutants. *Atlantic States Legal Foundation, Inc. v. Eastman Kodak Co.,* 12 F.3d 353, 357 (1993), *cert. denied*, 115 S. Ct. 62 (1994).

A. **State-issued permits:** A state may issue permits if it has an EPA-approved permit program. FWPCA §402(b), 33 U.S.C. §1342(b).

1. **Approval and review of permits:** Permit procedures are *governed by state law*, and subject to review in state courts. *Natural Resources Defense Council, Inc. v. Outboard Marine Corp.,* 702 F. Supp. 690 (N.D. Ill. 1988).

2. **EPA veto:** EPA may veto a state-issued permit if the permit is *outside the guidelines and requirements* of the Act. FWPCA §402(d), 33 U.S.C. §1342(d). If a veto occurs and EPA assumes permitting authority, review of EPA's decision is under §509.

B. **EPA-issued permits:** EPA has permitting authority in states without an approved program. FWPCA §402(a)(1), 33 U.S.C. §1342(a)(1).

   1. **Approval and review of permits:** Each federal permit involves a *full adjudication* of the issues. *Marathon Oil Co. v. EPA*, 564 F.2d 1253 (9th Cir. 1977). EPA's permit decisions are subject to review under §509.

   2. **State certification:** Each source must provide state certification that the discharges of the source *will comply* with the Act as a condition to EPA-permit issuance. FWPCA §401(a), 33 U.S.C. §1341(a).

# VII. ENFORCEMENT

Enforcement of FWPCA provisions is similar to the enforcement scheme under the Clean Air Act. For the details of the Clean Air Act's enforcement mechanism, see *supra*, p. 68.

A. **EPA enforcement:** EPA may issue a compliance order, may institute a civil action, or may pursue criminal sanctions against an alleged violator. FWPCA §309(a)(3), (b), 33 U.S.C. §1319(a)(3), (b).

   1. **Compliance orders:** The order must *state the violation with reasonable specificity* and must give the alleged violator *reasonable time to comply* with the order. FWPCA §309(a)(5)(A), 33 U.S.C. §1319(a)(5)(A).

   2. **Civil actions:** EPA should bring suit in the federal district court "for the district in which the defendant is located or resides or is doing business." FWPCA §309(b), 33 U.S.C. §1319(b). Relief available includes temporary or permanent injunctions or civil penalties. *Id*. Section 402(k), which allows compliance with a discharge permit to be deemed in compliance with the federal statute for enforcement purposes, has been interpreted as shielding the permit holder from suits based on discharges expressly allowed by permit and also for discharges reasonably anticipated by the Administrator as a result of disclosures made during the permitting process. See *Piney Run Preservation Association v. Carroll County Commissioners*, 268 F.3d 255 (4th Cir. 2001).

   3. **Criminal liability:** EPA may seek criminal penalties against a violator who *negligently or knowingly violated an Act provision*. FWPCA §309(c), 33 U.S.C. §1319(c). The criminal enforcement provisions of the CWA list four categories of criminal conduct. Convictions carry fines and imprisonment terms.

      a. **Negligent violations:** FWPCA §309(c)(1) punishes negligent violations of permit requirements and pollution control requirements, including *record-keeping violations*. 33 U.S.C. §1319(c)(1).

      b. **Knowing violations:** FWPCA §309(c)(2) results in felony convictions for violations of the above requirements if they are committed "knowingly." 33 U.S.C. §1319(c)(2). In *United States v. Weitzenhoff*, 35 F.3d 1275 (1994), *amending* 1 F.3d 1523 (1993), *cert. denied, Mariani v. United States*, 115 S. Ct. 939 (1995), the court held that "knowingly" violating a permit condition did not require that the polluter be aware of the requirements, or even the existence of the permit, but only that the ***polluter knowingly engaged in conduct that resulted in violation*** of the permit.

    **c. Knowing endangerment:** FWPCA §309(c)(3) states that any person who knowingly violates CWA provisions and knows at the time that he places another person in imminent danger of death or serious bodily injury is ***subject to a heavier fine and/or more lengthy imprisonment upon conviction.*** 33 U.S.C. §1319(c)(3). It further states that a defendant which is an "organization" can receive a steep fine.

    **d. False statements:** FWPCA §309(c)(4) imposes felony penalties on a person who knowingly makes any ***false*** material ***statement, representation, or certification*** in any document filed or required to be maintained under the Act. 33 U.S.C. §1319(c)(4).

    **e. Prohibition from contracts:** A final punishment for persons or firms found guilty of violating the CWA is their placement on a list which ***automatically prohibits*** them from contracting with the federal government until their violations are eliminated.

**4. Other enforcement options**

    **a. Administrative penalties:** These penalties are classified as per violation penalties (Class I) and per day penalties (Class II). FWPCA §309(g)(2), 33 U.S.C. §1319(g)(2).

    **b. EPA inspection:** EPA may require sources to ***maintain records*** and ***institute monitoring mechanisms.*** FWPCA §308, 33 U.S.C. §1318. EPA may visit sources and inspect these records and monitoring equipment. FWPCA §308(a)(4)(A)-(B), 33 U.S.C. §1318(a)(4)(A)-(B).

**B. Citizen suits:** Any person with standing may sue any alleged violator of an effluent limitation or an order issued by a state or EPA. FWPCA §505(a)(1), 33 U.S.C. §1365(a)(1). A citizen suit, however, may not be brought to enforce ***state regulations*** (*e.g.*, provisions of state pollutant discharge elimination system permits) ***which mandate stricter standards*** than required by the CWA. *Atlantic States Legal Foundation, Inc. v. Eastman Kodak Co.*, 12 F.3d 353 (1993), *cert. denied*, 115 S. Ct. 62 (1994); cf. *Northwest Environmental Advocates v. Portland*, 56 F.3d 979 (9th Cir. 1995), *cert. denied*, 116 S. Ct. 2550 (1996) (Ninth Circuit holding that §301 incorporated by reference the water quality requirements of §303, thus allowing citizen suits to enforce state water quality standards). In reaching their decision, the Ninth Circuit relied heavily on the Supreme Court's holding in *Pud No. 1 of Jefferson County*, but no other circuit has endorsed or adopted this extension of citizen enforcement. A citizen also may bring suit to compel the EPA to perform a non-discretionary duty. FWPCA §505(a)(2), 33 U.S.C. §1365(a)(2).

**1. Procedural requirements:** A citizen must give notice to EPA, the state, and the alleged violator 60 days prior to commencing suit. FWPCA §505(b)(1)(A), 33 U.S.C. §1365(b)(1)(A). If suing a discharger, the citizen must bring suit in the federal district court for the district in which the source is located. FWPCA §505(c)(1), 33 U.S.C. §1365(c)(1).

**2. Available relief:** A citizen may seek injunctive relief or civil penalties. FWPCA §505(a), 33 U.S.C. §1365(a). A court may award costs to the prevailing party. FWPCA §505(d), 33 U.S.C. §1365(d).

**3. Jurisdiction:** A citizen must allege an ***ongoing or repeated violation*** of the Act for subject matter jurisdiction to exist under the citizen suit provision; ***no suit exists for a "wholly past" violation.*** *Gwaltney of Smithfield, Ltd. v. Chesapeake Bay Found., Inc.*, 484 U.S. 49 (1987). Compare *Fried v. Sungard Recovery Services, Inc.*, 916 F. Supp. 465 (E.D. Pa. 1996) (holding that the CAA, after the 1990 Amendments, does allow for citizen suits for wholly past violations, *supra*, p. 70).

C. **Petitions for review:** Any interested person may seek judicial review of certain listed actions of EPA. FWPCA §509(b)(1), 33 U.S.C. §1369(b)(1).

   1. **Procedural requirements:** The person should sue in the United States Court of Appeals for the circuit in which the interested party resides or does business. FWPCA §509(b)(1), 33 U.S.C. §1369(b)(1). The person must bring suit within 120 days of EPA's action unless new grounds arise after the notice period has expired. *Id.*

   2. **Available relief:** The court may award the costs of litigation to the prevailing party. FWPCA §509(b)(3), 33 U.S.C. §1369(b)(3). *Roosevelt Campobello Int'l Park Commission v. EPA*, 711 F.2d 431 (1st Cir. 1983).

# VIII.  NONPOINT SOURCE POLLUTION

Nonpoint source pollution is usually *runoff,* or pollution *not channeled* through a discrete conveyance. The Act addresses nonpoint source pollution in §§208 and 319, but in application, these provisions have failed to control the significant amount of nonpoint source pollution that is produced.

A. **Act provisions:** The FWPCA provisions dealing with nonpoint source pollution involve federal funding of state programs.

   1. **Section 208:** This section provides for a *federal funding mechanism* to fund state programs developed to control nonpoint source pollution. 33 U.S.C. §1288. Most states' programs attempt to control runoff through land use controls, an intrusive and expensive method of control.

   2. **Section 319:** States are required to develop nonpoint source pollution *management programs* by 1988 with federal funding. 33 U.S.C. §1329.

      a. **Identification of problem:** Each state must *identify the waters threatened* by nonpoint source pollution. FWPCA §319(a)(1)(A), 33 U.S.C. §1329(a)(1)(A).

      b. **Promulgation of program:** Each state must develop a *state management program* that identifies "best management practices," sets up implementation programs and establishes a schedule of milestones. FWPCA §319(b)(2)(A)-(C), 33 U.S.C. §1329(b)(2)(A)-(C).

B. **Failure of provisions:** The programs under §§208 and 319 have failed to control nonpoint source pollution.

   1. **No adequate funding:** Both programs were designed to be funded by the federal government, yet Congress *did not adequately fund* these programs. States also were left to spend what money was provided without any oversight.

   2. **No sanctions:** If a state failed to implement programs to control nonpoint source pollution, EPA *had no authority* to develop a plan for the state, unlike the sanction of a federal implementation plan under the Clean Air Act.

   3. **Difficult to control:** Developing programs to control nonpoint source pollution is a difficult task because the most effective way of controlling such pollution is through *regional programs.* Yet, states do not organize their affairs on a regional basis, but on a state-wide or local basis.

4. **No meaningful enforcement:** EPA *cannot* use its enforcement authority to compel control over nonpoint source pollution, FWPCA §309, 33 U.S.C. §1309, and citizen suits are unavailable. FWPCA §505, 33 U.S.C. §1365.

# IX. WETLANDS

The Clean Water Act does not specifically address wetlands protection, but EPA and the Army Corps of Engineers have utilized the §404 permit process to provide some protection for wetlands.

A. **Definition of wetlands:** Both the Corps and the EPA utilize the definition of wetlands as *"those areas that are inundated or saturated by surface or ground water at a frequency and duration sufficient to support . . . a prevalence of vegetation typically adapted for life in saturated soil conditions."* 30 C.F.R. §328.3(b).

B. **Section 404 jurisdiction:** A §404 permit *must be* issued for the "discharge of *dredged or fill material* into the navigable waters at specified disposal sites." FWPCA §404(a), 33 U.S.C. §1344(a).

1. **Discharge:** *Redepositing* of materials may constitute a discharge. *Avoyelles Sportsmen's League, Inc. v. Marsh*, 715 F.2d 897 (5th Cir. 1983).

   **Example:** In *Avoyelles*, the defendants' landclearing activities constituted a discharge because the bulldozers and backhoes cleared the land and then redeposited the materials into the wetlands.

2. **Dredged and fill materials:** Dredged material is *excavated or dredged from the waters of the United States*. 33 C.F.R. §323.2(c). EPA and the Corps have different definitions of fill material. Both definitions focus on materials *used for replacing an aquatic area* with dry land or changing the bottom elevation of a water body, but the Corps' test requires a "primary purpose" of accomplishing such ends. Compare 33 C.F.R. §323.2(e) (Corps' definition) with 40 C.F.R. §232.2(i) (EPA definition).

   **Example:** In *Avoyelles*, the court determined that the unburned material that the defendants buried on the property was fill material because it had the effect of leveling the land so that farming operations could begin.

3. **Navigable waters:** The Corps and EPA broadly define navigable waters under §404 to include *wetlands adjacent to the waters of the United States*. 33 C.F.R. §328.3(a); 40 C.F.R. §230.3(s). The Supreme Court has upheld this interpretation. *United States v. Riverside Bayview Homes, Inc.*, 474 U.S. 121 (1985). The reasoning of the Court was that adjacent wetlands play an important role in protecting and enhancing water quality because of their part in the aquatic ecosystem. Thus, protecting wetlands furthers the Clean Water Act's goal of protecting water quality. *But* see *Hoffman Homes Incorporated v. EPA*, 999 F.2d 256 (7th Cir. 1993), where the court found that EPA had not presented substantial evidence that a small area of wetlands having no source of moisture other then rainfall which was partially filled by a developer had an effect on "interstate commerce" and was therefore beyond the jurisdiction of EPA under the CWA. Compare *Leslie Salt Co. v. United States*, 55 F.3d 1388 (9th Cir.), *cert. denied, Cargill, Inc. v. United States*, 516 U.S. 955, 116 S. Ct. 407 (1995), where isolated, seasonally dry intrastate waters used only by migratory birds were found to be within the regulatory scope of the CWA and the reach of the commerce clause.

**C. Exemptions from permit requirement:** Certain activities are *exempt* from the permit requirement for discharges of dredged or fill material. FWPCA §404(f)(1), 33 U.S.C. §1344(f)(1).

1. **Exemptions:** The exemptions include discharges from (1) normal farming activities, (2) maintenance or reconstruction of dams, (3) construction or maintenance of farm ponds or irrigation and drainage ditches, (4) construction of temporary sedimentation basins, (5) construction of farm roads, forest roads, or roads for mining operations, and (6) activities covered by nonpoint source pollution programs. FWPCA §404(f)(1), 33 U.S.C. §1344(f)(1).

    **Example:** In *Avoyelles*, the court held that the defendants' landclearing activities did not fall within the exception for normal farming activities because no such activities had occurred. The defendants were clearing and filling in the land so that they could farm.

    **Example:** In *Brace v. United States*, 41 F.3d 117 (3d Cir. 1994), *cert. denied*, 515 U.S. 1158, 115 S. Ct. 2610 (1995), the court held that farming activities were not "established" because the area was converted from non-suitable to suitable land for farming, and were not "ongoing" because "modifications to the hydrological regime [were] necessary to resume operations." The farming exemption excludes activities that *convert a wetland to a non-wetland use.*

2. **No exemption:** Any of the discharges exempted under §404(f)(1) *will be subject* to the permit requirement if the purpose of the activity is to convert the waters to a new use.

**D. Permit requirements:** Each §404 permit must meet certain substantive guidelines promulgated under §404(b)(1). 33 U.S.C. §1344(b)(1).

1. **Substantive requirements:** A permit will issue if:

    a. *no practicable alternative* exists to the proposed project;

    b. *no significant adverse impacts* on aquatic resources will result;

    c. *all reasonable mitigation measures are employed*; and

    d. the proposed project *will not violate any statute.* 40 C.F.R. §230.10(a)-(d).

2. **Practicable alternatives analysis:** If an *activity is not water-dependent*, a practicable *alternative is presumed* available unless the applicant demonstrates otherwise. 40 C.F.R. §230.10(a)(3); *Sylvester v. Army Corps of Eng'rs*, 882 F.2d 407 (9th Cir. 1989).

    **Example:** In *Sylvester*, the court determined that no practicable alternatives existed for the golf course proposed by the permit applicant. The court held that the Corps cannot reject an applicant's conclusion that a certain activity is economically necessary to his project and must consider the applicant's purpose for the project in reviewing the permit application in determining the existence of alternatives.

3. **Role of EPA:** EPA has the *power to veto* a §404 permit. FWPCA §404(c), 33 U.S.C. §1344(c).

    **Example:** In *Bersani v. Robichaud*, 850 F.2d 36 (2d Cir. 1988), *cert. denied, Bersani v. EPA*, 489 U.S. 1089 (1989), and *cert. denied, Robichaud v. EPA*, 29 Env't Rep. Cas. (BNA) 1384 (1989), the court held that EPA's veto of a §404 permit was reasonable. The applicant wanted to build a shopping mall, and the Corps granted the permit. EPA vetoed the permit because it decided that alternative sites should be determined at the time the applicant enters the market to search for a site, not at the time the applicant applies for a permit. The court found EPA's approach reasonable and consistent with the statute and its goals.

4. **General permits:** The Corps may issue a general permit as an alternative to a §404 permit. FWPCA §404(e)(1), 33 U.S.C. §1344(e)(1). These permits may be issued on a state, regional, or nationwide basis for categories of activities that are similar in nature if:

- each activity alone causes minimal adverse environmental effects, and

- the cumulative impacts on the environment are also minimal. *Id.*

**Example:** In *Shelton v. Marsh*, 902 F.2d 1201 (6th Cir. 1990), the court held that the Corps' issuance of a nationwide permit after issuing a §404 permit was proper because the same conditions were contained in both permits.

E. **The takings issue in wetlands regulation:** The Fifth Amendment prohibits the federal government from taking private property without just compensation. There have been many cases asserting that imposition of governmental restrictions on wetlands development constitutes a regulatory taking of the property without compensation. Of these cases, only a few before the late 1980s had succeeded on the taking claim.

1. **The effect of the navigational servitude:** In *Kaiser Aetna v. United States*, 444 U.S. 164 (1979), an artificially created pond was developed into a marina and connected to a bay through dredging and filling. The Corps of Engineers asserted regulatory authority over the pond under §10 of the RHA and demanded public access to the pond as navigable waters of the United States. The Ninth Circuit Court of Appeals concluded that the pond was subject to the federal government's navigational servitude, authorizing public access to the pond. The Supreme Court, however, viewed the navigational servitude as authorization for public access subject to traditional taking analysis for when compensation is required. Public access to the pond constituted a taking, according to the Court, because the ***pond was not a waterway*** traditionally subject to the navigational servitude, and public access would deprive the owners of an essential property right, the right to exclude others.

2. **Wetlands regulation under §404:** In contrast, taking challenges to §404 permit denials have utilized the more traditional taking analysis. Traditional taking clause analysis focuses on whether the regulation substantially ***advances a legitimate state interest*** and whether the landowner is ***deprived of all or almost all of the property***. Before the 1987 trilogy of Supreme Court takings cases, takings challenges to permit denials were rarely successful. A marked shift in the federal courts analysis occurred in *Florida Rock Indus., Inc. v. United States*. The Court of Claims ruled that a permit denial for limestone mining was a taking. On appeal, the Court of Appeals for the Federal Circuit reversed the Court of Claims' holding that ***only current uses and not future ones could be considered*** in determining whether economically viable uses of the property remained, and thus remanded the case to the court of claims for evaluation of the remaining fair market value of the property. The value of the property should be determined by examining a market of investors speculating on the property who are aware of the regulatory limits on the use of that property. 791 F.2d 893 (Fed. Cir. 1986).

On remand, the Court of Claims determined the value of the property through an examination of a market of investors who were speculating on the property and were aware of the regulatory limits on its use, and awarded damages for the full fair market value of the property. Once again, on appeal, the Federal Circuit Court of Appeals rejected the lower court's critical determinations — that all economically beneficial use of the 98-acre parcel had been taken and that there had been a 95 percent reduction in value of that parcel. As to the reduction in value, the court found the evidence demonstrated an "active though speculative investment market" for the land after the permit denial such that Florida Rock could have received a yet undetermined fair market value "certainly much higher than the nominal $500 per acre value accepted by the Court of Federal Claims." The speculative nature of the market did not render it so aberrational that the entire market should be disregarded in assessing fair market value.

As to whether a taking of all economic use had occurred, the court said the outcome is "no longer clear" if the 98 acres retained a value of $4,000. Having strongly intimated that a complete taking had not occurred, the court's opinion offers guidance on the ultimate unresolved issue under the takings clause: how far is too far under takings clause? In concluding that *a partial taking may be compensable*, the Federal Circuit Court of Appeals rejected any precise threshold of value loss as necessary to a partial taking.

---

## Quiz Yourself on
## THE FEDERAL WATER POLLUTION CONTROL ACT (FWPCA)

21. Point Source, Inc. is located along the Swimmingly River in Machez, Ember. The company's discharge amount of conventional pollutants into the river is controlled by their NPDES permit, but their company falls into a BAT standard through an EPA-promulgated classwide basis. Their sewage is discharged into the Machez municipal sewage treatment plant. Point Source has fallen on hard times in the last two years and they are no longer financially capable of keeping up with their water pollution controls. They are hoping to increase revenues through a plant expansion, but that would require building near wetlands adjacent to the Swimmingly River.

    (a) Can Point Source challenge the EPA classwide certification since they are no longer able to afford the controls? _____

    (b) Is Point Source responsible for any water quality regulations for their discharge into the Machez municipal system? _____

    (c) Disregarding wetlands protections, can Point Source obtain a variance from their current technological controls by expanding and discharging through a new source? _____

    (d) Can Point Source count on expansion into the wetlands area? _____

---

## Answers

**21a. Probably not.** The EPA is allowed to set effluent limitations on a classwide basis as opposed to an individual source basis. Since Point Source is subject to a BAT standard, economic inability to comply is not considered. Costs are only considered with the BCT standard.

**21b. Yes.** Pretreatment standards apply to the discharger as well as the POTW. Point Source is certainly limited by the general pretreatment standard and may be regulated under a categorical standard if their industry is so regulated. Finally, Machez may have locally imposed limitations for Point Source's indirect discharges.

**21c. No.** New sources are potentially subject to designing controls within the new system, so this may be more stringent than existing source controls. Additionally, new sources may not receive variances, even if they are subject to the BCT controls.

**21d. No.** Although the CWA does not specifically address wetlands, §404 has been interpreted to allow some protections. Building so close to the area will likely result in dug-up land being deposited into the wetlands area. Point Source would first have to apply for a permit to potentially discharge redeposited materials into the wetlands area. The expansion would certainly not fall into an exemption category nor are the waters being converted to a new use. Point Source could run into a problem when the EPA considers the purpose behind the application. Remember that there is a presumed practicable alternative when the activity is not water-dependent.

## *Exam Tips on* THE FEDERAL WATER POLLUTION CONTROL ACT (FWPCA)

☞ It may seem obvious, but remember that this Act also may be referred to as the Clean Water Act (CWA).

☞ Remember to love your acronyms! Here is another nonexhaustive list:

  ☞ FWPCA: Federal Water Pollution Control Act

  ☞ NPDES: National Pollutant Discharge Elimination System

  ☞ POTW: Publicly Owned Treatment Works

  ☞ BPT: Best Practicable Control Technology

  ☞ BAT: Best Available Control Technology

  ☞ BCT: Best Conventional Control Technology

  ☞ FDF: Fundamentally Different Factor

  ☞ TMDL: Total Maximum Daily Load

☞ Approach a fact pattern by first identifying the pollution source and the controlling regulations:

  ☞ A *point source* is a definite conveyance, which would be a specific building, such as a plant.

    ☞ Determine if the source is *private* and subject to strict *technology-based* standards, or a *POTW* subject to *primary* or *secondary* treatments.

    ☞ Evaluate whether the source is *existing or new*.

    ☞ If the source is *directly discharging* (*i.e.*, sending pollutants directly into water systems), move to the requirements of the *NPDES* permit system.

☞ If the source is ***indirectly discharging*** (*i.e.*, sending its sewage to the municipal sewage treatment center), then look at the ***pretreatment*** requirements.

☞ Read carefully to see if there is a ***variance*** allowed.

*Example:* BPT is the most stringent technological standard, but individual plants may seek an FDF variance if economic inability to meet costs is not the cause. The availability of variances depends on the reason it is being sought, the technological standard applied, and meeting the deadline.

☞ A ***nonpoint source*** has no specific pollutant building, but is something like ***runoff***. If the fact pattern involves this type of water pollution, then remember that the regulations have been rather ***unsuccessful***.

☞ A professor may want your opinion on a potential ''fix'' for the system. Consider ***additional federal funding***, meaningful ***enforcement authority***, or ***sanction*** options similar to those available under the Clean Air Act.

☞ You likely won't be asked about the ***oil spill program***, but remember that this deals exclusively with oil.

☛ ***Economic inability cannot*** be considered when granting ***BPT*** variances, so don't be sidetracked by cost issues. They ***can*** be considered for ***BAT*** variances if the source will use the best technology it can afford.

☛ The EPA is not the only voice in water quality — remember that the ***states*** must promulgate their own standards. States or the EPA may issue the NPDES permits.

☛ Enforcement authority includes ***civil or criminal penalties***, but the violator must have ***knowingly or negligently*** violated the Act to incur criminal penalties. Private individuals ***may not*** file citizen suits to enforce ***state regulations***.

☛ ***Wetlands*** are not specifically addressed in the CWA, but the EPA and the Army Corps of Engineers protect them under §404.

☞ A ***permit*** must be issued to discharge ***dredged or fill material***.

☞ Remember also that the definition of ***navigable waters*** is broadly defined to include wetlands near national waters.

☞ Look to ***alternatives*** and the ***applicant's purpose*** when the fact pattern involves a permit application.

## CHAPTER 8

# SAFE DRINKING WATER ACT (SDWA)

## *ChapterScope* ━━━━━━━━━━━━━━━━━━━━━━━━━━━━━━━━━━━━━━

The Safe Drinking Water Act of 1972 (SDWA) is designed to assure the safety of public water supplies for human consumption. Here are the key concepts in this chapter:

- ■ **Drinking water regulations:** The EPA promulgates these *health-based standards* to *specify and limit contaminants* in drinking water.

  - ■ **National Primary Drinking Water Standards (NPDWSs):** These standards *regulate the level of physical, chemical, biological, or radiological substances* in drinking water of *public water systems*.

  - ■ **National Secondary Drinking Water Standards (NSDWSs):** These standards are *non-enforceable aesthetic standards*.

- ■ **Underground water regulations:** This regulation *maintains the purity* of drinking water at its source.

## I. PURPOSE

The Safe Drinking Water Act of 1972 (SDWA) is designed to *assure the safety of public water* supplies for human consumption. Protection of underground sources of drinking water from toxic contaminants is of special concern.

## II. PROTECTION METHODS

The SDWA uses various methods to protect drinking water.

A. **National Drinking Water Regulations:** National Drinking Water Regulations are *health-based standards* promulgated by the EPA that regulate public water systems and *specify and limit contaminants* in drinking water through maximum *contaminant levels* (MCLs) and *treatment techniques*. The goal of these regulations is to protect public health and welfare to the extent feasible through ''the use of the best technology . . . available.'' SDWA §1412(b)(4)(D), 42 U.S.C. §300g-1(b)(4)(D). This best available technology (BAT) standard is limited only by additional health risk considerations that a BAT may introduce into the drinking water supply and by cost-benefit considerations. SDWA §1412(b)(5)-(6), 42 U.S.C. §300g-1(b)(5)-(6). Using a cost-benefit analysis, BAT is not often feasible for smaller public water systems; therefore the EPA is charged with identifying variance technologies for use by those smaller public water systems that are unable to implement the best technologies and treatment standards. SDWA §1412(b)(14), 42 U.S.C. §300g-1(b)(14).

   1. **National Primary Drinking Water Standards (NPDWSs):** NPDWSs are used to protect the public health by *regulating the level of physical, chemical, biological, or radiological substances* or matter in the drinking water of ''public water systems.'' A ''public water system'' is

"a system for the provision to the public of water for human consumption through pipes or other constructed conveyances, if such system has at least 15 service connections or regularly serves at least 25 individuals." SDWA §1401(4)(A), 42 U.S.C. §300f(4)(A). NPDWSs are enforceable standards and require compliance by public water systems with MCLs or treatment techniques for those contaminants that raise public health concerns and require regulation. SDWA §1401(4), 42 U.S.C. §300f(1). In addition to those contaminants that the EPA may deem necessary to regulate, the SDWA requires specific regulation for arsenic, sulfate, and radon. SDWA §1412(b)(12)-(13), 42 U.S.C. §300g-1(b)(12)-(13).

> A State may have *primary enforcement* responsibility for public water systems provided that it has adopted drinking water regulations that are at least as stringent as federal standards. SDWA §1413(a)(1), 42 U.S.C. §300g-2(a)(1).

2. **National Secondary Drinking Water Standards (NSDWSs):** NSDWSs are *non-enforceable aesthetic standards* established by the EPA to protect public welfare. Secondary drinking water regulations may apply to the odor, appearance, or other aesthetic quality of drinking water that may adversely affect the public welfare. SDWA §1401(2), 42 U.S.C. §300f(2).

3. **Public information and notice:** As of the 1996 Amendments to the SDWA, each person served by a public water system is *required to be informed* of any conditions affecting their drinking water that may have an impact on public health. Owners and operators of public water systems are *required to give notice of any failure to comply* with an MCL, any failure to perform a requirement, the existence of a variance or exemption, the existence of a concentration of any unregulated contaminant for which the EPA has required public notice. SDWA §1414(c)(1), 42 U.S.C. §300g-3(c)(1).

> In addition to requiring public notice, the SDWA also requires annual reports by the EPA, or the state, as the primary enforcement agency, informing the public of violations within the state. SDWA §1414(c)(3), 42 U.S.C. §300g-3(c)(3). Lastly, by August 1998, the EPA, in consultation with public water systems are required to produce consumer reports informing the public about their water systems and the regulations that apply to it. SDWA §1414(c)(4), 42 U.S.C. §300g-3(c)(4).

4. **Enforcement:** Whenever the EPA determines that a public water system does not comply with an applicable requirement such as an MCL, the EPA *must issue an administrative order* requiring the public water system to comply with the regulation, or the EPA must commence a civil enforcement action. SDWA §1414(2), 42 U.S.C. §300g-3(a)(2). In states that have primary enforcement responsibility, the EPA must first *notify the state and provide it with advice and technical assistance* to help bring the public water system into compliance. If 30 days after notification, the state has not commenced enforcement action, the EPA must either initiate a civil action against the public water system or it may issue an administrative order requiring compliance. SDWA §1414(1), 42 U.S.C. §300g-3(a)(1).

> Though secondary drinking water regulations are not enforceable by the EPA, the SDWA requires the EPA to notify a state when it determines that a public water system within the state is violating a secondary regulation and such non-compliance is due to the state's failure to take "reasonable action" to assure compliance. SDWA §1414(d), 42 U.S.C. §300g-3(d).

B. **Protection of underground sources of drinking water:** This category of regulation is aimed at *maintaining the purity* of drinking water at its source.

1. **Wellhead protection:** All states must have programs to protect "wellhead protection areas" from potentially dangerous contaminants. SDWA §1428(a), 42 U.S.C. §300h-7(a). A "wellhead protection area" consists of the *surface and subsurface area surrounding a well* that supplies a public water system and "through which contaminants are reasonably likely to move toward and reach such a water well or wellfield." SDWA §1428(e), 42 U.S.C. §300h-7(e). Each state program must have at a minimum: a protection area, a protection program, a contingency plan, and a requirement that all potential sources of contamination must be considered. SDWA §1428(a), 42 U.S.C. §300h-7(a).

2. **Sole source aquifer demonstration program:** This is a grant program that reimburses states for 50 percent of their costs in developing and implementing state programs to identify and preserve "critical aquifer protection area[s]." SDWA §1427(c), 42 U.S.C. §300h-6(c). The objective of this program is to "maintain the quality of ground water in the critical protection area in a manner reasonably expected to protect human health, the environment and ground water resources." SDWA §1427(f), 42 U.S.C. §300h-6(c).

3. **Underground injection control program:** The purpose of this program is to *regulate deep well injection of wastes into "dry" wells* in order to assure that underground injection will not endanger drinking water sources. SDWA §1421(d), 42 U.S.C. §300h(d). The extent of regulation depends upon which of five regulatory categories the well encompasses. Excluded from the program are aquifers that are not and will not be suitable for water supply purposes and aquifers that are "mineral, hydrocarbon or geothermal energy producing," or are capable of becoming commercially mineral or hydrocarbon energy producing. 40 C.F.R. §146.4. See *Legal Environmental Assistance Foundation, Inc. v. EPA*, 118 F.3d 1467 (11th Cir. 1997).

---

# *Quiz Yourself* on *SAFE DRINKING WATER ACT (SDWA)*

22. SmellsLikeFeet Waste Company has a long and proud history of burying its waste products deep into the earth. Their favorite dumping places are the dry wells of the city of Springfields, because the people of the city rarely check on them. After a number of years, the 2,000 residents of Springfields began noticing that their drinking water had a definite odor of sweaty feet. No one who works at SLF Waste lives in Springfields, so the odor was not immediately brought to their attention. Moe Reya, a resident of Springfields, became downright disgusted with the odor and the taste of the water and he complained to the city managers. Soon, complaints came pouring in and some of the residents began to fall ill.

    (a) If the city found no contaminants in their drinking supply, does the SDWA even apply to SLF Waste? _____

    (b) Do the NPDWSs apply to Springfields's water system? _____

## *Answers*

**22a. Yes.** The underground injection of waste into Springfields's dry wells is regulated under the SDWA. SmellsLikeFeet Waste must ensure that there is no contamination of the underground water supply. Since SLF has been dumping for a number of years, it is possible that waste contaminants have leeched into the water supply slowly and are just now appearing. It also is possible that their waste dumping has not contaminated the water, but just makes it smell like feet. In that case, NSDWSs would apply because of the odor.

**22b. Yes.** Springfields's public water system regularly serves 2,000 people, well over the requirement of at least 25. The NPDWSs would regulate any contaminants that had leeched into the water system after the years of SLF Waste's dumping practices.

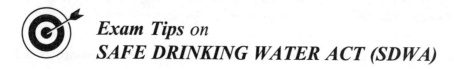

## *Exam Tips on*
## *SAFE DRINKING WATER ACT (SDWA)*

☞ Remember that the EPA can consider ***cost-benefits*** when determining the BAT standard implementation by smaller public water systems. If the cost seems too high, look to alternative technologies for protecting the public water supply.

☞ Read the facts carefully to determine whether the standard to apply is an ***NPDWS or NSDWS***, because the former is enforceable while the latter is not.

*Example:* Sue Reena's drinking water smells like dead fish and her neighbors are starting to complain of the same thing. They are so disgusted that they finally contact the city about the problem. The city determines that the water is clean and safe, just stinky. The EPA cannot enforce stricter regulations on the city, because the odor of water is just an aesthetic standard. The city should voluntarily comply with the NSDWS, however, or the EPA will notify the state.

☞ The states have the responsibility to maintain the ***cleanliness and safety*** of their drinking and underground water. They also may have the ***primary enforcement responsibility***, so they will be the first to try to bring the violator into compliance. Just remember that the water needs to be safe to drink, and you will be fine.

CHAPTER **9**

# CONTROL OF TOXIC SUBSTANCES

*ChapterScope* ────────────────────────────────────

Many substances can have a dual nature: while they can be extremely useful, they also can pose significant risks to human health. Several statutes have been passed relating to the production, use, storage, and disposal of such substances. In this chapter, we examine some of the most important laws relating to the control of toxins.

■ **Risk assessment:** Risks are divided into *public* and *private* risks. Policy-making involves *assessment* and *management* of these risks.

■ **The Resource Conservation and Recovery Act (RCRA):** RCRA is a comprehensive regulatory scheme for the management of both hazardous and non-hazardous waste.

■ The RCRA creates and regulates *four separate programs* to govern waste, but we focus on the identification, management, and regulation of *hazardous wastes*.

■ **The Comprehensive Environmental Response, Compensation, and Liability Act (CERCLA):** CERCLA was designed to provide for the *cleanup* of hazardous and toxic waste sites. CERCLA is *remedial* rather than regulatory and creates the *Superfund* to finance *governmental response activities*.

■ *Liability* under CERCLA is *strict* with *limited defenses*.

■ *Brownfields* Economic Redevelopment Initiative is designed to encourage *remediation and reuse* of contaminated sites.

■ **The Toxic Substances Control Act (TSCA):** The TSCA is a *two-tiered evaluation system*, which was designed to enable the *testing and gathering of information* on chemical toxicity.

■ **The Federal Insecticide, Fungicide, and Rodenticide Act (FIFRA):** FIFRA specifically regulates *pesticide use*, requiring pesticide product *registration* with the EPA.

## I. RISK ASSESSMENT AND MANAGEMENT

A. **Introduction:** Risks, from both natural and manmade sources, are inherent to life. These risks may be considered in two groups—private risks and public risks.

1. **Private risks:** Private risks are either of *natural origin* (such as earthquakes or natural disease) or *manmade* (such as automobiles), but are produced in relatively discrete units, with local impacts more or less subject to personal control.

2. **Public risks:** Public risks are man-made threats to human health or safety that are *centrally or mass-produced*, broadly distributed, and *largely outside* the individual risk bearer's direct understanding and control (such as nuclear power plants, mass-produced vaccines, or chemical additives). Public risks carry unique problems listed below.

a. **Long latency period:** Many public risks may take years or even decades to manifest themselves. This long latency period *may require preventive measures* long before the exact nature or extent of the risk posed is clear.

b. **Diffuse impact:** Public risks may impact on a *relatively small* number of persons in any community (*e.g.*, one in a hundred, or one in a thousand). When taken collectively, the *impact is quite extensive,* but this dispersion may cause the impact to be ignored within smaller, more discrete communities.

c. **Diffuse cost:** The costs of the risk also may be diffuse. The cost to each victim may be small, providing low incentive for individual action, but the *collective cost* to society of these minor individual injuries *may be high enough* to merit risk management.

d. **Discounting of risk:** Because of the factors mentioned above, specifically the low or unknown probability of injury and the delayed manifestation of the injury, people *may ignore or discount* the risks posed by a hazard.

e. **Lack of information:** Often the public lacks whatever information is available to make a knowledgeable assessment of risk.

B. **Process of risk assessment and risk management:** By the mid-1970s, environmental policymakers became aware that there were potentially thousands of environmental contaminants which could cause severe harm to a large number of persons exposed to even trace amounts of contaminants. This awareness was a *significant shift* from the previous view of environmental hazards as a limited number of contaminants that were hazardous only in large amounts and posed harm to large but discrete communities. In response to this paradigm shift, policymakers were forced to develop a new process for studying and regulating these hazards. Policy-making for these hazards involves two steps:

1. **Risk assessment:** Risk assessment is the use of a base of scientific research to *define the probability* and severity of some harm coming to an individual or a population as a result of exposure to a substance or situation.

2. **Risk management:** Risk management is the public process of deciding *what to do where risk has been determined* to exist, including integrating risk assessment with considerations of engineering feasibility and figuring out how to exercise our societal imperative to reduce risk in the light of social, economic, and political factors.

3. **Integration of risk assessment and risk management:** Theoretically, these are *two independent* processes, although they may be conducted within the same agency. The risk assessment phase is concerned solely with generating data, and is supposed to be value neutral. Since determining values and applying values is the very function of policymaking, these decisions are left to the second phase, risk management. Based upon the data derived in the risk assessment phase, policymakers in the risk management phase develop guidelines and regulations dealing with a particular hazardous substance.

C. **Dose-response assessment:** Although risk assessment attempts to develop neutral data, it is an *inexact science*. A common example of this is dose-response assessment. To determine the risk of a particular substance, lab animals are exposed to high-level doses of the substance until some reaction (usually cancerous tumors) develops. From this data, scientists extrapolate backwards from this process to determine the *probability of injury from some percentage* of that dosage. Based on the reaction of the lab animals, estimates are made for reactions in humans to the same substance.

However, this process is less than exact, and a number of choices which scientists make can influence the outcome.

1. **Choice of statistical models:** Scientists use statistical models to extrapolate probability of harm from different dosage levels. These models may be conservative (assigning the greatest risk plausible to a given exposure level) to liberal (assigning the smallest risk plausible to a given exposure level). The choice of a statistical model thus applies some values to data produced. Choosing a conservative model assumes a preference for safety, or a higher level of risk aversion, as data generated from a conservative model would necessarily dictate more conservative guidelines in the risk management phase. This problem can be complicated by trying to extrapolate data performed on healthy, mature individuals to sensitive population groups such as children and the elderly.

2. **Translating data from test animals to humans:** Scientists must use statistical models and other tools to translate the data they generate from animals to humans. These tools are *less than exact* and require choices which can *greatly affect* the results. There also may be different pathways of ingestion for animals and humans.

3. **Effects of marginal dosage:** The data generated in risk assessments states the probability of injury from some level of exposure, but *does not* provide information *about the marginal effect* of increased dosage. For some substances there may be a threshold dosage before any harm is done. If this threshold point is unknown, regulations may limit exposure to a level far below what is necessary to provide a safe environment. It is also difficult to isolate the effects of ingestion of a substance when there has been exposure to multiple substances.

   **Example:** At 1 part per million (ppm), substance X is relatively harmless; but at 10 ppm, it becomes harmful, and at 100 ppm it becomes potentially lethal. Using a statistical model to determine the hazards of the substance, 5 ppm is shown to have a 2 percent probability of causing death in humans. Because 2 percent is an unacceptably high level of risk for policymakers, they set exposure levels at 1 ppm. However, in reality there is no risk from exposure at levels below 10 ppm, the threshold point for substance X. Therefore the exposure level limits are far stricter than they actually need to be. The marginal risk from exposure to substance X below 10 ppm is near zero.

D. **Increasing neutrality in risk assessments:** Several suggestions have been made for ways to create more neutral risk assessments.

   1. **Presentation of data:** Currently, most risk assessments present their data as a *single set of numbers derived from a single set of assumptions* (*e.g.*, the risk from X at this level is 3 percent). Alternatively, the risk assessment could present a range of data, derived from a variety of estimates (*e.g.*, the risk from X at this level is between 2 percent and 5 percent). Presenting a range would provide a better understanding of the significance of the data and return some decision making to the risk management process by allowing them to choose between conservative and liberal estimates.

   2. **Assumptions inherent in the process:** Currently, risk assessments usually set forth data with little *explanation of processes used* to develop that data or assumptions made by the scientists in developing the data. A fuller presentation of this information could increase policymakers' understanding of the significance of the data and again transfer some choice back to the risk management phase (*e.g.*, if the risk assessment is based on the most conservative estimates, pol-

icymakers may not feel the need to adopt guidelines more stringent than the data suggests is necessary "just to be on the safe side," because a cushion is already built into the data).

**E. Problems with risk management:** Risk management is far from a perfect science, and it also contains a number of inherent difficulties.

   **1. Identifying societal attitudes regarding risk:** Before an agency can develop guidelines, it ***must know the societal attitude*** regarding risk. Is the society risk adverse, desiring the lowest level of risk possible regardless of cost, or is it willing to undertake a much higher level of risk? Does it wish to have a zero risk environment, a safe environment, or a riskier environment?

   **2. Costs of risk management:** Each risk bears costs to the society. Managing a risk can reduce its costs, but that management carries its own costs. The society must determine ***how it wishes to weigh the costs*** of prevention against the costs of the unmitigated risk. Does it wish to adopt best possible, best feasible, or a straight cost benefit analysis?

   **Example:** To avoid a cost of pollution, a factory may decide to install a filter in its smokestack. This filter will raise the cost of the factory's product, and it might make production too expensive to continue at all. Given these facts, is it worthwhile to require the filter?

   **3. Decision by experts:** Traditionally, risk management is performed by various governmental agencies, usually by scientists and other experts. These persons are regarded as having ***greater knowledge of, and experience with***, the technical process of risk management, and are given some deference in their decisions. This deference may be problematic.

      **a. Expert viewpoint:** Experts tend to view risk as a ***linear problem***, in terms of more or less risk being encountered.

      **b. Citizen viewpoint:** Most common citizens view risk as a ***multi-dimensional problem*** with several different factors. They are concerned not only with their chance of encountering the risk, but also with the ***type of harm*** that might occur, their ***ability to avoid the risk*** through their individual actions, and other considerations.

      **c. Result of conflicting viewpoints:** The dissonant views of the expert and the layman may lead to policies that ***are not*** in keeping with the sentiments of the society. There may also be conflicting viewpoints in the scientific community.

**F. Risk management and the judiciary:** The courts have not become actively involved in the actual balancing of interests involved in risk management. Rather, they have engaged in ***procedural reviews*** of agency decisions, seeking to determine the scope of an agency's review, the factors to be balanced, and whether the agency's actions are in keeping with the spirit of the legislature's intent.

   **1. When should risk management occur:** In *Reserve Mining Co. v. Environmental Protection Agency*, 514 F.2d 492 (8th Cir. 1975), the Court of Appeals reviewed a challenge to EPA regulation on the discharge of asbestos fibers into the Great Lakes. Although there was ***no showing*** that such discharge posed a health hazard, both airborne asbestos fibers and asbestos fibers had been shown to contribute to a risk of cancer. The Court held that Congress's provision in the Federal Water Pollution Control Act (FWPCA) authorizing action where discharges "endanger . . . the health or welfare of persons" was sufficient grounds for EPA regulation. The Court concluded that "endanger" was used in a "precautionary or preventive sense" and that evidence of "potential harm as well as actual harm" came within the purview of that term. See also *Ethyl Corp v. EPA*, 541 F.2d 1 (D.C. Cir.), *cert. denied, E.I. du Pont de Nemours & Co. v. EPA*, 426

U.S. 941 (1976), holding that the precautionary nature of the Clean Air Act gave the EPA a right to regulate lead additives in gasoline. Although data was inconclusive as to the health risks of exposure to lead from gasoline, the EPA can regulate where data suggest a "significant risk of harm."

2. **Factors to be considered:** Courts have also interpreted delegations from legislatures to administrative agencies as to what factors should be considered.

**Example:** In *American Textile Manufacturers Institute, Inc. v. Donovan*, 452 U.S. 490 (1981), the court found that OSHA was not required to perform a cost-benefit analysis in determining whether regulations are "feasible."

3. **Adequacy of agency's consideration:** In the vinyl chloride case (*NRDC v. EPA*, 824 F.2d 1146 (D.C. Cir. 1987)), the EPA had made a blanket determination that, since it considers vinyl chloride a carcinogen, there was no safe level of exposure. Then the EPA based regulatory decisions upon the cost and feasibility of controlling vinyl chloride emissions. Upon review, the court held that the requirement that EPA *identify a "safe" exposure level does not mean "risk free,"* and that the EPA must therefore identify a "safe" emission level as the basis for its regulatory scheme. See also *Industrial Union Dept., AFL-CIO v. American Petroleum Institute*, 448 U.S. 607 (1980) (the benzine decision), holding that OSHA could not issue occupational standards for exposure to benzine until it had identified the level of exposure that constituted a "significant risk." The Court looked to the OSHA Act that defined occupational standard as one "reasonably necessary or appropriate to provide safe and healthful employment." The Court then held that "reasonably necessary" implied that a workplace be safe, not risk free, and that to be unsafe a "significant risk" must be present. Until OSHA had determined what level of exposure created a "significant risk," it could not issue occupational standards to regulate that risk.

## II. THE RESOURCE CONSERVATION AND RECOVERY ACT (RCRA)

In 1976, Congress enacted the Resource Conservation and Recovery Act (RCRA) in response to *growing concerns* about the health and *environmental problems* associated with the rising tide of waste materials generated by an increasingly urban population.

A. **Purpose:** The RCRA, codified at 42 U.S.C. §§6901-6987, 9001-9010, provides a *comprehensive regulatory structure for managing both hazardous and non-hazardous solid wastes*. It fits into the federal statutory scheme as a "gap-filler" in that it regulates both *active and inactive* waste disposal sites. The Act contains regulatory standards but also has a health-oriented focus to achieve its goals of conservation, reducing waste disposal, and minimizing present and future threats to human health and the environment.

B. **Structure:** The Act creates *four separate programs* that govern hazardous wastes, non-hazardous wastes, underground storage tanks and used oil. The focus of this section is on RCRA's regulations of hazardous wastes.

1. **Hazardous wastes:** Subtitle C of RCRA sets out a *framework for the regulation and disposal of hazardous wastes*. It creates a "cradle-to-grave" system designed to track hazardous wastes from the point they are generated to the point at which they are disposed.

2. **Non-hazardous wastes:** Subtitle D of RCRA creates a regulatory program for *non-hazardous waste* and requires these wastes to be disposed of in *sanitary landfills*.

3. **Underground storage tanks:** Subtitle I governs storage of materials in *underground storage tanks* (USTs). The program applies to storage of a *range of both unused products* (including gasoline) *and wastes*. Owners and operators under the program are required to register their tanks, upgrade their tanks to achieve technological minimums, and ensure that tanks are properly closed when not in use. §3014, 42 U.S.C. §6935.

4. **Used oil:** RCRA regulates used oil *even if that oil is not a hazardous waste*. The regulations promulgated under this section apply to generators, transporters, sellers, and recyclers of used oil.

5. **Key statutory provisions of RCRA:** Understanding the control of toxic substances in our federal system requires a careful reading of the underlying statutory language. This section provides an overview of the most significant provisions of RCRA.

   - **Section 1004, 42 U.S.C. §6903:** General definitions.

   - **Section 3001, 42 U.S.C. §6921:** Sets forth procedures and requirements for the identification and listing of hazardous wastes; establishes a special subcategory of small quantity generators.

   - **Section 3002, 42 U.S.C. §6922:** Sets forth procedures and requirements for promulgating standards for generators of hazardous waste.

   - **Section 3003, 42 U.S.C. §6923:** Sets forth procedures and requirements for promulgating standards for transporters of hazardous waste.

   - **Section 3004, 42 U.S.C. §6924:** Sets forth procedures and requirements for promulgating standards for owners and operators of hazardous waste treatment, storage, and disposal facilities.

   - **Section 3005, 42 U.S.C. §6925:** Sets forth procedures and requirements for permits for treatment, storage, or disposal of hazardous waste.

   - **Section 3006, 42 U.S.C. §6926:** Authorizes states to develop and administer hazardous waste programs, subject to EPA approval.

   - **Section 3008, 42 U.S.C. §6928:** Establishes range and scope of federal enforcement powers.

   - **Section 3009, 42 U.S.C. §6929:** Permits states to develop hazardous waste regulations more stringent than federal regulations.

   - **Section 3012, 42 U.S.C. §6933:** Sets forth procedures and requirements for developing a hazardous waste site inventory.

   - **Section 3017, 42 U.S.C. §6938:** Sets forth procedures and requirements regarding the export of hazardous waste.

   - **Section 4004, 42 U.S.C. §6944:** Sets forth procedures and requirements for promulgating criteria for sanitary landfills.

   - **Section 4005, 42 U.S.C. §6945:** Prohibits dumping of solid and hazardous wastes at any place other than a sanitary landfill.

- **Section 7002, 42 U.S.C. §6972:** Sets forth procedures, requirements, and jurisdiction for citizen suits.

- **Section 7003, 42 U.S.C. §6973:** Sets forth procedures, requirements, and jurisdiction for government action against persons contributing to an imminent hazard.

- **Section 7006, 42 U.S.C. §6976:** Sets forth standards for judicial review.

C. **Cradle-to-grave program for hazardous wastes:** Subtitle C of RCRA provides a comprehensive system for the "cradle-to-grave" regulation of the *generation, transportation, and treatment, storage, and disposal of hazardous wastes.* See 42 U.S.C. §§6921-6934. This management system requires waste materials to be classified, written manifests to track waste shipments from generation until disposal, and certification of disposal facilities through a permit system.

   1. **Manifests:** A manifest *describing the waste material* accompanies a shipment of waste material throughout its life. §3002(a)(5), 42 U.S.C. §6922(a)(5). The generator, transporter, and disposal facility *must each sign* the manifest and a signed copy of the completed manifest must be returned to the original generator.

   2. **Disposal facility permits, TSDFs:** Hazardous wastes *may only be disposed of at a "treatment, storage, and disposal facility"* (TSDF). §3005(a), 42 U.S.C. §6925(a). TSDFs are required to obtain a *federal permit* before they will be allowed to receive and dispose of shipments of hazardous waste.

D. **Identification of hazardous wastes:** For hazardous materials to be subject to regulation under RCRA they must first *fall under the definition* of solid waste. Only after having made this determination is qualification of the material as hazardous explored.

   1. **Solid wastes:** The first question that must always be asked in deciding whether a material is subject to control as an RCRA hazardous waste is whether it *fits in the definition of "solid wastes."*

      a. **Broad definition of solid wastes:** Solid wastes are defined in §1004(27), 42 U.S.C. §6903(27) to include "any garbage, refuse, sludge from a waste treatment plant, water supply treatment plant, or air pollution control facility and other *discarded* material, including solid, liquid and semisolid, or contained gaseous material resulting from industrial, commercial, mining, and agricultural operations, and from community activities . . ." (emphasis added). This *extremely broad definition* makes RCRA applicable to a far wider range of materials than a common sense understanding of "solid waste" might suggest because it includes semi-solids, liquids, and contained gases.

         i. **Three solid waste groups:** EPA-promulgated regulations further divide the statutory definition of solid waste into three groups: (1) *garbage, refuse, or sludge*; (2) *solid, liquid, semisolid, or contained gaseous material*; or (3) *other substances*. Materials in the first category are always subject to RCRA and those in the third category are always excluded. Materials in the middle category are solid wastes unless specifically excluded by the Act.

         ii. **Excluded wastes:** The Act *does not apply* to certain materials and areas including domestic sewage (even where it contains otherwise hazardous waste), industrial and waste water discharges subject to Clean Water Act permits, irrigation return flows, otherwise regulated nuclear material, and certain mining wastes.

**b. Discarded materials:** RCRA jurisdiction *only* applies to those wastes that are "discarded." While the Act does not define discarded material, regulations promulgated by EPA have defined "discarded material" as any material which is either: (1) *abandoned*; (2) *recycled*; or (3) *considered inherently wastelike*. 40 C.F.R. §261.2(a)(2). EPA published a list of inherently wastelike materials; coverage issues arise under the other two categories.

   **i.    Abandoned materials:** A material is considered "abandoned" if it is *disposed of, burned or incinerated, or accumulated, stored, or treated* (but not recycled) before or in lieu of disposal, burning, or incineration. 40 C.F.R. §261.2(b).

   **ii.    Disposal:** To define disposal, refer to the statutory definitions to see that disposal includes the *discharge, deposit, injection, dumping, spilling, or leaking of waste into the environment*. §1004(3), 42 U.S.C. §6903(3).

   **Example:** Four million pounds of lead shot built up within a trap and skeet shooting range have been held to be hazardous waste that had been "discarded." The lead shot is therefore subject to RCRA regulation. *Connecticut Coastal Fisherman's Ass'n v. Remington Arms Co.*, 777 F. Supp. 173 (D. Conn. 1991), *aff'd in part, rev'd in part on different grounds*, 989 F.2d 1305 (2d Cir. 1993). But see *Long Island Soundkeeper Fund, Inc. v. New York Athletic Club*, 42 Env't Rep. Cas. (BNA) 1421, No. 94 Civ. 0436, 1996 WL 131863 (S.D.N.Y. Mar. 22, 1996) where the court, at the urging of EPA, held that spent shot and target fragments from a trap shooting range did not fall within the regulatory definition of solid waste under RCRA. The court found that the regulatory definition of "solid waste" is narrower than the statutory definition, and that EPA's interpretation of its own regulations is reasonable. Relying on *Chevron, U.S.A., Inc. v. Natural Resources Defense Council*, 467 U.S. 837 (1984), the court gave deference to EPA's interpretation.

**c. Recycled materials:** RCRA's restrictions on waste materials *do not apply to those materials that are recycled, reclaimed, or are still useful*. Unfortunately, the regulations do not define with great precision what constitutes recycled material. Materials that are used in a manner *constituting disposal, burned for energy recovery, reclaimed, or accumulated speculatively are considered solid waste and subject to RCRA*. 40 C.F.R. §261.2(c). However, other recycled materials such as those used as a substitute for a commercial product or those returned as a substitute for raw material feedstock are excluded from RCRA's coverage. 40 C.F.R. §261.2(e). Because the regulations have left many gray areas, the courts have often been called upon to determine whether or not a material is considered recycled or discarded.

   **i.    *American Mining Congress v. EPA*:** In *American Mining Congress*, 824 F.2d 1177 (D.C. Cir. 1987), the court held that EPA *could not treat secondary materials* that were being recycled and reused in an ongoing manufacturing or industrial productions process as RCRA solid wastes. The court noted that the materials had "not yet become part of the disposal problem" because they were "destined for beneficial reuse or recycling in a continuous process by the generating industry itself." 824 F.2d at 1186.

   **ii.    *American Petroleum Inst. v. EPA*:** *American Petroleum Inst.*, 906 F.2d 729 (D.C. Cir. 1990), involved EPA's decision *not to prescribe treatment standards* for K061 slag, even though the material fell within the agency's rules covering materials "derived from" hazardous waste. EPA claimed the material ceased to be discarded when it reached a metals reclamation facility. The court rejected EPA's ruling, reasoning that once K061 had been "discarded," it remained so throughout the waste treatment process.

iii. ***American Mining Congress v. EPA (American Mining Congress II)***: Shortly after the *API* case, industry contested a decision by EPA to relist six wastes generated from primary smelting operations as hazardous. The court in *American Mining Congress II*, 907 F.2d 1179 (D.C. Cir. 1990), stated that the possibility that some of the ***waste might eventually become reclaimed*** in the future ***did not preclude its present characterization*** as solid waste for RCRA regulation. 907 F.2d at 1187.

iv. ***Zands v. Nelson***: In *Zands*, 779 F. Supp. 1254 (S.D. Cal. 1991), the court determined that gasoline leaking from an underground storage tank ***constituted the abandonment***, and ***therefore discarding***, of a solid waste for RCRA purposes. 779 F. Supp. at 1262.

2. **Determining which wastes are hazardous:** RCRA requires EPA to develop criteria for identifying hazardous wastes in one of two ways: (1) by ***"listing" a waste as hazardous*** or (2) by ***determining a waste to be hazardous because of certain "characteristics."*** A solid waste becomes subject to the cradle-to-grave requirements if it is classified as hazardous ***under either approach***. The regulations that actually implement these statutory requirements are very technical, complex, and frequently ambiguous.

   a. **Definition of hazardous wastes:** Hazardous wastes are defined in §1004(5), 42 U.S.C. §6903(5) as:

      a ***solid waste***, or combination of solid wastes, which because of its quantity, concentration, or physical, chemical, or infectious characteristics may —

      (A) cause, or significantly contribute to an increase in mortality or an increase in serious irreversible, or incapacitating reversible illness; or

      (B) pose a substantial present or potential hazard to human health or the environment when improperly treated, stored, transported, disposed of, or otherwise managed (emphasis added).

   b. **Listed hazardous wastes:** The simplest way EPA can designate a waste as hazardous is to ***place the waste on a list*** after a rulemaking proceeding. This can be done if the waste meets any one of three criteria.

      ■ A waste may exhibit ***one of the four hazardous waste characteristics*** (ignitability, corrosivity, reactivity, or toxicity). 40 C.F.R. §261.11(a)(1).

      ■ A waste may be considered ***"acutely toxic" based on studies*** that show even low doses would be fatal to humans. 40 C.F.R. §261.11(a)(2).

      ■ Finally, if a waste ***contains certain toxic constituents*** and, after considering a variety of enumerated factors, the agency determines the waste is ***capable of posing substantial harm*** if managed improperly. 40 C.F.R. §261.11(a)(3).

   c. **Characteristic hazardous wastes:** The second and more common way a waste may be classified as hazardous is by ***looking to a waste's characteristics*** and to the ***knowledge of the waste generator***. EPA regulations lay out the criteria used to identify characteristics of hazardous wastes. Waste that, when tested, meet those criteria qualifies as hazardous waste.

    **i.**    **Identifying characteristic hazardous wastes:** A material is deemed to be hazardous if it is determined that:

        (1) A solid waste exhibits the characteristic that may:

            (i) Cause, or significantly contribute to, an increase in mortality or an increase in serious irreversible, or incapacitating reversible, illness; or

            (ii) Pose a substantial present or potential hazard to human health or the environment when it is improperly treated, stored, transported, disposed of, or otherwise managed; and

        (2) The characteristic can be:

            (i) Measured by an available standardized test method which is reasonably within the capability of the generators of solid waste or private sector laboratories that are available to serve generators of solid waste; or

            (ii) Reasonably detected by generators of solid waste through their knowledge of the waste. 40 C.F.R. §261.10.

    **ii.**    **Four characteristics:** EPA regulations state that a waste is hazardous if it exhibits any one of four characteristics: (1) *ignitability*; (2) *corrosivity*; (3) *reactivity*; or (4) *toxicity*. 40 C.F.R. §§261.21-261.24. Ignitability is the tendency of the waste to catch fire. Corrosivity is a measure of the pH (acidity or alkalinity). Reactivity is the likelihood that the material will explode. EPA provides waste generators with *identification numbers* for these wastes and requires generators to comply with various notification, record keeping, and reporting procedures under the Act. 40 C.F.R. §§261.20, 261.12.

    **iii.**    **Toxicity:** Toxicity is determined by a *complicated "toxicity characteristic leaching procedure"* (TCLP) which tests whether the amount of certain toxins in the waste materials *exceeds allowable levels*. The TCLP approach to toxicity testing was adopted in 1990 and may have tripled the amount of waste classified as hazardous compared to the pre-1990 testing methods. See generally D. Stever, *Law of Chemical Regulation*, §5.02[2][b].

> The toxicity test of EPA has been challenged by several groups; the courts, however, have upheld this test and its procedures. *Edison Electric Institute v. EPA*, 2 F.3d 438 (D.C. Cir. 1993) (holding that the toxicity test that seeks to identify waste which, if mismanaged, may release hazardous materials into the environment was valid and reasonable; EPA need only explain adequately the application of the test to certain mineral processing and electric utility wastes).

  **d.**  **Mixtures and "derived from" wastes:** EPA regulations define hazardous wastes *to include certain mixtures of hazardous and non-hazardous materials*. 40 C.F.R. §261.3(c)(2)(i), (d)(2). The "mixture" rule was written out of concern that *certain industries might avoid RCRA by mixing their hazardous waste* with non-hazardous materials such as dirt in an effort to dilute the waste even though the resulting mixtures would still be environmentally hazardous.

    **i.**    **Mixture rule:** The mixture rule *treats "listed" and "characteristic" hazardous wastes differently*. If a "listed" waste is mixed with non-hazardous material, the resulting mixture will *still be considered hazardous* under RCRA regardless of the actual threat posed by the mixture. 40 C.F.R. §261.3(a)(2)(iii). However, a "characteristic" hazardous waste that is *mixed with a non-hazardous* material *will no longer be considered hazardous* if the generator can show that the *mixture no longer exhibits the hazardous characteristics*. 40 C.F.R. §261.3(a)(2)(iv). Note that the generator has the burden of demonstrating the mixture is no longer hazardous. If he fails to meet this burden, his waste will be presumed hazardous.

ii.   **"Derived from" rule:** Waste "derived from" a *listed hazardous* waste is *deemed hazardous*, but waste "derived from" a *characteristic hazardous* waste *is not unless* it exhibits one of the four characteristics. For example, classification of incinerated waste will depend on what was incinerated. The "derived from" rule sought to close another RCRA loophole in which owners and operators of treatment, storage, and disposal facilities could escape RCRA by limited processing of a hazardous waste.

iii.  **"Contained-in" wastes:** Consistent with the policy of the "mixture rule," EPA has also followed a policy that *any material "containing" a listed hazardous waste is treated as a hazardous waste as well.*

iv.   **Used oil mixture rule:** EPA has had difficulty in establishing rules in this area. One example is seen in its problems with its used oil mixture rule. Under this rule, which issued in 1992, management standards were established which *allowed some oil and mixtures of used oil to escape RCRA hazardous waste regulation.* After several groups challenged these regulations as being inconsistent with *Chemical Waste Management, Inc. v. EPA*, 976 F.2d 2 (D.C. Cir. 1992), Order for Stay of Mandate until Jan. 5, 1993 (D.C. Cir. Nov. 24, 1992), *reh'g denied*, 985 F.2d 1075 (D.C. Cir.), *cert. denied*, 113 S. Ct. 1961 (1993) (holding that dilution is not an appropriate treatment for deactivating intangible, corrosive or reactive wastes if unacceptable levels of hazardous materials remain after treatment), the EPA attempted to rescind the rule using an administrative stay. The D.C. Circuit Court of Appeals, however, held that EPA could not use a stay once a regulation has already been adopted. See *Safety-Kleen Corp. v. EPA*, No. 92-1629 (D.C. Cir. Jan. 19, 1996) (*per curiam*) (finding that the agency could not suspend the regulation absent notice and comment procedures).

e.   **Exclusions:** EPA regulations exclude *certain extremely common materials* from classification as hazardous wastes. Although excluded as hazardous waste, they *may still qualify as solid waste*.

i.   **Household wastes:** These wastes are not considered hazardous even though they *may contain small quantities of hazardous wastes* in them.

   **Example:** In *City of Chicago v. Environmental Defense Fund*, 114 S. Ct. 1988 (1994), the EDF sued, alleging that municipal waste combustion ash generated by a waste-to-energy facility was toxic enough to qualify as a hazardous waste under EPA regulations. The court interpreted the statute to provide an exemption under subsection C to the facility and not the ash. The court reasoned that an ash could be hazardous, even if the product from which it was generated was not because the ash is a new medium in which the contaminants are more concentrated, and the statute specifically omitted "generating" from activities a facility could be engaged in and still be excluded from the regulations.

ii.   **Mining/oil production wastes:** Mining wastes and wastes associated with exploration and production of oil and gas are *excluded* by the Act itself. §3001(b)(2)-(3), 42 U.S.C. §6921(b)(2)-(3). Petroleum and used oil are not excluded.

**E. Requirements for generators, transporters, and treatment, storage, and disposal facilities:** RCRA imposes *specific requirements* on generators and transporters of hazardous waste as well as on those *who treat, store, and dispose* of hazardous waste. Generators and treatment, storage, and disposal facilities must have RCRA permit to operate.

1. **Generators:** Generators *must obtain an EPA identification number* used for all of its waste manifest and reports. The generator *must determine if its wastes are hazardous* by looking at EPA's "listed" hazardous wastes or determining if it is a characteristic hazardous waste. Hazardous waste sent off site *must be accompanied by a manifest* that identifies the type of waste being disposed of and its destination. A generator *may accumulate* waste on-site for up to 90 days *subject to certain restrictions*. Finally, facilities that generate less than 100 kilograms per month are largely exempt from subtitle C and face fewer restrictions on where they dispose of their waste. §3001(d)(4), 42 U.S.C. §6921(d)(4).

   The 1976 Act required all hazardous waste disposal facilities to operate with a permit issued by EPA. Because it was impossible for EPA to process all permit applications by the 1980 deadline, the Act provided that any facility in existence prior to November 19, 1980 could receive an "interim status" *allowing it to operate until a decision could be made on its final permit application* if it turned in "Part A" and met certain minimum requirements. By 1984, Congress became concerned about these interim status facilities and dealt with them in the Hazardous and Solid Waste Amendments (HSWA) to RCRA. The HSWA declared that all interim status facilities which received their interim status prior to November 8, 1984, would lose their interim status on November 8, 1985, unless they (A) turned in "Part B" of the final permit application and (B) certified that they met applicable groundwater monitoring financial responsibility requirements. 42 U.S.C. Section 6925(e)(2). Facilities that failed to meet these new requirements were subject to injunctive relief sought by EPA. See *EPA v. Environmental Waste Control, Inc.*, 917 F.2d 327 (7th Cir. 1990), *cert. denied*, 499 U.S. 975 (1991).

2. **Transporters:** Like generators, transporters *must also obtain* an *EPA identification number*. They may *only transport* hazardous wastes if the wastes are accompanied *by a hazardous waste manifest* provided by the generator, and they may only deliver hazardous wastes to a permitted treatment, storage, and disposal facility. If a transporter fails to return a manifest to the generator within a specified number of days, the generator must notify the relevant environmental agency. Transporters are also regulated by the Department of Transportation under other statutes and regulations.

3. **Treatment, storage, and disposal facilities (TSDFs):** RCRA imposes *stringent requirements* on all treatment, storage, and disposal facilities (TSDFs). The general requirements are laid out in §3004(a), 42 U.S.C. 6924(a).

   a. **Permit required:** All TSDFs *must obtain a permit* before they may receive any hazardous waste. These permits are issued by EPA but may be issued by the state in which the TSDF is located if EPA has delegated authority over the permitting program to the state in question.

   b. **Permit conditions:** Permits *impose many technical requirements* to prevent contamination such as specialized liners in landfills to prevent leakage of pollutants. Permit conditions also require monitoring programs to guard against release of hazardous substances. TSDFs must also demonstrate that they have *sufficient financial* strength to pay for any damages caused by operation of the facility. In addition, the permit may require the TSDF to take *corrective action* to remove hazardous waste and solid waste that are found at the facility or a separate corrective action order may be issued by EPA.

**F.  Land disposal of hazardous wastes, "land ban":** Land disposal of hazardous wastes presented serious problems during the first years of the Act because materials buried in these sites inevitably leak out. Consequently, Congress *generally prohibited land disposal* of hazardous wastes in a move often referred to as the "land ban," although land disposal is still permissible under certain conditions.

**1.  1984 Hazardous and Solid Waste Amendments (HSWA):** In 1984, Congress passed the Hazardous and Solid Waste Amendments (HSWA) in which it issued *tough new schedules* regarding EPA's administration of its hazardous waste management program, set stringent design and performance standards for landfills to prevent leaking, and contemplated a phaseout of land disposal of hazardous wastes. The statute stated outright that landfills and surface impoundments were "the least favored method" for managing hazardous wastes. RCRA §1002(b)(7), 42 U.S.C. §6901(b)(7).

**2.  Land disposal of hazardous wastes generally prohibited:** Generally, the amended RCRA *prohibits all land disposal of hazardous wastes* except when substances are *treated satisfactorily* or a *special petition* is granted. This prohibition on land disposal includes disposal in landfills or underground injection wells. The 1984 RCRA Amendments mandated that EPA come up with *alternative ways* to treat hazardous wastes other than disposing of them on land. To do this, the statute created phased compliance requirements and had EPA divide hazardous wastes into three groups (thirds).

**a.  Treatment exception, BDAT:** An exception will be granted where substances are *"treated" prior to disposal* according to nationally uniform technology requirements. RCRA §3004(m), 42 U.S.C. §6924(m). The treatment exemption was inspired by technology driven provisions in the Clean Water and Clean Air Acts and *requires waste to be treated with the "best demonstrated technology"* (BDAT) before disposal. See 40 C.F.R. Part 286, Subpart D (setting treatment standards for wastes subject to land disposal prohibition). Technology-based standards specify either the *type of pretreatment technology* that must be used or the *levels of toxicity* of the waste that must be achieved. BDAT requirements even set some waste levels below the hazard characteristic level.

**b.  Petition exception if no migration of waste:** EPA can also grant an exemption if a petitioner shows that *its disposal will result in "no migration"* of hazardous substances. RCRA §3004(d)(1), 42 U.S.C. §6924(d)(1). This exemption for which individual petitioners may apply is *extremely difficult to acquire* because §3004 requires the petitioner to show that there will be "no migration" from the hazardous waste disposal site for "as long as the wastes remain hazardous." RCRA §3004(d)(1), (e) and (g); 42 U.S.C. §6924(d)(1), (e) and (g); 40 C.F.R. §268.6(a).

**Example:** As an example of what was required for an exemption, a court held that an EPA standard requiring no migration of hazardous wastes from a deep well injection zone for 10,000 years was reasonable. *Natural Resources Defense Council, Inc. v. EPA*, 907 F.2d 1146, 1158 (D.C. Cir. 1990), *reh'g denied, Natural Resources Defense Council, Inc. v. Reilly*, 1990 U.S. App. LEXIS 18527 (D.C. Cir. Oct. 5, 1990).

**3.  Groundwater contamination from hazardous waste sites:** One of Congress's greatest concerns in passing the 1984 Amendments was the release of liquids from hazardous waste disposal sites into groundwater supplies.

**a. Landfill liquid ban:** Consequently, the amendments placed a *total ban* on the placement of liquid hazardous wastes into landfills. RCRA §3004(c), 42 U.S.C. §6924(c).

**b. Monitoring required:** The amendments also focused on groundwater monitoring as the *best means to detect leaks and implement quick corrective actions*. EPA regulations require three tiers of groundwater monitoring: a basic detection system, more extensive requirements if leachate reaches groundwater, and corrective action if certain tolerance levels are exceeded. RCRA §3004(p), (u), (v); 42 U.S.C. §6924(p), (u), (v); 40 C.F.R. §§264.98-.100.

**G. Export of hazardous wastes:** RCRA requires the *informed consent* of the recipient country before *export of hazardous waste* may take place. §3017, 42 U.S.C. §6938. Anyone seeking to export hazardous wastes *must also notify the EPA*. EPA must then contact and seek the approval of both the receiving country and any country through which the waste is transported. The Basel Convention and other bilateral agreements between the U.S. and receiving countries also govern the export of hazardous waste. See *infra*, p. 181.

**H. Regulation of non-hazardous wastes:** Subtitle D of RCRA primarily deals with disposal of non-hazardous waste in municipal landfills and consists of two major parts.

**1. Sanitary landfills:** Under §4004, 42 U.S.C. §6944, EPA has issued regulations governing landfills receiving *non-hazardous waste*. These facilities are known as *"sanitary landfills."* EPA has also imposed more detailed requirements on certain landfills known as *Municipal Solid Waste Landfills*.

**2. Open dumping ban:** The Act completely *bans dumping of a solid waste*, including non-hazardous wastes, *anywhere other than* at a *sanitary landfill*. §4005(a), 42 U.S.C. §6945(a).

**I. Judicial review:** Section 7003 of RCRA authorizes *judicial review of EPA regulations* and of *EPA's denial or issuance* of permits. Petitions for review of regulations are to be filed only in the U.S. Court of Appeals for the District of Columbia while petitions for review of a permit denial or issuance may be filed in any appropriate court of appeals. Both types of petitions must be filed within ninety days of the EPA action. Section 7002(a)(2) is a citizen suit provision *authorizing suits against EPA for failure to perform acts or duties that are "non-discretionary."*

**J. EPA's powers of remedial action under RCRA §7003:** Section 7003 of RCRA provides the government with a means of responding to existing contamination problems. It states:

> [n]otwithstanding any other provision of this Act, upon receipt of evidence that the past or present handling, storage, treatment, transportation or disposal of any solid waste or hazardous waste may present an *imminent and substantial endangerment* to health or the environment, the Administrator may bring suit on behalf of the United States in the appropriate district court against any person (including any past or present generator, past or present transporter, or past or present owner or operator of a treatment, storage, or disposal facility) who *has contributed or who is contributing to* [such practices] to restrain such person from such handling, storage, treatment, transportation, or disposal, to order such person to take such other action as may be necessary, or both.

RCRA §7003, 42 U.S.C. §6973(a) (emphasis added).

**1. Injunction:** Note that the relief the courts may provide under §7003 is equitable. Compensatory damages for personal injury or property damage are *not available under* this section.

**2. Common law expanded:** In *United States v. Waste Indus. Inc.*, 734 F.2d 159 (4th Cir. 1984), the court stated that while Congress intended RCRA to be interpreted in light of the common law of nuisance, the Act was *meant to be interpreted more liberally* than the former common law. 734 F.2d at 167.

3. ***Prima facie* case for injunction under §7003:** For the government to make a *prima facie* case under §7003, it must show three elements:

- the *conditions* at the site *present an imminent and substantial endangerment*;

- the *danger stems from the handling, storage, treatment, transportation, or disposal* of any solid or hazardous waste; and

- the *defendant has contributed to or is contributing* to that handling, storage, treatment, transportation, or disposal. *United States v. Bliss*, 667 F. Supp. 1298, 1313 (E.D. Mo. 1987).

Once EPA has shown the three required elements, *liability is strict*. Unfortunately, the statute does not define the terms ''contributing to'' or ''imminent and substantial endangerment.''

Notice that a violation of a regulatory provision of RCRA is not necessary to seek relief under §7003.

4. **Section 7003 applies to inactive sites:** In *United States v. Waste Indus. Inc.*, 734 F.2d 159 (4th Cir. 1984), a variety of toxic substances seeped out of a landfill and into an aquifer that provided drinking water for Flemmington, North Carolina. In a ruling that clarified the reach of §7003, the court held that the section *allowed suits to be brought against inactive sites* as well as active ones. 734 F.2d at 167.

5. **Endangerment:** Courts have generally defined endangerment in RCRA by looking to other statutes. In *United States v. Vertac Chem. Corp.*, 489 F. Supp. 870 (E.D. Ark. 1980), the court relied on *Reserve Mining Co. v. EPA*, 514 F.2d 492 (8th Cir. 1975), a case involving the Clean Water Act. In *Vertac*, the government sought an injunction to abate continuing discharge of hazardous pollutants into the soil and groundwater from a landfill. The court stated that *''endangerment'' included a risk of harm that was less than a certainty*. Since toxic materials were escaping from the site, the court held that an abatement order was permissible even though no actual harm had yet occurred. The court observed that injunctive relief was particularly appropriate in circumstances involving scientific uncertainties regarding either the significance of the risk or the probability of exposure.

6. **Expansiveness of §7003:** In *United States v. Price*, 688 F.2d 204 (3d Cir. 1982), toxic waste escaped from a landfill and contaminated an aquifer that served as the public water supply for Atlantic City, New Jersey. The government sought to require the defendants to fund a diagnostic study of the nature of the threat to the water supply and also to provide potable water for landowners with contaminated wells. Although the injunction was not issued for procedural reasons, the court read §7003 very expansively.

> By enacting the endangerment provisions of [RCRA], Congress sought to invoke the broad and flexible powers of the federal courts in instances where hazardous wastes threatened human health. Indeed, these provisions have enhanced the courts' traditional equitable powers by authorizing the issuance of injunctions when there is but a risk of harm, a more lenient standard than the traditional requirement of threatened irreparable harm. 688 F.2d at 211 (citations omitted).

In *Price*, the court stated that *equitable relief could include payment or expenditure of money*. 688 F.2d at 212-213.

7. **Significance of §7003:** After passage of CERCLA, §7003 continues to be important because it applies to endangerment from *non-hazardous* as well as hazardous waste. Also ''contribute to'' may be broader in its reach than CERCLA §106.

**K. Government enforcement:** RCRA gives the federal government a *wide range of enforcement provisions* to ensure compliance with the regulator of provisions hazardous waste management under the Act. RCRA §3008(a), 42 U.S.C. §6928(a). EPA is authorized to assess civil penalties for past or current violations, issue compliance orders, revoke permits, or seek temporary or permanent injunctive relief. RCRA also contains criminal provisions for knowing violations of the Act. RCRA §3008(d), 42 U.S.C. §6928(d).

1. **Civil fines and orders:** Section 3008 authorizes civil penalties and temporary or permanent injunctions against violators. §3008(a), (g), 42 U.S.C. §6928(a). Although the agency may penalize violators as much as $25,000 per day, it is *directed to consider the seriousness of the violation and good faith efforts to comply* with the Act in awarding a fine. Civil enforcement actions are brought in federal district court.

2. **Administrative orders and penalties:** The EPA also has the *option of issuing an administrative order* or penalty without using the courts. §3008(a)-(c), 42 U.S.C. §6928(a)-(c). Penalties of up to $25,000 a day are authorized and the order may direct the violator to take specific actions to comply with the Act. Orders and penalties are subject to administrative and judicial review.

3. **Criminal prosecution:** The RCRA allows for criminal liability, generally premised upon demonstrating a "knowing" violation or endangerment. See RCRA §3008(d), (e), 42 U.S.C. §6928(d).

   a. **Responsible parties:** Both corporations and their responsible officials *can be held criminally liable for company violations* of environmental regulations. Corporations can be held responsible for the *actions of their officers or employees* under the doctrine of respondeat superior. Individual corporate officers can be sentenced to prison terms for their *own actions and for the acts of individuals* under their supervision.

      i. **Corporate liability:** In *Illinois v. O'Neil*, 194 Ill. App. 3d 79, 550 N.E.2d 1090 (Ill. App.), *appeal denied*, 131 Ill. 2d 564, 553 N.E.2d 400 (1990), the court recognized that a corporation can be convicted of a crime, based on the reasoning that the mind and mental state of a corporation is the mind and mental state of the directors, officers, and managers.

      ii. **Liability for corporate officials:** As with other environmental statutes, *corporate officers can be found criminally liable* under RCRA.

         **Example:** In *United States v. MacDonald & Watson Waste Oil Co.*, 933 F.2d 35 (1st Cir. 1991), corporate officers appealed an RCRA criminal conviction of knowingly transporting or causing the transportation of a hazardous waste to a facility which had an RCRA permit, but not for that particular waste, toluene-contaminated soil. The court held that a responsible corporate officer in a position to ensure compliance with the laws could be held criminally liable if the government could show that the officer had actual knowledge of the particular shipment of hazardous waste that violated the Act. 933 F.2d at 55. The court in *MacDonald* also observed that knowledge could be inferred from circumstantial evidence, such as the position and responsibility of the officer and "willful blindness" to the facts constituting the offense. *Id.*

         **Example:** In *United States v. Park*, 421 U.S. 658 (1975), the president of a corporation was convicted under the Federal Food, Drug and Cosmetic Act of causing contamination of food which had traveled in interstate commerce. As president and CEO, the defendant was held to have been advised of and responsible for the operations of the company. The Court held that a *prima facie* case is established when the government introduces evidence sufficient to warrant a finding that the defendant had, by reason of his position in the corporation, responsibility and authority either to prevent or correct the violation, and that he failed to do so.

4. **Knowledge and intent:**  Generally, the government ***need not prove that the defendant knew of the specific statute or regulation*** that he is charged with violating in a criminal prosecution.

  i. **Knowledge as an element of the offense:** The courts have disagreed over precisely what one must know to be criminally liable under RCRA.

   (a) ***Hayes***: In *United States v. Hayes Int'l Corp.*, 786 F.2d 1499 (11th Cir. 1986), the court found that RCRA required a two-fold showing: (1) that the ***defendant knew the material was a hazardous waste*** and (2) that the ***disposal site lacked a permit***. Additionally, the court in *Hayes* stated that the government may prove guilty knowledge with circumstantial evidence. 786 F.2d at 1504-1505.

   (b) ***Johnson***: In *United States v. Johnson & Towers, Inc.*, 741 F.2d 662 (3d Cir. 1984), *cert. denied sub nom., Angel v. United States*, 469 U.S. 1208 (1985), the Third Circuit held that ***knowledge of RCRA permit requirements and knowledge that a company lacks a permit are elements of a criminal violation***. The "knowing" requirement is implied from subsection (d)(2) into 2(A) under RCRA §6928(d)(2)(A).

   (c) ***Hoflin***: In *United States v. Hoflin*, 880 F.2d 1033 (9th Cir. 1989), *cert. denied*, 493 U.S. 1083 (1990), the Ninth Circuit rejected the knowledge requirements of *Johnson* in an RCRA prosecution. It held that ***knowledge of the absence of a permit is not a required element*** of the criminal offense under RCRA §3008(d).

   (d) ***Laughlin***: In *United States v. Laughlin*, 10 F.3d 961 (2d Cir. 1993), *cert. denied, Goldman v. United States*, 114 S. Ct. 1649 (1994), the court held that the knowledge element is satisfied upon a showing that a ***defendant was aware*** that he was performing the proscribed acts. Knowledge of the regulatory requirements or that a permit is lacking is not a necessary element. The court applied this reasoning to RCRA and CERCLA violations.

   (e) **Sentencing guidelines:** Sentencing guidelines for criminal violations of environmental laws ***abolished parole and severely restricted the use of probation*** for environmental crimes. The development of mandatory sentencing guidelines has the potential to increase the sentences received by criminal defendants.

   **Example:**  *United States v. Rutana*, 18 F.3d 363 (6th Cir. 1994), illustrates how sentencing guidelines can be applied in environmental cases. A corporate CEO pled guilty to knowingly discharging pollutants into a public sewer system in violation of the CWA. The Sixth Circuit has remanded the case twice, assigning error to the district court's failure to apply sentencing guidelines by its lenient sentences for the defendant, and demanding stricter sentencing.

L. **Citizen suits:**  Section 7002 of the Act permits individuals to commence an action in Federal District Court to ***enforce RCRA's waste disposal*** requirement or remedy contamination. Using citizen suits, prevailing plaintiffs can obtain equitable relief, civil penalties awards, litigation costs and expert witness fees, and reasonable attorney's fees. RCRA §7002(b)(2), 42 U.S.C. §9672(b)(2). Citizens also may sue *to compel* the Administrator to perform a non-discretionary duty under the Act.

1. **Imminent and substantial endangerment:**  Section 7002(a)(1)(B) permits citizen suits if the citizen can show that someone is creating an *"imminent and substantial endangerment"* from their handling of solid or hazardous wastes. §7002(a)(1)(B), 42 U.S.C. §6972(a)(1)(B). The language mirrors that of §7003 and raises many of the same problems. See pp. 112-113.

2. **Suits barred if agency diligently prosecuting:**  Citizen suits are *barred if EPA or a delegated state has commenced* and is *diligently prosecuting an enforcement action*, although citizens have a right of permissive intervention in enforcement actions. RCRA §7002(b)(2), 42 U.S.C. §9672(b)(2).

3. **Sixty-day notice requirement:**  Before an individual can file suit, he *must* notify the alleged violator, the state, and the EPA of the intent to sue 60 days prior to filing suit.

   **Example:**  In *Hallstrom v. Tillamook County*, 493 U.S. 20 (1989), *reh'g denied*, 493 U.S. 1037 (1990), a suit in which the plaintiff had prevailed on the merits at trial, the District Court was reversed after it was established that the plaintiff's attorney had failed to notify the State and EPA prior to filing the initial claim. The court strictly enforced the 60-day notice provision even though both state and federal agencies indicated that they would not pursue any enforcement action. The court justified its 60-day notice provision and its harsh result by stating that:

   ■ the alleged violator, once on notice of his alleged violation, would have an opportunity to correct the offending conduct;

   ■ government agencies have primary enforcement responsibility which could be undermined by hastily filed citizen suits; and

   ■ judicial efficiency would be improved.

4. **Suits against federal agencies:**  The citizen suit imposes liability on federal agencies for both *"coercive" fines imposed to induce compliance and "punitive" fines imposed to punish for past violations*; sovereign immunity for government agencies is waived in these instances. See generally *United States Dept. of Energy v. Ohio*, 503 U.S. 607 (1992). This waiver of immunity is for all state civil penalties imposed upon an agency under RCRA. *United States v. Colorado*, 990 F.2d 1565 (10th Cir. 1993).

5. **Past cleanup costs:**  The Supreme Court, in *Meghrig v. KFC Western, Inc.*, 116 S. Ct. 1251 (1996) held that the plain language of RCRA §7002 precludes recovery of cleanup costs for a site that, at the time the suit was filed, no longer posed an imminent and substantial endangerment. Pursuant to a health department order, KFC had cleaned up a site it owned which had been previously contaminated with petroleum, and then sought to recover its cleanup costs from the prior owners. The Court suggested that only two types of remedies are available under §7002; a mandatory injunction that orders a party to undertake cleanup or a prohibitory injunction which restrains a party from further violating RCRA. Neither, according to the Court, contemplates past cleanup costs. The Court refused to decide whether a party could obtain cleanup costs after a citizen suit is properly commenced.

6. **Significance of §7002:**  CERCLA only authorizes parties, other than the federal government, to recover cleanup costs under §107. To compel cleanup, a state or private party must use §7002. Also, courts have suggested that the term "contribute to" under §7002 is broader than the term

''arrange for'' in CERCLA §107. Finally, recall that §§7002 and 7003 protect against imminent and substantial endangerment from *non-hazardous* waste as well as hazardous waste. CERCLA §106(a) allows for injunctive relief, but only the EPA may pursue such a course of action.

# III. COMPREHENSIVE ENVIRONMENTAL RESPONSE, COMPENSATION, AND LIABILITY ACT (CERCLA)

A. **Introduction:** The Comprehensive Environmental Response, Compensation, and Liability Act (CERCLA), 42 U.S.C. §§9601-9662, as amended by the Superfund Amendments and Reauthorization Act of 1986 (SARA) has come to have a tremendous impact on real estate *transactions*. Unfortunately, because CERCLA was passed after extensive political compromise during the final months of the 96th Congress, it is far from a model of legislative draftsmanship.

1. **Purpose:** CERCLA is essentially a *tort-like, backward-looking* statute designed to clean up hazardous waste sites and respond to hazardous spills and releases of toxic waste into the environment. In many cases, hazardous waste sites have been abandoned by their original owners or the owners have become bankrupt. Consequently, CERCLA provides *mechanisms for reaching a range of liable parties* to pay cleanup costs which frequently run into the tens of millions of dollars per site or, alternatively, financing for government cleanup of ''orphan'' sites.

2. **Remedial nature of CERCLA:** CERCLA is remedial, rather than regulatory. In contrast to RCRA, which provides for ''cradle-to-grave'' management of *present* hazardous waste activities, CERCLA focuses on remediation of *past* activities. This includes liability for both the past and future cleanup costs of sites. *O'Neil v. Picillo*, 883 F.2d 176 (1st Cir. 1989), *cert. denied sub nom. American Cyanamid Co. v. O'Neil*, 493 U.S. 1071 (1990).

3. **The Superfund:** CERCLA creates the ''Superfund'' which the government may use *to finance governmental response activities*, to pay claims arising from response activities of private parties who are not themselves liable parties under CERCLA, and to compensate federal and state governments for damage to natural resources. CERCLA §111(a), 42 U.S.C. §9611(a). The Superfund is funded largely by excise taxes on industries such as the oil industry and the chemical industry.

4. **Liability generally:** The federal government, state governments and private parties may sue *those responsible for the generation, transportation, or disposal of hazardous substances to recover the costs of cleanup*. CERCLA §107(a), 42 U.S.C. §9607(a). While liability is strict, it is *subject to very limited defenses that the hazardous release was caused solely by an act of God, an act of war, or an act or omission of a third party* unrelated to the defendant. CERCLA §107(b), 42 U.S.C. §9607(b).

Section 107(a) attaches liability to a person *only if there is a release or threatened release* from a facility of hazardous substances. Release applies to an act involving the *spilling or leaching* of hazardous substances and excludes most releases in a workplace covered by the Occupational Safety and Health Act or worker compensations provisions. Likewise, the broad definition of facility includes most areas from which hazardous substances may be released but excludes any consumer product in consumer use.

5. **Delegation of authority:** CERCLA also provides that the President is authorized to take certain actions to respond to releases of hazardous substances, but by Executive Order the President has delegated to EPA the authority to implement activities subject to Presidential control.

6. **Notification of releases:** Notification to the National Response Center of a *release of hazardous substances* is required under §103(a) (42 U.S.C. §9603) by any person who knows of release of a reportable quantity (generally one pound of the substances within a 24-hour period). Section 109 authorizes penalties for the failure to report. 42 U.S.C. §9609.

7. **Key statutory provisions of CERCLA**

   ■ **Section 101, 42 U.S.C. §9601:** General definitions under CERCLA; §101(20)(E) limits lender liability under certain circumstances.

   ■ **Section 102, 42 U.S.C. §9602:** Sets forth procedures and requirements for designation of hazardous substances.

   ■ **Section 103, 42 U.S.C. §9603:** Sets forth notification requirements for substance releases.

   ■ **Section 104, 42 U.S.C. §9604:** Sets forth procedures and requirements for removal or remedial actions by the federal government.

   ■ **Section 105, 42 U.S.C. §9605:** Sets forth procedures and requirements for the promulgation of the National Contingency Plan and a hazard ranking system.

   ■ **Section 106, 42 U.S.C. §9606:** Sets forth procedures and requirements for additional abatement actions, cleanup orders.

   ■ **Section 107, 42 U.S.C. §9607:** Defines potentially responsible parties, scope of liability, and defenses.

   ■ **Section 109, 42 U.S.C. §9609:** Sets forth procedures and requirements for the imposition of civil administrative penalties.

   ■ **Section 111, 42 U.S.C. §9611:** Sets forth procedures and requirements for the use of the Hazardous Substances Superfund.

   ■ **Section 112, 42 U.S.C. §9612:** Sets forth procedures and requirements for claims against the Superfund for response costs.

   ■ **Section 113, 42 U.S.C. §9613:** Sets forth procedures, requirements, and standards of judicial review for civil proceedings under CERCLA.

   ■ **Section 122, 42 U.S.C. §9622:** Sets forth procedures and requirements for settlement agreements under CERCLA.

   ■ **Section 310, 42 U.S.C. §9659:** Sets forth procedures, requirements, and jurisdiction for citizen suits under CERCLA.

B. **Scope of liability:** The central focus of the Act is the liability scheme found in §107(a), 42 U.S.C. §9607(a).

1. **Cost recovery actions:** In CERCLA, Congress created a bifurcated method for cleaning up hazardous waste sites by providing both government and private parties with *authority to respond to hazardous releases at abandoned and inactive waste* disposal sites. The federal government may look to the Superfund in responding to hazardous waste disposal problems and

then seek cleanup costs from any responsible parties or proceed directly against responsible parties. Private parties, even if partially responsible themselves, may sue other responsible parties for their share of the cleanup costs.

a. **CERCLA does not provide a cause of action for all hazardous waste related injuries:** The Act is not intended to create a cause of action for toxic torts *to compensate for every injury* resulting from toxic waste contamination. See *Exxon Corp. v. Hunt*, 475 U.S. 355, 375 (1986). This does not mean, however, that CERCLA prevents states from enacting law to supplement CERCLA and relating to the cleanup of hazardous waste. *Manor Care, Inc. v. Yaskin*, 950 F.2d 122 (3d Cir. 1991).

**Example:** CERCLA does not compensate for economic losses or for personal injuries sustained that are attributable to the release of hazardous waste. *Artesian Water Co. v. Government of New Castle County*, 659 F. Supp. 1269, 1285 (D. Del. 1987).

**Example:** Similarly, diminished property value of a home was deemed a nonrecoverable type of economic loss under CERCLA. *Wehner v. Syntex Corp.*, 681 F. Supp. 651, 653 (N.D. Cal. 1987).

b. *Prima facie* ease for a private cost recovery action: Courts differ somewhat in what a plaintiff must show to recover the costs of cleaning up a site under CERCLA §107. However, the principal required elements are:

- the waste disposal site is a "facility";

- a "release" or "threatened release" of any "hazardous substance" (§101(22), 42 U.S.C. §9601(22)) from that facility has occurred;

- which has caused the claimant to incur cleanup and response costs;

- the costs sought to be recouped were "necessary";

- the actions taken were consistent with the national contingency plan; and

- that the defendant is within one of the four classes of "covered" persons subject to liability.

i. **Facility:** CERCLA defines "facility" in part as "any site or area where a hazardous substance has been *deposited, stored, disposed of, or placed, or otherwise come to be located.*" CERCLA §101(9)(B), 42 U.S.C. §9601(9)(B). Courts have interpreted "facility" very broadly to include "virtually any place at which hazardous wastes have been dumped, or otherwise disposed of." *United States v. Northeastern Pharmaceutical & Chem. Co., Inc.*, 810 F.2d 726 (8th Cir. 1986), *cert. denied*, 484 U.S. 848 (1987).

ii. **Response:** "Response" in CERCLA means two types of actions: *short-term cleanup measures* called "removal" actions and more comprehensive long term *"remedial"* measures involving permanent containment or disposal. While the distinction between the two response types is not always clear, it can have significance to parties seeking to recover costs.

**Example:** A private party undertaking a *remedial* action cannot seek reimbursement from Superfund unless the site is listed on the National Priorities List, but is not limited to Superfund sites in seeking recovery from potentially responsible parties.

**Example:** Since CERCLA does not define "response," courts have had to determine whether medical monitoring and testing for air, soil, and water contamination constituted response costs. In *Ambrogi v. Gould, Inc.*, 750 F. Supp. 1233 (M.D. Pa. 1990), the court found that medical monitoring costs were not recoverable while air, soil, and water testing costs were recoverable. The court explained that the latter were "necessary" for removal of hazardous wastes from the environment which is the purpose of the Act. Medical testing, however, does not remove hazardous wastes from the environment. 750 F. Supp. at 1238.

2. **CERCLA imposes strict and joint and several liability:** Courts have held that CERCLA imposes both *strict liability* and *joint and several liability*. Consequently, a person responsible for only a small fraction of the waste at a site could conceivably be liable for 100 percent of the cleanup costs if no other *responsible parties* could be found. Courts, however, have held that damages should be apportioned if the defendant can demonstrate that the harm is in fact divisible. *O'Neil v. Picillo*, 883 F.2d 176 (1st Cir. 1989), *cert. denied sub nom. American Cyanamid Co. v. O'Neil*, 493 U.S. 1071 (1990). The defendant in such a case has the burden of proving that the harm is divisible. *United States v. Alcan Aluminum Corp.*, 964 F.2d 252 (3d Cir.), *reh'g, en banc, denied*, 1992 U.S. App. LEXIS 17371 (3d Cir. July 27, 1992).

3. **Liable parties under CERCLA:** If a person falls into one of the categories listed in §107(a) that is related to a Superfund site, they become known as *"potentially responsible parties"* (PRPs) until a legal determination is made regarding liability. Section 107(a) makes four classes of persons liable:

■ *current owners or operators* of a facility at which there is a release or threatened release of hazardous substances;

■ *past owners or operators* of such a facility at any time in the past when hazardous substances were "disposed of";

■ any person who *"arranged for"* the treatment or *disposal* of a hazardous substance "owned or possessed by such person" at the facility (usually a generator); and

■ the *persons who transported hazardous* substances to the facility and selected the site.

a. **"Arranged for":** A number of cases have attempted to determine what "arranging for" treatment and disposal of a hazardous waste means. As the following cases indicate, courts have interpreted "arranged for" very broadly.

i. *Aceto Agricultural Chemicals*: In *United States v. Aceto Agric. Chems. Corp.*, 872 F.2d 1373 (8th Cir. 1989), EPA and the state of Iowa attempted to recover ten million dollars in response costs incurred in the cleanup of a pesticide formulation facility. All defendants in the case had contracted with Aidex Corporation to make pesticides for them. The court looked to the common law of abnormally dangerous activities and found the defendants *responsible for the activities of their independent contractor*. 872 F.2d at 1384. Liability existed even though the defendants did not actually manage the disposal of the hazardous waste. As owners of the waste, they were deemed to have authority to control the management and disposal of waste and were therefore found liable for cleanup costs.

ii. *NEPACCO:* In *United States v. Northeastern Pharmaceutical & Chem. Co.*, 810 F.2d 726 (8th Cir. 1986), *cert. denied*, 484 U.S. 848 (1987), a number of NEPACCO's 55 gallon drums filled with hazardous waste were disposed of on Denny farm. Among others, the U.S. sued NEPACCO, Lee, vice president and supervisor of the manufacturing plant, Mills, the shift supervisor, and Michaels, a major shareholder and president of NEPACCO. NEPACCO was clearly responsible as a person that arranged for waste disposal as was Mills who actually took the waste to the farm. The court also found Lee personally responsible because he was personally involved in the disposal decision and because his corporate position gave him authority over management and disposal of hazardous waste sufficient to find that Lee "possessed" the waste within the meaning of §107(a)(3) based on his ***authority to control*** the waste. 810 F.2d at 743. Michaels's liability as an "arranger" was more problematic because he had not been personally involved in the decision. The court declined to address his liability, under §107, finding instead that he could be held liable under the reach of §7003.

iii. **The Superfund Recycling Equity Act (SREA):** In 1999, Congress passed H.R. 3194, exempting certain types of recycling from Superfund liability. Recycling is no longer to be considered "arranging for disposal." Recyclers of paper, scrap rubber, scrap metal, and scrap glass, among other products, are shielded from Superfund liability if they meet certain predetermined factors (*i.e.*, a market exists for the product, the recycled material is substantially used in the creation of a new product, the recycled material meets commercial grading requirements).

b. **Owner/operator:** One of the more noted cases discussing what constitutes an owner/operator is ***State of New York v. Shore Realty Corp.***, 759 F.2d 1032 (2d Cir. 1985). Defendant Leogrande created Shore Realty for the purpose of buying a small tract of land in New York for condominium development. Leogrande was the sole officer and stockholder in the corporation and was aware that tenants had been illegally operating a hazardous waste storage facility. Hundreds of thousands of gallons of hazardous substances were found on the property in deteriorating tanks. The State of New York cleaned up the site and sued Leogrande and Shore to recover costs. Shore Realty was liable as the current owner under Section 107(a)(1). Leogrande was found liable for operating the site. The court noted that an "owner or operator" excludes a person who, without participating in management of a facility, holds indicia of ownership primarily to protect his security interest in the facility. However, Leogrande was found liable under §107(a)(1) because he was a stockholder who owned and managed the corporation.

> It has been held that an "owner" under CERCLA ***need not exercise actual control*** in order to qualify as an "operator" so long as ***authority to control the facility is present***. *Nurad, Inc. v. William E. Hooper & Sons Co.*, 966 F.2d 837, *cert. denied sub nom. Mumaw v. Nurad, Inc.*, 506 U.S. 940 (1992). See also *Union Gas Co. v. Pennsylvania*, 35 Env't Rep. Cas. (BNA) 1750 (E.D. Pa. Sept. 30, 1992) where the court held that ownership of an easement on contaminated land may constitute operator liability, and that owner liability may stem from state ownership of a creek bed as a navigable waterway.

**Example:** In *New York v. General Electric Co.*, 592 F. Supp. 291 (N.D.N.Y. 1984), the state of New York sought to recover cleanup costs of used transformer oil containing PCBs and other hazardous materials that had been sold to a dragstrip by G.E. The court found that GE had knowledge or imputed knowledge that the oil would be placed on land surrounding the dragstrip and stated that liability under CERCLA could not be avoided by characterizing arrangements as sales or by contracting away responsibilities.

**Compare:** Compare *Florida Power and Light Co. v. Allis Chalmers Co.*, 27 Env't Rep. Cas. (BNA) at 1558-1560 (S.D. Fla. 1988) (Allis Chalmers was far removed from disposal because *Florida Power* had purchased electrical transformers for forty years and then disposed of them) and *Prudential Insurance Co. of America v. U.S. Gypsum*, 711 F. Supp. 1244 (D.N.J. 1989) (the court held that the sale of asbestos-containing products used in the construction of a building did not constitute disposal for the purpose of CERCLA liability because the manufacturer had not acted to get rid of the asbestos beyond the sale transaction).

**Sale of waste:** Sale of waste ***does not provide per se insulation from liability*** under CERCLA. *Nurad, Inc. v. William E. Hooper & Sons Co.*, 966 F.2d 837 (4th Cir. 1992), *cert. denied sub nom. Mumaw v. Nurad, Inc.*, 506 U.S. 940 (1992). Nevertheless, if the substance is sold for incorporation into useful products, then the seller will retain no liability.

c. **Parent corporation liability:** Often PRPs are subsidiary companies, owned in whole or in part by another company. May the parent company be held liable under CERCLA? In *United States v. Bestfoods*, 524 U.S. 51 (1998), the Supreme Court held that parent companies may be held liable under two distinct theories — direct or derivative liability. Under a direct liability theory, courts are to look at the relationship between the parent company and the *facility*. If the parent manages, directs, or conducts operations specifically related to disposal, leakage, or compliance with environmental regulations, they may be held liable as an operator under §107(a)(2). The Court was less clear on the principles of derivative liability, declining to rule on whether state or federal common law should be applied in "piercing the corporate veil." The case was remanded to the United States District Court for the Western District of Michigan, where that court found that Bestfoods's involvement with the facility was insufficient to establish direct liability.

d. **Successor liability:** What happens when the assets of a PRP have been purchased by another corporation? The issue of successor liability was addressed by the First Circuit in *United States v. Davis*, 261 F.3d 1 (1st Cir. 2001). Citing *Bestfoods*, the First Circuit held that Connecticut's "mere continuation" test for successor liability was appropriate, rather than the federal "substantial continuation" test. Under this test, the First Circuit looked at a number of factors, including the transfer of assets by the divesting corporation, continuation of the same business by the buyer, commonality of officers between the buyer and the seller, and transaction costs. However, two district courts have applied federal common law and the "substantial continuation" test. See *Norfolk Southern R.R. v. Gee Co.*, 2001 WL 710116 (N.D. Ill. 2001) and *New York v. National Services Industries*, 134 F. Supp. 2d 275 (E.D.N.Y. 2001). See also *United States v. Exide Corp.*, 2002 WL 319940 (E.D. Pa. 2002) (holding that where a corporation continues the business of its corporate predecessor with the same employees, shareholders, facilities, and management, it may be found liable under Superfund after applying the "de facto merger" or "substantial continuity of business" test).

e. **Individual liability:** May individuals acting in a corporate capacity be held liable under CERCLA? Both the Connecticut and the Indiana Supreme Courts have adopted the "responsible corporate officer" doctrine, which imposes liability on corporate officers who are in a position of control or influence, actually influence the actions of the corporation, and whose actions lead to the violation. *BEC Corp. v. Connecticut Department of Environmental Protection*, 775 A.2d 928 (Conn. 2001); *Indiana Department of Environmental Management v. RLG, Inc.*, 755 N.E.2d 556 (Ind. 2001). The Fourth Circuit also relied on the responsible officer doctrine to uphold a criminal conviction of a defendant under the Clean Water Act. *United States v. Hong*, 242 F.3d 528 (4th Cir. 2001).

4. **RCRA §7003 compared to CERCLA §§106(a) and 107(a):** EPA frequently seeks to impose liability on potentially responsible parties under both RCRA §7003 and CERCLA §107(a) or CERCLA §106(a). Conceptually, RCRA §7003 is broader than CERCLA because it *includes those who "contribute"* to the offending conduct while CERCLA includes those who *"arrange for"* hazardous waste disposal. However, CERCLA provides the government with several powerful tools.

   a. **Section 106(a):** CERCLA §106(a) is *available only to the federal government* and allows EPA to issue abatement orders. Unlike RCRA §7003 and CERCLA §107(a), CERCLA §106(a) contains no limitation on the class of persons subject to abatement orders.

   b. **Threat levels that trigger each section:** Both RCRA §7003 and CERCLA §106(a) are triggered by conduct which *"may present an imminent and substantial endangerment."* While this is a broad standard, it is more rigorous than the mere showing of a "threat of a release" required under CERCLA §107(a).

   c. **Private parties and states seeking abatement:** Private parties and states seeking abatement of potential harms from hazardous substances *will be forced to use RCRA §7002* since §106(a) of CERCLA is available only to EPA and §107 only allows for cleanup costs.

5. **Hazardous substances:** One of the requirements for private cost recovery under CERCLA §107(a) is the *presence of a hazardous substance at the site*. By covering hazardous and non-hazardous "solid wastes," RCRA reaches a broader range of substances than CERCLA, which only covers "hazardous substances" as defined in §101(14).

   a. **Definition incorporates hazardous substances from other environmental acts:** However, the definition of "hazardous substances" in CERCLA *incorporates by reference* hazardous or toxic substances under RCRA, the Clean Water Act, the Clean Air Act, and the Toxic Substances Control Act. See §101(14), 42 U.S.C. §9601(14). Consequently, a material that is not considered a "hazardous waste" under RCRA may be considered a "hazardous substance" under CERCLA. EPA can also designate a substance as hazardous for purposes of CERCLA.

   b. **Other pollutants or contaminants:** CERCLA gives EPA broad authority to respond to "pollutants or contaminants" which have not been designated as hazardous in circumstances which *"may present an imminent and substantial endangerment"* to health or the environment. See 42 U.S.C. §9604(a)(1)(B); §9601(33) (defining "pollutant or contaminant").

   c. **Petroleum and natural gas excluded:** CERCLA *specifically excludes* petroleum and natural gas from the definition of "hazardous substances" under §101(14) and from "pollutants or contaminants" under §101(33). The exclusion *does not apply*, however, *to petroleum products or contaminants*. Leakage of petroleum from underground storage tanks is addressed by RCRA §9003, 42 U.S.C. §6991b, but it does not allow for private cost recovery.

6. **Disposal:** Liability under §107(a) also *requires a showing that the hazardous substances were "disposed of."* Courts have held that strict liability under §107(a) will not attach unless the disposal is characterized as *an affirmative act to "get rid of" or "dump" the waste*. Sales

or transfers of a useful product are not considered disposal. Since courts will examine the character of a transaction, merely labeling something as a "sale" will not exculpate the person from liability. See *supra*, p. 122.

**Example:** In *Prudential Ins. Co. of America v. United States Gypsum,* 711 F. Supp. 1244, 1254 (D.N.J. 1989), the court held that sale of asbestos-containing products used in the construction of a building did not constitute disposal.

> The definition of "disposal," however, has been held to have a range of meanings, with both active and passive conduct of the owner/operator constituting "disposal." *Nurad, Inc. v. William E. Hooper & Sons Co.*, 966 F.2d 837 (holding that the "reposing of hazardous waste and its subsequent movement through the environment" fits within the definition of "disposal"), *cert. denied sub nom. Mumaw v. Nurad, Inc.*, 506 U.S. 940 (1992). But see *Carson Harbor Village Ltd. v. Unocal Corp.*, 270 F.3d 863 (9th Cir. 2001), *cert. denied*, 122 S. Ct. 1437 (2002) (holding that contaminants which spread passively into the soil do not constitute "disposal" under CERCLA). It is hoped that the Supreme Court will resolve the array of views currently held by five of the circuits.

7. **Retroactivity:** In *United States v. Northeastern Pharmaceutical Chem. Corp.*, 810 F.2d 726, 734 (8th Cir. 1986), *cert. denied*, 484 U.S. 848 (1987), the court determined that Congress intended CERCLA to be applied retroactively to acts committed before the effective date (December 11, 1980) of the statute and that such retroactivity *did not violate due process*. Most courts have upheld CERCLA as constitutional despite its retroactive impact. More controversial as a policy matter is the fairness of holding a party liable for extensive cleanup costs for disposal practices which were legal at the time the practices occurred. Should the parties pay who benefitted from less expensive (and less safe) disposal practices, or should the parties who benefit from cleanup pay (*i.e.*, the public at large)?

8. **Burden of proof regarding consistency with NCP:** One of the elements for a cost recovery action is that costs incurred cleaning up the site be *consistent* with the National Contingency Plan (NCP).

   a. **National Contingency Plan:** The NCP is authorized by §105 of CERCLA, 42 U.S.C. §9605, and is designed to establish *procedures and standards for preparing for and responding to* releases of hazardous substances. See 40 C.F.R. §300.1.

   b. **Recovery by private parties:** A private party *can only recover costs that it shows are consistent* with the NCP. Private parties must show that their cleanup actions were in *"substantial compliance"* with enumerated requirements and resulted in a "CERCLA-quality cleanup." 40 C.F.R. §300(c)(3)(i).

   c. **Recovery by government:** Unlike private parties, the court in *United States v. Northeastern Pharmaceutical Chem. Corp.*, 810 F.2d 726, 747 (8th Cir. 1986), *cert. denied*, 484 U.S. 848 (1987), noted that §107(a)(4)(A), 42 U.S.C. §9607(a)(4)(A) means that the government's costs are presumptively recoverable unless the defendant proves *inconsistency* with the NCP.

   d. **Opportunity for public comment:** Courts have held that a *failure to provide an opportunity* for public comment regarding a response action is *inconsistent* with the NCP and therefore bars recovery. See *Channel Master Satellite Systems, Inc. v. JFD Elec. Corp.*, 748 F. Supp. 373, 389-390 (E.D.N.C. 1990).

9. **National Priorities List (NPL):** In giving EPA broad authority to respond to hazardous waste sites, CERCLA authorizes EPA to create a *list of the worst hazardous waste sites* in the country. These sites are then placed on the National Priorities List (NPL).

   a. **Hazard Ranking System (HRS):** Recognizing that the number of potential hazardous waste sites requiring remediation far exceeds the EPA's administrative and financial resources, CERCLA requires the agency to establish a procedure for *identifying and ranking which sites warrant the highest priority* for remedial action. CERCLA §105, 42 U.S.C. §9605. The EPA employs a Hazard Ranking System (HRS) for determining which waste sites should be placed on the National Priorities List (NPL). The HRS assigns a "score" to each site based on various risk assessment criteria such as the potential for contamination of drinking water supplies and the destruction of sensitive ecosystems.

   b. **Superfund and NPL:** The EPA can use Superfund resources for undertaking a *remedial* action *only* at sites on the NPL. 40 C.F.R. §300.425(b). *Removal* actions, however, may be conducted by the government or private parties regardless of the listing status of the site.

   c. **NPL and recovery of non-Superfund costs:** Inclusion on the NPL is *not a precondition* for agency action pursuant to §106 or §122 or for recovery of non-Fund financed costs under §107. See 40 C.F.R. §300.425(b)(4).

   **Example:** In *State of New York v. Shore Realty Corp.*, 759 F.2d 1032, 1045 (2d Cir. 1985), the court determined that although the site was not on the NPL, inclusion on the NPL was not a requirement for New York to be able to recover cleanup costs from defendant Leograndc.

10. **EPA's enforcement options:** When EPA determines that an actual or threatened release of hazardous substances presents an "imminent and substantial endangerment" to health or the environment, the EPA may *issue the responsible party an abatement order* to compel cleanup pursuant to §106(a) or go to federal district court to obtain such an order. 42 U.S.C. §9606(a). Alternatively, the agency may conduct the cleanup itself using funds from the Superfund for sites on the NPL. The statute also authorizes EPA to obtain reimbursement of its actual costs incurred in performing the cleanup (§107(a)(4)(A)).

    a. **Fines:** The EPA may bring an action in federal district court to hold the violator in contempt or to impose fines of up to $5,000 per day for noncompliance.

    b. **Punitive damages:** Section 107(c)(3), 42 U.S.C. §9607(c)(3), states that EPA may recover *three times* the cleanup costs against a responsible party who fails to comply with an abatement order "without sufficient cause."

    c. **No pre-enforcement judicial review:** To expedite cleanup of hazardous waste sites, §113(h) of CERCLA *precludes pre-enforcement judicial review* of the merits of EPA's compliance and abatement orders.

    **Note:** The combination of possible treble damages and no pre-enforcement judicial review can place defendants in a very difficult position. See *Solid State Circuits, Inc. v. EPA*, 812 F.2d 383 (8th Cir. 1987) (finding that treble damages and §113(h) do not violate due process). If an innocent party cleans up a site pursuant to a §106 abatement order or the order is found to be arbitrary and capricious, the party may petition EPA for reimbursement from Superfund under §112(h), 42 U.S.C. §9612(h).

11. **Jury trial:** An important question in evaluating the nature of remedies sought for environmental harm is whether the parties have a constitutional right to a jury trial. The jury right is *consti-*

*tutionally mandated if the relief sought is characterized as a legal action pursuant to common law or statute*, but is not recognized for equitable claims. *Ross v. Bernhard*, 396 U.S. 531 (1970).

**Example:** In *Northeastern Pharmaceutical*, the court characterized the government's recovery of response costs under CERCLA as equitable and therefore not implicating defendant's right to jury trial. The court reasoned that reimbursement of such costs in effect was in the form of restitution rather than legal damages. The court cited *United States v. Mexico Feed & Seed Co., Inc.*, 729 F. Supp. 1250, 1254 (E.D. Mo. 1990).

**Example:** In *Acushnet River v. New Bedford Harbor: Proceedings re Alleged PCB Pollution*, 712 F. Supp. 994 (D. Mass. 1989), the court held that the Seventh Amendment required a jury trial for issues regarding claims for injuries to natural resources brought by the government under CERCLA. The court noted that although the statute was silent with respect to the right of jury trial, the type of relief sought under CERCLA was analogous to common law tort claims for diminution in value and loss of use of natural resources. Consequently defendant had a right to a jury trial.

12. **Attorneys' fees:** Courts have sharply split over whether the prevailing party in a private cost recovery suit under CERCLA may be awarded attorneys' fees.

   a. **American Rule:** Under the "American Rule," a successful plaintiff in federal court *cannot receive litigations costs absent a showing of bad faith* litigation or a statutory authorization. The Supreme Court embraced this view in *Alyeska Pipeline Serv. Co. v. Wilderness Soc'y*, 421 U.S. 240 (1975), in which it denied attorneys' fees to a citizens' group which successfully challenged a government action under federal environmental laws. After this ruling, many environmental statutes were amended to authorize recovery of attorneys' fees for prevailing parties.

   b. **CERCLA:** Under CERCLA, attorneys' fees are *expressly authorized* for government response actions in §104(b)(1), 42 U.S.C. §9604(b)(1), and for citizen's suits under §310(f), 42 U.S.C. §9659(f), but are not explicitly provided for in private cost recovery actions.

   c. **Courts prohibiting attorneys' fees:** Several courts have viewed the lack of an explicit provision for fee awards in private cost recovery actions as a reflection of *congressional intent to preclude* an award of attorneys' fees under this section. See, *e.g., T & E Indus., Inc. v. Safety Light Corp.*, 680 F. Supp. 696, 708 (D.N.J. 1988).

   d. **Courts allowing attorneys' fee awards:** A number of courts have found *sufficient authorization* for attorneys' fees in the definition of response costs which includes "enforcement activities" and from the underlying policies of CERCLA as a remedial statute. See, *e.g.,* 42 U.S.C. §101(25); *General Elec. Co. v. Litton Indus. Automation Sys., Inc.*, 920 F.2d 1415, 1422 (8th Cir. 1990), *cert. denied*, 499 U.S. 937 (1991); *Pease & Curren Refining, Inc. v. Spectrolab, Inc.*, 744 F. Supp. 945, 951 (C.D. Cal. 1990).

C. **Defenses:** While liability is strict under CERCLA it is not absolute.

1. **CERCLA liberalizes causation requirement:** Instead of the traditional concept of limiting accountability to the harms directly traceable to the offending conduct, CERCLA *dispenses with any "fingerprinting"* of the defendant's waste and the release which required expenditure of response costs. This treatment of causation reflects two policies — one scientific and the other a public interest.

a. **Scientific rationale:** The scientific rationale recognizes that *waste sites often contain chemicals and substances from numerous generators* which have commingled, making a specific causal link of a particular waste to the harm virtually impossible. Consequently, CERCLA shifts the burden to the defendant to *prove* that its waste is not responsible for the harm.

b. **Public interest:** The moderated causation requirement reflects an *effort to impose liability more readily* and effectively on the actors responsible.

**Example:** In *City of New York v. Exxon Corp.*, 744 F. Supp. 474 (S.D.N.Y. 1990), the court held that a party may be liable under the Act merely by showing that the defendant disposed of hazardous waste at a facility which now contains substances of "the kind" attributable to the defendant and that a release or threatened release of that or any hazardous substance caused response costs to be incurred. 744 F. Supp. at 483.

**Example:** Similarly, in *United States v. Monsanto Co.*, 858 F.2d 160 (4th Cir. 1988), *cert. denied*, 490 U.S. 1106 (1989), the court held that the statute was satisfied by proof that hazardous substances "like" those contained in the generator defendants' waste were found at this site. 858 F.2d at 169.

**Example:** In *Artesian Water Co. v. Government of New Castle County*, 659 F. Supp. 1269 (D. Del. 1987), the plaintiff water company sought to recover its costs of cleanup of a polluted aquifer under CERCLA. The defendant challenged the causal link necessary to establish liability because leachate from several nearby landfills could have caused the contamination. The court rejected a "but for" causation approach and instead held that causation was satisfied if the release of contamination from defendant's landfill was a *substantial factor* in producing plaintiff's injury. 659 F. Supp. at 1283.

c. **Joint and several liability exists if harm is indivisible:** The court in *Monsanto* also held that *joint and several liability existed*, in accordance with common law principles, where the *defendants caused a single indivisible harm*. 858 F.2d at 172. Since the harm is almost always indivisible at Superfund sites, joint and several liability is almost always applied.

2. **Three narrow affirmative defenses:** Three narrow affirmative defenses to causation-based liability exist under §107(b).

- The hazardous substance release was caused *solely* by an act of God.

- The hazardous substance release was caused *solely* by an act of war.

- The hazardous substance release was attributed *solely* to a third party unaffiliated and unrelated to the defendant.

3. **Defendant bears burden of proof:** The defendant bears the burden of *establishing one of the defenses* by a preponderance of the evidence.

4. **Innocent landowner defense:** One important manifestation of the third party defense is the innocent landowner defense. This allows a landowner to *escape liability* by showing that the harm was *caused "solely" by a third party*. Unfortunately for most defendants, the defense is narrowly construed since it was largely intended to preclude liability in cases where vandals cause damage to hazardous waste sites.

a. **Elements:** Section 107(b)(3) describes the elements of the innocent landowner defense.

■ The release or threat of release and damages were caused *solely* by the third party.

■ The third party's act or omission *did not occur in connection* with a contractual relationship with the defendant.

■ The defendant *exercised due care* with respect to the hazardous substance.

■ The defendant "*took precautions against* foreseeable acts or omissions of any such third party and the consequences that could foreseeably result from such actions."

The essence of the defense is demonstrating a *complete absence of responsibility* for causing the harm and exercising due diligence in managing the property. Partial fault by the landowner invalidates the defense. See also, *United States v. Pacific Hide & Fur Depot, Inc.*, 716 F. Supp. 1341, 1346-1347 (D. Idaho 1989).

**b. United States v. Monsanto:** In *United States v. Monsanto Co.*, 858 F.2d 160 (4th Cir. 1988), *cert. denied*, 490 U.S. 1106 (1989), hazardous substances leaked from decaying drums and commingled with incompatible chemicals, generating noxious fumes, fires, and explosions. The government brought suit against the site owners and non-settling waste generators under CERCLA §107(a). The site owners claimed that they were merely innocent landowners and had no involvement in disposal. However, the defense failed. First, the owners had entered into a lease agreement with the site operators and therefore a contractual relationship related to the harm existed. Second, the site owners presented no evidence that they took precautionary action against the foreseeable conduct of the site operators. As the court stated, "the statute *does not sanction such willful or negligent blindness* on the part of absentee owners." 858 F.2d at 168.

**c. "Contractual relationship":** The second element in the innocent landowner defense requires that the defendant had *no contractual relationship* with the third party connected to the harms caused by the third party. In 1986, Congress added CERCLA §101(35)(A), 42 U.S.C. §9601(35)(A), which explained what was meant by a contractual relationship.

**i. Real estate transactions included:** The definition includes real estate transactions *unless* the defendant acquired the property *after* the disposal of hazardous waste and the defendant did not know or have reason to know of the presence of hazardous waste at the site.

**ii. Landowner's knowledge:** The investigation into a landowner's knowledge of hazardous waste asks whether the landowner exercised due care in *investigating the property* "consistent with good commercial practice" and takes into account any "specialized knowledge or experience" on the part of the defendant. CERCLA §101(35)(A), 42 U.S.C. §9601(35)(A). Consequently, a large business will be expected to do a more comprehensive land inspection than the average home buyer.

**5. Lender liability:** Section 101(20)(A) of CERCLA, 42 U.S.C. §9601(20)(A), excludes from the definition of owner/operator those institutions that hold the property as a security interest, such as a bank. This exclusion *does not apply if the lender "participated in management"* rather than simply held the property on paper. *United States v. Fleet Factors Corp.*, 901 F.2d 1550 (11th Cir.), *reh'g denied, en banc*, 911 F.2d 742 (11th Cir. 1990), *cert. denied*, 498 U.S. 1046 (1991). The uncertainty created in *Fleet Factors* prompted the EPA to promulgate regulations that broadly defined actions that would not destroy a lender's exemption from CERCLA.

In 1994, however, the D.C. Circuit vacated the EPA regulations in *Kelley v. EPA*, 15 F.3d 1100 (1994), *reh'g denied, Kelley ex rel. Michigan v. EPA*, 25 F.3d 1088 (D.C. Cir. 1994), *cert. denied by, American Bankers Ass'n v. Kelley*, 115 S. Ct. 900 (1995), finding that EPA did not have the authority to issue regulations defining lender liability. Then, in 1995, the EPA responded to this judicial invalidation and issued a new policy statement. The statement recognized that while the EPA lacked the authority to issue a binding regulation, it intended to use the 1992 Lender Liability Rule as enforcement policy.

In 1996 Congress passed legislation as part of the Omnibus Budget Act that amended §107 of CERCLA. Among other things, the legislation, entitled the Asset Conservation, Lender Liability and Deposit Insurance Protection Act of 1996, further defined the liability of fiduciaries. In the definition of owner or operator, it amended §101(20) by excluding from the definition a person that did not participate in management "notwithstanding that the person forecloses on the facility. In addition, the legislation further defined participation in management for purposes of CERCLA to include a lender who "exercises decisionmaking control over the environmental compliance . . . such that the person has undertaken responsibility for the hazardous substance handling or disposal practices," and a lender who "exercises control at a level comparable to that of a manager . . . such that the person has assumed or manifested responsibility (aa) for the overall management . . . encompassing day-to-day decisionmaking with respect to environmental compliance; or (bb) over all or substantially all of the operational functions . . . other than the function of environmental compliance."

In *Canadyne-Georgia Corp. v. Nations-Bank N.A.*, 183 F.3d 1269 (11th Cir. 1999), the Eleventh Circuit held that a bank acting as a trustee for a business may be held liable under CERCLA because of their partnership interest. Whether this is consistent with congressional intent in amending §101(20) is unclear.

6. **Bankruptcy:** Some claims that arise before the debtor files bankruptcy are discharged under the federal Bankruptcy Code. Courts are split as to when a claim under CERCLA arises for this issue. Some courts have found the CERCLA action to become a claim *when the waste is released*; this formula could discharge a debtor before the person asserting the CERCLA claim could identify the debtor as responsible. Other courts have held CERCLA actions to be claims for discharge only if the person asserting the claim *had reason to know* of the potential claim before the bankruptcy. In either case, bankruptcy will not discharge liability of injunctive orders concerning ongoing problems.

D. **Settlement:** Section 122 of CERCLA, 42 U.S.C. §9622, clearly reflects Congress's view that *settlement should be pursued* where the public interest in cleanup of hazardous waste sites can be accomplished. While §122 encourages settlement where practicable and in the public interest, the ultimate decision regarding settlement rests with EPA.

1. **Settlement through consent decrees:** CERCLA litigation typically involves complex technical and scientific issues implicating numerous parties with diverse interests and concerns. From the government's perspective, settlement through consent decrees offers an attractive vehicle to *economize limited administrative resources* while expeditiously cleaning up hazardous waste sites.

   a. **PRPs have incentive to settle:** CERCLA contains several provisions which give PRPs *tremendous incentives to forego litigation* and agree to settlement even under relatively unfavorable terms. These provisions include the following:

   ■ A statutory scheme of strict liability with narrow defenses;

- ▪ Imposition of joint and several liability irrespective of fault;

- ▪ Settling parties shielded from contribution claims;

- ▪ Non-settlors effectively penalized by bearing a risk of disproportionate liability.

   **b. Adding PRPs in consent decrees:** After PRPs are held liable in a CERCLA contribution action, other PRPs may be added in consent decrees even if they have not been sued by the United States. See *United States v. Davis*, 261 F.3d 1 (1st Cir. 2001).

2. **Three types of settlement:** Three distinct types of settlements are provided for in CERCLA §122: (1) *agreements for the cleanup* of a hazardous waste site; (2) *de minimis settlement* with small volume generators; and (3) *cost recovery settlements*. EPA has considerable discretion in deciding which, if any, settlement route to pursue.

3. *De minimis* **waste contributors:** The *system* of joint and several liability employed by CERCLA may result in certain parties bearing a disproportionate amount of cleanup costs. The harshness of this scheme is partially alleviated by providing *special settlement alternatives* for *de minimis* waste contributors. Parties who enter into a *de minimis* settlement are shielded from later contribution claims. CERCLA §122(g)(5), 42 U.S.C. §9622(g)(5). There are two general classes of *de minimis* contributors:

   **a. Small volume contributors:** A small volume contributor whose volume and toxicity of *waste are minimal compared* to the *waste* at the site may be considered *de minimis*. CERCLA §122(g)(1)(A), 42 U.S.C. §9622(g)(1)(A). Typically, a *de minimis* contributor is one who has contributed no *more than 1 percent* of the volume of waste sent to a given site.

   **b. Property owners:** *De minimis* treatment also may be given to property owners who *did not contribute* to the release of hazardous substances through act or omission, provided they *acquired the property without knowledge* of the toxic waste.

   **Example:** In *United States v. Cannons Eng'g Corp.*, 899 F.2d 79 (1st Cir. 1990), a case involving over 400 PRPs, 384 different defendants were classified as *de minimis*. EPA established a cutoff that allowed parties to be considered *de minimis* if they contributed less than one percent of the total volume of waste found at the site. Many of these PRPs entered into a consent decree with EPA which absolved them of further liability on the condition that they pay EPA 160 percent of their volumetric share of the projected cleanup costs.

4. **Contribution:** When Congress amended CERCLA in 1986, it provided that any potentially responsible party had the *right to seek contribution* from other PRPs during or following an action under §§106 or 107. See CERCLA §113(f)(1), 42 U.S.C. §9613(f)(1). A party seeking contribution must be or have been a defendant to a CERCLA §§106 or 107 action; however, CERCLA does not affect a party's ability to seek contribution under state law. See *Aviall Services, Inc. v. Cooper Ind. Inc.*, 263 F.3d 134 (5th Cir. 2001).

   **a. Factors considered in allocating costs:** Courts have considered a wide variety of factors in allocating costs including:

- ▪ The *degree of fault* in the generation, transportation, treatment, storage, or disposal of hazardous waste;

- ▪ The *amount* of hazardous waste involved;

- ▪ The *degree of toxicity* of the hazardous waste involved;

- The *degree of cooperation* by the parties with government officials to prevent any harm to the public health or the environment; and

- The *benefits received* from the contaminating activities.

See *Weyerhauser Corp. v. Koppers Co., Inc.*, 771 F. Supp. 1406, 1426 (D. Md. 1991); *United States v. Monsanto Co.*, 858 F.2d 160, 168 n.13 (4th Cir. 1988), *cert. denied*, 490 U.S. 1106 (1989); *United States v. A & F Materials Co., Inc.*, 578 F. Supp. 1249, 1256 (S.D. Ill. 1984).

b. **Nonbinding allocation of responsibility (NBAR):** To facilitate the negotiating process, §122 gives EPA *the discretion to allocate 100 percent of the response costs* among PRPs prior to cleanup by assessing non-binding allocations of responsibility (NBAR). CERCLA §122(e)(3). The NBAR serves as a useful framework for PRPs to allocate cleanup costs among themselves and to develop settlement offers.

c. **Settling parties immune from further liability:** The contribution amendments to CERCLA encourage settlement of CERCLA cases by making the *settling party immune from future liability* if the settlement is administratively or judicially approved. See *United States v. Alcan Aluminum Corp.*, 25 F.3d 1174 (3d Cir. 1994). Section 113(f) thus extinguishes the contribution rights of PRPs against parties that have settled with the United States or a state with respect to matters contained in the settlement. However, the settling parties are still entitled to seek contribution from other potentially responsible parties.

d. **Settlement reduces remaining liability by amount of settlement:** When a party settles with the government, the nonsettling defendant's liability is reduced by the *amount* of settlement rather than by a proportional share of the settlement. §113(f)(2), 42 U.S.C. §113(f)(2); §122(g)(5), 42 U.S.C. §9622(g)(5). Consequently, if it is later discovered that a site will cost $2 million more to clean up than initially estimated, the nonsettling defendants must pay for the entire $2 million increase instead of just their proportional share of the increase.

5. **Judicial review of consent decrees:** "A consent decree is in essence a 'settlement agreement subject to judicial policing.'" *Kelley v. Thomas Solvent Co.*, 717 F. Supp. 507, 514 (W.D. Mich. 1989). Courts view voluntary settlement of environmental disputes between the government and potentially responsible parties *very favorably* and this is reflected in their highly deferential approach to reviewing consent decrees.

a. **Standard of review:** The standard of review for a consent decree is not whether the settlement is one which the court itself might have fashioned, but whether the proposed decree is *fair, reasonable, and faithful* to the objectives of the governing statute. *United States v. Cannons Eng'g Corp.*, 899 F.2d 79, 85 (1st Cir. 1990).

b. **Disallowed consent decrees:** A consent decree will not be approved where the agreement is *illegal, a product of collusion, inequitable, or contrary to the public good*. 717 F. Supp. at 514.

**Example:** In *United States v. Cannons Eng'g Corp.*, 899 F.2d 79 (1st Cir. 1990), EPA reached administrative settlements with 300 generators who were all classified as *de minimis* PRPs. Eighty-four PRPs who were eligible for *de minimis* status rejected the agreement. The settlement agreement reached with the first 300 PRPs required them to pay 160 percent of their volumetric share of the projected response costs. The 60 percent premium was intended to cover unforeseen costs. A later offer was made to the remaining *de minimis* generators to resolve their liability if they paid 260 percent of their volumetric share of response costs. A separate settlement offer was made to the major waste generators. The additional 100 percent premium was imposed as a penalty for delaying settlement. Some of the non-settling *de minimis* PRPs brought this suit. Since the public interest supported early settlement, the court found the negotiation process and the offers procedurally fair, substantively fair, and reasonable, and ordered the consent decrees upheld.

E. **Cleanup costs:** CERCLA contains two liability schemes, both contained in §107(a), 42 U.S.C. §9607(a). The first authorizes recovery of response costs from dealing with contaminated sites and another which establishes liability for damages to natural resources. Overall, the requirements for recovering damages for injuries to natural resources are ***much tougher*** to meet than the requirements for recovering damages to reimburse the cost of cleaning up a hazardous waste site.

1. **Motivation for natural resource damage provisions:** A major motivating factor behind CERCLA's natural resource damage provisions was Congress's ***dissatisfaction with common law damage rules***. The traditional approach for measuring damages to real property involves a choice between examining diminution in value or cost to restore. Because natural resource damages are difficult to value, Congress was concerned that courts would tend to undervalue natural resources and not award the cost of restoration.

2. **Liability under §107(a)(4)(C):** Section 107(a)(4)(C) states that liability includes "***damages for injury to, destruction of, or loss of natural resources***, including the reasonable costs of assessing such injury, destruction, or loss resulting from such a release."

3. **Natural resources defined:** Natural resources are defined to include "land, fish, wildlife, biota, air, water, ground water, drinking water supplies, and other such resources." 42 U.S.C. §101(16); 40 C.F.R. §300.5.

4. **Government appointed trustees:** CERCLA authorizes "trustees to bring natural resource damage claims ***on behalf of state and federal governments and Indian tribes***." 42 U.S.C. §101(16); 40 C.F.R. §300.5. Federal trustees are designated in the National Contingency Plan. 40 C.F.R. §300.600(a). State trustees are designated by the governor of the affected state and tribal trustees are ordinarily appointed by the tribal chairman. 40 C.F.R. §§300.605, 300.610.

5. **Private recovery not allowed:** CERCLA ***does not*** provide for private recovery of natural resource damages, nor does it authorize private attorney general suits for such claims.

6. **Government need not possess title to land:** A government is ***not required to possess title*** to the affected resource in order to seek damages. To recover for harm to resources, it need only show that it ***substantially controls, regulates, or manages*** the resources. *Ohio v. Department of the Interior*, 880 F.2d 432, 461 (D.C. Cir.), *reh'g denied, en banc*, 897 F.2d 1151 (D.C. Cir. 1989). However, the government cannot recover natural resource damages for harms to privately owned property.

7. **Valuation of natural resources:** In *Ohio v. Department of the Interior*, 880 F.2d 432, 461 (D.C. Cir.), *reh'g denied, en banc*, 897 F.2d 1151 (D.C. Cir. 1989), regulations put out by the Interior Department would have made damages for natural resources the lesser of restoration or replacement costs, or diminution of use values. The court ruled that this approach undervalued the damage since diminution of use values would almost always be much lower than restoration cost. Instead, ***diminution of use*** value could only be considered as ***one of a number of factors***

in valuing damages. Likewise, in *Kennecott Utah Copper Corp. v. Interior Dept.*, 88 F.3d 1191 (D.C. Cir. 1996), the court invalidated Department of Interior regulations governing the assessment of natural resource damages. Finding the language of the preamble and the language of the regulations inconsistent because the regulations could be read to require both restoration of the services provided by damages resources, as put forth in the preamble, and also restoration of the injured resource, the court stated that Interior's failure to explain which methodology is required and what it requires natural resources trustees to do rendered the regulation arbitrary and capricious. Under *United States v. Asarco*, 28 F. Supp. 2d 1170 (D. Idaho 1998), a Superfund trustee must prove the extent of environmental injury underlying its natural resource damages assessment.

**F. Brownfields Economic Redevelopment Initiative:** As part of the EPA's attempt to encourage independent cleanup, a series of programs have been announced to encourage and empower states, localities, and other agents of economic redevelopment to prevent, assess, clean up, and sustainably reuse contaminated community property. Among the program components are *liability reform, tax incentives*, and *pilot programs* with grants.

1. **What are Brownfields?:** Brownfields are *abandoned, idled, or under-used industrial and commercial facilities for which development is stymied because of real or perceived environmental contamination*. In January 1995, the EPA announced the Brownfields Action Agenda which outlined EPA's plans to encourage the remediation and reuse of contaminated sites.

   On January 11, 2002 President George W. Bush signed the "Small Business Liability Relief and Brownfields Revitalization Act" (Public Law 107-118; H.R. 2869). The purpose of this Act is to provide relief from liability under CERCLA §107 for small businesses (under 100 employees) that do not contribute any hazardous wastes and contribute insignificant amounts of non-hazardous wastes to a site. Liability exemptions also were created for adjacent property owners, prospective site buyers, and landowners who do not themselves contribute to the contamination of their property. The Act also amends CERCLA to promote increased cleanup and reuse of Brownfields, to allocate increased financial resources toward Brownfields revitalization (increasing annual Brownfields funding from $92 million to $250 million), and to enhance the response programs of individual states.

2. **The Action Agenda:** The Brownfields Action Agenda has *several categories* of efforts intended to assist states, localities, and individuals.

   a. **Pilot program:** EPA has a Brownfields pilot program designed to test redevelopment models, direct special efforts toward removing regulatory barriers without sacrificing protectiveness and facilitate coordinated efforts. As of November 1996, EPA had funded 76 pilot programs with grants up to $200,000.

   b. **Coordination of efforts:** EPA *states and localities work together* to develop and issue guidances clarifying liability of prospective purchasers, lenders, and property owners which clearly state EPA's decision not to use its enforcement discretion to pursue such parties in certain situations. EPA's goal is to facilitate cleanup and redevelopment by removing fear of prosecution and liability.

   c. **Encourage community participation:** EPA has committed itself to work with states and localities to encourage public participation and community involvement and to develop jobs and job training programs. To encourage such activities, some states have initiated state voluntary remediation programs to help clarify liability and cleanup issues for groups who voluntarily agree to clean up contaminated sites. For example, in July of 1997, Virginia's Voluntary Remediation Program will become effective and will allow persons who own, operate, have a security interest in, or enter into a contract for the purchase of contaminated property to voluntarily clean up releases of hazardous substances, hazardous wastes, solid wastes, or petroleum where the cleanup is not clearly mandated by EPA. Va. Code §10.1-1429.1.

# IV.  TOXIC SUBSTANCES CONTROL ACT

A significant number of chemical substances and mixtures are manufactured and processed annually in the United States and appear in a vast array of socially useful products. Prior to the enactment of the Toxic Substances Control Act (TSCA) in 1976, though, no mechanism existed under federal law to evaluate the potential health risks associated with exposure to these often toxic chemicals. In TSCA, Congress gave EPA considerable latitude *to gather and assess data on the toxicity* of these chemicals but also required EPA to consider the potential economic consequences and burdens of regulation on industry.

**A.  Principal goals of TSCA:**  TSCA has essentially two principal goals:

- *to gather information* regarding chemical toxicity, use, and exposure,

- to *utilize that data* to protect human health and the environment from unreasonable risks, and

- to accomplish these goals *without creating unnecessary barriers* to technological innovation.

**1.  Information gathering:**  The Act provides EPA with a variety of means to generate information on chemical substances. These tools allow the agency to *ascertain gaps in coverage* in information from existing reported toxicological studies and determine what tests would produce the desired information.

**a.  Required testing:**  EPA has authority to adopt rules *requiring testing by manufacturers* for both new and existing chemicals if the agency finds that manufacturing, distribution, processing, use, or disposal of the chemical "may present an unreasonable risk of injury to human health or the environment." (TSCA §4, 15 U.S.C. §2603).

**b.  Premanufacture notification (PMN):**  The Act also requires industry to submit a premanufacture notification (PMN) *before producing a new chemical substance* or making significant new uses of an existing chemical (TSCA §5(a), 15 U.S.C. §2604(a)).

**c.  Reporting and record-keeping:**  Finally, TSCA imposes *extensive reporting and record-keeping* duties on industry and mandates the EPA to compile an inventory of chemicals manufactured and processed in the United States. (TSCA §8, 15 U.S.C. §2607).

**2.  Health and environment protection via regulation:**  The Act also gives EPA broad authority *to take regulatory measures* to protect against *risks* posed by hazardous chemical substances and mixtures. TSCA §6(a), 15 U.S.C. §2605(a).

**B.  Two-tier evaluation system:**  TSCA provides for a two-tier system for evaluating and regulating chemical substances. First, the Act permits EPA to *require health and environmental effects testing* of chemicals by and at the expense of their manufacturers and processors. TSCA §4, 15 U.S.C. §2603. Second, it empowers EPA to *regulate substantively the manufacturing and processing* of those chemicals. TSCA §6, 15 U.S.C. §2605.

1. **Required testing:** EPA may require testing by a manufacturer under §4 in two instances:

   ■ Where the agency finds that the manufacture, distribution, processing, use, or disposal of a particular chemical substance *"may present an unreasonable risk* of injury to human health or the environment." 15 U.S.C. §2603(a)(1)(A)(i); and

   ■ Where there has been substantial human exposure to chemical substances or where chemicals may reasonably be anticipated to enter the environment in **substantial quantities.** 15 U.S.C. §2603(a)(1)(B)(i).

   In both cases, the underlying assumption is that *insufficient information exists* regarding the health risks associated with a given chemical and that the required tests will fill the knowledge gaps.

   a. **"May present an unreasonable risk":** The crux of EPA's testing authority turns on an assessment of whether or not a chemical substance "may present an unreasonable risk." This relatively low trigger standard makes it *very difficult for industry to challenge a testing order.*

   **Example:** In *Ausimont U.S.A., Inc. v. EPA*, 838 F.2d 93 (3d Cir. 1988), EPA adopted a rule requiring manufacturers to conduct extensive testing of certain chemicals to determine their potential for producing adverse health effects. Industry estimated that total testing costs would range between $5 million and $9 million. Industry argued that EPA had no evidence that the chemicals were unusually toxic and claimed that the number of persons potentially exposed to the chemicals was insignificant. The court held that although mere scientific curiosity cannot form an adequate basis for a rule, EPA had produced substantial evidence to demonstrate uncertainty over whether the chemicals presented an unreasonable risk. In finding that enough persons were potentially exposed to the chemical, the court held that the statute "allows the agency to act when an existing possibility of harm raises reasonable and legitimate causes for concern." 838 F.2d at 97. In short, Congress granted EPA broad discretion in determining when toxicological data must be produced.

   **Example:** In *Chemical Mfrs. Ass'n v. EPA*, 859 F.2d 977 (D.C. Cir. 1988), the court rejected an industry argument that agency testing orders must be predicated on a finding that the risk was "more probable than not." Instead, it upheld EPA's view that the statute was satisfied simply by finding a "substantial probability" of harm. 859 F.2d at 984.

   b. **"Substantial quantities":** In addition to situations where a chemical may present an unreasonable risk, EPA may order testing if *"substantial quantities" of a chemical are entering the environment.* Naturally, industry and EPA often disagree over what constitutes "substantial quantities."

   **Example:** In *Chemical Mfrs. Ass'n v. EPA*, 899 F.2d 344 (5th Cir. 1990), industry challenged EPA's rule requiring manufacturers and processors to perform toxicological testing of cumene. EPA estimated that three million pounds of cumene escaped during manufacturing and more escaped from vehicle exhaust. Industry claimed EPA's figures were exaggerated and that EPA had failed to articulate criteria for "substantial quantities." The court rejected plaintiff's view and rejected the argument that "substantial" was limited to chemicals presenting a high degree of risk. The court also stated that infrequent or intermittent emissions could be considered substantial for testing purposes and that persistence of the chemical in the environment was not required.

c.  **Voluntary testing agreements not allowed:** In *NRDC v. EPA*, 595 F. Supp. 1255 (S.D.N.Y. 1984), the NRDC challenged EPA's practice of accepting voluntary testing agreements by manufacturers. While the court acknowledged some benefits from these agreements, the court held that *EPA could not allow de facto voluntary testing programs to replace statutory rulemaking duties* because they allowed no opportunity for public comment and often had no enforcement mechanism.

2.  **Implementation of regulations:** The data developed under §4 provides EPA with the information *necessary to decide* whether or not to regulate under §6.

    a.  **EPA has broader testing authority than regulatory authority:** The level of certainty of risk warranting a §4 test rule is lower than that warranting a §6 regulatory rule. EPA must pass rules to *"protect adequately"* against unreasonable risks yet do so by using the *"least burdensome"* means. TSCA §6(a), 15 U.S.C. §2605(a).

    b.  **Regulations based on risk, not harm:** Since EPA never has as much information as it would like, *it must issue regulations and testing orders based on an assessment of risk rather* than a certainty of harm.

    c.  **EPA must consider economic consequences:** In addition to considering the impact of a regulation on human health and the environment, EPA must take into account the *potential economic consequences* to industry.

    d.  **Least burdensome:** One of the principal difficulties in utilizing TSCA as an effective environmental risk management tool is the requirement that EPA regulate in the *"least burdensome" manner possible.* TSCA §6(a), 15 U.S.C. §2605(a).

    **Example:** In *Corrosion Proof Fittings v. EPA*, 947 F.2d 1201 (5th Cir. 1991), EPA promulgated a staged ban of asbestos. EPA estimated that the ban would save 148 to 202 lives at a cost of $450 to $800 million. Since EPA instituted the most burdensome regulation — a total ban — the agency bore a high burden to show that this ban was the least burdensome alternative available that would meet the requirements of TSCA. The court held that EPA needed to consider and rule out less burdensome regulations. Since EPA had only closely considered the effects of no regulation at all or a total ban, the court remanded the regulation to EPA to consider less burdensome alternatives.

    e.  **Judicial review:** Unlike most other environmental statutes, Congress permits EPA regulations *to be set aside* where not supported by "substantial evidence in the rulemaking record . . . *taken as a whole.*" 15 U.S.C. §2618(c)(1)(B)(i). This is far less deferential than the "arbitrary and capricious" standard of review used under the APA (5 U.S.C. §706(2)(E)). For more detailed discussion of judicial review, see the chapter "Judicial Role in Environmental Litigation," *supra*, p. 16. This heightened standard of review places a considerable burden on the agency.

    **Example:** In *Corrosion Proof Fittings v. EPA*, 947 F.2d 1201 (5th Cir. 1991), the court explained that substantial evidence supporting EPA requires something less than the weight of the evidence where it is possible to reach inconsistent conclusions. 947 F.2d at 1213. After careful scrutiny of EPA's analysis supporting the asbestos ban, the court rejected the analysis stating that it found no reasonable basis for EPA's regulation.

3.  **Interagency Testing Committee (ITC):** To carry out the goals of the Act, Congress established a committee of representatives from specified agencies and federally funded institutions,

known as the Interagency Testing Committee (ITC). The ITC's principle charge is to *recommend to EPA a list of no more than the 50 most dangerous chemicals* for priority consideration for testing. EPA is then required to initiate rulemaking proceedings to require testing of the designated chemicals or to publish reasons for not doing so.

**C. Enforcement:** TSCA contains a wide range of both civil and criminal remedies. TSCA §16, 15 U.S.C. §2615.

**1. Penalties:** TSCA provides a hearing and judicial review of penalties imposed by the EPA. However, if a penalty goes unpaid or an order becomes final, the validity, amount, and appropriateness of the final administrative civil penalty *is not reviewable*. TSCA §16(a)(4), 15 U.S.C. §2615(a)(4); see also *United States v. Carolina Transformer Co.*, 739 F. Supp. 1030, 1039 (E.D.N.C. 1989), *aff'd*, 978 F.2d 832 (4th Cir. 1992).

**2. Attorneys' fees:** TSCA provides awards of attorneys' fees in "appropriate cases." TSCA §19(d), 15 U.S.C. §2618(d). In *Environmental Defense Fund, Inc. v. EPA*, 672 F.2d 42 (D.C. Cir. 1982), following a partly successful challenge to EPA's PCB regulations, EDF sought an award of its attorneys' fees. The court held that TSCA allowed awards not only to the prevailing party but permitted fee awards even with respect to issues unsuccessfully litigated because the public interest was served by more fully considering the issues at stake.

**3. Emergency enforcement:** TSCA provides for emergency *enforcement* measures where chemical substances present an *imminent* and unreasonable risk of serious or widespread injury to health or the environment. TSCA §7, 15 U.S.C. §2606.

**D. Miscellaneous provisions:** In addition to regulating toxics generally, the Act also contains provisions *specifically dealing* with asbestos, *PCBs, and radon*.

**1. Regulation of asbestos:** A 1986 amendment to TSCA added Title II, which *specifically addresses* the health hazards associated with exposure to asbestos-containing building materials in public and commercial buildings and in schools. TSCA §§201-215, 15 U.S.C. §§2641-2655.

  **a. Principal requirements:** Title II establishes four principal goals to combat the asbestos problem:

  - *Inspection* of school buildings;

  - Development of asbestos *management plans* by local educational agencies;

  - Determination and implementation of *appropriate response actions;* and

  - *Training and accreditation* of asbestos contractors and laboratories. TSCA §§203 and 206, 15 U.S.C. §§2643 and 2646.

  **b. Enforcement:** In addition to the enforcement options discussed above, TSCA §208, 15 U.S.C. §2648, *empowers EPA* to take *emergency measures*, including seeking injunctive relief, whenever airborne asbestos fibers or friable asbestos in a school building presents an *"imminent and substantial endangerment."*

**2. Regulation of PCBs, §6(e):** Section 6(e) of TSCA sets forth a *detailed scheme* to dispose of polychlorinated biphenyls (PCBs), to *phase out* manufacturing, processing, and distributing of PCBs, and to limit the use of PCBs. EPA's principal charge under TSCA §6(e), 15 U.S.C. §2605(e), is protecting against potential health hazards associated with PCBs.

**a. Exemptions:** Congress provided an exemption for *"totally enclosed" use of PCBs*. The statute also allows the Administrator to grant an exemption for one year in cases where use "will not present an unreasonable risk of injury to health or the environment." 15 U.S.C. §2605(e)(2)(B).

**b. Implementation of §6(e):** In *Environmental Defense Fund, Inc. v. EPA*, 636 F.2d 1267 (D.C. Cir. 1980), the Environmental Defense Fund (EDF) petitioned EPA for a review of the regulations implementing §6(e).

    **i.   50 ppm cutoff:** One part of the regulations *limited application of the disposal and ban* of PCBs to materials containing concentrations of at least 50 parts per million (ppm). The court remanded this part of the regulations and demanded a more rigorous explanation than EPA was able to provide. The court noted that the 50 ppm cutoff *contravened the purpose* of §6(e), which is to prevent the introduction of additional PCBs into the environment.

    **ii.  Enclosed uses:** EDF also contested EPA's decision to include non-railroad transformers, capacitors, and electromagnets as totally enclosed uses. The court noted that these devices *all had the capacity to leak* and that the regulations provided *no mechanism to report* leaking. Consequently, the court found no substantial evidence that classification of these devices as totally enclosed uses "will ensure that any exposure of human beings or the environment to a polychlorinated biphenyl will be insignificant," 15 U.S.C. §2605(e)(2)(C), and set aside that portion of the regulation.

**3. Regulation of radon:** A 1988 Amendment which deals with indoor radon pollution added Title III to TSCA. TSCA §§310-311, 15 U.S.C. §§2661-2671. The health risks posed by radon arise when the gas escapes to the surface and becomes trapped in buildings in large concentrations. EPA estimates that radon may be responsible for 20,000 lung cancer deaths per year, making it a greater health risk than asbestos. Rather than establishing a comprehensive regulatory scheme, TSCA's Title III provisions are principally aimed at *providing information to the public describing the health risks* associated with radon (TSCA §303, 15 U.S.C. §2663) so that detection and mitigation steps can be taken.

**4. Regulation of biotechnology:** Substances created through genetic engineering or biotechnology present special regulatory problems because of the *scientific uncertainty over the risks associated* with their release and questions over whether or not they fit in the federal regulatory system. Under FIFRA and TSCA, EPA has declared its authority to regulate deliberately released genetically engineered commercial microbial products. 51 Fed. Reg. 23,313 (1986). Although TSCA's application to these products is controversial because its jurisdictional grant applies to "chemical substances," EPA has asserted that the statutory language encompasses living organisms. The premanufacture notice program and the information gathering authority under §4 may provide authority for establishing regulatory controls by the agency.

**5. Coordination with other federal agencies and laws:** TSCA provides for *coordination of actions* between the EPA and other federal agencies with respect to the health risks presented by chemical substances. TSCA §9, 15 U.S.C. §2608. Where coordinating efforts have not been taken, conflicts over compliance standards inevitably develop.

**Example:** In *Environmental Transp. Sys., Inc. v. ENSCO, Inc.*, 763 F. Supp. 384 (C.D. Ill. 1991), *aff'd*, 969 F.2d 503 (7th Cir. 1992), the plaintiff trucking company sought contribution for cleanup costs against the company that had hired it to transport transformers containing

PCBs to a disposal site. Where Department of Transportation (DOT) and TSCA regulations conflicted, the court held that TSCA should control since its provisions dealt directly with PCBs. Ironically, the defendant had no liability under the supposedly more stringent TSCA regulations but would have been partially responsible under the DOT approach.

# V. FEDERAL INSECTICIDE, FUNGICIDE, AND RODENTICIDE ACT (FIFRA)

American farmers have increasingly relied on chemical pesticides to minimize damage caused by crop disease and pests. The widespread application of these chemicals in the agricultural process, however, also presents collateral risks to human health and the environment. Thus, a difficult balance must be struck between society's needs and demands for adequate food production and protecting environmental quality.

A. **Regulatory framework:** The cornerstone of the regulatory framework requires *registration with the EPA of pesticide products* in the United States, coupled with provisions for review, cancellation, and suspension of registration in certain circumstances.

   1. **Registration:** The registration process revolves around an agency determination that the *pesticide will not present* unreasonable *adverse risks* to human health or the environment when used appropriately.

      a. **No unreasonable adverse effects on the environment:** The primary condition for registering a pesticide under FIFRA involves a determination by the EPA that the product will not cause "unreasonable adverse effects on the environment" when used properly. 7 U.S.C. §136a(c)(5)(D). This phrase takes into account the *"economic, social, and environmental costs and benefits"* of the pesticide. §136(bb).

      b. **Public disclosure of information:** One of the most controversial provisions of FIFRA allows EPA *to disclose some testing information* about a pesticide that has been submitted to it by an applicant.

         i. **Trade secrets:** Both the company submitting the application for approval and the EPA *may designate* information as "trade secrets or commercial or financial information." FIFRA §10(a) and (b), 7 U.S.C. §136h(a) and (b).

         ii. **Use of data in considering an application by a subsequent company:** FIFRA also allows EPA to consider data submitted by one applicant for registration in *support of another application* pertaining to a similar chemical. However, such consideration can only occur during the first ten years after the date of submission if the original company gives its permission. §3(c)(1)(D)(i). After the ten year period expires, EPA may use the data without permission. §3(c)(1)(D)(ii).

         iii. **Compensation must be provided:** Up until the 15th year from the date of submission, EPA can use the data from the original applicant in considering another application but the subsequent applicant *must offer to compensate the applicant who originally submitted the data.* FIFRA §3(c)(1)(D), 7 U.S.C. §136a(c)(1)(D). In the event that the original submitter and the applicant cannot reach an agreement regarding the terms of compensation, the statute provides that the dispute will be settled by binding arbitration. 7 U.S.C. §136a(c)(1)(D)(ii).

**Note:** The binding arbitration provision was challenged in *Thomas v. Union Carbide Agric. Prods. Co.*, 473 U.S. 568 (1985), as contravening Article III of the Constitution. The court upheld the arbitration procedure, concluding that Congress, pursuant to its powers under Article I, could vest decisionmaking authority in tribunals other than Article III courts. 473 U.S. at 593-594.

    **iv. Congressional purpose:** In writing these provisions, Congress hoped the provisions would eliminate costly duplication of research and *streamline the regulatory process*, making new end-use products available to consumers more quickly.

**Note:** In *Ruckelshaus v. Monsanto Co.*, 467 U.S. 986 (1984), Monsanto incurred costs in excess of $23.6 million in developing the health, safety, and environmental data submitted by it under FIFRA. Monsanto challenged the data disclosure provisions and the data consideration provisions of FIFRA as a "taking" of property without just compensation. While the court found that Monsanto had a property interest in the information at issue, it stated that Monsanto's "reasonable investment backed expectation" could not have been that the information would remain completely private since the company was aware of FIFRA's disclosure provisions at the time it made its investment.

**2. Experimental use permits:** FIFRA provides for the issuance of experimental use permits (EUPs) by EPA to *allow testing of unregistered chemicals or for the application of registered pesticides* for an approved use. 7 U.S.C. §136c. The grant of an EUP is limited to situations where the applicant needs to develop certain information in order to register a pesticide.

**3. Local regulation of pesticides:** FIFRA does not contain any express language *preempting* local regulation. However, it does provide some authority for states to regulate the use of federally registered pesticides and *precludes states* from imposing labeling or packaging *requirements different from the Act*. See 7 U.S.C. §136v(a) and (b).

**Example:** In *Wisconsin Pub. Intervenor v. Mortier*, 501 U.S. 597 (1991) the Court held that FIFRA did not expressly or impliedly preempt a town ordinance which required a permit for certain applications of pesticides to public and private lands. The Court viewed the relationship between federal, state, and local governments as a "partnership" of cooperation and joint regulation over a wide range of matters involving pesticides.

**4. Reregistration:** One of the amendments Congress passed in 1988 required the reregistration of approximately 600 older pesticides (registered prior to 1984). Pesticides previously registered under less stringent testing standards must now be tested for health and safety considerations *under current standards*. This reregistration involves a complex five phase process and was expected to take nine years. 7 U.S.C. §136a-1.

**5. Pesticide contamination of groundwater:** FIFRA currently *does not regulate* pesticide contamination of groundwater, despite serious concerns about the significant risks posed by such chemicals to human health and the environment. EPA has attempted to fill this regulatory gap by regulatory action which would place primary responsibility on states to implement a groundwater plan.

**6. Export of pesticides:** FIFRA provides an exemption for pesticides produced solely for export to a foreign country. 7 U.S.C. §136o(a); 40 C.F.R. §152.30(d). The exemption requires that the pesticide meet certain labeling requirements to avoid being misbranded and be produced by a registered applicant subject to the Act's recordkeeping requirements.

**a. Rationale:** The rationale for exempting exports is that other *countries can weigh the risks and benefits* of pesticide usage in light of their own circumstances and needs.

**b. Notification of foreign governments:** The foreign purchaser must sign a statement acknowledging restrictions on resale and distribution in the United States. Copies of the statement are then given to foreign government officials informing them that unregistered pesticides are being shipped to their country. EPA, acting through the State Department, is *obligated to notify* the governments of foreign countries and appropriate international organizations *when a pesticide registration, cancellation, or suspension becomes effective or is terminated*. 7 U.S.C. §136o(b).

**B. Cancellation and suspension:** FIFRA contains several mechanisms designed to ensure that the public and environment *continue to be protected* from dangerous pesticides. The most important measures involve cancellation and suspension of registration of the pesticide.

**1. Trigger action:** The trigger for agency action to *initiate proceedings for removal* of a product from the market mirrors the type of cost-benefit analysis involved in the original registration process. Whether and to what extent EPA acts to cancel or suspend registration of a pesticide presents a difficult balancing of competing public interests.

**Example:** Suppose a particular pesticide proves extremely and uniquely effective at abating pests and diseases which would otherwise harm an important crop in a specific region of the country. Evidence then comes to light that application of the pesticide in normal usage may pose a more serious health problem than originally believed. If farmers in that locale need to use the pesticide immediately in order to achieve a successful crop, should EPA wait for additional studies regarding the safety of the pesticides or issue an order removing the pesticide from the market? In this example, the dilemma faced by EPA of imposing economic hardship on farmers if it bans usage or risking the public's health if it chooses to pursue a more restrained course of action is typical of these cases.

**2. Cancellation:** Cancellation *bans a pesticide from shipment or use in interstate commerce*. Despite its name, cancellation is considered less drastic than suspension because it often involves protracted administrative proceedings before a pesticide is actually banned.

**a. "Appears [to cause] generally unreasonable adverse effects":** Cancellation proceedings may be initiated whenever it "*appears* to the [EPA] that a pesticide . . . generally causes unreasonable adverse effects on the environment." 7 U.S.C. §136d(b) (emphasis added). Courts have interpreted this standard to mean that EPA must only find a "substantial question of safety" in order to initiate proceedings. *National Coalition Against Misuse of Pesticides v. EPA*, 867 F.2d 636 (D.C. Cir. 1989); see also *Environmental Defense Fund, Inc. v. Ruckelshaus*, 439 F.2d 584, 594 (D.C. Cir. 1971).

**b. "Generally causes unreasonable effects":** In *Ciba-Geigy Corp. v. EPA*, 874 F.2d 277 (5th Cir. 1989), a pesticide manufacturer challenged EPA's decision to cancel registration of diazinon for use on golf courses and sod farms because of the agency's concern about the effect of the chemicals on birds. The parties disagreed over what "generally causes unreasonable effects" meant. The court chose a middle ground between what the two parties advocated and stated that *both the likelihood of the occurrence and the seriousness of the injury* were proper factors to take into account in the cancellation determination.

**3. Suspension:** Suspension may be used *to remove pesticides more swiftly* from the market than cancellation. Absent an emergency, EPA may not issue a suspension order until it has done two things:

■ *Notified registrants* that it intends to cancel registration of the pesticide and that it will issue a suspension order based on a finding of "imminent hazard" which it must include in the notice; and

■ Given registrants an *opportunity for an expedited hearing* on whether an imminent hazard exists. FIFRA §6(c)(1), 7 U.S.C. §136d(c)(1).

**a. Imminent hazard:** The key requirement for issuance of a suspension notice is a showing that *the product constitutes* an *"imminent hazard"* to man or the environment.

**Example:** In *Environmental Defense Fund, Inc. v. EPA*, 548 F.2d 998 (D.C. Cir. 1976), *reh'g denied*, 9 Env't Rep. Cas. (BNA) 1575 (D.C. Cir. 1977), *cert. denied, Velsicol Chemical Corp. v. EPA*, 431 U.S. 925 (1977), EPA suspended the registration for heptachlor and chlordane pending the outcome of the cancellation proceeding. Plaintiffs contended that substantial evidence did not support EPA's conclusion that continued use of chlordane posed an "imminent hazard to human health." EPA relied on studies that showed the pesticides caused cancer in mice and rats. The court upheld the extrapolation of the animal data to man. In addition, the court found that once a risk was shown, responsibility to demonstrate that the benefits outweigh the risks shifted to the proponents of continued registration. The court also held that once a risk of cancer was shown by one method of exposure, the plaintiffs had the burden of showing that other methods of exposure (inhalation and direct contact) did not pose a threat.

**b. Emergency suspension:** EPA may issue an emergency suspension order *only if unreasonable harm would be likely to materialize* while ordinary suspension hearings were pending. Courts have characterized emergency suspension orders as "draconian," implying that they should only be sparingly applied and as a last resort.

**Note:** In *Environmental Defense Fund, Inc. v. EPA*, 465 F.2d 528 (D.C. Cir. 1972), the court addressed the relationship between the cancellation and suspension provisions of FIFRA. EPA issued notices of cancellation of several registered pesticides after it found "substantial question[s] of safety." However, in the interim, the agency did not order an emergency suspension pending a final determination of the administrative decision on cancellation. Plaintiffs challenged EPA's decision not to suspend registration during the cancellation proceedings. The court held that once EPA made a determination of harm by issuing a cancellation notice, it triggered responsibilities to evaluate the need for suspension as well.

**4. Existing stocks:** When a cancellation or suspension order is issued, *provisions must be made for handling the existing stocks* of the pesticide. FIFRA allows EPA to allow continued sale and use of existing stocks of pesticides as long as doing so is not inconsistent with the purposes of the Act and has no unreasonable adverse effects on the environment. 7 U.S.C. §136d(a)(1).

**a. Indemnification required:** FIFRA requires EPA *to indemnify registrants and applicants holding unused stocks of suspended and canceled pesticides*. Critics claim that this policy deters rigorous enforcement efforts by EPA since the agency would bear the financial costs of taking unsafe products off the market. A 1988 FIFRA Amendment tightened the provision by denying payment to registrants unless Congress approved a specific line item appropriation of funds. 7 U.S.C. §136m(a)(4).

  **b. Settlement agreements:** EPA frequently attempts to reach settlement agreements with registrants regarding existing stocks to ***encourage them to accept a cancellation notice*** without contesting it.

  **Example:** In *National Coalition Against Misuse of Pesticides v. EPA*, 867 F.2d 636 (D.C. Cir. 1989), EPA allowed sale and commercial use of the termiticides heptachlor and chlordane as part of a settlement agreement where the producers agreed to a voluntary cancellation of the pesticide's registration. Plaintiffs sought an injunction forbidding the sale and use of existing stocks claiming that EPA had failed to determine that continued sale and use would not have unreasonable adverse effects on the environment. Because fundamental scientific questions about the effects of these pesticides existed at the time of settlement, the court found the settlement reasonable.

**5. Economic consequences:** Before suspending a given pesticide, EPA must consider ''the ***economic, social, and environmental costs and benefits*** of the use of any pesticide.''

  **Example:** In *Love v. Thomas*, 858 F.2d 1347 (9th Cir. 1988), *cert. denied, AFL-CIO v. Love*, 490 U.S. 1035 (1989), EPA issued an emergency suspension order prohibiting the sale, distribution, and use of dinoseb pending completion of cancellation proceedings. With the growing season about to begin in the Northwest, farmers sought relief from EPA's suspension order. Unlike other farmers using dinoseb elsewhere in the country, farmers in the Northwest had no replacement for dinoseb due to the unique climate and types of pests on their crops. Without dinoseb, crop losses were estimated to be $39.2 million. The court found that EPA had not gotten around to studying the economic consequences of suspension on plaintiff's crops given its tight schedule. Although the loss may have appeared minor on a national scale, the court held that EPA's insensitivity to the local economic consequences of its suspension was arbitrary and capricious and an abuse of discretion.

**C. Pesticides and the Federal Food, Drug, and Cosmetic Act:** Section 409 of the Federal Food, Drug, and Cosmetic Act (FFDCA), known as the Delaney Clause, provides that ***no food additive shall be deemed safe if it induces cancer.*** Citing this Delaney Clause, the Ninth Circuit struck down EPA regulations that had permitted use of pesticides as food additives since the chemicals permitted only *de minimis* risk of causing cancer. *Les v. Reilly*, 968 F.2d 985 (9th Cir. 1992), *cert. denied, National Agric. Chems. Ass'n v. Les*, 507 U.S. 950 (1993). The court held that use of any additive that is carcinogenic is prohibited ***regardless*** of the degree of risk. This Delaney Clause was repealed in Pub. L. No. 104-170, and 21 U.S.C. §348(a)(1) now states that a food additive will be ''unsafe unless its use conforms to an exemption under the Federal Food, Drug, and Cosmetic Act or the additive is or will be safely used under prescribed conditions.

**D. Pesticides and the Clean Water Act:** In *Headwaters, Inc. v. Talent Irrigation District*, 243 F.3d 526 (9th Cir. 2001), the Ninth Circuit held that approval of an aquatic herbicide label under FIFRA does not relieve the obligation to obtain a National Pollutant Discharge Elimination System (NPDES) permit under the Clean Water Act. The court found that though FIFRA and the CWA had complementary purposes, FIFRA was not designed to take local and specific conditions into account.

## *Quiz Yourself on*
## *CONTROL OF TOXIC SUBSTANCES*

23. Village A on the East Coast had one case. Village B on the West Coast had two cases. Villages C, D, and E in the Midwest and South had two cases each. The physicians for each did not know what was causing the illness, nor did they have a way to find out about the other patients. A few cases continued to pop up in various places over the next twenty years. Enough physicians finally alerted Agency that a possible environmental risk was causing harm to their patients.

   **(a)** Did Agency have to wait for proof of harm before seeking to assess and manage the risk? _____

   **(b)** Is this a risk that should have been noticed before it actually was discovered? _____

   **(c)** Since the hazard seems to affect a relatively small number of individuals scattered throughout the country, should Agency regulate the risk? _____

24. Spewer, Inc. emits a foul gaseous substance as a waste product of its production operations. Does this substance fall under EPA regulations as a "solid waste"? _____

25. The EPA sought to save time and regulate the liquid wastes as well as the gaseous materials generated by Spewer, Inc. As part of Spewer's operations, the liquid wastes were generated, stored, and then reused in the production process that then produced the gaseous material waste. Can the EPA regulate the liquid wastes under the RCRA at this time? _____

26. Wutizit is a discarded waste, but it is not listed as an EPA-identified hazardous waste. Tests show that it is not toxic or corrosive. Future tests are scheduled to determine if it is ignitable or reactive. The company which produces the Wutizit waste does not want it classified as a hazardous waste because of the increased regulatory costs that will be incurred. If the future tests show that Wutizit is ignitable or reactive, can the company mix Wutizit with a definitely non-hazardous waste to avoid hazardous classification? _____

27. The government is charging Mr. Poe Looter with a criminal violation of the RCRA. Mr. Looter claims that he knew his company's waste was hazardous, but he did not know that he needed a permit. Will he be found guilty of the violation? _____

28. Muck Movers, Inc. transports hazardous substances daily. Most of its transport drivers are very responsible and conscientious every day. Unfortunately, one of them was very tired from the prior evening's bachelor party festivities. This driver just "rested his eyes" for one minute even though he was mid-transport. Next, the inevitable happened . . . the driver's carelessness resulted in the spill of hazardous wastes across the highway and onto Farmer Amy's property.

   **(a)** Is Muck Movers liable for the cleanup costs? _____

   **(b)** Is the driver personally liable for the cleanup costs? _____

   **(c)** Is the government liable for the cleanup costs? _____

   **(d)** Is Farmer Amy liable for the cleanup costs? _____

29. Chemicals R Us had been regulating its chemicals under a voluntary testing agreement with the EPA. Now that they are no longer allowed to do this, they are claiming their chemicals are not harmful. There is no hard scientific evidence that the chemicals are harmful, but quite a lot of them are released into the environment during use. Will the EPA prevail in regulating under the TSCA?

---

## Answers

**23a.** **No.** Risks may be addressed before actual harm occurs.

**23b.** **Not necessarily.** Public risks with diffuse impact may affect many people who are scattered throughout an area before experts begin to put the numbers together. Additionally, the lack of information among the physicians may have prevented earlier notice.

**23c.** **Possibly.** Agency will have to look at the collective cost to society of regulating the hazard which is causing the illnesses of a few people over many years. If the cost outweighs the benefits, people may just live with the risks. If the impact is too great, the Agency should regulate.

**24.** **Yes.** Gaseous waste materials fall under the second group of EPA-promulgated regulations within the very broad definition of ''solid wastes.''

**25.** **No.** The RCRA only regulates discarded material. That is, only material which is not being recycled or reused. Since Spewer is reusing the liquid waste, the EPA may only regulate the gaseous waste under the RCRA at this time.

**26.** **Maybe.** If Wutizit had been listed as hazardous, the mixture definitely would not avoid hazardous classification. Mixture is not a way to avoid hazardous classification entirely, because it is still possible that the mixture will exhibit hazardous characteristics. For example, Wutizit may be ignitable. If the mixture is still ignitable, then the mixture will still be considered hazardous. If not, then hazardous classification is successfully avoided.

**27.** **Depends on the jurisdiction**. Some jurisdictions require a showing of knowledge about the permit requirement while others have rejected knowledge as an element. Make sure you know the case law of the jurisdiction your case is in.

**28a.** **Yes.** Strict liability attaches to those responsible for the transport, generation, or disposal of hazardous wastes. The only defenses available are act of God, act of war, or an act of third party unrelated to the defendant. None of those apply here because it was an employee's carelessness. Muck Movers could seek contribution from other PRPs, if any, and courts will consider the several factors involved in allocating costs.

**28b.** **No.** Liability does not attach to the individual under §107(a) unless there is a release from a facility. ''Facility'' is broadly defined, but the transportation device does not fall within that definition.

**28c.** **Yes.** The government will clean up the site and seek reimbursement from the other liable parties. The Superfund will reimburse the state government for damage, if any, to the natural environment.

**28d.** **No.** Farmer Amy may have to pay initially to clean up her land, but she can then seek reimbursement from Muck Movers and the Superfund.

**29.  Yes.** Although there is no hard scientific evidence of harm, the EPA may regulate the risk even without a showing of harm. Additionally, the EPA just needs to make a showing that the chemicals "may present an unreasonable risk" and are released in "substantial quantities." "Substantial" is not explicitly defined, so large numbers being released will likely fit.

---

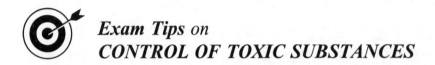

## Exam Tips on
## CONTROL OF TOXIC SUBSTANCES

☞ Environmental risks are grouped into two groups: ***public*** and ***private***. Remember that ***only private risks*** are possibly of ***natural origin***.

    ☞ ***Risk assessment*** seeks to ***define the scientific probability*** of harm after exposure, while ***risk management*** seeks to ***decide what to do*** where risk has been determined. Remember that the ***same agency*** may conduct both processes.

    *Example:* Agency is given a mandate to set acceptable human exposure levels for substance Q. Agency first uses a scientific base to define the risk assessment, and discovers that unacceptable levels of substance Q occur at 25 ppm. Substance Q is merely an irritant at 3 ppm. Agency conducts risk management processes and decides to set exposure levels at 2 ppm maximum to reduce the risk to humans.

    ☞ Don't forget that risk assessment is an ***inexact science*** and that risk management may be affected by ***societal attitudes*** and/or ***costs***.

    ☞ ***Judicial review*** of agency decisions regarding risk management is available as ***procedural review*** rather than review of the balancing of interests.

☞ The ***RCRA*** manages ***both hazardous and non-hazardous solid wastes*** through ***regulation of both active and inactive*** waste disposal sites. An exam hypothetical will likely address hazardous wastes, but be familiar with all ***four programs*** and tailor your outline to your class lectures.

    ☞ Remember that ***Subtitle C*** is a ***cradle-to-grave*** program requiring ***classification, written documentation, and certification of facilities.***

    ☞ First, ***identify*** the materials under consideration as a ***solid waste.*** Remember that the definition of *solid waste* is very ***broad*** and separated into ***three groups***.

    ☞ Second, remember that RCRA ***only applies to discarded*** materials. It ***does not apply to recycled*** materials.

    ☞ Third, identify the material as ***hazardous***: It will either be ***listed*** or will have any or all of the ***four certain characteristics***. The latter is more common.

    *Example:* Waste Z is under consideration. It is liquid waste from an industrial source, therefore it meets the definition of "solid waste" under the second group in the statutory definition. It is on the EPA list of inherently wastelike materials, but it is not on the hazardous wastes list. Waste Z's characteristics must be examined to determine whether it is hazardous. Waste Z is not toxic, corrosive, or reactive. It is, however, ignitable. Since it meets one of the four characteristics, Waste Z is considered hazardous and will fall under RCRA hazardous waste regulations.

☞ Don't forget that *mixtures* of hazardous and non-hazardous materials may still fall under the definition of hazardous wastes. Look for an industry attempting to avoid RCRA regulation by mixing its waste.

☞ Determine if there is a *permit requirement* that a business must meet. They need a permit if they are acting as a *generator, treatment, storage, or disposal facility.* In addition to these businesses, *transporters* also have *specific requirements* under RCRA for dealing with hazardous wastes.

☞ The RCRA has ''bite'' because it has a wide range of *enforcement mechanisms* available under it. *Citizen suits* in federal court also are allowed.

☛ *CERCLA* is designed to *clean up* hazardous waste sites and *respond to* hazardous spills and releases of toxic wastes. Remember that it is *remedial rather than regulatory*.

☞ *Liability is the most important issue* under CERCLA because someone needs to pay to clean up or address hazardous wastes and toxic spills. An exam hypothetical likely will involve determination of liability. The government will want to find at least one responsible private party so that they are not responsible for 100 percent of the costs. That private party will want to find other responsible parties to share the burden. *Try to spot all PRPs* and whether or not *reimbursement* or *private cost recovery* is even possible.

☞ Look to the *liability scheme* to determine who needs to pay for the cleanup and remember that CERCLA imposes *strict, joint, and several liability*. Determine if a party in an exam hypothetical is a *potentially responsible party (PRP)*.

☞ Strict liability is *not absolute*, so determine if there is an *appropriate defense* available to a party.

☞ The *Superfund* provides the *financing* for *governmental response activities*. Cleanup costs may be sought from *responsible private parties*, but don't forget that *not all injuries are compensable.*

☞ Verify that the costs of cleanups are consistent with the *National Contingency Plan* and check to see if the site is listed on the *National Priorities List*. Both affect cost recovery.

☛ The *TSCA* is to *gather and assess data on toxic substances.*

☞ Verify that any chemical has undergone the *two-tier evaluation system*. The EPA requires *health and environmental effects testing* and *substantive regulation of manufacturing and processing* of the chemicals.

☞ Remember that the testing standard is whether the chemical *''may present an unreasonable risk''* or if *substantial quantities* of the chemical are entering the environment.

☛ *FIFRA* requires *registration with the EPA of pesticide products*.

☞ The question is whether or not the pesticide will present *unreasonable adverse risks to human health or environment.*

☞ Remember that the EPA is allowed to *disclose* some testing information, which may create controversy.

☞ States *may not* impose labeling or packing requirements which *differ from FIFRA*.

☞ The most important enforcement mechanisms are registration *suspension or cancellation.*

## CHAPTER 10

# LAND USE

## *ChapterScope*

When land use controls become necessary to preserve a critical resource, frequently nothing less than a *complete ban* on further development can ensure preservation. The legal issues then posed do not involve how much development is permissible, but whether development is permissible at all. Here are the key concepts of this chapter:

■ **Coastal zone management:** States *preserve* the *coastal lands and adjacent waters* using federal *grants* under the *Coastal Zone Management Act* of 1972 (CZMA).

    ■ Grants for controlling *nonpoint source pollution* are regulated under the *Coastal Zone Enhancement Grant (CZEG)* program.

    ■ The first environmental law that *coordinated federal fiscal policy with environmental preservation* was the 1982 *Coastal Barrier Resources Act (CBRA)*. This Act was intended to *preserve coastal areas* and *minimize human endangerment* from poorly located coastal development.

    ■ The federal government is active in *floodplain regulations*. Implementation of the *National Flood Insurance Program (NFIP)* is evidence of the federal government's concern.

■ **Takings:** The government *may prevent development* in certain areas both to preserve the environment and protect human life, even from owners willing to take risks in floodplains areas, for example. The taking is *compensable only* when the owner *loses* all economically feasible use of the *parcel as a whole*.

■ **Soil conservation:** There are numerous federal programs designed to control *soil erosion*, including the *Environmental Conservation Acreage Reserve Program (ECARP)* and the *Environmental Quality Incentives Program (EQIP)*.

■ **Farmland preservation:** There are various programs designed to *slow the loss* of agricultural land, including the *Farmland Protection Policy Act (FPPA)*.

    ■ *Right-to-farm* laws protect farms that existed before residential developments began springing up around them.

    ■ Farmland also is preserved through *agricultural zoning*.

■ Some states have developed *special management techniques* for land planning and control.

■ **Endangered Species Act (ESA):** This was enacted in 1973 to *conserve endangered and threatened species*, which are determined by the *Secretary of the Interior*.

# I. COASTAL ZONE MANAGEMENT

The United States' coastal zone is rich in resources used for transportation, food, water, dilution of waste, and aesthetics and acts as a buffer zone for the dispersion of pollutants and sediments. The coasts offer attractive areas for homes and recreation and are often the site of major ports and industry.

**A. Coastal Zone Management Act:** Passed by Congress in 1972, the Coastal Zone Management Act (CZMA) *declared a national interest in land use decisions* previously viewed as local in nature by acknowledging that a rapidly growing population endangered the fragility and beauty of the coastal zone.

   1. **Purpose:** The purpose of CZMA is to *preserve the unique values of coastal lands and waters* by encouraging states to devise land and water use plans for coastal protection.

   2. **Operation and funding:** The Act provides funds to states that *develop programs for management of land and water uses* consistent with the Act's standards. The Secretary of Commerce must approve these programs upon a finding that they satisfy the requirements of §§305 and 306 of the CZMA. After approval, the Secretary must award grants to the state for the costs of administration of the approved state management program. 16 U.S.C. §§1454-1455. In addition, federal agencies, permittees, and licensees must show that their proposed developments, including certain oil and gas activities on the outer continental shelf, are *consistent with the state's management program*. 16 U.S.C. §1456(c).

   3. **Definition of coastal zones:** The CZMA defines coastal zones as "the *coastal waters* (including the lands therein and thereunder) and the *adjacent shorelands* (including the waters therein and thereunder), *strongly influenced by each other* and in *proximity to the shorelines* of the several coastal states, [which] includes islands, transitional and intertidal areas, salt marshes, wetlands, and beaches." 16 U.S.C. §1453(1).

      a. **Amendment of definition:** In 1990 the definition was *amended to limit the seaward boundary* to the extent of state ownership and title under the Submerged Lands Act, 43 U.S.C. §§1301-1356. The zone now extends inland "to the extent necessary to control shorelands, the uses of which have a direct and significant impact on the coastal waters, and to control those geographical areas which are likely to be affected by or vulnerable to sea level rise." Coastal Zone Act Reauthorization Act Amendments of 1990, Pub. L. No. 101-508, §6204, 104 Stat. 1388, 1388 (codified as amended at 16 U.S.C. §1453(1)).

      b. **Vague definition:** The definition of the coastal zone is intentionally vague, giving states *great discretion* in setting their own jurisdiction. This discretion is necessary since different types of areas, developed and undeveloped, may exist within a single state's coastal zone.

      c. **Exclusions from definition:** Excluded from the definition of coastal zone is land "*the use of which is by law solely subject to the discretion of or which is held in trust by the Federal government*, its officers or agents." 16 U.S.C. §1453(1).

         **Example:** In *California Coastal Commission v. Granite Rock Co.*, 480 U.S. 572 (1987), the Supreme Court clarified state authority over federal lands within the coastal zone holding that federal forest regulations preempted state regulations regarding land use, but not environmental regulation. Even though federal land is excluded from the definition of coastal zone, the state laws are not automatically preempted by CZMA.

4. **Funding of state management programs:** Under the CZMA, coastal states are given grants for the development and administration of *federally approved state management programs* for coastal zones.

   a. **General requirements for funding:** In order to receive these grants, the state must *coordinate the program* with other state and local plans applicable to areas within the coastal zone, *establish an effective mechanism for continuing consultation and coordination* between the designated management agency and other agencies within the coastal zone to assure full participation of these agencies, and *obtain approval* from the Assistant Administrator of the Office of Ocean and Coastal Resource Management (OCRM) after complying with the requirements of the management program. 16 U.S.C. §1455(d)(3)(A)(i), (d)(3)(b), (d)(2).

   b. **Technical requirements for management programs:** Before a management program can be funded it must first satisfy certain requirements. These requirements are:

      i. *identification of the boundaries* of the coastal zone;

      ii. a *definition of what constitutes permissible land and water uses* which have a direct and significant impact on the coastal waters;

      iii. an *inventory and designation* of areas of particular concern;

      iv. an *identification of the means* to exert control over land and water uses, including a listing of relevant constitutional provisions, laws, regulations, and judicial decisions;

      v. *broad guidelines* or priorities of uses in particular areas including specifically those of lowest priority;

      vi. a *description of organizational structure* proposed to implement the program, including the responsibilities and interrelationships of local, areawide, state, regional, and interstate agencies in the management process;

      vii. a *definition of the term "beach"* and a planning process for the protection of, and access to, public beaches and other public coastal areas of environmental, recreational, historical, aesthetic, ecological, or cultural value;

      viii. a *planning process for energy facilities* likely to be located in, or which may significantly affect, the coastal zone, including, but not limited to, a process for anticipating and managing the impacts from such facilities; and

      ix. a *planning process for assessing the effects* of shoreline erosion and studying and evaluating ways to control, or lessen the impact of, such erosion, and to restore areas adversely affected by such erosion. 16 U.S.C. §1455(d)(2).

   c. **Further requirements:** Grants for the management and administration of these programs are administered separately and states *must satisfy additional requirements* in order to receive them. Prior to granting approval the Secretary must find that the requirements of §1455(d)(2), *supra*, have been met and also that:

      i. the management program has been adopted in accordance with the applicable regulations after notice and with opportunity for full participation by the relevant federal agencies, state agencies, local governments, regional organizations, port authorities, and other public and private interested parties;

    ii.  the state has held public hearings in its development;

    iii.  the management program and any changes have been reviewed and approved by the Governor;

    iv.  the Governor of the state has designated a single agency to receive and administer the administrative grants;

    v.  the state is organized to implement the management program;

    vi.  the state has the authority necessary to implement the program;

    vii.  the management program provides for adequate consideration of the national interests involved in planning for, and in the siting of, facilities that are necessary to meet requirements that are not local in nature; and

    viii.  the management program makes provision for procedures whereby specific areas may be designated for the purpose of preserving or restoring their conservation, recreational, ecological, or aesthetic values. 16 U.S.C. §1455(d)(l)-(9).

5. **Methods of regulation:** States may choose the method of regulation of their programs. These choices include:

    a.  state *establishment of criteria and standards* for local implementation, subject to administrative review and enforcement compliance;

    b.  *direct state land and water use planning* and regulation;

    c.  state *administrative review for consistency* with the management program of all development plans, projects, or land and water regulations, including exceptions and variances thereto proposed by any state or local authority or private developer, with power to approve or disapprove after public notice and an opportunity for hearings. 16 U.S.C. §1455(d)(l)(A)-(C).

6. **Federal participation and consistency review:** Certain categories of activity *trigger review* of federal actions for consistency with state CZMA plans. The main categories of activity subject to this review are:

    a.  activities conducted or supported by a federal agency ''affecting any land or water use or natural resource of the coastal zone'';

    b.  federal development projects ''in the coastal zone'';

    c.  federally licensed and permitted activities ''affecting any land or water use or natural resource of the coastal zone'';

    d.  federally licensed or permitted activities described in detail in OCS plans ''affecting any land or water use or natural resource of the coastal zone''; and

    e.  federal assistance to state and local governments ''affecting any land or water use or natural resource of the coastal zone.'' 16 U.S.C. §1456(c), (d).

7. **Controversial consistency determinations:** The most controversial consistency determinations have involved oil and gas lease activities in the outer continental shelf.

a. ***Secretary of the Interior v. California:*** In *Secretary of the Interior v. California,* 464 U.S. 312 (1984), the Court, relying upon Congress's rejection of four proposals to extend the CZMA beyond three miles and a specific proposal to make OCSLA leasing subject to consistency review, held that ***only federal activities within the coastal zone could directly affect the coastal zone***. In addition, the separation of OCSLA development into four stages was interpreted as a congressional decision to separate OCSLA lease sales from the latter two stages of development for purposes of consistency review under §307(c)(3)(B).

b. **Criticism and response:** This opinion was intensely criticized and was overturned by the 1990 Amendments to the CZMA. Section §307(c)(l) was amended to include "each Federal agency activity ***within or outside the coastal zone that affects any land or water use or natural resource*** of the coastal zone." 16 U.S.C. §1456(c)(l)(A). A Presidential exemption is authorized if the activity is in the paramount interest of the United States. 16 U.S.C. §1456(c)(l)(B).

B. **Coastal Zone Enhancement Grants (CZEG):** The 1990 Amendments to the CZMA created the Coastal Zone Enhancement Grant (CZEG) Program. 16 U.S.C. §1456b.

1. **Program implementation:** States must submit their programs to the Secretary and the Administrator of EPA within 30 months of publication of the national guidelines. 16 U.S.C. §1455b(a)(l). After approval, the state must implement the program through changes in the state plan ***for control of nonpoint source pollution*** approved under section 319 of the Clean Water Act, 33 U.S.C. §1328, and through changes in the state's coastal zone management program. 16 U.S.C. §1455b(c)(2). If a state fails to submit an approved program, the Secretary ***may withhold*** a percentage of any §306 grant under the CZMA, and EPA may withhold portions of any §319 grant under the Clean Water Act. 16 U.S.C. §1455b(c)(3), (4). These grants are to be provided to coastal states for the purpose of attaining any one or more of the coastal zone enhancement objectives.

2. **CZEG objectives:** The CZEG Program is aimed at the:

   a. ***protection*** of existing coastal wetlands or creation of new coastal wetlands;

   b. ***minimization or elimination of development*** in natural hazard areas in order to protect life and property;

   c. ***increased public access*** to coastal areas having recreational, historical, aesthetic, ecological, or cultural value;

   d. ***reduction of marine debris*** through increased management of uses and activities which contribute to the presence of such debris in the coastal and ocean environment;

   e. ***development and adoption*** of procedures to control the cumulative and secondary impacts created by coastal growth and development;

   f. ***preparation and implementation*** of special area management plans for important coastal areas;

   g. ***planned use*** of ocean resources; and

   h. adoption of ***enforceable procedures*** and policies regarding the siting of coastal energy and government facilities having greater than local significance. 16 U.S.C. §1456b(a).

3. **Nonpoint source pollution control measures required:** The 1990 Amendments *require* every state with a federally approved program to develop a program to implement coastal land use management measures for controlling nonpoint source pollution. 16 U.S.C. §1455b. The EPA Administrator must publish *national guidelines on "management measures"* to control coastal nonpoint sources. 16 U.S.C. §455b(b)(l).

   a. **Management measures:** "Management measures" are defined as *"economically achievable measures"* for the control of pollutants from new and existing nonpoint sources that reflect the *"greatest degree of pollutant reduction achievable"* through application of the best available nonpoint pollution control practices and other methods. 16 U.S.C. §1455b(g)(5).

C. **The Coastal Barrier Resources Act (CBRA):** Enacted in 1982, the Coastal Barrier Resources Act (CBRA), 16 U.S.C. §§3501-3510, was the first environmental law that *coordinated federal fiscal policy with environmental preservation.* Coastal barriers, or barrier islands, are long, narrow, low-lying land forms, partially or almost completely surrounded by water, such as New York's Fire Island and North Carolina's Outer Banks.

   1. **Purposes of CBRA:** The purposes of CBRA were to *minimize danger to human life* from poorly located coastal development, to end *federal expenditures* for such development, and to *preserve the natural resources* of the coastal barriers. 16 U.S.C. §3501(b).

      a. **Accomplishment of purposes:** The CBRA accomplishes these purposes by *restricting new federal assistance or expenditures*, including financial assistance for construction or purchase of structures, roads, bridges, facilities, and related infrastructure, within coastal barrier areas.

      b. **Costs borne by developers and property owners:** Thus, the costs of development, and the costs from risks of development, *must be borne by the developer and consumer* of coastal barrier property. The Act was enacted despite challenges from realtors and developers that the Act was federal land use which failed to distinguish between coastal barriers suitable for development and those which are not.

   2. **New expenditures:** *No new expenditures or new financial assistance* may be made available under authority of any federal law for any purpose within the Coastal Barrier Resources System. 16 U.S.C. §3504(a). Financial assistance includes any form of loan, grant, guarantee, insurance, payment, rebate, subsidy, or any other form of direct or indirect federal assistance. 16 U.S.C. §3502(3). Although this definition is very broad, it is subject to many exemptions. See 16 U.S.C. §§3502(3), 3505(a).

   3. **Challenge to validity:** In a district court decision affirmed by the Fourth Circuit Court of Appeals, a general challenge to the validity of the CBRA failed. *Bostic v. United States*, 581 F. Supp. 254 (E.D.N.C. 1984), *aff'd*, 753 F.2d 1292 (4th Cir. 1985).

D. **Floodplain regulation:** Substantial regulation of land use, development, construction practices, and insurance coverage in areas prone to flooding exists at the federal, state, and local levels. The federal government is particularly active in flood control in structural terms, through the efforts of agencies such as the Army Corps of Engineers.

   1. **National Flood Insurance Program (NFIP) (42 U.S.C. §§4001-4128):** Since flood insurance is not widely available through the private insurance market, participation in the federal flood insurance scheme is a *practical necessity* for the owners of the many residences and businesses

erected in floodplain areas. The federal government has in turn used this leverage to exert powerful pressures on state and local governments to enact effective land use measures mitigating the potential damage in areas prone to flooding. The program was upheld as constitutional in *Texas Landowners Rights Ass'n v. Harris*, 453 F. Supp. 1025 (D.D.C. 1978), *aff'd*, 598 F.2d 311 (D.C. Cir. 1979), *cert. denied*, 444 U.S. 927 (1979).

a.  **Who is regulated?:** The persons regulated under the NFIP are *property owners in flood-prone communities that agree to meet federal requirements* for reducing potential flood damage.

b.  **"100 year floodplain":** The regulatory measure is the "100 year floodplain," an area exposed to damage from a "100 year flood." A 100 year flood refers to a statistical calculation whereby hydrologists determine that the flood *will be equaled or exceeded once in every 100 years on average* — thus creating a roughly 1 percent chance of occurrence in any given year.

c.  **Administration:** The NFIP is administered by the *Federal Insurance Administration* within the *Federal Emergency Management Agency* (FEMA). FEMA works to reduce exposure to flood hazards by encouraging the adoption of appropriate land-use construction regulations. See 44 C.F.R. §205.32(f).

d.  **Liability of federal government:** The United States government is *not liable* for damages arising from floods or the administration of the NFIP. See, *e.g., Baroni v. United States*, 662 F.2d 287 (5th Cir. 1981), *cert. denied*, 460 U.S. 1036 (1983); *Britt v. United States*, 515 F. Supp. 1159 (M.D. Ala. 1981); *Oahe Conservancy Sub-District v. Alexander*, 493 F. Supp. 1294 (D.S.D. 1980). Indeed, Congress has disclaimed all liability arising from flooding: "No liability of any kind shall attach to or rest upon the United States for any damages from or by floods or flood waters at any place." 33 U.S.C. §702c. This applies to claims of property damage and claims of personal injury. See *United States v. James*, 478 U.S. 597 (1986), discussed in Note, *United States v. James: Expanding the Scope of Sovereign Immunity for Federal Flood Control Activities*, 37 Cath. U. L. Rev. 219 (1987).

e.  **Disaster Relief Act of 1974**, 42 U.S.C. §§5121-5202, is primarily designed to provide financial assistance to state and local governments, individuals, and businesses in the event of a Presidentially declared *"emergency"* or *"major disaster."*

    i.   **Emergency:** An "emergency" is any natural disaster that *occurs or threatens to occur* beyond the response capabilities of state and local governments which necessitates federal assistance to protect lives, property, health, and safety. 44 C.F.R. §205.34(a).

    ii.  **Disaster:** A major disaster is one for which federal assistance is *necessary to supplement the efforts and resources* of state and local governments and disaster relief organizations. 44 C.F.R. §205.33(a).

f.  **Executive Order 11988 — practical alternatives:** Promulgated in 1977, an executive order requires federal agencies to avoid direct or indirect support of floodplain development when there is a "practicable" alternative.

E.  **Takings in coastal and floodplain regulation:** The Supreme Court's 1987 trilogy of decisions, *Keystone Bituminous Coal Ass'n v. DeBenedictis*, 480 U.S. 470 (1987), *First English Evangelical Lutheran Church of Glendale v. Los Angeles County*, 482 U.S. 304 (1987), and *Nollan v. Califor-*

*nia Coastal Comm'n*, 483 U.S. 825 (1987), indicated a shift in the Court's formulation of what constitutes a "regulatory taking."

**Example:** South Carolina's Beachfront Management Act, S.C. Code Ann. §§48-39-10 to -220, prohibits the replacement of some buildings and structures in an area 20 feet behind the first row of dunes, and limits rebuilding and new construction in a much larger area. Other regulations are even more restrictive in prohibiting all or almost all use of coastal or floodplain property.

1. **Landowner response:** Real estate owners and developers challenge these regulations by alleging violations of the takings clause based on the fact that the regulations limit the use of their property, often despite the fact that the landowners are willing to self-insure the property.

2. **Government rationale:** While the landowners' arguments are not without merit, they ignore the fact that the ***government has a compelling interest*** in protecting the lives and property of beachfront owners despite their willingness to take risks. In addition, because construction and development in high-risk floodplain areas increases the size of the floodway and causes floodwaters to damage property and endanger lives, government regulation is justified as nuisance regulation.

3. **Deprivation of all economically viable use:** In *Lucas v. South Carolina Coastal Council*, 112 S. Ct. 2886 (1992), the Supreme Court held that a compensable taking occurs when landowners are deprived of ***all economically feasible use of "the parcel as a whole,"*** even if the taking is only temporary. See *supra*, p. 34.

F. **Public trust doctrine:** This doctrine protects public access to water resources. It generally requires that the ***resources cannot be sold and must be maintained for uses that serve the public***. This limitation is particularly controversial because it often conflicts directly with the interests of private landowners.

**Example:** In *Phillips Petroleum Co. v. Mississippi*, 484 U.S. 469, *reh'g denied*, 486 U.S. 1018 (1988), the Supreme Court held that upon entering the Union the states gained title to all land influenced by the tide, whether navigable or non-navigable, and held such lands in trust for the public.

1. **Expansion of doctrine to include recreational and ecological value:** The public trust doctrine has been expanded to include the ***preservation of tidelands*** in their natural state for recreational and ecological value. See *National Audubon Soc'y v. Superior Court of Alpine County*, 33 Cal. 3d 419, 658 P.2d 709 (1983), *cert. denied, Los Angeles Dep't of Water & Power v. National Audubon Soc'y*, 464 U.S. 977 (1983).

# II. SOIL CONSERVATION

Agriculture is the primary contributor to soil loss, with about one-half of the total soil loss in the United States occurring on a small percentage of highly erodible cropland. Agriculture is also a major contributor to nonpoint source water pollution.

A. **Soil loss:** Soil loss per acre is estimated by one of two methods, the universal soil loss equation (USLE) or the wind erosion equation (WEE), both of which ***estimate the average annual tonnage of soil lost from each soil type*** as a result of climate, topography, cropping systems, and management practices. Once calculated, these losses are compared to loss tolerances (T-values) which reflect the amount of annual loss that can be sustained without adversely affecting the productivity of the land. Because the majority of this soil loss occurs on a small portion of highly erodible cropland, soil conservation efforts should be targeted to these specific areas. See generally, Linda A. Malone, *The Renewed Concern on Soil Erosion: The Current Federal Program and Proposal*, 10 J. Agric. Tax'n & L. 310, 315-317 (1989). In addition to affecting the productivity of the land, soil erosion harms air and water quality and also impacts toxic contamination from nutrients and pesticides.

1. **Nonpoint source pollution:** *Agriculture is a primary contributor* to nonpoint source water pollution due to the fact that sediment from soil erosion and water runoff contains pollutants, fertilizer residues, insecticides, herbicides, fungicides, dissolved minerals, and animal-waste-associated-bacteria.

B. **Federal programs designed to control soil erosion:** There are more than 27 federal programs under 8 different agencies designed to control soil erosion.

1. **Programs are voluntary:** All of these programs are voluntary and *provide technical assistance and cost-sharing* for conservation measures. Until recently, there have been no meaningful sanctions or penalties for contributing to or failing to control soil erosion.

2. **1985 Farm Bill:** The 1985 Farm Bill was the first program to impose *meaningful* sanctions on landowners guilty of contributing to or failing to control excessive soil erosion. It contained conservation provisions that were new to agricultural programs: the so-called sodbuster, swampbuster, conservation compliance, and conservation reserve programs. 16 U.S.C. §§3801-3845.

   a. **Purpose:** The basic purpose of programs under the Farm Bill is to *ensure cross-compliance* between the conservation programs and the price and income support programs of the USDA.

   b. **Costs of noncompliance:** Although compliance with these provisions is voluntary, a producer will receive *no USDA program payments*, such as price and income supports, disaster payments, and crop insurance unless the producer is in compliance with the conservation provisions.

3. **1990 Farm Bill:** Congress reauthorized the conservation programs created by the 1985 Farm Bill in the 1990 Farm Bill, known as the Conservation Program Improvements Act. This reauthorization *expanded the scope* of the conservation program and *broadened the exemptions* in and weakened enforcement of the sodbuster and swampbuster programs and also created several new conservation programs. See generally, Linda A. Malone, *Conservation at the Crossroads: Reauthorization of the 1985 Farm Bill Conservation Provisions*, 8 Va. Envt'l L.J. 215 (1989).

4. **1996 Farm Bill:** Congress reauthorized the conservation programs created in the earlier farm bills in the 1996 Farm Bill, known as the *Federal Agriculture Improvement and Reform Act*. The principal innovation of the Act was the establishment of *seven years of guaranteed but annually declining* program payments to producers who contract with the USDA. With respect to conservation, the Act continued the programs begun in 1985 with provisions allowing for somewhat more flexibility in their administration, and created several new, primarily voluntary conservation programs.

   a. **More flexible approach:** The 1996 Farm Bill provides for *more flexibility* in the administration of provisions of the Act.

i.  **New definitions:** The 1996 Farm Bill provided new definitions for ''conservation plan'' and ''conservation system.'' Pub. L. No. 104-127, §301(a)(2) and (3), 110 Stat. 888 (1996). These new definitions allow for increased flexibility in both conservation plans and systems.

ii.  **More flexible guidelines:** There is a new provision that requires the Secretary to ensure that the standards and guidelines for conservation systems permit a landowner to use a system that: (1) is *technically and economically* feasible; (2) is based on *local resource conditions* and available *conservation technology*; (3) is cost-effective; and (4) does not cause undue economic hardship on the landowner. Pub. L. No. 104-127, §315, 110 Stat. 888 (1996).

b.  **Sodbusting and conservation compliance:** This provision is designed to ensure that *no highly erodible land will be placed into production of an agricultural commodity* for the first time without full application of a compliance plan. The Act requires a conservation plan for highly erodible land which was not in production or set aside any year from 1981 to 1985. For highly erodible land that was in production or set aside in that period, the conservation compliance provision *requires active application of a conservation plan or system* in most cases by January 1, 1990 with full implementation by January 1, 1995. 16 U.S.C. §§3811, 3812.

i.  **Liability restricted:** There are a number of provisions restricting liability in the event that a violation has occurred, most of which were added in the 1990 Amendments. 16 U.S.C. §§3812(a)(4), 3812(e); 7 C.F.R. §12.9; 16 U.S.C. §3812(f)(4).

ii.  **Graduated sanctions:** Furthermore, graduated sanctions are *authorized for good faith violations*, whereby failure to ''actively apply'' a conservation plan for conservation compliance will not result in ineligibility for program payments acted in good faith without intent to violate the Act. Pub. L. No. 104-127, §313, 110 Stat. 888 (1996). In addition, the 1996 Amendments give the producer a *''reasonable period of time*, as determined by the Secretary, but not to exceed one year, during which to implement the measures and practices necessary to be considered to be actively applying the person's conservation plan.'' *Id.*

iii.  **Ineligibility not permanent:** In addition, program ineligibility resulting from failure to *actively apply a conservation plan* is not permanent. Eligibility may be regained if, prior to the beginning of a subsequent crop year, the Secretary determines that the individual is actively applying an approved conservation plan according to schedule, 16 U.S.C. §3812(f)(3).

c.  **The Environmental Conservation Acreage Reserve Program (ECARP):** Created by the 1990 Farm Bill, the ECARP's goals are to assist *owners and operators of highly erodible lands, other fragile lands, and wetlands* in conserving and improving the soil and water resources of their farms and ranches. Between 40 million and 45 million acres of land, including the acreage already in the conservation reserve program, were to be placed into the ECARP program by the Secretary during the 1986 through 1995 calendar years. 16 U.S.C. §3830(b). The 1996 Farm Bill limits enrollment in the program to 36.4 million acres of land and reauthorizes those enrollments through 2002. Pub. L. No. 104-127, §331, 110 Stat. 888 (1996).

The 1996 amendments incorporate into the statutory provisions for ECARP the concept of conservation priority areas previously included in the regulations. The Secretary may designate watersheds, multistate areas, or regions for special environmental sensitivity as conservation priority areas to comply with nonpoint source pollution requirements under federal and state law and "to meet other conservation needs." Pub. L. No. 104-127, §331, 110 Stat. 888 (1996). Assistance payments to producers in these areas may be based on the significance of the resource problems and the practices that best address those problems and "maximize environmental benefits for each dollar expended . . . " Pub. L. No. 104-127, §331, 110 Stat. 888 (1996).

i.   **Eligible land:** Lands eligible under the Farm Bill include highly erodible croplands, marginal pasture lands, and croplands that the Secretary determines *contribute to the degradation of water quality*.

ii.  **Requirements for placing eligible land into the conservation program:** In order to put eligible land into the conservation program, the owner must agree by contract to:

- apply an approved conservation plan removing the land from production and putting it to a less intensive use; and

- not use the land for agricultural purposes except as permitted by the Secretary. 16 U.S.C. §3832(a)(11).

iii. **Landowner assistance:** If the requirements are met, the owner of the land receives *technical assistance and cost-sharing* for all the conservation measures required. 16 U.S.C. §3833. This often consists of 50 percent of the cost of establishing water quality and conservation measures and annual rental payments to compensate for the retirement of the land during the period of the contract. 16 U.S.C. §§3833(b) and 3834(b)(l).

iv.  **Duration of contract:** Conservation reserve program contracts under the Act range in duration from *not less than 10 years to no more than 15 years*. 16 U.S.C. §3831(e)(l). During 1996 through 2000, the Secretary may extend, for up to 10 years, conservation reserve contracts entered into prior to November 28, 1990, or place such land in an environmental easement program at the option of the owner or operator.

v.   **Environmental Quality Incentives Program (EQIP):** In order to reduce paperwork and bureaucratic involvement, the 1996 Farm Bill consolidated programs created under the prior farm bills into *one conservation cost-share program*, the Environmental Quality Incentives Program (EQIP). The EQIP is under the ECARP umbrella.

(1) **Benefits:** From 1996 to 2002, the Secretary can provide *technical assistance, cost-share payments, incentive payments, and education* to producers who enter into contracts under the program. Pub. L. No. 104-127, §1240B, 110 Stat. 888 (1996). Generally, the total amount of cost-share and incentive payments paid may not exceed $10,000 annually or $50,000 for the term of the contract. Pub. L. No. 104-127, §1240G(a), 110 Stat. 888 (1996).

(2) **Self-certification:** The 1996 Act allows a sort of self-certification of compliance. To determine eligibility for program payments, the landowner *may simply certify that there is compliance* with the conservation plan, and the Secretary will not be required to review the status of the person's compliance. Pub. L. No. 104-127, §315, 110 Stat. 888 (1996). In addition, the landowner who makes such a certification is *permitted to*

*revise the conservation plan* ''in any manner if the same level of conservation treatment'' is maintained. Pub. L. No. 104-127, §315, 110 Stat. 888 (1996). The Secretary cannot revise a person's conservation plan without consent.

(3) **Notice and investigation:** A new section of the Act outlines the notice and investigation process for noncompliance with a conservation plan. If a USDA employee observes a possible violation of a plan while providing onsite technical assistance, the employee must *give notice*, within 45 days, of the actions needed to be in compliance. The responsible person must attempt to *correct the violation* as soon as practicable after receiving the information, but no later than one year after receipt. If corrective action is not fully implemented after one year, only then may a review of compliance with the plan be conducted. Pub. L. No. 104-127, §315, 110 Stat. 888 (1996).

d. **Swampbusting:** Under this provision, a person is *totally or partially ineligible* for USDA benefits if that person produces an agricultural commodity on wetlands converted after December 23, 1985, or who, after December 23, 1990, converts a wetland by any means so as to make possible the production of an agricultural commodity. The 1996 Farm Bill for the first time provides that ineligibility, with respect to wetlands, will be proportionate to the severity of the violation. Pub. L. No. 104-127, §321, 110 Stat. 888 (1996).

   i. **Exemptions:** A number of exemptions exist for land converted to wetlands before December 23, 1985 or for production of an agricultural commodity on a wetland *using normal farming or ranching techniques*. §§3822(b)(l)(A), (B), (C), (D), (b)(2)(A), (b)(2)(B), 3834. The 1996 Act added several additional exemptions. Pub. L. No. 104-127, §322, 110 Stat. 888 (1996). In addition, the Secretary may grant an exemption if the action *has a minimal effect* on the wetland, or if the wetland values and functions are *mitigated by the restoration of another converted wetland* in accordance with a restoration plan. 16 U.S.C. §3822(f)(l)-(3). The 1996 Act broadened the minimal effects exemption. The Secretary is directed to identify by regulation categorical minimal effect exemptions on a regional basis. Pub. L. No. 104-127, §322, 110 Stat. 888 (1996).

   ii. **Graduated sanctions:** In addition, there is a provision for graduated sanctions in the case of a *good faith violation* in the conversion of a wetland. 16 U.S.C. §3822(h). The 1996 Farm Bill provides that the Secretary must provide the person with a reasonable period, up to one year, to restore the wetland. Pub. L. No. 104-127, §322, 110 Stat. 888 (1996).

e. **Wind erosion:** The 1996 Farm Bill creates a wind erosion estimation pilot project to *review the wind erosion factors* used in the wind erosion equation to determine the rate of erosion of land. Pub. L. No. 104-127, §310(b), 110 Stat. 888 (1996).

f. **Additional programs created:** The 1996 Act created several *focused, voluntary conservation programs*, including the conservation farm option (Pub. L. No. 104-127, §335, 110 Stat. 888 (1996)), forestry incentives program (§373), resource conservation and development program (§383), conservation of private grazing land program (§386), wildlife habitat incentives program (§387), farmland protection program (§388), Everglades ecosystem restoration program (§390), flood risk reduction program (§385), and an environmental quality incentives program applicable to livestock as well as agricultural procedures (§334).

# III. FARMLAND PRESERVATION

Concern about irreversible conversion of agricultural land to nonagricultural uses in the 1970s led to a wave of farmland preservation measures at the state and local levels.

A. **Introduction:** Governmental measures include right-to-farm laws, exceptions for agriculture in county zoning, agricultural zoning, agricultural districts, differential assessment, purchases of development rights, and transferable development rights to farmland. These measures are generally *aimed at reducing the attractiveness of farming areas* for development, reducing burdens on farmers caused by encroaching development, or directly preventing change from agricultural to nonagricultural uses.

B. **National Agricultural Lands Study (NALS):** This study concluded that development and the problems created by farmland from surrounding development threatens farmers and *causes them to reduce ongoing, long-term investments* in land improvements, soil and water conservation, and farm structures. This effect, known as the "impermanence syndrome," leads to the sale of the farmland for development. In order to avoid this result, the NALS report recommended that a variety of farmland preservation measures be adopted.

C. **The Farmland Protection Policy Act:** Adopted in 1981, the FPPA's purpose is to preserve the United States' ability "to produce food and fiber in sufficient quantities to meet domestic needs and the demands of our export markets." 7 U.S.C. §4201(a) and (b).

   1. **Applicability:** The FPPA is limited to procedures "to assure that the actions (of federal agencies) do not cause United States farmland to be *irreversibly converted* to nonagricultural uses in cases in which other national interests do not override the importance of the protection of farmland or otherwise outweigh the benefits of maintaining the farmland resources." §4201(a)(7).

   2. **Limitations of the Act:** The Act is very limited in the protection that it gives to agricultural land since there are very few restrictions on whether the agency ultimately decides to continue or abandon a project. In addition, the Act does not provide a private enforcement provision.

D. **Right-to-farm laws:** These laws are essentially a codification of the common law "coming to the nuisance defense" and provide protection to agricultural operators that were in place *before* neighboring residential development.

   1. **Model right-to-farm laws:** There are four model right-to-farm laws on which most right-to-farm laws have been based.

      a. **New York model:** This model prohibits *local laws that unreasonably restrict* agricultural operations.

      b. **North Carolina model:** This is the most frequently utilized model. It *prohibits nuisance lawsuits that occur as a result of changed conditions* in the locality if the agricultural facility has been in operation for one year or more before the changed conditions. In examining a North Carolina-type statute, the Supreme Court of Georgia concluded that "changed conditions . . . in the locality of the facility refers solely to the extension of nonagricultural land uses, residential or otherwise, into existing agricultural areas." *Herrin v. Opatut*, 248 Ga. 140, 281 S.E.2d 575 (1981).

      c. **Tennessee model:** This model provides the *broadest protection* but applies to the *most limited types* of agricultural facilities. For feedlots, dairy facilities, and egg production facilities, if the agricultural facility has been in operation for one year or more before the complaining party's ownership of the land, the agricultural facility is protected from a nuisance cause of action and exempted from other forms of state and local regulation.

    **d. Washington model:** This model provides that an agricultural facility is *presumed reasonable if it is operated in accordance with good agricultural practices* and was established prior to the surrounding nonagricultural uses.

**E. Agricultural zoning:** Zoning is one of the *most popular types* of farmland preservation. Agricultural zoning can be exclusive or nonexclusive.

    **1. Exclusive zoning:** Exclusive zoning *prohibits nonagricultural* use of land within the district. This is unpopular with landowners and is not used frequently. The essential characteristics of this form of zoning are (1) non-farm dwellings are prohibited; (2) there is a direct focus on preserving farm use rather than defining a farm by a large minimum lot size; and (3) each proposed farm dwelling usually requires some individual evaluation under the ordinance.

        **a. Advantage:** The main advantage of this type of zoning is that it insures that there will be *no conflict* between residential and agricultural uses in those areas where non-farm dwellings are prohibited.

        **b. Disadvantages:** The disadvantage of this form of zoning is the fact that there are *higher administrative costs* because of the more extensive restrictions and the requirement for review of farm dwellings. In addition, these ordinances are more difficult to get adopted because they prohibit residential development and upset farmers who might someday want to sell their land to developers.

    **2. Nonexclusive zoning:** With nonexclusive zoning ordinances, preservation is accomplished through the *limiting of density of residential development* by establishing agricultural use as one of the permitted uses within the district. There are four types of nonexclusive zoning:

        **a. Conditional use zones:** This is a direct and effective form of zoning where non-farm dwellings are a *conditional or special use for which a permit must be obtained* upon satisfaction of an ordinance's criteria. Such criteria are usually designed to direct development to land unsuitable for agricultural use. Conditional zones are usually combined with small lot size.

        **b. Large-lot zones:** This is the most common form of nonexclusive zoning. *A minimum lot size is set* in an area in which non-farm development is permitted, thereby limiting the density of development. The lot size usually corresponds to the usual size of farms in the area.

        **c. Fixed area-based allocation zoning:** In this form of zoning there is a *direct linear relationship* between the size of the tract and the number of dwelling units permitted on the tract. Usually this is combined with a small lot size so that development can be clustered thereby leaving a larger area free for agricultural use.

        **d. Sliding-scale area-based allocation zoning:** With this form of zoning the number of dwelling units permitted *does not increase* in direct linear proportion to the size of the parcel. There is usually a clustering of development on a small lot of unproductive soil.

**F. Agricultural districting:** Districting programs provide *incentives* to farmers to join in the voluntary creation of districts to resist the pressures of development. Membership in the district entitles farmers to an array of benefits which vary from state to state.

1. **Benefits:** Benefits may include differential assessment, protection against nuisance ordinances, limits on public investments for non-farm improvements, prohibitions on eminent domain, limitations on special assessments, protection from subdivisions and unregulated development on adjoining land, programs for the purchase of development rights, and agricultural zoning protection.

2. **Formation:** Formation of a district is initiated by one or more farmers and approved by an authorized governmental agency. The districts are created for fixed but renewable periods of time, with an average time for enrollment being from four to ten years. The minimum amount of agricultural land acceptable within an agricultural district is approximately 350 to 500 acres.

## IV. SPECIAL MANAGEMENT TECHNIQUES

Traditionally, land use planning and controls have been the function of local governments, however some states do have state or regional agencies that have supervisory authority over the local governments.

A. **Model Land Development Code (1975):** The Model Land Development Code authorizes the designation of *areas of critical concern* in which the state may establish general principles for guiding development and the review of local decisions or developments of regional impact (DRIs).

B. **Regional planning and development controls:** Regional programs ordinarily govern regions contained entirely within a state but also *may* govern an interstate region, such as the California/Lake Tahoe region.

C. **Development rights programs:** Programs for the purchase and transfer of development rights developed in response to the deficiencies in zoning as a preservation tool.

1. **Purchase of developmental rights:** In a program for the purchase of developmental rights (PDRs), a state or local planning board *purchases* the developmental rights and *holds them* indefinitely (land banking) or until a decision is made to release the rights for development.

2. **Transferable developmental rights:** In a program for TDRs the rights are purchased by *private buyers to be transferred for use in another area*. The standard TDR program establishes a preservation district and a development district. TDRs can be used to allow building at a higher density than ordinarily allowable under the applicable zoning guidelines.

## V. THE ENDANGERED SPECIES ACT (ESA)

The Endangered Species Act has become one of the most controversial limitations on land development. The Endangered Species Act of 1973, Pub. L. No. 93-205, 87 Stat. 884 (codified at 16 U.S.C. §§1531-1544 (1988)).

A. **Purpose:** Congress enacted ESA in 1973 to conserve both endangered and threatened species and also to protect the ecosystems upon which those species depend. The ESA requires the Secretary of the Interior to *take action to avoid jeopardizing the continued existence of a species*. Also, the Secretary is to conserve threatened and endangered species until they are no longer threatened or endangered. *Carson-Truckee Water Conservancy District v. Clark*, 741 F.2d 257 (9th Cir. 1984), *cert. denied, Nevada v. Hodel*, 470 U.S. 1083 (1985). The ESA requires the Secretary to give the highest priority to protecting the endangered species. *Tennessee Valley Authority v. Hill*, 437 U.S. 153 (1978).

**B. Listing a species — §4:** Section 4 provides the Secretary of the Interior with authority to determine whether any species is endangered or threatened.

    **1. Endangered species:** The Secretary considers the following factors in determining if a species is endangered:

        **a.** Degree of habitat destruction;

        **b.** Overutilization for commercial or other purposes;

        **c.** Disease or predation;

        **d.** Failure of existing regulatory mechanisms to protect; and

        **e.** Any other factors affecting its continued existence. ESA §4(a)(l).

    **2. Threatened species:** A species is considered threatened if it is *likely to become endangered in the foreseeable future*. ESA §3(20).

    **3. Critical habitat designated:** Whenever the Secretary decides to list a species as endangered and publishes this listing in the Federal Register, he is required to *specify the range* over which the species is *endangered* and designate areas of *critical habitat*. However, only about 10 percent of listed species have critical habitat designations.

    **4. Fish and Wildlife Service:** The Secretary receives recommendations from the Service; the Service's role is to *assess technical and scientific data* against relevant listing criteria. If the Service disregards expert scientific opinions, it must offer a credible alternative explanation for its listing decision. *Northern Spotted Owl v. Hodel*, 716 F. Supp. 479 (W.D. Wash. 1988). Prior to 2001, the Fish and Wildlife Service usually declined to designate critical habitat for species under the logic that designation under an ''adverse modification'' standard would not add to the protections already provided for under the ''no jeopardy'' standard of §7. In *Sierra Club v. Fish and Wildlife Service*, 245 F.3d 434 (5th Cir. 2001), however, the Fifth Circuit held that basing the ''no jeopardy'' and ''adverse modification'' prohibitions on the effects of the action on recovery *and* survival of the species was improper, as critical habitat designation is only concerned with recovery of a species.

**C. Limits on federal agency action — §7:** Section 7 of ESA prohibits a federal agency from engaging in any action that is *likely to jeopardize* the continued existence of endangered or threatened species or that destroys or adversely affects the critical habitat of such species. ESA §7.

    **1. Consultation required:** Any federal agency proposing an action which may adversely impact an endangered or threatened species *must consult* with the Fish and Wildlife Service before carrying out that action. ESA §7(a).

    **2. Federally funded projects included:** Section 7 covers a wide array of activities because *all projects* funded by the federal government are covered by the section.

        **a. Direct threat:** In *TVA v. Hill*, 437 U.S. 153 (1978), construction of the substantially completed Tellico Dam on the Tennessee River had to be halted due to the threat posed by the endangered snail darter found in the river. The Supreme Court held that once a violation had been established, an injunction had to be issued. See *supra*, p. 23.

   b. **Indirect threat:** In *National Wildlife Fed'n v. Coleman*, 529 F.2d 359 (5th Cir. 1976), *reh'g denied*, 532 F.2d 1375 (5th Cir. 1976), *cert. denied, Boteler v. National Wildlife Federation*, 429 U.S. 979 (1976), the court granted an injunction to prevent the construction of a highway which would lead to future commercial and residential development in the "critical habitat" of the Mississippi Sandhill Crane.

3. **Violations:** Section 7 includes procedural and substantive guidelines. A violation of the Act occurs if either set of guidelines, procedural or substantive, are not followed. *Thomas v. Peterson*, 753 F.2d 754 (9th Cir. 1985).

   **Example:** In *Sierra Club v. Lyng*, 694 F. Supp. 1260 (E.D. Tex. 1988), harms to the endangered red-cockaded woodpecker such as interference with breeding patterns, impairment of essential behavioral patterns, and limitations on foraging areas were enough for a court to order a Forestry Service to change its current forest management system.

D. **Limits on private development — §9:** This section has the greatest impact on private land development activities.

1. **Takings prohibited:** Section 9 makes it unlawful for any person to *"take"* an endangered or threatened species. ESA §9(a)(l).

   a. **"Person" defined:** Person is defined *very broadly* under the Act to include:

   > [A]n individual, corporation, partnership, trust, association, or any other private entity; or any officer, employee, agent, department, or instrumentality of the Federal government, of any State, municipality, or political subdivision of a State, or of any foreign government; any State, municipality, or political subdivision of a State; or any other entity subject to the jurisdiction of the United States. ESA §3(13).

   b. **"Taking" defined:** A "taking" means *"to harass, harm, pursue, hunt, shoot, wound, kill, trap, capture, or collect, or attempt to engage in any such conduct."* ESA §3(19). The terms "harass" and "harm" have received special attention from those interested in private development.

   c. **"Harm" defined:** The regulations define "harm" *very broadly* as:

   > [A]n act which actually kills or injures wildlife. Such an act may include significant habitat modification or degradation where it actually kills or injures wildlife by significantly impairing essential behavioral patterns, including breeding, feeding, or sheltering. 50 C.F.R. §17.3 (1990).

   d. **Harm definition challenged in *Sweet Home*:** In *Sweet Home Chapter of Communities for a Great Oregon v. Babbitt*, 17 F.3d 1463 (D.C. Cir. 1994), the D.C. Circuit Court invalidated the regulation discussed above that included habitat modification in the definition of harm. The Supreme Court, however, overruled the D.C. Circuit and ruled that the FWS regulation defining harm was within the Interior Department's rulemaking discretion under the ESA. *Babbitt v. Sweet Home Chapter of Communities for a Greater Oregon*, 515 U.S. 687, 115 S. Ct. 2407 (1995). The Court found that the Interior Department's interpretation of "harm" was *reasonable and was in accord with the broad purposes* of the ESA.

      i. **O'Connor's concurrence:** Justice O'Connor's concurring opinion suggests the unresolved issues with which the lower courts must struggle. The majority opinion states that the ordinary meaning of harm "naturally encompasses habitat modification that results in actual injury or death to members of an endangered or threatened species.'' 115 S. Ct. at 2418. Justice O'Connor's concurrence is predicated on that assumption and limitation on the regulation's application by proximate causation notions of foreseeability. With those limitations in mind, she proceeds to conclude that *Palila* was wrongly decided because ''destruction of the seedlings did not proximately cause death or injury to identifiable birds; it merely prevented the regeneration of forest land not currently inhabited by actual birds.'' *Id.* at 2421. See also *Loggerhead Turtle v. County Council of Volusia County*, 896 F. Supp. 1170 (M.B. Fla. 1995) (holding that *Sweet Home* did not weaken protection available to listed species and that no case-by-case consideration of the social and economic effects of species protection was needed).

    ii. **Response of Congress:** Congress is reviewing the ESA, in part in response to the Court's decision. The Senate, for example, has recently proposed limitations on the authority of the executive branch to impose habitat restrictions on private landowners.

    iii. **Response of the Executive Branch:** In response to the Senate proposals, the Clinton Administration has introduced new regulations that would *exempt small landowners* from the more demanding provision for the ESA.

  e. **"Harass" defined:** The regulations define ''harass'' to mean

> ''an intentional or negligent act or omission which creates the *likelihood of injury* to wildlife by annoying it to such an extent as to *significantly disrupt normal behavioral patterns* which include, but are not limited to, breeding, feeding or sheltering.'' 50 C.F.R. §17.3 (1990).

While this definition is even more broad than that for ''harm,'' the courts have not yet evaluated its validity.

  f. **Actual and present injury:** In an unusual case, the Ninth Circuit held that actual and present injury had occurred to a species when wild sheep were allowed to eat seedlings which might have provided habitat for the endangered bird. *Palila v. Hawaii Dep't of Land & Natural Resources*, 649 F. Supp. 1070, at 1076-1077 (D. Haw. 1986), *aff'd*, 852 F.2d 1106 (9th Cir. 1988). O'Connor's concurrence in *Sweet Home* questions the analysis of the decision.

2. **Exceptions:** Section 10(a) provides for issuance of permits in two situations: scientific studies and incidental takings.

  a. **Scientific purpose:** If the prohibited activity is to be carried out for *scientific purposes or to enhance the survival* of the species, a permit may be issued. ESA §10(a)(l)(A).

  b. **Incidental taking:** More importantly, the Secretary may permit any taking otherwise prohibited by §9 ''if such taking is *incidental to, and not the purpose of*, the carrying out of an otherwise lawful activity.'' ESA §10(a)(l). However, ESA limits the Secretary's discretion to issue incidental takings permits. ESA §10(a)(2)(A). For example, no incidental taking permit may be issued unless the permit applicant submits a habitat conservation plan. Upon review of habitat conservation plans, courts consider issues such as whether the taking will appreciably reduce survival likelihood and any measures taken to ''minimize and mitigate'' possible adverse effects. *Friends of Endangered Species, Inc. v. Jantzen*, 760 F.2d 976 (9th Cir. 1985). In order to assure the rules and standards under which a permit is issued do not change to the detriment of the landowners, the Fish and Wildlife Service and the National

Marine Fisheries Service adopted a "No Surprises" rule. In the event of extraordinary circumstances, or a foreseeable change in circumstances, the "No Surprises" rule provides for exceptions. Habitat Conservation Plan Assurances ("No Surprises") Rule, 63 Fed. Reg. 8859 (1998) (amending 50 C.F.R. parts 17 and 222).

**E.   Enforcement:** The Act provides four avenues for enforcing §9 prohibitions.

**1.   Civil penalties:** The Secretary of the Interior may impose civil penalties of up to $25,000 for each *knowing violation* of §9 or up to $500 for *any other* violation. ESA §11(a)(1).

**2.   Criminal charges:** The United States may bring criminal charges *for knowing violations*. ESA §11(b)(1). If convicted, a violator may face up to $50,000 in fines and/or up to one year in prison.

**3.   Attorney General injunction:** The Attorney General may bring suit to enjoin any person alleged to be in violation of §9. ESA §11(e)(6).

**4.   Citizen suits:** Private citizens may bring suit in federal court for *injunctive relief*. ESA §11(g). Environmental groups have standing to bring suit on behalf of their members and these suits may only be brought in federal court. However, no suit may be brought *to compel the Secretary to enforce prohibitions* of the Act if the Secretary has already commenced an investigation. ESA §11(g)(2)(B)(ii).

In addition, citizen suits can be brought against persons whose action is imminent and reasonably certain to harm endangered species. Proof by showing a past or current injury to that species is not necessary. *Forest Conservation Council v. Rosboro Lumber Co.*, 50 F.3d 781 (9th Cir. 1995).

**Example:**  The citizen suit provision, however, does not allow anyone to sue under the ESA. In *Bennett v. Plenert*, 63 F.3d 915 (9th Cir. 1995), *cert. granted*, 116 S. Ct. 1316 (1996), the Court of Appeals held that "plaintiffs who assert no interest in preserving endangered species may [not] sue the government for violating the procedures established in" the ESA. 63 F.3d at 916. In this case, plaintiffs were ranchers and irrigation districts who wanted to challenge the water level in two reservoirs that the government determined necessary to preserve two species of fish based on economic reasons. The court found that plaintiffs' suit did not fall within the zone of interest test and, therefore, they did not have standing to sue under the ESA. To allow a suit, the court reasoned, would "permit plaintiffs to sue even though their purposes were plainly inconsistent with, or only 'marginally related' to, those of the Act." 63 F.3d at 919.

---

## *Quiz Yourself* on
## *LAND USE*

**30.**  The CEO of Beautihomes Development Company recently visited the lovely coastal state of Beachachusetts and fell in love with the wild, undeveloped coastal lands. She loved them so much that she purchased a large strip of beachfront, coastal cliffs property. Beautihomes began marketing the potential home sites to many interested buyers. Most of the buyers wanted to own the homes as summer homes, but a few were considering living there year-round. The CEO knew that Beachachusetts might be wary of the development of the property, so she required all the final home purchasers to sign contracts accepting the risks and liabilities of living in such an area.

**(a)** The CEO believes that her land is not regulated under the CZMA because it is not federal land. Is she correct? _____

**(b)** Alternatively, the CEO believes that the contracts with her homeowners allow Beautihomes to move forward with the development even if the state determines that development would be risky. Is she correct? _____

**31.** Beachachusetts is located on the U.S. East Coast. Westachusetts is located on the U.S. West Coast. Both have coastal lands to regulate. Does the federal government simply provide each state with blanket coastal zone regulations? _____

**32.** The CEO of Beautihomes is outraged that her beautiful, beachfront property is not suitable for development according to government regulation. She claims that the federal government enacted the CZMA and CZEG solely to obtain more land under their control. Is she correct? _____

**33.** The Zwimmer family has lived on their land for 45 years. Unfortunately, they live smack-dab in the middle of a floodplain. They got together with their neighbors and decided to purchase flood insurance. The private insurers they approached either did not offer it or were charging astronomical amounts. Do the Zwimmers and their neighbors have any other options? _____

**34.** Constant farming over the past century has turned three acres of Mr. Agri's land into a highly erodible area. He would like to seek federal assistance under ECARP, but cannot afford to lose the agricultural aspect of the land. May he still qualify for assistance? _____

**35.** Pig farms stink. Mr. Agri's farm is a pig farm. Suburbs R Us has purchased all of the land surrounding Mr. Agri's farm and has begun residential development. The homeowners have enthusiastically taken up residence in their new suburbia . . . except they have begun noticing the stink. The new homeowners finally cannot take the odor any longer, their talks with Mr. Agri led nowhere, so they take their complaints to the developer. Suburbs R Us sues Mr. Agri on a nuisance claim. Will they succeed? _____

**36.** Same facts as above. Could Mr. Agri have prevented the development from beginning in the first place? _____

**37.** Suburbs R Us decides to build elsewhere in Ember state. They choose the middle of the state — away from floodplains, farmlands, and coastal zones. After building the first few homes, an ecologically astute person notes that the Bearded Ant habitat is located near the building sites. The head developer does some research and finds out that, in fact, the *only* Bearded Ant habitat in the state is located just yards from their next plot.

**(a)** Is Suburbs R Us automatically prevented from building because of the existence of the Bearded Ant habitat? _____

**(b)** Can Suburbs R Us argue collectively that they are not a "'person'" under the statute? _____

**(c)** Is there anything Suburbs R Us can do besides stop development? _____

---

## *Answers*

**30a.  No.** Federal land is not defined as "'coastal zone'' land, but states are the ones that develop and implement the coastal zone regulations under the CZMA. The regulatory programs are approved and then funded by the federal government. Beautihomes could begin development only if allowed under state regulations.

**30b.  No.** Landowner assumption of risk is irrelevant, as is the suitability of the land for development. If the state determines that the coastal zone is a protected area, not even private ownership trumps that determination.

Consider, however, that Beautihomes could seek compensation from the government under a takings claim if, and only if, every feasible economic use of the entire parcel of land is prohibited.

**31.  No.** Each state designs and implements regulations and protections appropriate for their own state. This allows states with varied coastal zones that may or may not be suitable for protection or development to consider its own needs rather than having blanket regulations enforced on them.

**32.  No.** These Acts were enacted to protect the life and property of landowners, not to place land under federal control. The states are in charge of protecting the land within their own boundaries. If the land was under federal control, it would not be subject to the CZMA at all.

**33.  Yes.** The Zwimmers and their neighbors may participate in the National Flood Insurance Program if they agree to meet federal requirements for reducing potential flood damage.

**34.  Yes.** Although his contract could require him to engage in a less intensive use of his land, the Secretary could permit Mr. Agri to continue agricultural use.

**35.  Not likely.** Mr. Agri is protected by the right-to-farm laws. He was there before the residential development sprung up, so he has protected rights.

The Washington model would serve Mr. Agri best, so long as he is reasonably operating in accordance with good agricultural practices.

**36.  Maybe.** If Mr. Agri could have changed the zoning laws surrounding his land, he could have fought for exclusive zoning. That would have prevented the surrounding land from being used for nonagricultural purposes.

**37a.  No.** The Secretary of the Interior must make a determination that the Bearded Ant is either an endangered or a threatened species before it is a species protected under the ESA. Since the locale is the only one in the state, however, the Secretary is likely to determine that the Bearded Ant is a threatened species at least.

**37b.  No.** "Person" is defined broadly to include corporations such as Suburbs R Us.

**37c.  Yes.** They could submit a habitat conservation plan to the Secretary and receive an incidental taking permit.

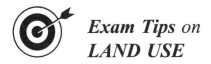 *Exam Tips on*
*LAND USE*

☞ *States have authority and discretion* as far as developing and implementing land use programs and regulations, but never forget that the *federal government holds the purse strings*. Grant applications may be denied or federal funding decreased if the states do not adequately protect their lands.

☞ Few professors will test on the details of the *management programs*, but remember the *nine requirements* that must be satisfied before the program will be funded.

☞ Coastal states must control *nonpoint source pollution* under both the Clean Water Act and the *Coastal Zone Enhancement Grant* (CZEG) program. There are *eight objectives* which CZEG seeks to achieve, and *every coastal state* must develop a program.

    ☞ The EPA publishes *guidelines for management measures* to achieve the *greatest degree of pollutant reduction possible*.

☞ Remember that the Coastal Barrier Resources Act (CBRA) was the first environmental law that *coordinated federal fiscal policy with environmental preservation*. This Act will be important if the fact pattern involves potential development along coastal barriers or barrier islands.

*Example:* Developer A would like to begin construction on new residential condos along the state of Watersedge's coastal barrier. He attempts to obtain a federal loan to offset some of the building costs, but no financial assistance is available according to CBRA regulations. This is true regardless of the suitability or unsuitability for development of Watersedge coastal barriers.

☞ Floods are a problem throughout much of the United States, but few private insurance companies offer flood insurance. The *National Flood Insurance Program (NFIP)* fills that gap, but *does not place liability on the federal government* for flood damage.

    ☞ Remember that property owners in floodplains *must agree to meet federal requirements* for reducing potential flood damage.

☞ *Takings* are a source of contention between the government and the private coastal or floodplain property owners. These owners may be willing to assume the risks of potentially dangerous development, but the government takes the decisions out of their hands through *prohibiting all or almost all use* of coastal or floodplain property. The government can do this because of the *compelling interest* to protect the citizens' lives and the property of beachfront owners.

☞ *Soil erosion* and *nonpoint source pollution* are both related to agriculture and should be addressed in any answer involving agriculture.

    ☞ *Sanctions* may be applicable to those guilty of *contributing to or controlling excessive soil erosion*.

    ☞ The *Environmental Conservation Acreage Reserve Program (ECARP)* assists owners and operators of highly erodible lands and wetlands in conserving and improving their soil and water resources.

☞ Remember that the landowner can receive *technical assistance and cost-sharing* for the conservation measures if she meets all the requirements under the contract to place eligible land into the conservation program.

☞ The *Environmental Quality Incentives Program (EQIP)* falls under ECARP and consolidates the cost-sharing into one program.

☞ Remember that production on a wetland *using normal farming or ranching techniques* is allowed under an exemption to the *swampbusting* regulations.

☛ Development has begun to threaten the nation's farms and *farmland preservation* has become important. The *Farmland Protection Policy Act* is meant to guarantee that federal agencies do not convert too much land to nonagricultural uses. There are few enforcement mechanisms built into this Act, however.

☞ Farms in operation prior to residential development are protected under the *right-to-farm laws*. Remember the *four models* (New York, North Carolina, Tennessee, and Washington) and apply the facts in the hypothetical to the model that fits the best.

☞ *Zoning* is another important protection for agricultural lands. Distinguish between *exclusive and nonexclusive* zoning to determine which fits the facts.

☛ The *Endangered Species Act* is a beloved testing subject because it is considered to be so controversial. The *Secretary of the Interior* is responsible for determining which species are *endangered or threatened*. Remember the *five factors* considered in making the "endangered" determination.

☞ Federal agencies are prohibited from engaging in any action that is *likely to jeopardize* endangered or threatened species. This covers many activities, because *federally funded programs* are included in the prohibition.

☞ When confronted with a fact pattern involving the ESA, first determine if the species is endangered, threatened, or neither. Then determine if the potential activity is being sponsored or performed by the federal government. If it is, then evaluate the likelihood of jeopardy to the species.

☞ Remember also that the ESA has the *greatest impact on private land development*.

*Example:* Developer A has purchased 25 acres of wooded land and is ready to begin development. He soon learns that the Bearded Ant is a threatened species with its main habitat in the middle of his woods. His development will be prohibited because it constitutes a taking under ESA §9.

☞ Remember that the definitions under the ESA are very *broad* and can cover an array of activities, public and private.

☞ *Civil and criminal penalties* are available to the ESA.

## CHAPTER 11

# INTERNATIONAL ENVIRONMENTAL LAW

## *ChapterScope* ━━━━━━━━━━━━━━━━━━━━━━━━━━━━━━━━━━━━━━

As the world becomes increasingly industrialized, the global community has begun to develop a greater awareness of the importance of environmental issues. Maintaining environmental resources on the global level often requires the involvement of multinational organizations and international cooperation. This chapter provides an overview of the most significant issues and statutes in international environmental regulation.

- **History:** The evolution of general principles of international environmental regulations began with the Stockholm Conference of 1972 and continued to the 1982 Rio Earth Summit.

    - A specialized subsidiary of the United Nations, *United Nations Environment Program (UNEP)*, coordinates environmental protection activities for the United Nations as a whole.

    - In 1982, the World Conservation Union drafted the *World Charter*, which sets forth global environmental principles.

- **Transboundary pollution:** States may not injure another state or that state's citizens through pollution. Several leading cases and treaties relate to transboundary pollution and theories of liability.

- **Ozone depletion and global warming:** Several treaties have been developed to prevent the depletion of the *ozone layer* and to protect climate through the control of *greenhouse gases*.

- **Wildlife preservation:** International laws govern areas such as *whaling control*, protection of *endangered species*, and *biodiversity*.

- **Hazardous waste, radioactive pollution, and environmental emergencies:** The 1986 *Chernobyl* accident in the former Soviet Union was the impetus for the regulation and control of *hazardous and radioactive wastes*.

- **Antarctica:** This is the only continent that has *not been commercially exploited*. There are several international laws relating to the protection of Antarctic resources.

- **Deforestation:** The primary concern is for the *destruction of tropical rainforests*, but regulations exist to protect all *forests' genetic resources*.

- **Desertification/land degradation:** Regulations are in place to attempt to prevent land degradation from the *adverse human impact*.

- **Marine environment:** Fewer formal regulations exist to protect the marine environment, so a crucial issue is whether the Conventions on the High Seas *reflect international law* or are *binding only on parties* to the Conventions.

    - *Vessel source pollution* is one of the marine areas controlled through international regulations. Each state must establish *international guidelines*.

- **International trade and environment:** The *General Agreement on Tariffs and Trade (GATT)* codifies most international trade rules. There is not, however, environmental protection under

GATT. The ***North America Free Trade Agreement (NAFTA)*** is unique in that it does ***incorporate environmental protections.***

■ **Military activities and the environment:** International agreements may ***impose liability*** on military activities that harm the environment.

# I. EMERGENCE OF INTERNATIONAL ENVIRONMENTAL LAW

Several international organizations, including the United Nations, have played a fundamental role in developing general principles of international environmental law. The modern development of international environmental law is marked by the 1972 Stockholm Conference and culminated in the 1992 ''Earth Summit'' in Rio de Janeiro, Brazil.

A. **Stockholm Conference:** In 1972, the United Nations sponsored the ***first global conference*** on the environment in Stockholm. The 113 parties to the Stockholm Conference adopted the Stockholm Declaration on the Human Environment, and an Action Plan for the Human Environment.

1. **Stockholm Declaration on the Human Environment:** In this Declaration, the Stockholm Conference parties set forth 26 principles which addressed the major ***environmental themes*** of the time, and ***established a global approach*** to the problem of environmental protection.

    a. **Principle 1:** Principle 1 recognizes a ''fundamental right to freedom, equality and adequate conditions of life, in an environment of a quality that permits a life of dignity and well-being . . .''

    b. **Principle 21:** This principle provides that although states have the ***right to exploit their own resources***, states must ensure that ''activities within their jurisdiction or control do not cause damage to the environment of other states or of areas beyond the limits of national jurisdiction.''

    c. **Principle 22:** This principle affirms that states should cooperate in developing international law regarding liability and compensation ***for victims of pollution and other environmental damage*** produced outside boundaries.

2. **Action Plan for the Human Environment:** In this Plan, the parties to the Conference adopted 109 resolutions which addressed the following items: a ***global environmental assessment program, environmental management activities, and supporting measures***.

B. **United Nations Environment Program (UNEP):** Partly as a result of the Stockholm Conference, the United Nations General Assembly created UNEP in 1973, a specialized subsidiary organ of the United Nations which coordinates ***environmental protection activities*** for the United Nations as a whole.

1. **Structure of UNEP:** UNEP has a Governing Council of 58 members; a Secretariat based in Kenya; and an Environment Fund.

2. **Functions of UNEP:** These functions include gathering information on environmental problems and existing efforts to solve them, recommending and initiating environmental protection

programs, and funding chosen environmental protection programs through utilization of UNEP's Environment Fund.

3. **UNEP's legal activities:** UNEP plays a lead role in the formulation of international environmental law, and sponsored major international environmental agreements including, *inter alia*, the Vienna Convention for the Protection of the Ozone Layer, the Montreal Protocol on Substances that Deplete the Ozone Layer, and the Convention on Biological Diversity.

C. **World Charter for Nature:** Drafted by the World Conservation Union (IUCN) in 1982, the World Charter sets forth global environmental principles. The Charter contains a preamble and 24 articles divided into three sections: general principles, functions, and implementation.

1. **General principles:** These principles state that *nature shall be respected* (Principle 1), and that unique areas of the globe should receive special protection (Principle 3).

2. **Functions:** These principles stress the *importance of integrating nature conservation* into social and economic development planning (Principle 7), and the *necessity of avoiding destruction* of natural resources through either waste, pollution, natural disaster, or other adverse processes (Principles 10-11).

3. **Implementation:** These principles focus on the *importance of incorporating the UN Charter* principles into the law and practice of each state. Of particular importance, Principle 21 provides that states and other entities shall . . .

   a. Cooperate through common activities, such as information exchanges, to conserve nature;

   b. Establish standards for products and manufacturing processes with adverse effects on nature;

   c. Implement international legal provisions for nature conservation and environmental protection;

   d. Ensure that their own activities do not harm the natural systems of other jurisdictions or those areas beyond national jurisdiction; and

   e. Safeguard and conserve natural areas beyond national jurisdiction.

D. **Draft Articles on state responsibility:** The International Law Commission (ILC) has drafted various articles focusing on state responsibility and liability for *transboundary pollution* and other environmental damage. Since 1978, it has separately addressed state responsibility for activities not otherwise prohibited by international law.

1. **Article 1:** Article 1 of the Draft Articles states that "*every internationally wrongful act* of a State entails the international responsibility of that state."

2. **Article 3:** Article 3 states that an intentionally wrongful act occurs when (1) conduct is an act or omission "*attributable to the state* under international law," and (2) "that conduct constitutes a breach of an *international obligation* of the state."

3. **Article 19(3)(d):** In this Article, the ILC listed among international crimes "*a serious breach* of an international obligation of essential importance for the safeguarding and preservation of the human environment, such as those prohibiting massive pollution of the atmosphere or of the seas."

4. **Articles 29, 30, and 31:** These articles describe three circumstances that preclude a state's liability for an otherwise wrongful act under international law: (1) the affected state has *consented* to the act, (2) the act was *a response* to an internationally wrongful act of the other state, and (3) the act was due to "*an irresistible force or to an unforeseen external event* beyond its control." An act consented to by the affected state that is not in conformity with an existing obligation to that state is not wrongful "to the extent that the act *remains within the limits* of that consent." This defense, however, "does not apply if the obligation arises out of a peremptory norm of general international law." An act done in response to a wrongful act of another state is not wrongful only if the act also "constitutes a measure legitimate under international law against that other state, in consequence of . . . [the] wrongful act of the other state." Finally, the "*force majeure* and fortuitous event" defense requires that the extraordinary event made it "materially impossible" for the state to act in conformity with its international obligations, and that the state in question "has [not] contributed to . . . the situation of material impossibility."

E. **Restatement (Third) on Foreign Relations Law in the United States:** The American Law Institute has also addressed state responsibility for environmental damage in the Restatement on Foreign Relations Law. Section 601 provides:

1. A State is obligated to take such measures as may be necessary, to the extent practicable under the circumstances, to ensure that activities within its jurisdiction or control

   a. *conform* to generally accepted international rules and standards for the prevention, reduction, and control of injury to the environment of another state or of areas beyond the limits of national jurisdiction; and

   b. are *conducted so as not to cause significant injury* to the environment of another state or of areas beyond the limits of national jurisdiction.

2. A state is responsible to all other states

   a. for *any violation* of its obligations under Subsection (1)(a), and

   b. for *any significant injury*, resulting from such violation, to the environment of areas beyond the limits of national jurisdiction.

   c. A state is responsible for any significant injury, resulting from a violation of its obligations under Subsection (1), to the environment of another state or its property, or to persons or property within that state's territory or under its jurisdiction or control.

F. **The 1982 Rio Earth Summit:** On the tenth anniversary of the Stockholm Conference, the United Nations sponsored in Rio de Janeiro, Brazil, the U.N. Conference on Environment and Development (UNCED), the largest global conference on the environment, also known as the "Earth Summit."

1. **Summit documents:** The Earth Summit produced *five* major documents: the Convention on Biological Diversity, the Climate Change Convention, the Declaration of Principles on Forest Conservation, the Rio Declaration, and Agenda 21.

2. **The Rio Declaration:** The modern equivalent of the 1972 Stockholm Declaration, the Rio Declaration is a *non-binding* declaration of 27 principles adopted by the Conference and endorsed by the U.N. General Assembly. It is a result of *compromise between the developed and developing nations*, and reflects a balance of the goals of each, including the "right to development" insisted on by the developing countries. Important principles include:

a. **Principle 2:** This principle is a revision of Principle 21 of the Stockholm Declaration with greater emphasis on *states' right to develop their own resources*. It provides:

> States have, in accordance with the Charter of the United Nations and the principles of international law, the sovereign right to exploit their own resources pursuant to their own environmental and developmental policies, and the responsibility to ensure that activities within their jurisdiction or control do not cause damage to the environment of other States or of areas beyond the limits of national jurisdiction.

b. **New elements:** New concepts not encompassed in the Stockholm Declaration include the *precautionary approach* to environmental management (Principle 15), the right to development (Principle 2), and an *obligation to undertake environmental impact assessments* of proposed activities likely to have a significant adverse impact on the environment (Principle 17).

c. **Other key environmental principles:** A number of other concepts address problems associated with transboundary pollution: *notification of environmental emergencies or disasters* (Principle 18), notification and consultation with states regarding transboundary effects of proposed activities (Principle 19), liability and compensation for pollution victims (Principle 13), and warfare (Principle 24).

3. **Agenda 21:** Agenda 21 is an 800 page comprehensive program of action for sustainable development and environmental preservation. It includes a set of priority actions and means for accomplishing the priority actions. There are six priorities:

a. *achieving sustainable growth*, through integrating environment and development in decisionmaking;

b. *fostering an equitable world*, by combating poverty and protecting human health;

c. *making the world habitable* by addressing issues of urban water supply, solid waste management, and urban pollution;

d. *encouraging efficient resource use*, a category which includes management of energy resources, care and use of fresh water, forest development, management of fragile ecosystems, conservation of biological diversity, and management of land resources;

e. *protecting global and regional resources*, including the atmosphere, oceans and seas, and living marine resources; and

f. *managing chemicals and hazardous and nuclear wastes*. A Commission for Sustainable Development, which reports to UNESCO, is established to monitor and review implementation of Agenda 21.

## II. TRANSBOUNDARY POLLUTION

A. **General rule:** As indicated in several of the sources above, *no state may use or permit the use of its territory in a manner that is injurious to another state, or that other state's persons or property*.

1. *Trail Smelter Case:* The *Trail Smelter Case (United States v. Canada)*, 3 R.I.A.A. 1911 (1949) established two fundamental principles of liability for transboundary pollution under international law: (1) a state must show *material damage and causation* to be entitled to legal relief,

not merely that emissions or releases from one state have crossed into the territory of another state, and (2) a state has a ***duty to prevent, and may be held responsible*** for pollution by private parties within its jurisdiction if such pollution results in demonstrable injury to another state.

> In *Trail Smelter*, a smelter near Trail, Canada, emitted 300-350 tons of sulfur dioxide daily. The United States contended that these emissions were harming forests vital to Washington state's lumber industry. The United States and Canada submitted the dispute for arbitration. An arbitration tribunal found that fumes from the smelter had already caused $78,000 damage to the forests, and would continue to cause damage there in the future. The Tribunal held that Canada was legally responsible for the actions of the smelter, ordered Canada to pay damages, and required the smelter to refrain from causing further damage to the United States.

2. ***Corfu Channel Case:*** The *Corfu Channel Case (United Kingdom v. Albania)*, 1949 I.C.J. 4., established the principles that ***every state has an obligation not to knowingly allow its territory to be used for acts contrary to the rights of other states***, and every state has a ***duty to notify states of any imminent danger*** that might harm another state.

> In *Corfu Channel*, the United Kingdom sued Albania in the International Court of Justice (ICJ) for physical damage and loss of life sustained by two British warships which ran into moored contact mines in the Straits of Corfu. The ICJ determined that the laying of the minefield could not have been done without Albania's knowledge, and that Albania did not notify the United Kingdom of the minefield's existence or warn the approaching warships. The ICJ recognized that permitting extraterritorial damage from intrastate activity which is in and of itself lawful may, nevertheless, render a state responsible for the damage inflicted, and held Albania responsible for the damages caused to the United Kingdom.

3. ***Lake Lanoux Arbitration:*** The *Lake Lanoux Arbitration (France v. Spain)*, 12 R.I.A.A. 281 (1957), held that ***downstream states do not have a right of veto*** over an upstream state's use of water, but the panel also stated that an upstream state must consider the counterproposals of a downstream state offered to it.

4. ***Nuclear Test Cases:*** The *Nuclear Test Cases (Australia v. France)*, 1973 I.C.J. 99 and *(New Zealand v. France)*, 1973 I.C.J. 135, left the legality of atmospheric nuclear testing unresolved on the merits, although the International Court of Justice did preliminarily enjoin France from testing while it heard the dispute.

> In the *Nuclear Test Cases*, Australia and New Zealand claimed that atmospheric nuclear testing by France was causing them to incur risks and damages. The ICJ enjoined France from further testing until final judgment. The merits of the case were never reached, however, because the French government unilaterally decided to halt its testing, thus rendering the case moot according to the ICJ.

B. **Possible theories of liability for transboundary pollution under international law:** Such theories include: (1) an absolute duty to protect against harm from ultrahazardous activities which, if violated, results in a state being held strictly liable; (2) responsibility for negligent or intentional acts ("abuse of rights"); and (3) liability for a state which permits transboundary pollution to exceed that which its neighbors can reasonably be expected to endure ("good neighborliness"). Of these theories, the least clearly established in customary international law is strict liability for ultrahazardous activities.

1. **Specific treaties focusing on transboundary pollution:** Treaties in this area take a variety of approaches, such as agreeing to try to reach agreement ("framework conventions"), establish-

ing substantive standards, "freezing" pollution at current levels, providing for notification and consultation, and authorizing an international organization to establish applicable rules.

a. **Acid rain treaties:** Various treaties and agreements have been negotiated in response to the growing problem of acid rain. Acid rain is caused by gases, such as sulfur oxides and nitrogen oxides, dissolving into water carried in the air. These gases form acids in the atmosphere, and the acids descend to land through precipitation.

   i. **Convention on Long-Range Transboundary Air Pollution 1979:** This Convention was adopted in Geneva and went into force March 16,1983. As of December 1991, 33 states including the United States were parties to the Convention. The purpose is to "limit, and as far as possible, gradually reduce and prevent air pollution including long-range transboundary air pollution." The Convention provides for enforcement through *research, exchange of information, and an Interim Executive Body* (IEB). The IEB was established to carry out a cooperative program for monitoring pollution in Europe. The Convention also includes *notice and consultation* requirements. The Convention's weakness is the lack of ceilings and timetables to achieve reduction in acid rain.

      (a) **Sulphur Emissions Protocol:** This Protocol went into force in 1987. Using 1980 levels as a basis, the Protocol requires the reduction of sulfur emissions or their transboundary fluxes by 30 percent by 1993. The Protocol also requires annual reporting of sulfur emissions. Several major sulfur producers — including the United States and the United Kingdom — did not ratify this Protocol.

      (b) **Nitrogen Oxides Protocol:** This Protocol requires the stabilization of nitrogen dioxide emissions or their transboundary fluxes at 1987 levels by 1994. The Protocol covers major stationary sources and vehicle emissions. The Protocol also requires use of the best available technology for national emissions standards, and eventual negotiation of internationally accepted "critical loads."

# III. OZONE DEPLETION AND GLOBAL WARMING

A. **Protection of the ozone layer:** Several treaties address the problem of the depletion of the ozone layer. The ozone layer in the atmosphere filters out harmful ultraviolet radiation from the sun. Chlorofluorocarbons (CFCs) are *primarily responsible* for the depletion of the ozone layer. CFCs are used in air conditioning, aerosols, styrofoam, and refrigerators. As more radiation reaches the earth due to the depletion of the ozone layer, the incidence of cancer, smog, and eye disease increases.

1. **Vienna Convention for the Protection of the Ozone Layer 1985:** This framework convention primarily focuses on information exchange, and cooperation among states in research and scientific assessments on the depletion of the ozone layer. The Convention's goal is to *develop appropriate measures* to protect human health and the environment against adverse effects resulting from or likely to result from activities which modify or are likely to modify the ozone layer. The Convention also allows the parties to the Convention to adopt protocols to implement the goals of the Convention.

2. **Montreal Protocol on Substances that Deplete the Ozone Layer:** This Protocol to the Vienna Convention was originally adopted in 1987, and was amended in 1990.

a. **1987 Protocol:** This Protocol was in force in 1989. The Protocol *sets forth a timetable* for the reduction in use of CFCs — 50 percent by 1999. The Protocol also bans CFC imports of nonparties unless the nonparties meet the reductions of the Protocol. The Protocol freezes halons at 1986 levels.

b. **1990 Amendments:** These amendments placed a *total ban on CFCs by the year 2000* (by the year 2010 for developing countries). The amendments provide for graduated reduction in CFCs: 20 percent by 1993, 50 percent by 1995, and 85 percent by 1997 (based on 1986 levels). The amendments also establish a 14-member executive committee, and a $240 million fund to assist developing countries in the transition to technology free of CFCs.

B. **Protection of the climate:** Another serious environmental problem is climate change due to the *greenhouse effect*. The greenhouse effect results when gases in the air, such as carbon dioxide, methane, CFCs, and nitrogen dioxide, trap infrared radiation near the surface of the earth, preventing the radiation from escaping into the atmosphere and thus elevating global temperatures.

1. **United Nations resolutions on climate change:** Two resolutions passed in 1989 recognize climate change as a common concern of mankind and a topic to be given high priority by United Nations organizations and programs. These resolutions *emphasize the need for governmental and intergovernmental efforts* to prevent detrimental effects on the climate. The resolutions also review possible elements that may be included in an international convention on climate change.

2. **United Nations Framework Convention on Climate Change (UNFCCC):** This Convention was signed at the Earth Summit held in Rio de Janeiro during June 1992. The Convention emphasizes the *concern over changes in the Earth's climate*, especially those changes caused by greenhouse gases, and has as its objective the stabilization of greenhouse gas concentrations in the atmosphere. No specific controls or deadlines are set, although the Convention has an implicit goal of returning to 1990 levels of emissions by 2000.

   a. **Commitments of the parties:** The parties to the Convention commit themselves to the following goals: periodic national inventories of anthropogenic emissions and removal by sinks of greenhouse gases; mitigation programs on a national and regional level; the development of technology to control emissions; the consideration of climate change in various decision-making processes; and cooperation in the exchange of information, education, and public awareness. In addition, developed countries commit to the adoption of national policies and mitigation measures; the use of the best available scientific technology for calculation; and the financing of developing countries to help them meet their obligations under the Convention.

   b. **Structure of the Convention:** The Convention establishes a Conference of the Parties to review implementation of the Convention and to adopt protocols, amendments, and annexes as needed. A Secretariat is also established to arrange for sessions of the Conference and to prepare reports on climate change. The Convention also provides for two subsidiary bodies, one for implementation and another for scientific and technological advice. A financial mechanism is included in the Convention to enable developing countries to meet the demands of the Convention.

# IV. WILDLIFE PRESERVATION

**A. Provisions under the Stockholm Declaration and the World Charter for Nature:** Both the Stockholm Declaration and the World Charter for Nature contain provisions focusing on the preservation of wildlife.

1. **Stockholm Declaration:** In Principle 4, the Declaration states that the plants and animals of the earth are a world heritage, and that man has a *special responsibility* to safeguard nature. Principle 4 also states that nature conservation should receive a place of importance in economic development planning.

2. **World Charter for Nature:** In Principle 2, the World Charter stresses the need to *safeguard necessary habitats* so that the genetic viability of the earth is not compromised, and the necessity of maintaining population levels of all life forms is sufficient for survival. In Principle 3, the World Charter states that all areas of the earth are subject to conservation, and that special protection should be provided for unique areas.

**B. International Convention for the Regulation of Whaling:** The International Whaling Commission was established by the International Convention for the Regulation of Whaling of 1946. The original intent of the Convention's framers was to negotiate a fishing treaty to regulate the whaling industry. Implementation of the Convention has been *increasingly directed to conservation of whales.*

1. **Structure of the Commission:** The Commission has one member from each contracting government. The Commission holds annual sessions to analyze information about the whaling industry and adopt recommendations for regulation. Three standing committees are the technical, scientific, and finance and administration committees.

2. **Functioning of the Convention:** A schedule with whaling regulations is published annually. The Commission has the power to modify the schedule. The Convention also contains an opt-out provision — any member may exempt itself from compliance with any regulation by objecting. The Commission adopted a three-year moratorium on commercial whaling in 1982 and extended that moratorium in 1990 for ten more years.

**C. Convention on International Trade in Endangered Species of Wild Fauna and Flora (CITES):** With over 100 parties, this Convention sets up a complex system of *import and export permits* and regulations to safeguard endangered species from over-exploitation.

1. **Structure of the Convention:** The Convention establishes a Secretariat operated under UNEP which prepares scientific and technical studies. The Secretariat also coordinates the national recordkeeping and reporting required by the Convention. The Convention establishes a Conference of State Parties which meets every two years to adapt the Convention to evolving conditions.

2. **Functioning of the permit system:** The import and export permits required under the Convention are *nationally administered* and are *keyed to categories of endangered species.* Exemptions from the permits system exist, and *states are permitted to take stricter measures* if they wish. The categories of endangered species are contained in the appendices to the Conventions. Appendix I contains all species threatened with extinction which are or may be affected by trade; Appendix II contains those species which are not currently threatened but which may become so; and Appendix III contains species which states designate as "locally endangered."

No permit may be issued for commercial use of an Appendix I species or a recognizable part or derivative of such a species.

**D. United Nations Convention on Biological Diversity:** This Convention was signed at the Earth Summit held in Rio de Janeiro in June 1992. The objectives of the Convention include conserving biological diversity and the sustainable use of its components, and the equitable sharing of benefits of utilizing genetic resources.

1. **Commitments of the parties:** The parties of the Convention obligate themselves to the following: developing national strategies for the conservation of biological diversity; integrating conservation into sectoral or cross-sectoral plans; developing identification and monitoring schemes; establishing a system of protected areas, adopting incentive measures; cooperating in the establishment of research and training programs; public education and awareness programs; and impact assessment procedures.

2. **Structure of the Convention:** The Convention establishes a Conference of the Parties to review implementation, and to adopt protocols, amendments, and annexes. A Secretariat is also established to arrange meetings of the Conference and prepare reports on biological diversity. The Convention sets up a subsidiary body to provide scientific, technical, and technological advice to the Conference. The Convention also contains an arbitration mechanism, and the opportunity for a conciliation commission.

# V. HAZARDOUS WASTE, RADIOACTIVE POLLUTION, AND ENVIRONMENTAL EMERGENCIES

**A. Early conventions on civil liability for nuclear damage:** These conventions include the Paris Convention of Third Party Liability in the Field of Nuclear Energy of 1960, the Brussels Convention Supplementary to the Paris Convention, the Vienna Convention on Civil Liability for Nuclear Damage of 1963, and the Joint Protocol Relating to the Application of the Vienna Convention and the Paris Convention of 1988.

1. **Vienna Convention on Civil Liability for Nuclear Damage 1963:** Based on the Paris Convention and its Brussels Supplementary Convention, this Convention gives jurisdiction to the courts of the state in whose territory the damage occurred. The operator of a nuclear installation is *absolutely* liable for nuclear damage, but exemptions exist. A victim of nuclear damage must present a claim within ten years from the date of the accident or the claim is barred by the Convention. The Convention also requires the installation state to insure payment of the claim against the operator. Few states are parties to the Convention, and none of the parties are major nuclear powers.

2. **Joint Protocol Relating to the Application of the Vienna Convention and the Paris Convention 1988:** This Protocol was negotiated by the International Atomic Energy Agency (IAEA) in cooperation with the Nuclear Energy Agency (NEA) of the Organization for Economic Cooperation and Development (OECD). The purposes of the Protocol are to *eliminate conflicts of law* when both conventions apply, and to require the parties of each convention to grant each other a right of compensation under each instrument.

**B. The Chernobyl accident and resulting conventions:** On April 26, 1986, an explosion occurred in a reactor at the Chernobyl nuclear power plant in the Soviet Union. The accident raised questions about the adequacy of international law in compensating victims of nuclear accidents, and utilizing international law to prevent such accidents in the future and to inform states when such accidents occur. As a result of the accident, two conventions were negotiated.

1. **Convention on Early Notification of a Nuclear Accident:** This Convention was signed by 58 states on September 26, 1986. The Convention provides for *notification ''forthwith''* and information regarding nuclear accidents ''which has resulted or may result in an international transboundary release that could be of radiological safety significance for another state.'' States are also required to notify the IAEA of the authority responsible for the accident.

2. **Convention on Assistance in the Case of a Nuclear Accident or Radiological Emergency 1986:** Also signed on September 26, 1986, this Convention provides that parties should *cooperate in coordinating emergency response and assistance* in the event of a nuclear accident that could involve transboundary radiological release. Under this treaty, any exposed state can claim assistance. The Convention focuses on efforts prior to and after nuclear accidents. Prior to accidents, the Convention requires the identification of experts, equipment, and materials available; financial assistance; and elaboration of emergency plans. After accidents, states which require assistance are required to indicate the scope and type of assistance needed. The IAEA has a central role under the Convention in facilitating cooperation among the parties, receiving and dispersing information about accidents, and coordinating emergency response to nuclear accidents.

C. **Basel Convention on the Control of Transboundary Movements of Hazardous Wastes and their Disposal:** This Convention seeks to *limit and regulate international traffic in hazardous waste products*.

1. **Obligations of the parties:** General obligations include prohibiting the export of hazardous waste without prior approval of the importing country, and proof that the importing country has adequate facilities to dispose of the waste; prohibiting trade with nonparties; minimizing the generation of hazardous waste; managing exported waste in an environmentally sound manner; labeling and packaging shipments of waste in accordance with generally accepted international rules and standards; and cooperating in training of technicians, the exchange of information, and the transfer technology.

2. **Structure of the Convention:** The Convention establishes a Conference of the Parties to review implementation, and to adopt protocols, amendments, and annexes. The Convention also establishes a Secretariat to arrange meetings of the Conference and to prepare reports.

# VI. ANTARCTICA

Antarctica comprises about ten percent of the earth's land and water mass, and is the *only continent that has not been economically exploited*. The principal mechanisms for protection of the Antarctic environment are described below.

A. **Antarctic Treaty of 1959:** The Antarctic Treaty was the first international agreement governing the use of Antarctica. Its goal was to *assure continued scientific research* while suspending states the right to claim ''sectors'' of the continent.

1. **Antarctic Treaty Consultative Parties (ATCPs):** The ATCPs include 38 states: the 12 original signatories (the Antarctic Directorate) and 26 other states who have since signed the treaty

and have conducted substantial scientific research activity there. Other signatories are referred to as non-consultative parties.

2. **Environmental provisions:** Two provisions are environmentally important: Article 5 *prohibits nuclear explosions and disposal* of radioactive waste material; and Article 9(1) *requires the original signatories to meet regularly* to exchange information, consult on matters of common interest, and, if necessary, formulate measures to further the objectives of the Treaty — which may concern preservation and conservation of living resources in Antarctica. State representatives have adopted several measures designed to protect living organisms on the continent, including the establishment of a "special conservation zone" within the boundaries of the treaty, and "Specially Protected Areas" within that zone.

B. **Convention for the Conservation of Antarctic Seals:** This Convention, signed in 1972, recognizes the necessity to protect Antarctic seals, which had almost disappeared from excessive hunting. The Treaty *does not ban* hunting, but instead establishes a regulatory system to prevent overexploitation. Some species are totally protected by the Treaty.

C. **Convention on the Conservation of Antarctic Marine Living Resources:** This Convention, signed in 1980, covers conservation of Antarctic marine resources within the entire Antarctic marine ecosystem. This zone, called the Antarctic Convergence, extends beyond the original Antarctic Treaty area to the physical boundaries of the Antarctic Ocean. Its objectives, described in Article 11(3), reflect its ecological perspective: maintenance of the levels of population sufficient to ensure their viability, protection of ecological relations, and prevention of changes that could have irreversible effects. The *"rational use" of resources is permitted* within this context. The Convention has created two organs to implement the Treaty, the Commission for the Conservation of Antarctic Marine Living Resources, which must meet at least once a year, and a Scientific Committee to assist the Commission.

D. **Agreed Measures for the Conservation of Antarctic Fauna and Flora:** The ATCPs adopted these measures in 1964. The most significant provision is the declaration of the Antarctic Treaty Area as a "Special Conservation Area." It establishes a *regulatory permit system* for the killing or harming of mammals or birds and requires states to take steps to minimize habitat interference and water pollution. Areas of outstanding scientific interest are designated as "Specially Protected Areas" subject to special regulatory protections.

E. **The 1991 Madrid Protocol:** The Madrid protocol provides the *first comprehensive protection of the Antarctic environment*.

1. **Specific protection:** Article 3 establishes the basic environmental principle underlying the Protocol, with paragraph 1 stating that protection of the Antarctic environment "shall be the fundamental consideration[] in the planning and conduct of all activities in the Antarctic Treaty Area." In furtherance of this principle, paragraph 2 of Article 3 provides for the first time a *basis for a uniform standard to assess all human activity* on Antarctica. It states that all activities "shall be planned and conducted so as to limit adverse impacts on the Antarctic environment . . . [and] on the basis of information sufficient to allow prior assessments of . . . their possible impacts on the Antarctic environment." Subparagraph (d) of Article 3(2) provides for "regular and effective monitoring . . . to allow assessment of impacts . . . including the verification of predicted impacts." Article 11 establishes a Committee for Environmental Protection, an independent body meant to oversee compliance with the Protocol. Under Article 9 of the Protocol, the Annexes constitute an integral part of the agreement. They include: Annex I (establishing

procedures for environmental impact assessment, including a provision for public notice and comment), Annex II (conservation of wild flora and fauna), Annex III (procedures on waste disposal and management that aim to reduce and remove waste "to the maximum extent possible"), Annex IV (prevention of marine pollution), and Annex V (area protection and management). The most controversial aspect of the Protocol is that it effectively bans mining on Antarctica for at least 50 years. Article 7 expressly prohibits "any activity relating to mineral resources other than scientific research."

2. **Amending the Protocol:** Although Article 12 contains amendment and modification procedures which may be invoked at any time, amendments to ban require unanimity of the consultative parties. In 2041, the Protocol will be open for review by the parties, who will have an opportunity to amend the agreement. An amendment requires adoption by a majority of the parties, including three-quarters of the states which are consultative parties at the time of adoption of the Protocol. However, no amendment takes effect until ratification by three-quarters of the consultative parties, including all of the states which were consultative parties at the time of adoption of the Protocol. Under Article 25, a party may opt-out from Article 7, effective two years after giving notice, if an amendment to the Article has been successfully adopted but fails to be entered into force within three years of its adoption.

# VII. DEFORESTATION

Deforestation involves the ***unsustainable use of forests and their genetic resources***. Of primary concern today is the destruction of tropical rainforests.

A. **Consequences:** Although states have not agreed on a definition of the problem, a ***fundamental cause is thought to be poverty***. Local impacts include floods and droughts, siltation of rivers, destruction of breeding areas, and the threat to the survival of over 140 million forest dwellers worldwide. Globally, deforestation is thought to be the primary cause of loss of biodiversity, including medicinal plants, and a major contributor to the greenhouse effect due to the release of carbon dioxide from forest burning and the loss of tropical forests as consumers of carbon dioxide.

B. **The 1984 International Tropical Timber Agreement:** This agreement, administered by the International Tropical Timber Organization (ITTO), is the ***only international agreement regulating tropical timber***. It includes 22 producing states and 24 consuming states and accounts for over 95 percent of the international trade in tropical timber. Although any trade restrictions on tropical timber would likely require action by the ITTO, the Timber Agreement is based on the principle of free trade, and is unlikely to be changed for environmental reasons alone.

C. **The Rio Forest Principles:** The United States ***proposed a binding deforestation agreement*** during a preparatory meeting for UNCED, but was met with considerable opposition from developing countries concerned about threats to sovereignty over their natural resources. The result was an agreement adopted by the Conference called the ***Non-Legally Binding Authoritative Statement of Principles for a Global Consensus on the Management, Conservation and Sustainable Development of All Types of Forests***, or Rio Forest Principles. In the Rio Forest Principles, the parties agree to promote international cooperation on forestry, but do not commit to any specific actions or deadlines.

D. **Debt-for-nature swaps:** Debt-for-nature swaps, first introduced in 1987 by non-governmental organizations (NGOs), involve the ***purchase of foreign debts of debtor countries in exchange for*** *the creation of domestic forest reserves* or other environmental projects. Countries such as Bolivia, Ecuador, and Costa Rica have already participated in such swaps, and many other countries are currently considering similar plans.

1. **Public vs. private debt-for-nature swaps:** The first generation of debt-for-nature swaps were ''private,'' meaning at least one of the parties involved was private. A ''second generation'' of swaps has recently emerged, called ''public'' swaps. These occur between sovereign states and, to date, have provided a greater amount of debt reduction than private swaps.

2. **Three new types of public debt-for-nature swaps:** Three types of public swaps have emerged, each with different enforcement mechanisms:

   a. **Government debt purchases:** Similar to private debt exchanges, this swap involves the government of one country agreeing to buy private debt of another in exchange for reforestation or conservation projects. Enforcement mechanisms are determined by the nature of the agreement between the parties. To date, these agreements have lacked traditional enforcement provisions, and instead rely on the friendly relations between the parties.

   b. **Government grants to environmental groups:** In the United States, the U.S. Agency for International Development has statutory authority to make grants to NGOs, which in turn may support reforestation efforts in countries that have ''the capacity, commitment and record of environmental concern to oversee the long-term viability of . . . the project.'' Although legal agreements are required prior to a grant, specific terms and enforcement provisions have not been mandated.

   c. **Debt forgiveness:** The largest debt-for-nature exchange is contained in the Enterprise for Americas Initiative (EAI) proposed by the United States. Within the EAI, the United States has structured a number of environmental framework agreements with countries such as Chile, Bolivia, and Jamaica that *are designed to replace old debt with new, and funnel funds* directly to environmental projects. By statute, enforcement provisions of these agreements must be ''reasonable.'' One example is a strong mechanism for dispute resolution: the host country can cut off all future funds to a country if a dispute cannot be solved. Other exchanges proposed in Europe focus on environmental cleanup efforts rather than conservation.

# VIII.  DESERTIFICATION/LAND DEGRADATION

Desertification is identified in Agenda 21 as one of the key global environmental problems that not only affects the quality of the environment but also is *critically linked* to the goal of achieving sustainable development in all countries. Desertification affects about one sixth of the population and one quarter of the total land area of the world. While some degraded lands can be reclaimed with a reasonable amount of effort and resources, severely or totally degraded land may be permanently lost.

A. **Definition:** Desertification is defined by the United Nations as land degradation in arid, semi-arid and dry sub-humid areas (including irrigated cropland) *resulting mainly from adverse human impact* (improper land use). A number of factors are involved, including demographics, overgrazing, deforestation, sources of energy, water resources and irrigation, and erosion.

**B.  The Lome IV Convention:** Signed in 1989 between the EEC and the African, Caribbean, and Pacific States (ACP), this agreement specifically addresses the problem of desertification in Title I, which calls for specific actions on national, regional, and international levels to *preserve resources* and *protect ecosystems* against desertification and drought.

**C.  Past U.N. efforts to combat desertification:** The U.N. Conference on Desertification (UNCOD), held at UNEP in Nairobi in 1977, was the first world conference to set out a Plan of Action for *initiating and sustaining a cooperative effort* to combat desertification. Focusing on technical and economic reforms, the Plan attempted to reinforce and integrate national, regional, and global actions within and outside of the U.N. The status of the Plan of Action was reviewed in 1992, when it was found that little progress was made.

**D.  Current U.N. efforts:** Chapter 12 of Agenda 21 includes six program areas countries agree to focus on:

1. **Strengthening the knowledge base and developing information and monitoring systems** for regions prone to desertification and drought;

2. **Combating land degradation** through, *inter alia*, intensified soil conservation and reforestation activities;

3. **Creating integrated development programs** for the eradication of poverty and promotion of alternative livelihood systems in areas prone to desertification;

4. **Developing comprehensive anti-desertification programs** and integrating them into national development plans and national environmental planning;

5. **Developing drought preparedness and relief schemes** and programs to cope with environmental refugees; and

6. **Promoting environmental education** about desertification and drought.

**E.  Treaty envisioned:** Paragraph 12.40 of Agenda 21 requires the U.N. General Assembly to establish a committee to oversee the creation of an international convention to combat land degradation and drought. The committee, established in 1992, is currently formulating an agreement.

# IX.  MARINE ENVIRONMENT

Prior to the 1960s there was very little protective regulation of the marine environment. The limited provisions of the 1958 Convention on the High Seas contemplated future action. In the 1970s, general rules for the preservation of the global environment imposed a few limitations on pollution of the seas. Growing concern with marine pollution led to inclusion of extensive provisos in the LOS Convention for protection and preservation of the marine environment. A crucial issue is whether these provisions can be said to reflect *customary international law* or whether they are only binding on parties to the Convention.

**A.  The 1958 Conventions:** The only provisions of the 1958 Convention specifically addressed to preservation of the marine environment are articles 24 and 25 of the Convention on the High Seas. Article 24 requires states to *regulate to prevent pollution* of the seas by oil discharge from ships, pipelines, or deep seabed activities. Article 25 calls on states to take *measures to prevent pollution* of the seas from radioactive materials.

B. **The Stockholm Declaration and general obligation to preserve the environment:** In 1972, the Stockholm Declaration was adopted at the United Nations Conference on the Human Environment. Principle 7 of the Declaration requires states to take ''all possible steps'' to *prevent pollution* of the seas. Principle 21 provides that states must ensure, in exercising their sovereign rights to exploit their resources, ''that activities within their jurisdiction or control do not cause damage to the environment or other states or of areas beyond the limit of national jurisdiction.'' Principle 21 expanded upon the international law principle that no state could use or permit its territory to be used in a manner injurious to another state's territory. See, *e.g., The Trail Smelter Case (U.S. v. Canada)*, 3 R.I.A.A. 1905 (1941). Principle 22 further requires states to cooperate to develop international law for liability and compensation for damage caused by states to areas beyond their jurisdiction.

C. **Third United Nations Conference on the Law of the Sea:** Article 192 of the LOS Convention outlines the general obligations of states to *protect and preserve the marine environment*. States are required to meet this obligation by taking all measures necessary to prevent pollution of the marine environment from any source. *LOS Convention*, art. 194, ¶1. All sources of pollution of the marine environment must be considered, such as: (1) the release of toxic, harmful, or noxious substances from land-based sources, from or through the atmosphere, or by dumping; (2) pollution from vessels; (3) pollution from installations and devices used in the exploration or exploitation of the natural resources of the seabed and subsoil; and (4) pollution from other installations operating in the marine environment. Art. 194, ¶3. The provisions apply to commercial ships; states have only to ensure that warships, as far as practicable, act consistently with international rules and standards. Art. 236.

1. **Regional standards adopted:** States are required to *harmonize their policies on a regional level* with regard to pollution from land-based sources and from seabed activities within zones of national jurisdiction. *LOS Convention*, arts. 207, ¶3,208, ¶4.

2. **Global standards adopted:** States are requested to *harmonize their policies on a global level* with regard to pollution from land-based sources, seabed activities subject to national jurisdiction, pollution from dumping, and pollution of the marine environment through or from the atmosphere. *LOS Convention*, arts. 207, ¶4,208, ¶5,210, ¶4,212, ¶3.

D. **Vessel-source pollution:** States are required to establish *international guidelines* governing vessel-source pollution through international organizations, such as the International Maritime Organization or through general diplomatic conference. *LOS Convention*, art. 211.

1. **Flag state jurisdiction:** Flag states are *required to adopt* laws and regulations for the prevention of pollution of the marine environment from ships flying their flag or of their registry. Areas of regulation include: (1) the design, construction, equipment, operation and manning of vessels; (2) accident prevention; (3) emergency procedures; (4) operations of sea safety standards; and (5) prevention of intentional and unintentional discharges. *LOS Convention*, arts. 194, ¶3, cl. b, 211.

2. **Coastal state regulation in ports, in internal waters, and in the territorial sea:** Coastal states may adopt laws and regulations for the prevention, reduction, and control of marine pollution from foreign vessels within their territorial sea but *may not hamper innocent passage*. States may set standards for pollution prevention as a condition for entrance into their ports or for internal waters. *LOS Convention*, art. 211, ¶¶3-4.

3. **Coastal state jurisdiction in the EEZ:** States *may regulate vessel-source pollution in the EEZ* in accordance with generally accepted rules and standards through a competent interna-

tional organization or diplomatic conference. Coastal states may request a competent international organization to authorize the states to adopt additional regulations if the reviewing organization finds that the international rules and standards are inadequate to protect an area of their exclusive economic zones. *LOS Convention*, art. 21, ¶6.

E.  **Pollution from land-based sources:** All states must adopt laws or regulations to ***prevent pollution of the marine environment from land-based sources***. *LOS Convention*, art. 207.

F.  **Ocean dumping:** States are required to adopt laws and regulations to ***prevent pollution of the marine environment by the dumping of sewage, sludge, and other waste materials into the ocean***. *LOS Convention*, art. 210. These laws must be no less stringent than global standards. Dumping in the territorial sea, exclusive economic zone, or continental shelf of a state, requires permission from the proper state authorities. The 1972 Convention on the Dumping of Wastes at Sea sets forth regulations regarding three categories of waste. The Convention prohibits the dumping of materials listed in Annex I: (1) high level radioactive wastes; (2) materials produced for biological and chemical warfare; and (3) non-biodegradable synthetic materials. Dumping of wastes in the second category, which includes low-level radioactive wastes, requires a special permit. The third category of waste materials requires only a general prior permit. Annex III to the Convention specifies terms and conditions upon which general and special permits are issued.

G.  **Pollution from seabed activities subject to national jurisdiction:** States are required to adopt all laws and regulations necessary to ***prevent pollution of the marine environment arising from or in connection with their exploration and exploitation of the seabed and subsoil***, or from artificial islands, installations, and structures under their jurisdictions, taking into account any internationally agreed upon standards. *LOS Convention*, art. 194, ¶3, cl. e, art. 208.

H.  **Pollution from deep seabed mining:** Part XI of the *LOS Convention* authorizes the Authority to adopt appropriate rules and regulations to prevent pollution of the marine environment from ***deep seabed activities***.

I.  **Pollution from or through the atmosphere:** All states are required to adopt laws and regulations to prevent pollution of the marine environment ***from or through the atmosphere***, taking into account internationally agreed upon rules. All vessels flying a state's flag or aircraft under the state's registry must abide by the regulations. *LOS Convention*, art. 212.

J.  **Protection of fragile ecosystems:** States are obligated specifically to take measures necessary to protect and preserve ***rare or fragile ecosystems as well as the habitat of depleted, threatened, or endangered species and other forms of marine life***. *LOS Convention*, art. 194, ¶5,211. A Coastal state also may adopt and enforce ***non-discriminatory*** laws and regulations for the prevention, reduction, and control of marine pollution from vessels in ice-covered areas within its exclusive economic zone, where severe climatic conditions and the presence of ice for most of the year create obstructions or exceptional hazards to navigation. Art. 234.

K.  **Liability:** A state which fails to fulfill its obligations to protect and preserve the marine environment is ***liable in accordance with international law***. States must ensure resource is available for ***prompt and adequate relief*** for damage caused by pollution. States must cooperate to be developed to assure prompt and adequate compensation for damage caused by pollution of the marine environment, such as compulsory insurance or compensation funds. *LOS Convention*, art. 235.

1.  **Liability for nuclear accidents:** Article 2 of the 1962 Nuclear Ships Convention provides that the operator of a nuclear ship ''shall be ***absolutely liable*** for any nuclear damage upon proof

that such damage has been caused by a nuclear incident involving the nuclear fuel of, or radioactive products or waste produced in, such ship.'' The licensing state is obligated to insure payments are made for the claims for compensation for injuries resulting from a nuclear accident.

2. **Liability for oil pollution:** The 1969 Convention on Civil Liability for Oil Pollution Damage governs injuries caused by oil pollution in a state party's territory or territorial sea. Because the Convention did not provide *full compensation* for victims of oil pollution injuries, the 1971 Convention concerning an International Fund for Compensation for Oil Pollution Damage was promulgated.

L. **Enforcement:** Flag states, coastal states, and port states may enforce rules and regulations relating to the marine environments. The extent of their enforcement powers varies, depending on the source of pollution, the location of the violation, and the degree of harm to the environment.

1. **Flag state enforcement:** Flag states are obligated to ensure that all ships flying their flags or registry *comply with international rules and standards* established by the competent international organization or diplomatic conference, and state laws adopted in accordance with the Convention. *LOS Convention*, art. 217, ¶1. Flag states must inspect ships to issue and periodically verify certificates of compliance with the laws of the state. Other states must accept these certificates as evidence of the condition of the ship. Art. 217, ¶¶2-3. Flag states must establish penalties harsh enough to discourage violations by their ships. Art. 217, ¶8. In the event a ship violates international rules and standards, the flag state must investigate immediately and institute proceedings if appropriate. Art. 217, ¶4.

2. **Coastal state enforcement:** When a ship is in port, a coastal state *may institute proceedings* against it for violation of its laws adopted under the Convention or any international standards if the violation occurred on its *territorial sea or exclusive economic zone*. When a ship is in the territorial sea of a state, the state may undertake *physical inspection if it has clear grounds* for suspecting a violation and institute proceedings if the violation occurred during its passage through the territorial sea. When a ship is in the exclusive economic zone or territorial sea, the coastal zone *may require it to provide relevant information* if it has clear grounds for believing the ship committed a violation in the exclusive economic zone. Whether the coastal state may take further steps for violations in the EEZ depends upon the extent of damage caused or threatened by the violation. *LOS Convention*, art. 220.

3. **Port state enforcement:** If a ship in a foreign port is responsible for a discharge beyond the port state's EEZ in violation of international standards, the port state *may investigate and, if warranted, institute enforcement proceedings*. If the discharge occurred within the EEZ, territorial sea, or internal waters of another state, the port state *cannot* institute proceedings *unless so requested* by that state, the flag state of the ship, or another state damaged by the discharge, unless the waters of the port state itself have been or are likely to be polluted by the discharge. As far as practicable, the port state is obligated to investigate or institute proceedings if so requested by the flag state of the ship, any state whose coastal waters are damaged by the discharge, or any state within whose waters the discharge occurred. *LOS Convention*, art. 218.

4. **Liability for wrongful enforcement:** A state is obligated to compensate the flag state for *any injury or loss attributable to unlawful or excessive measures taken against a foreign ship*. The legal systems in all states must provide for private actions in respect to such injury or loss. *LOS Convention*, art. 232. Also, under the 1973 Convention for the Prevention of Pollution from

Ships (MARPOL), a ship "shall be entitled to compensation for any loss or damage suffered" from a state's measures that cause the ship to be unduly delayed or detained. International Convention for the Prevention of Pollution from Ships, art. 7, ¶2, 12 I.L.M. 1319 (1973).

**M. Notification and cooperative action:** As soon as a state is aware that injury to the marine environment has occurred or is imminent, it must *notify* immediately the appropriate global or regional international organizations and all states likely to be affected. *LOS Convention,* art. 198. In order to eliminate or minimize the effect of an accident causing marine pollution, neighboring states have a duty to develop contingency plans to respond to pollution. Art. 199.

**N. Government noncommercial ships:** Ships that are used by governments for noncommercial purposes *are not subject* to the international rules, standards, and enforcement procedures discussed above. Each state must adopt measures to insure that such ships follow the international rules and standards as far as practical. *LOS Convention*, art. 236.

# X. INTERNATIONAL TRADE AND ENVIRONMENT

There is a growing recognition that trade and environment are inextricably linked, and trade implications of environmental policy, and environmental implications of the world trade system are emerging as issues of international concern.

**A. The GATT:** Most of the rules governing international trade are codified in the General Agreement on Tariffs and Trade, which was first established in 1948 and is periodically negotiated by the parties. The rules are based primarily on the ideology of *free trade*, with a view that is skeptical of regulations that inhibit trade. Thus, many proponents of free trade see environmental regulations as a type of non-tariff barrier to be forbidden under GATT.

    **1. Lack of environmental protection under GATT:** There is *no mention* in GATT of environmental protection as a justification for limiting trade; however, states may legitimately restrain trade under Article XX if "necessary to protect human, animal or plant life or health" and impose measures "relating to the conservation of natural resources."

    **2. The Uruguay Round:** The Uruguay Round of GATT talks, begun in 1985, was the *first round to link international trade and the environment* in the contexts of agricultural subsidies, harmonization of certain environmental standards, prohibition of export controls, and the liberalization of import restrictions. Although these issues were not resolved, the participants signed an agreement pledging to undertake a dialogue on the "interlinkages between environmental and trade policies."

    **3. GATT Group on Environment Measures and Trade:** First established in 1971, the Group on Environment Measures and Trade was dormant until first activated in 1991 following a GATT debate on environment and trade. The Group's initial agenda includes: (1) trade provisions in existing multilateral environmental agreements, (2) national environmental regulations likely to have an international effect, and (3) trade effects of packaging and labeling requirements aimed at protecting the environment.

**B. Conflicting views of traditional free trade theorists and environmentally oriented economists:** GATT negotiators have a difficult time coming to an agreement about issues concerning trade and environment because economists' theories in this area conflict. According to environmentally oriented economists, when the prices of goods that enter the international market do not reflect the environmental costs of production, the producers are receiving an effective subsidy equal to the resources used in the process. Thus, they claim that these goods distort the trade process, giving an unfair advantage to producers who degrade the environment, termed "ecological dumping." However, under the GATT *no such explicit environmental subsidy is recognized*. Instead, these goods are viewed as having only an "implicit subsidy," one that is unforbidden.

C.   **The Tuna/Dolphin Decision:** In February of 1991, Mexico filed a formal complaint against the United States claiming a U.S. embargo on Mexican yellowfin tuna was protectionist in nature, and a violation of GATT. The U.S. had imposed the embargo pursuant to the Marine Mammal Protection Act as a trade sanction to compel Mexico (and other states) to bring its kill rate of dolphin in the harvesting of yellowfin tuna in the Eastern Tropical Pacific in line with U.S. standards. The U.S. argued that the measure was justified under Article III of GATT, which requires only that imported products be accorded no less favorable treatment than products of national origin, or under the exemptions in Article XX for protection of natural resources and animals. The panel concluded that the import ban violated GATT. Dispute Settlement Panel Report on United States Restrictions on Imports of Tuna, Aug. 16, 1991, *reprinted at* 30 I.L.M. 1594. According to the panel, Article III only allows for regulation of a product based on the qualities of the product itself, not on the process by which it is made. The Article XX exemptions *can only be used to protect living or natural resources under the jurisdiction of the party invoking the exemptions*. A second panel has been established to hear the European Community's claim that GATT is also violated by the U.S. embargo on intermediary nations that import and then export yellowfin tuna harvested in violation of U.S. standards.

D.   **The Global Environment Facility (GEF):** The Global Environment Facility was established by the World Bank in 1991 as a pilot program under which grants or loans will be provided to developing countries *to help them implement programs addressing problems of global environmental significance*. These include: protection of the ozone layer, limiting emissions of greenhouse gases, protection of biodiversity, and protection of international waters. GEF is currently considering the inclusion of desertification programs. A number of global environmental treaties that address these problems contain funding mechanisms provided by GEF, including the 1992 biodiversity treaty and the Montreal Protocol. Multilateral contributions to the GEF are currently made by participant states on a voluntary basis. Programs funded under GEF are implemented through a "tripartite arrangement" by the World Bank, UNEP, and UNDP.

E.   **North America Free Trade Agreement (NAFTA):** NAFTA is a unique trade agreement for its *incorporation of environmental protections*. The preamble states that trade must be *consistent* with environmental protection and conservation. The agreement calls for "harmonization of the parties domestic standards with international environmental standards, while preserving in certain circumstances each country's ability to maintain domestic environmental standards which exceed prevailing international standards." Disputes over environmental standards may be resolved by an arbitral panel, with the burden under NAFTA on the party challenging the environmental measure. Although NAFTA by its terms is generally to be given priority over conflicting international agreements, exceptions are made for several major international environmental treaties. A separately negotiated environmental agreement focuses on cleanup of the Mexico/U.S. border area and establishment of a Commission on Environmental Cooperation to ensure enforcement of environmental standards by the parties.

In *Public Citizen v. U.S. Trade Representative*, 5 F.3d 549 (D.C. Cir. 1993), *cert. denied*, 114 S. Ct. 685 (1994), the D.C. Circuit Court of Appeals held that an environmental impact statement did not have to be prepared for NAFTA because it was not "final agency action" under the Administrative Procedure Act and NEPA itself does not create a private right of action.

# XI. MILITARY ACTIVITIES AND THE ENVIRONMENT

The international community is increasingly willing to condemn military acts that harm the environment, and may impose legal liability on an aggressor. Liability for environmental harm that results from military activities may arise from a number of international agreements.

**A.** **Protocol I to the 1949 Geneva Conventions Relating to the Protection of the International Armed Conflicts:** Article 35 prohibits methods of warfare which *"are intended, or may be expected, to cause widespread, long-term and severe damage to the natural environment."* Article 55 of Protocol I of the Geneva Conventions states that "care shall be taken in warfare to protect the natural environment against widespread, long-term and severe damage . . . Attacks against the natural environment by way of reprisals are prohibited." The status of the Protocol as customary international law is controversial.

**B.** **Environmental Modification Convention of 1977 (ENMOD):** This Convention was drafted during the Vietnam War in response to concern over the use of "deliberate manipulation of natural processes" that change the "dynamics, composition or structure of the earth . . . ." ENMOD prohibits member states from engaging in environmental modification techniques that have *"widespread, long-lasting, or severe" effects* as a means to harm another state.

**C.** **General customary laws of war:** The customary laws of war impose a requirement of *proportionality and necessity* on all methods of warfare. It has also been argued that the body of law restricting use of certain weapons gives rise to a more general prohibition of *any method of warfare that causes unnecessary suffering*. Finally, it is unclear whether or not the general norms of international environmental law are suspended in the context of armed conflict.

---

## *Quiz Yourself* on *INTERNATIONAL ENVIRONMENTAL LAW*

**38.** World Foods is working in the desert country of Sofada. They are teaching the citizens planting, harvesting, and storage techniques. Could this be an outgrowth of the Earth Summit? _____

**39.** Sofada citizens have noticed a growing dark cloud of fumes continues to pass through the atmosphere. Sofada government heads learn that the fumes are originating from the nearby country of Armcharido. Is Sofada entitled to legal relief? _____

**40.** Jay Sunn and his wife, Capri, traveled to Armcharido on safari. One evening Capri encountered an adorable Blue Monkey that took quite a shine to her. When it came time to return home, Capri packed her new friend into her purse to sneak on the plane and keep as a pet. Jay knew that Blue Monkeys were endangered, but he wanted his wife to be happy and he knew they'd give the little guy a good home. Can the Sunns keep their new pet? _____

41. Same characters as above, but this year's trip takes them to Antarctica as part of a touring scientific expedition. Everyone in the group is assigned a marine ecosystem specimen to obtain. Are the Sunns in trouble when they fulfill their assignment? _____

42. The logging industry is the primary source of revenue for the country of Tundrana. Unfortunately, the steady logging has seriously depleted the natural forests in the nation. Tundrana owes a significant debt to the country of Fiscalio. Tundrana can stay on budget only if it continues logging or reduces its debts another way. Is there a way to save the national forests and reduce the debt? _____

---

## Answers

38. **Yes.** The Earth Summit produced Agenda 21. One of the six priorities of Agenda 21 is fostering an equitable world through combating poverty and protecting human health.

39. **Not necessarily.** Under the principles of liability established in the *Trail Smelter Case*, a nation must first show material damage and causation.

40. **No.** Endangered species are regulated through import-export permits. The Sunns did not have a permit, so their import of the Blue Monkey is against environmental regulation.

41. **No.** The Convention on the Conservation of Antarctic Marine Living Resources allows for the rational use of the marine ecosystem resources. Participating as part of a scientific expedition could easily fall within "rational use."

42. **Yes.** Debt-for-nature swaps purchase foreign debts in exchange for the creation of domestic forest reserves. The two governments of Tundrana and Fiscalio could form an agreement and rely on their friendly relations.

---

## Exam Tips on
## INTERNATIONAL ENVIRONMENTAL LAW

☞ There are several treaties, conventions, and agreements to understand in this chapter. Your professors will likely not expect you to memorize each one and its purpose, but here is a suggestion: Write down the names and a one-sentence description of each treaty, convention, and agreement. Bring that list with you into your exam (provided that is allowed, of course) and incorporate the information into your answer.

☞ The *first global conference* on the environment was the 1972 Stockholm Conference. The resulting 26 principles *established a global approach* to environmental protection.

☞ This conference led to the ***United Nations Environment Program (UNEP)*** of 1973, which was created as a U.N. subsidiary to ***coordinate environmental protection*** activities for the United Nations.

☞ Remember that all of these initial conferences and treaties were designed to broadly address the ***goals*** of environmental protection and the preservation of the world's unique resources through avoiding ***adverse human impact*** and destruction.

☞ Individual nations became ***responsible and liable*** for transboundary pollution and other environmental damage.

☛ The ***largest global conference*** on the environment occurred in Rio de Janeiro, Brazil in 1982 — the ***Earth Summit***. This resulted in a ***compromise between developing and developed nations*** on environmental protections.

☞ Remember the ***six priorities*** of ***Agenda 21***. These general principles are nice to add to an exam answer.

☛ ***Transboundary pollution*** protects states from other states' pollution and damage to its citizens and property.

*Example:* Acid rain is a problem for the international community. It definitely crosses boundaries, so no one country can truly be responsible for its control. International agreements provide countries with incentives to reduce the pollution they create which causes acid rain.

☞ Love the cases addressing transboundary pollution! Remember the ***two principles of liability*** emerging from the ***Trail Smelter Case*** and the ***duty to notify*** from the ***Corfu Channel Case***.

☛ The ***ozone layer and the greenhouse effect*** are hot topics for exam hypotheticals. The United Nations has given these subjects top priority and many nations are addressing concerns on the ***changes in the Earth's climate***. Remember the structure of the U.N. Convention on Climate Changes and consider why some countries would/would not be interested in participating in serious regulations.

☛ ***Wildlife protection*** is globally important, and remember that the most protections are afforded to ***whales***, and other ***endangered or threatened species***.

☛ Given the current global political climate regarding potential nuclear activities, regulations of ***hazardous waste, radioactive pollution, and environmental emergencies*** is a topic ripe for an exam hypothetical. Remember that treaties and agreements exist to ***compensate victims*** of nuclear accidents and to ***prevent future accidents***.

☛ Remember that Antarctica is the ***only continent not commercially exploited***. There are numerous treaties and conventions designed to protect the natural resources of this last continent.

*Example:* It would be a financial windfall for Country A if they could begin developing some of the more inhabitable areas of Antarctica. Country A is not allowed to simply begin development, because protections exist for the habitat, natural resources, and wildlife of the continent.

☛ Deforestation is a great concern to many nations. Remember that the primary cause is thought to be ***poverty***, so weigh the benefits of revenue-producing activities versus loss of biodiversity and contribution to greenhouse effect.

☛ Remember that *Agenda 21* identified *desertification* as a key global environment priority. U.N. countries focus on the *six program areas*.

☛ Consider again the critical issue of the *marine environment*: whether Convention provisions reflect *customary international law* or are only *binding on the parties*.

   ☞ Review the *required international guidelines* for vessel-source pollution.

   ☞ Nations also must regulate pollution from national jurisdiction *seabed activities*.

   ☞ *Liability* is established according to international law.

   ☞ *Enforcement* rights and responsibilities fall to *flag* states, *coastal* states, and *port* states.

☛ *GATT* does *not explicitly mention* restriction of trade for environmental protection, but *protections are allowed* under specific circumstances.

☛ *NAFTA* does *explicitly incorporate* environmental protections.

# Essay Exam Questions

**QUESTION 1:** After several years of financial difficulties following an accident at the Sorry Nuclear Reactor (Sorry), Sullivan Edison Co., the company that owns the Sorry nuclear power plant, announced its decision to terminate operation of the reactor pending approval by the Nuclear Regulatory Commission (NRC). In response, NRC officials conducted an environmental study of the reactor site. The conclusions of the study are as follows:

> It would be economically infeasible for any company to assume responsibility for the operation of Sorry. It has been determined by the NRC that it would be in the best interests of the environment to terminate operation and decommission the Sorry Reactor as expeditiously as practicable by immediate dismantlement. In the course of the study of the site, it has also come to light that chemicals, including lead, benzene, and arsenic, subject to regulation under the Resource Conservation and Recovery Act (RCRA) and the Comprehensive Environmental Response, Compensation, and Liability Act (CERCLA) are buried on site in deteriorating gallon drums which could leak into public drinking water wells. It has also been demonstrated during this study that the incidence of leukemia in residents near the Sorry plant is significantly higher than that found in the general population.

**Part A.** Assume that you are an attorney for the Sierra Club. The Sierra Club wants to bring suit under NEPA, challenging the NRC's recommendation to dismantle the Sorry reactor. Write a memo discussing fully those issues which would be relevant to the filing of a complaint under NEPA, what requirements would have to be met under NEPA, and what remedies might be available to the Sierra Club under NEPA.

**Part B.** EPA's study revealed that benzene found at the Sorry reactor site may have been generated by Jim's Plastics, Inc., whose president and sole stockholder is Jim Delaney. In 1979, the plant supervisor, Seymour Shore, had hired a transporter to take the benzene to a disposal site without Delaney's knowledge. When the transporter, Waste-On-Wheels (WOW), asked Shore where to take the waste, Shore named a couple of places in Sorry as possible disposal sites even though he knew none of them were authorized to accept hazardous waste. The transporter subsequently took the waste to the disposal site on which the Sorry reactor is now located. At the time, the disposal site was owned and operated by William Want. Want ceased accepting waste at the site in 1980, and sold the property to Sam and Beulah Smith in 1981. When the Smiths asked Want if any hazardous wastes were at the site, Want truthfully replied, ''To the best of my knowledge, no.'' The Smiths subsequently sold the site to the current owner, Sullivan Edison Co., in 1983. The Sorry site is not on the National Priority List.

The residents near the Sorry reactor are outraged by the findings of the EPA study, Delaney, Shore, WOW, Want, the Smiths, and officers of the Sullivan Edison Co. have come to you for legal advice. They want to know who, if anyone, can sue them for the contamination and their potential liability.

**QUESTION 2:** A group of electric utilities (the ''Intermountain Power Project'' or ''IPP'') is planning to construct a coal-fired power plant at a remote site in the southern part of the state of Haze. The southern part of the state of Haze is a nonattainment area for ozone, a Class II prevention of significant deterioration (PSD) area for sulfur dioxide, and particulates for all other pollutants for which a national ambient air quality standard has been set. The proposed plant would emit 250 tons per year of particulates but would emit less than 100 tons per year of ozone and sulfur dioxide. What review process or processes must the proposed plant go through under the Clean Air Act? What must be demonstrated by the IPP to satisfy the requirements of the Act? What changes, if any, have the 1990 amendments to the Clean Air Act made in the requirements applicable generally to such a nonattainment area? Be sure to refer to specific pollutants when necessary.

**QUESTION 3:** On March 1, 1989, EPA published a final regulation for a newly designated conventional water pollutant, ''goo,'' applicable to all widget-producing plants. You are counsel for Acme, Inc., a widget company presently emitting goo into the Mississippi River. You have been called into the office of Acme's president. He tells you that no widget company in the country has the technology to meet the standard, that Acme's goo discharges into the Mississippi have no effect on water quality, and that Acme cannot, in any event, afford whatever equipment would be necessary to comply unless they try a promising but still experimental technology that would take a year or two to implement. He wants you to prepare a memo explaining all possible ways in which to attack the regulation and, alternatively, all strategies for getting Acme out of having to comply with the regulations. Prepare such a memo, evaluating the likelihood of success of each avenue of attack.

**QUESTION 4:** Assume that you are clerking for a federal Circuit Court of Appeals judge Reinhardt. The judge hands you the following introduction for an opinion, with instructions to finish drafting the opinion in accordance with the final sentence of the introduction, being sure to argue fully the plaintiffs' and the government's positions before explaining why the suit must be dismissed:

> This case requires us to determine whether plaintiffs who assert no interest in preserving endangered species may sue the government for violating the procedures established in the Endangered Species Act.

I.

The plaintiffs are two Oregon ranch operators and two irrigation districts located in that state. They challenge the government's preparation of a biological opinion which concludes that the water level in two reservoirs should be maintained at a particular minimum level in order to preserve two species of fish. The plaintiffs, who make use of the reservoir water for commercial (and recreational) purposes, bring this action under the Endangered Species Act (ESA), 16 U.S.C. §1531 *et seq.*, the Administrative Procedure Act (APA), 5 U.S.C. §701 *et seq.*, and the National Environmental Policy Act (NEPA), 42 U.S.C. §4332(2)(C).

The two reservoirs in question are part of the federal government's Klamath Project, which the Bureau of Reclamation administers. The Bureau concluded that the long term operation of the Klamath Project might adversely affect two species of fish: the Lost River and shortnose suckers. Pursuant to the requirements of the ESA, the Bureau consulted with the United States Fish and Wildlife Service in order to assess the impact of the Klamath Project on the fish. 16 U.S.C. §1536(a)(2).

As a result of the consultation, the Service prepared a biological opinion. 16 U.S.C. §1536(b)(3)(A). The opinion concluded that unless mitigating actions were taken the ''long-term operation of the Klamath Project was likely to jeopardize the continued existence of the Lost River and shortnose suckers.'' The opinion ''recommended a number of measures the [Bureau] could take to avoid jeopardy to the suckers . . . including the recommendations regarding maintaining minimum lake level at issue in this case.'' The Bureau informed the Service that it accepted the opinion's recommendations and intended to comply with them.

The plaintiffs filed suit for declaratory and injunctive relief in an effort to compel the government to withdraw portions of the biological opinion. Their complaint alleges that there is no evidence to support the opinion's conclusion that the long-term operation of the Klamath Project will adversely affect suckers. In fact, the complaint alleges that the evidence shows that the fish are ''reproducing successfully'' and are not in need of special protection. The complaint then explains that the plaintiffs' objective in seeking to prevent the government from raising the minimum reservoir levels is to ensure that more water will be available for their own commercial (and recreational) use. In short, they wish to use for their own purposes some of the water that the government maintains is needed to ensure the survival of the suckers.

The complaint alleges that in preparing the opinion, the government violated the consultation provisions set forth in 16 U.S.C. §1536(a) of the ESA. It also alleges that the government violated 16 U.S.C. §1533(b)(2) of the ESA by failing to consider the economic impact of its determination that the reservoirs constituted critical habitats for the suckers. They bring related claims pursuant to the APA and NEPA.

The government moved to dismiss the complaint for lack of standing. The district court concluded that the plaintiffs' interest in utilizing the Klamath water for commercial and recreational purposes "conflict[s] with the Lost River and shortnose suckers' interest in using water for habitat." Accordingly, it concluded that the plaintiffs lacked standing because their claims were premised on "an interest which conflicts with the interests sought to be protected by the Act."

The issue before us is not whether the plaintiffs have satisfied the constitutional standing requirements but whether their action is precluded by prudential standing limitations that the district court deemed dispositive. The plaintiffs argue that the question is an open one because our past cases did not consider whether the ESA's citizen suit provision overrides such limitations on standing.

*Because the plaintiffs lack standing to sue under either the ESA or the APA, and because they have failed to state a claim under NEPA, we affirm the district court.*

II.

[Continue with your text of the opinion.]

**QUESTION 5:** We Ogle Whales (WOW), a company that organizes whale watching expeditions, has hired you to challenge the validity of a regulation promulgated by the Department of the Interior. The regulation they seek to invalidate is the regulatory definition of "harass" for purposes of the §9 (16 U.S.C. §1538(a)(l)) prohibition on "takings" under the Endangered Species Act.

You explain to your client that §3(19) of the Act defines the statutory term "take":

> The term "take" means to harass, harm, pursue, hunt, shoot, wound, kill, trap, capture, or collect, or to attempt to engage in any such conduct. 16 U.S.C. §1532(19).

The Act does not further define the terms it uses to define "take." The Interior Department regulations that implement the statute, however, define the statutory term "harass":

> "Harass" in the definition of "take" in the Act means an intentional or negligent act or omission which creates the likelihood of injury to wildlife by annoying it to such an extent as to significantly disrupt normal behavioral patterns which include, but are not limited to, breeding, feeding, or sheltering. 50 C.F.R. §17.3.

You tell WOW you are certain that it can bring a suit challenging the substantive validity of the definition of "harass" on its face (procedurally the regulation clearly was promulgated in conformity with all the procedures required by the Administrative Procedure Act). Your client asks you for a memo fully assessing the likelihood of success on the substantive merits of your claim. Write such a memo, assessing all the arguments for and against the validity of the regulation.

# Essay Exam Answers

**SAMPLE ANSWER TO QUESTION 1:**

**Part A:**

MEMORANDUM

**TO:** Sierra Club

**FR:** Attorney

**RE:** Potential causes of action to challenge NRC's recommendation regarding dismantling the Sorry Nuclear Reactor and available remedies.

NEPA has no express provisions for a citizen suit. Citizens, like the Sierra Club and its members, may enforce agency compliance with NEPA through the APA unless the agency action is specifically exempted by APA §701. This principle was established in *Calvert Cliffs*, which held that NEPA establishes a strict standard of compliance and therefore creates judicially enforceable duties when an agency has failed to comply with all the procedural elements in reaching its decision. Sierra Club may file a complaint alleging that NRC failed to comply procedurally with NEPA's action forcing provision, §102(2)(c) before reaching its decision to approve the dismantling of the Sorry Nuclear Reactor.

As a prerequisite to getting into court, Sierra Club must demonstrate standing. Sierra Club must satisfy APA's statutory standing requirements, constitutional requirements, as well as any prudential limitations. The constitutional requirements are injury-in-fact, causation, and redressability. The Sierra Club has based its standing on representational standing, informational standing, or procedural injury. Sierra Club should have no difficulty in satisfying the additional requirement under the APA that Sierra Club's interest (environmental preservation) fall within the "zone of interest." The statute, NEPA, was intended to protect.

To fulfill the representational standing requirements, the Sierra Club must satisfy the following three conditions: An individual member would have standing; the interest the suit seeks to protect is related to the Sierra Club's purpose; and, the relief requested does not need the participation of the individual member. Sierra Club clearly satisfies the last two requirements. In an environmental suit the available remedy is an injunction against the NRC which naturally does not require any individual participation. The Sierra Club's asserted organizational purpose is to preserve the environment. This suit seeks to force NRC compliance with NEPA, a statute to improve the environment through informed agency decisions. The remaining condition, an individual member with standing, ensures that there is someone with a personal stake in the outcome. Sierra Club will be successful in establishing representational standing if it has a willing member living near the Sorry Nuclear Reactor who will be injured by the plant's toxic leaks.

The Sierra Club may also assert standing predicated on "informational standing." The Sierra Club would be suing on its own behalf and alleging an informational injury caused by the NRC's failure to comply with NEPA's environmental impact statement requirement. The Sierra Club must demonstrate that the information a complete EIS would have provided is essential to the Club's activities. The lack of agency information on the hazards and benefits of nuclear dismantling negatively impacted the Club's ability to provide information to the public.

The last potential avenue for the Sierra Club is to assert a procedural injury. The Supreme Court still remains divided on the adequacy of procedural injury to satisfy the injury-in-fact requirement, however, some of the opinions in *Defenders of Wildlife* lend support to the position that a procedural injury under an environmental statute is sufficient to satisfy the injury-in-fact requirement. The Sierra Club will have to argue that the NEC's procedural duty under NEPA is so enmeshed with the prevention of a substantive harm, an increase of risk of leukemia, that the breach of this procedural duty demonstrates the likelihood of the substantive injury. At best, asserting a procedural injury in this suit is tenuous. However, if the Sierra Club is able to demonstrate any one of the above standing alternatives, it should be successful in fulfilling the constitutional and statutory requirements.

Turning to Sierra Club's allegations against the NRC, Sierra Club's suit seeks to establish that the NRC failed to comply with §102(2)(c) by not completing an environmental impact statement. NEPA fulfills its purpose, to require consideration of environmental impacts or the quality of the environment, by requiring agencies to prepare detailed explanations of the environmental consequences of its action through an EIS. To be successful in its suit, Sierra Club must demonstrate that the NRC did not meet all the NEPA requirements.

The NRC's first obligation was to prepare an environmental assessment (EA) assessing whether there were no significant effects on the environment by the agency's proposed activity. The NRC's proposed activity is to dismantle a nuclear reactor known to be leaking toxic, harmful chemicals. This type of activity obviously has enormous effects on the environment because of the potential for careless dismantling and the fact that the toxic chemicals will have to be relocated, and that residual leakage could damage the public drinking water.

The EA serves to assess whether the NRC needs to complete a full and detailed Environmental Impact Statement (EIS) by outlining the proposal and its possible environmental impact. To do so the EA must consider whether there is a major federal proposal which will have significant impacts on the human environment. Secondly, the EA must also consider alternatives to the proposed actions as well as the environmental impacts of the alternatives.

The threshold requirement for whether an EIS is required is answered by examining whether there is a major federal proposal significantly affecting the quality of the human environment. The NRC is a federal agency which has the power to control the termination and dismantling of a nuclear reactor. Furthermore, the NRC is directly involved and in fact is the sole agency which may give the requisite approval to Sullivan to dismantle Sorry nuclear plant. Second, the proposal to dismantle a nuclear plant is major. Any proposal is major if the effects of it may be significant, therefore this aspect of the analysis is answered by the fourth step. Third, the EA must assess if the NRC has even made a proposal. A bright line test, "the proposal test," is an established standard for determining what is a proposal and is delineated in *Kleppe v. Sierra Club*. The court held that if the federal agency is merely contemplating an action, there has not been a proposal. This standard rejects the *SIPI* balancing test and is criticized for being too mechanical and for discouraging full consideration of comprehensive environmental effects. The *SIPI* test balances several factors to determine whether the agency action is a proposal. The core of the test considers the extent to which meaningful information is presently available, balanced against the extent to which irretrievable commitments have been made. The CEQ guidelines are a hybrid of both the *Kleppe* and the *SIPI* analysis and simply states that a proposal exists when an agency has set a goal and is actively preparing to make a decision on means to pursue the goal. Under both the *Kleppe* and *SIPI* analyses, the NRC's decision would be deemed a proposal because the NRC's end goal was to grant or deny Sullivan Co. approval. This decision is made and is no longer being contemplated, as indicated by the completed environmental study. Still, the NRC has not yet made extensive commitments to the dismantling of Sorry, but the NRC's study has provided it with all the relevant information needed to do a complete assessment under NEPA.

The last factor assessed whether the proposal will have a significant environmental impact. Socioeconomic factors alone cannot trigger an EIS. Once the threshold is crossed, however, a broad range of impacts must be assessed. In considering what, if any, significant environmental impacts exist, the proposal needs to determine what are the relevant environmental impacts. Relevant impacts include impacts on the human environment, the urban environment, impacts on quality of life, effects on human physical and psychological health. Each impact is relevant if there is a reasonably close causal relation between the impact and the proposal's change to the physical environment. Last, in considering the environmental impacts, the EA must consider both direct and indirect effects which may be remote but are reasonably foreseeable. The risk of leukemia and the general safety of the local public water system are environmental impacts to be duly weighted in the EA.

In considering what is a significant impact, the EA must assess the context and intensity of the impact. *Hanley II* established a two-part test to evaluate significance: first, the incremental effects and second, any cumulative effects. These requirements ensure that the proposal is not considered in isolation. The NRC will have to look at the increase or decrease in toxic leakage by a dismantling, as well as the fluctuation in the risk of leukemia. A cumulative effect that the NRC will need to consider is the depletion of a nuclear energy source if Sorry is dismantled, as well as the absolute impact of the transportation and disposal of the toxic waste.

After the above impacts and alternatives are assessed in the EA, then the NRC needs to decide if an EIS is necessary. If the NRC found that the contested proposal failed to meet the threshold requirements for an EIS, then the NRC is required to prepare a FONSI (finding of no significant impact) to be publicly disseminated. An agency's decision not to do an EIS is judicially reviewed under an arbitrary and capricious standard. A reviewing court would only ask if the agency was arbitrary and capricious in not preparing an EIS rather than question the substantive decision. Based on the magnitude that a decision to dismantle a nuclear plant is, it is most likely that an EIS would have to be prepared by the NRC. NRC may seek to avoid an EIS by arguing that the dismantlement will have a beneficial impact on the environment.

The first requirement in preparing an EIS is to outline the scope and timing of the proposal. The scope seeks to determine the extent of the EIS. The scope of the EIS is essentially dictated by the scope of the proposal, thus how the agency frames its proposal becomes very important. The NRC can narrowly frame its proposal by stating that it seeks only to approve or disapprove of the dismantling and not include any mandatory procedural requirements the dismantling company would have to follow. Generally an EIS must be detailed, concise and clear. Scoping avoids segmentation of projects which can lead to evasion of completing an EIS. The NRC is in danger of segmenting a proposal if it does not include as part of the proposal the decision regarding the transportation and dumping of the toxic waste.

The timing element sets a completion deadline for the EIS. The EIS must be completed in time to effect the decision-making process in order to serve the broad purpose of NEPA and to avoid allowing an agency to use an EIS to justify a pre-selected course of action, but late enough for meaningful information.

The EIS report must address the following: the positive and negative environmental impacts of the proposal; alternative actions, their merits and reason for elimination from consideration; mitigation measures; and, a no-action alternative. The identification and analysis of possible alternatives is the heart of the EIS process. The goal in considering alternatives is to force the agency to closely examine the proposal and to assist the agency in making an environmentally sound decision. The court in *Morton* established the range of what alternatives need to be addressed. The *Morton* rule of reason stipulates that the EIS needs only to discuss alternatives which are reasonably available but includes alternatives not within the jurisdiction of the agency making the proposal. *Morton* also establishes a rule regarding the length of discussion per alternative by basing it on a sliding scale grounded on the likelihood the alternative would be implemented. This sets the depth and degree to which each alternative needs to be discussed. *Vermont Yankee* narrowed the scope of which alternatives needed to be included in the EIS by saying that "crystal ball inquiries do not have to be explored."

The no-action alternative is considered the most serious alternative to the proposed action and its evaluation needs to include the environmental impacts which cannot be avoided if the proposal is implemented. Next, mitigation measures must be included in the EIS. While an EIS is not required to include a complete mitigation plan, it is essential to the EIS to insure that the agency has taken a hard look at their proposal. NRC must detail possible mitigation plans that will allow the reactor to be dismantled with a lower risk of toxic waste damage, of improving the drinking water and pinpointing the cause of the increase in leukemia. Under new regulations the analysis only requires that the EIS summarize the existing credible scientific evidence that relates to the environmental impacts. Such a summary usually includes a probability analysis. No "worst case" analysis is required.

Ultimately, substantive review by a court is limited by an arbitrary and capricious standard, essentially leaving the courts with no substantive review of the agency's decision. Thus, even if dismantling the Sorry Reactor is determined to have a very detrimental impact, the agency after preparing a complete EIS may decide to continue with its proposed course of action so long as its decision is not arbitrary and capricious judicial review is limited to ensuring that agencies like the NRC complied with the NEPA requirements in formulating its EA and EIS. The only remedies available to the Sierra Club in its federal suit are injunctive relief and attorneys' fees.

**Part B:**

The following will outline the potential suits and liability of Delaney, Shore, WOW, Want, the Smiths and the officers of the Sullivan Edison Co. for the disposal of benzene at the Sorry Nuclear Reactor. Under the Resource Conservation and Recovery Act (RCRA) and Comprehensive Environmental Response, Compensation, and Liability Act (CERCLA), both citizens and the EPA may file suits against those deemed responsible for the existing benzene contamination problem.

RCRA created a cradle-to-grave program for the regulation of hazardous wastes. Under this management system wastes may only be disposed of at federally permitted disposal facilities (dubbed TSD facilities [treatment, storage and disposal].) Sorry reactor site was not "authorized" to accept hazardous waste. RCRA regulates "solid wastes" which includes contained gaseous material. Benzene is a contained gaseous material. Under the RCRA, waste generators, transporters, and disposal sites all must meet specific requirements. The focus of RCRA is to prevent groundwater contamination from hazardous waste sites, which is the existing potential threat from the Sorry site.

RCRA §7003 grants EPA the ability to sue those responsible for creating or maintaining a hazardous waste site. To establish a case the EPA must satisfy three elements: (1) the site presents an imminent and substantial endangerment to health or the environment; (2) the danger is caused by the past or present handling, storage, treatment, transportation or disposal of a hazardous waste; and, (3) the defendant contributed to the handling, storage, treatment, transportation or disposal of the hazardous waste. The EPA will be able to satisfy all three elements for several of the listed potential defendants. The question is whether Delaney, the Smiths and Sullivan Edison would be liable for contributing to any aspect of the handling, storage, transportation or disposal of the benzene.

Responsible parties, will be strictly liable. At issue is what encompasses "imminent and substantial endangerment." Section 7003 does not define this phrase. However, courts have interpreted endangerment to include a "risk of harm that was less than a certainty"; thus, an actual harm is not necessary. Present knowledge of leaking toxic waste materials implies a sense of imminent danger and this knowledge was supplied by the EPA's study of the Sorry Reactor site. The study disclosed that benzene was stored at Sorry in deteriorating drums, which suggests potential leakage. Further, the EPA study established that any leakage would adversely harm the public drinking water. Linked together, these two facts constitute a risk of harm satisfying the court's interpretation of "imminent and substantial endangerment," even though it may not amount to a threatened irreparable harm. The risk is directly associated with the improper disposal of the benzene fulfilling element two: causation.

Section 7003 is expansive enough to include suits to be brought against inactive as well as active sites, so even though Want ceased to accept waste in 1980, those involved with the handling of the waste disposal are still liable under §7003.

Only equitable relief is available under §7003, making the primary remedy an injunction. However, equitable relief may require payment of money to satisfy the injunction requirements. Outside of judicially awarded relief, the government may also apply civil penalties in amounts up to $25,000 per day to enforce RCRA. Both the civil penalties and injunctions are authorized by §3008(a) and (g).

RCRA under §3008(d) provides for criminal prosecution. Corporations and the responsible officials can be held criminally liable for company violation of the regulations. An individual official can be found liable in lieu of the corporation. To be criminally liable the corporate official will have to be proven to have had actual knowledge of the hazardous waste violations. A corporate officer's "willful blindness" will not release him from liability. Courts allow knowledge to be inferred from the fact that waste disposal was part of the officer's usual scope of duties.

The above named "defendants" are also open to citizen suits under RCRA §7002. To proceed with the citizen suit, the residents near Sorry need only show that the defendants created an imminent and substantial endangerment. If the conclusions of the EPA study were made public, the residents will be able to meet the standard of "risk of harm," thus satisfying the imminent and substantial endangerment requirement.

CERCLA, as a remedial statute, seeks to impose the cost of waste cleanups on potentially responsible parties. Under §107(a), the federal government, the state governments, or private parties may sue anyone responsible for the generation, transportation or disposal of hazardous substances. The standard for the injury is a mere showing of a "threat of a hazardous substance release." There are three potential but very limited defenses: an act of God; an act of war; or an act of an unrelated third party, over which the defendant had absolutely no control and could not possibly foresee. At the Sorry site, none of these defenses seem available to the potentially responsible parties (PRP).

PRPs must fall within one of four established classes. For the Sorry site the PRPs are: the Sullivan Edison Company as current owner and operator of Sorry; William Want as a past owner/operator at time of the waste disposal occurred; Jim Delaney as owner/president of the generator, Jim's Plastics; and Waste-On Wheels as the transporter of the hazardous substance. WOW could avoid liability if it is found that Seymour Shore selected the site rather than WOW. However, it appears that Shore recommended four possible sites and that WOW then had to choose one of the four. Because WOW's choices were restricted to the Sorry reactor site, WOW truly did not choose the site, only a location on the site.

While as supervisor of Jim's Plastics, Seymour Shore does not fall into one of the traditional four classes, nevertheless he can be found to be personally liable. As the supervisor who arranged the disposal, Shore was personally involved in the disposal decision. Because he held this position of authority to dispose of waste, Shore will be deemed to have "possessed" the waste as defined in §107(a)(3). This principle was established in *United States v. Northeastern Pharmaceutical & Chem. Co.*

Jim Delaney may attempt to avoid liability for the reason that he did not participate in the management of Jim's Plastics. However, as the sole stockholder Delaney is the owner. As President, he "managed" the corporation even though he did not actually control the company's day to day operations, as president his position conveyed to him the authority to control the facility.

The Smiths may attempt to invoke the innocent landowner defense to avoid liability. CERCLA provides that innocent landowners with no knowledge of the past hazardous waste disposal are not subject to liability. Smiths may argue that no waste was disposed while they were owners and that they had no reason to know of potential disposal sites. However, the adequacy of the defense rides on whether the Smiths exercised due care in investigating the property "consistent with good commercial practice" before purchasing. Large businesses are expected to conduct a more extensive pre-purchase inspection than average homeowners. While a homeowner could be expected to simply inquire whether the land was a waste disposal site, the Smiths may be held to a more stringent "commercial" standard.

None of the PRPs can escape liability for acts committed before CERCLA's enactment date, December 1980, because CERCLA applies retroactively to prior acts.

The extent of the PRP's liability is broad. Liability does not include economic losses, personal injuries, or diminished property value of private homes. Liability under CERCLA is divided into two branches under §107(a). The first branch allows recovery of the cost of cleanup (response costs) and the second extends liability for any damage to health and natural resources (resource damages).

Response damages are straightforward: liable parties must pay for the cost of the cleanup. Cleanup must comply with the National Contingency Plan (NCP), established procedures for cleaning up disposal sites. Private citizens, the residents near Sorry, can only win response damages which are consistent with the NCP guidelines. This could limit the PRP's potential response damages liability. However, the government may recover all cleanup costs unless the defendants are able to prove that the costs incurred are inconsistent with the NCP. The burden is placed on the liable parties.

Resource damages are difficult to value. Natural resources include land, fish, air, water, ground water and drinking water. The defendants here are liable for the cost of reconstructing the water supply. Damages are assessed by the cost of restoration or replacement of the natural resource with the diminution of use as an applicable factor to evaluate the monetary loss. The government need not own the affected resource to recover resource damages, but private parties can never recover resource damages.

CERCLA imposes strict as well as joint and several liability. Under joint and several liability, Jim Delaney, as president of the facility which generated the benzene, admittedly as small part of the disposal equation, could be held 100 percent liable for all cleanup costs if no other responsible parties can be located. The only possible escape from imposed joint and several liability is if Delaney could prove that the harm is divisible.

Last, defendants have no defense in arguing that the Sorry reactor is not listed on the NPL list. The National Priorities List targets the worst hazardous waste sites, but being listed on the NPL is not a precondition for a government or citizen suit action under CERCLA.

## SAMPLE ANSWER TO QUESTION 2:

The review process for proposed plants under the Clean Air Act (CAA) starts with a determination that the pollutants which Intermountain Power Project (IPP) will emit are criteria pollutants regulated by the EPA under established NAAQS. The EPA regulates criteria pollutants because they have been characterized as an endangerment to public health and welfare. The pollutants in question for IPP's plant include particulates, ozone, and sulfur dioxide, which are all criteria pollutants. IPP seeks to construct a plant in southern Haze, thus IPP may have to go through preconstruction review for a nonattainment area for ozone and for a Prevention of Significant Deterioration (PSD) for all other pollutants for which the act attempts to preserve the air quality at a level higher than the NAAQS standards. The classification of each area is pollutant specific, therefore, the same area may have different classifications as to different pollutants.

To comply with the CAA all proposed plants must undergo preconstruction review and obtain a permit if the plant is found to be a major emitting source. A plant's emission or potential to emit is determined by the plant's full design capacity to emit. Under nonattainment, therefore, preconstruction review, a plant is a major stationary source if it may potentially emit 100 tons per year of any nonattainment pollutant. IPP is not a major emitting source for a nonattainment area for ozone. Under PSD preconstruction review, it is also necessary to determine if IPP will be a major emitting source. In a PSD area, a major source is one that emits or potentially emits 250 tons per year of a regulated pollutant or emits 100 tons per year of a regulated pollutant in one of the 28 listed categories or 250 tons of any pollutant subject to regulation. Because IPP emits 250 tons per year of particulates it is a major emitting source in a PSD area.

If IPP were a major emitting source for purposes of nonattainment review, it would have to obtain a preconstruction permit under CAA §172(c)(5). To obtain the permit IPP must meet the lowest achievable emission rate (LAER) as well as meet the offset requirements for all nonattainment pollutants (a *de minimis* exemption exists for emissions which do not exceed specified amounts under the regulations).

The nonattainment offset requirement also applies to IPP's ozone emission. A new source must offset its pollutant emission by obtaining a reduction in another source's emission of the nonattainment pollutant, which in this case is ozone.

PSD areas also have a preconstruction review and permit procedure. PSD requirements attempt to balance the two contradicting policies of preserving clean air areas against beneficial economic growth. For the emission of sulfur dioxide and particulates IPP must seek a permit in order to proceed with construction of its plant.

PSD review requires IPP to establish that its plant can meet both control technology review and air quality impact review. IPP must use BACT (best available control technology) for every regulated pollutant emitted, which is determined on a case by case basis. Again, *de minimis* exemptions exist and nonattainment pollutants are exempt from PSD requirements.

Further, IPP must satisfy an air quality impact analysis which applies to sulfur dioxide, nitrogen dioxide, and particulars. Air quality impact review seeks to ensure that none of the three pollutants will violate any NAAQS or any other allowable increment. Air quality impact review procedure was clearly defined in *Alabama Power*. The analysis involves determining two things: the baseline concentration for an area and the percentages of increases in emissions allowed over the baseline concentration. The baseline concentration is the existing ambient pollution level in a PSD area at the time of the first application for a PSD permit in southern Haze. Then southern Haze is divided into three classes, with each class having a designated maximum allowable increment which sets the amount that the air quality can deteriorate past the initial baseline concentrations for each of the three pollutants. As a class II area, the baseline is set for moderate economic growth to allow for a moderate amount of industrial growth. IPP is required to demonstrate that its emission of sulphur dioxide and particulates will not deteriorate the air quality beyond the allowable class II increment.

The 1990 Amendments to the Clean Air Act incorporated several special provisions for nonattainment areas. In an ozone nonattainment area, additional requirements may be imposed depending upon the classification of the ozone nonattainment area.

**SAMPLE ANSWER TO QUESTION 3:**

MEMORANDUM

**TO:** President Acme, Inc.

**FR:** Counsel Acme, Inc.

**RE:** Possible challenges to Goo water pollutant regulations and measures for permissible noncompliance with the regulations

The Federal Water Pollution Control Act (FWPCA) provides framework for technology based discharge standards imposed on point sources through a NPDES permit system based on FWPCA §301 and §402. Technology-based limitations are imposed on an industry-by-industry basis for existing sources. There are three methods for Acme, Inc. to seek to avoid compliance with the newly promulgated goo regulation.

Acme may challenge the EPA's promulgation of the goo standard. Acme may request review of the EPA's actions under FWPCA §509. Judicial review of EPA action is governed by §509. This section authorizes judicial review of specific administrative actions, including the promulgation of effluent limitations. Section 509 specifies that Acme must sue EPA in the Court of Appeals for the district in which the plaintiff resides or transacts business. Furthermore, the suit must be brought within 120 days of the EPA's action.

Acme's potential claim under §509 is that EPA acted arbitrarily and capriciously in promulgating the goo regulation. The FWPCA requires the EPA to follow a two-step process before designating the best conventional control (BCT). A double-comparison procedure applies to a potential BCT standard. First, the EPA must consider the costs to the industry of meeting the proposed BCT standard in relation to the benefits that would result from the proposed BCT standard. Secondly, the EPA must compare that industrial cost/benefit ratio to the cost and level of reduction of such pollutants from the discharge from the publicly owned treatment works.

Acme may present the argument that the cost of industry compliance far outweighs the benefits. Compliance cost would be prohibitively high as indicated by the fact that no widget company has the technology to meet the standard, thus, the cost to the industry and to Acme is not reasonable. Any potential benefits are outweighed by the costs. The benefit to the environment is assessed by the potential effluent reduction.

Acme's argument is weakened because the EPA in creating a new regulation may only consider certain factors set forth in FWPCA §301. These factors do not include any consideration of water quality. The congressional intent in FWPCA indicates that the statute seeks to introduce technology-based standards to point sources and to avoid making water quality determinations.

A last alternative for Acme to avoid compliance with the new regulation rests on seeking a variance. Variances serve to accommodate for differences in individual industry plants. The types of variances available to industries depend on which technological standard is involved. There are two potential variances available for conventional pollutants subject to BCT: the fundamentally different factor (FDF) variance and an innovative technology variance.

The FDF variance is allowed under FWPCA §301(n). It serves as a corrective measure to the EPA's standard-setting process. Acme's complaint, economic inability to meet technology costs, is not grounds for granting an FDF variance. FDF variances focus on adjusting requirements based on an acknowledgment that a limitation was set without reference to the full range of current practices. Therefore, costs are relevant to granting a variance but economic inability of a particular source is not.

An innovative technology variance is also allowed under FWPCA §301(k). Under the innovative technology variance, Acme would have to demonstrate that the innovative system has potential for industry-wide application. Further, this waiver is only good for two years, so Acme would only be temporarily excused from compliance. Acme has a strong chance of success with this variance because as indicated the experimental technology available to Acme presently would only take up to two years to implement. Assuming Acme widget company operates in a similar manner to other widget companies, Acme may be successful in being awarded this variance.

Both the economic inability variance under FWPCA §301(c) and the water quality variance under FWPCA §301(g) are unavailable to Acme because the contested regulation designated goo as a conventional water pollutant. These variances apply to other types of pollutants.

## SAMPLE ANSWER TO QUESTION 4:

### *Opinion of the Circuit Court of Appeals*

At issue first is whether plaintiffs satisfied the prudential standing limitations for the court to appropriately adjudicate their claim. Plaintiffs must be able to establish that they have a personal stake in the outcome. In order to have appropriate standing, plaintiffs must satisfy the APA's standing requirements established in 5 U.S.C. §702: a final agency action; adverse effect on the plaintiff; and last the zone of interest test.

The final agency action requirement considers the ripeness of the suit and whether the agency action falls within the parameters of APA §551. Plaintiffs assert that the government's decision to maintain two reservoirs at a particular minimum level pursuant to its findings in a prepared biological opinion is a final agency action. Plaintiffs support their argument stating that the government's decision to act constitutes a final agency action within the definition of agency action in APA §551(13). Section 551(13) incorporates the whole or part of an agency rule or order, including a failure to act. The contested government action is the preparation of the biological opinion. This action constitutes an agency action within the meaning of the statute; thus, the government has no further steps to take to complete its biological opinion.

Although Defendant argues that the opinion is not a final action because the government only accepted the opinion's recommendation but has not begun to implement it, this court holds that the completion of the opinion is a final agency action. Furthermore, if courts were estopped from adjudicating suits until the contested action was irreversibly completed, then the purpose of injunctive relief could never be served. Last, the precise action Plaintiffs are contesting is the preparation of the opinion, not the maintenance of a minimum reservoir water level.

The last consideration regarding final agency action is the policies of the ripeness doctrine. Plaintiffs argue that the issue is ripe for litigation because they would suffer a hardship, loss of use of the reservoir, if a resolution was delayed. This litigation will not constitute an untimely interference with the agency's work as the opinion and the decision to accept the opinion are formulated. The government suffers no apparent hardship by delaying implementation of its plan, with the possible exception of the potential damage to the two species of fish. However, this risk is low, as the biological opinion gives no sense of immediacy of endangerment to the fish, stating only that long term operation of the reservoir might damage the fish. Finally, this is not premature litigation because the contested procedure is completed, thus allowing the court to fully evaluate it. In balancing these ripeness doctrine policies, this claim appears to be fit for adjudication as a final agency action.

The second APA standing requirement is a demonstration that Plaintiffs are adversely affected or aggrieved. Plaintiff argues that the ESA's decision will compromise or harm their use of the reservoir water for commercial and recreational purposes. This harm must at least be imminent but not necessarily current. Also, Plaintiffs' harm must be particular to them. Plaintiffs satisfy the so-called user test because plaintiffs' use of the reservoir will be negatively impacted by curtailing their recreational and commercial use. This negative impact is a result of the contested biological opinion.

The last APA standing requirement is the zone of interests test, which is a prudential limit on standing. The zone of interest test requires that the plaintiffs' stated interest be arguably within the class of interest that the statute was intended to protect. Plaintiff reminds the court that the zone of interest test is in most circumstances easily satisfied, as demonstrated by *Clarke v. Securities Industry Ass'n*, which held that Plaintiffs were within the zone of interest unless their interest was only marginally related to the statute. Plaintiffs contend that their interest in ensuring that the proper procedure is met in determining a water level which could affect endangered animals is within the zone of interests of the Endangered Species Act. Plaintiffs state that their interest in showing that the government failed to follow §1533(b)(2) by not considering the economic impact and not balancing the commercial benefits of excluding the reservoir from critical habitat status against the harm to the threatened species is relevant to the statute.

Defendants profess that Plaintiffs' asserted claim seeks only to guard against an injury to their commercial use of the reservoir and these interests are not within the zone of interest of the Endangered Species Act (ESA). The Endangered Species Act's purpose as delineated in §1531 is to provide the means to preserve ecosystems on which endangered and or threatened species depend. The congressional intent in creating the statute was to hold the goal of animal preservation as a paramount interest over economic growth.

This court holds that Plaintiffs' commercial interests do not comport with the class of interest the statute seeks to protect. Plaintiffs' claim simply cannot be reconciled with the ESA's purpose clearly set out in §1531(b) & (c). Addressing Plaintiffs' argument, while an economic interest may be a balancing factor in determining whether to make an area a critical habitat, an economic interest still does not speak to the relevant meaning of the statute: protecting endangered animals and their ecosystems. Plaintiffs fail the zone of interest test.

The Endangered Species Act's citizen suit provision grants private citizens an expressed cause of action to sue the government to enforce the government's compliance with the congressionally mandated purpose and policy. Plaintiffs attempt to argue that this express citizen suit overrides prudential limitations on standing. Private citizens may bring suit for injunctive relief under ESA §11(g).

Again, Plaintiffs have not asserted an interest in preserving endangered animals. Implicit in the zone of interest test is each individual statute's citizen suit expressed cause of action. The zone of interest test demands that the best suited claim come before the court in efforts to maximize judicial economy. A well situated claim is one which claims a harm that the citizen suit is designed to address. In this sense the two work together, thus neither overrides or limits the other.

The court will now consider the merit of plaintiffs' allegation that the biology opinion was prepared in a procedurally improper manner. The government's biological report designated a critical habitat under the Endangered Species Act. The first issue is whether designating a critical habitat is within the agency's scope of authority. It clearly was as set forth in 16 U.S.C. §1536(a)(2), which explicitly requires due consideration of all things which affect endangered species. The applicable language of the statute reads:

> Each Federal agency shall . . . insure that any action authorized . . . or carried out by such agency . . . is not likely to jeopardize the continued existence of any endangered species.

As the government's action was within its scope of authority, the court must assess whether the biological report's decision was made after considering the relevant factors and with no clear error. The plaintiff argues that neither an EA nor an EIS was prepared as dictated by NEPA in its action-forcing clause in §102(2)(c). The action-forcing clause states that federal actions which significantly affect the quality of the environment require an Environmental Impact Statement (EIS). Defendant's action would clearly fall under the EIS requirement, however, procedurally a full EIS does not have to be prepared under NEPA regulations if the preliminary assessment the EA determines that a full EIS is unnecessary.

Plaintiffs argue that the biological report cannot be substituted for an EIS or EA. Defendant asserts that its agency did not need to meet the EIS obligation because an EIS conflicts with the Endangered Species Act statutory obligations. Defendants cite to *Flint Ridge v. Scenic Rivers Ass'n* to support its proposition. Defendant explains that its obligations under the ESA make it impossible to fully comply with the NEPA requirements and that *Flint Ridge* held that the NEPA requirements then become secondary.

Defendant's alternative argument regarding an exemption is that its biological opinion as prepared under the guidance of the ESA's provisions in §1536(b)(3)(A) and with consultation to §1536(a)(2) adequately serves as a functional equivalent to NEPA's §102(2)(C) procedural requirements, and, therefore, the government is exempted from the NEPA regulations. This court finds that the government is exempted from following NEPA's EIS requirements under the functional equivalent exemption if the ESA procedure adequately replaces the NEPA procedures.

Plaintiff argues that the government's report lacks supporting evidence to support its conclusion. As dictated by *Overton Park*, the defendant's procedural compliance is reviewable with an arbitrary and capricious standard because the government's action is an "everything else" or an informal adjudication. The Court looks solely at if the government made no clear error in making its habitat determination "from the record." Plaintiff seems to want the court to include its own post-decision and ad hoc theories by claiming that there is evidence which contradicts the biological report. We will not entertain Plaintiffs' assertion regarding contradictory evidence because under *Vermont Yankee* and *Robertson v. Methow* procedural requirements are purely precatory; thus, the court has no authority to review the report's substance. Indeed, under these constructs, the government's decision was based on the relevant factors set out in the biology report and there is no clear error in the record, as the Court is obligated to give deference to the government agency's expertise and technological experience in determining if the scientific or "hard data" included in the report is adequate.

Finally, this court must determine whether the government's decision followed the relevant procedure. As stated above, the biology opinion is standing in place of traditional EIS as formulated by NEPA. This determination can be made by ensuring that the biological report's scope was consistent with the scope of an EIS.

The scope of an EIS is dictated by the action and the action's purpose. The action in question is whether to maintain minimum water levels of a reservoir to uphold the purpose of protecting two endangered species. There is no issue that a comprehensive report needs to be completed, because this is a single, independent decision, and not a connected, cumulative or same action decision. Therefore, this court will discuss this.

To be comparable to an EIS, the scope of the report needs to include alternatives, no-action alternatives, and mitigation measures. Finally, a procedurally complete report comporting with EIS requirements will consider the direct effects, indirect effects, and cumulative impacts of both the alternatives and the proposed action. Effects include ecological, aesthetic, and economic, among others. Plaintiffs contest that the biological report as a substitute for an EA ought to have considered the positive effect of their proposed action on the economy and commercial businesses. However, social and economic effects do not trigger an EIS. *Metro Edison* narrowed the scope of what constitutes an environmental effect and confirmed the exclusion of economic effects in determining whether an EIS is needed. Under the *Metro Edison* rule, a report comparable to an EIS is not necessary.

The alternatives that need to be discussed are subject to *Morton*'s Rule of Reason; thus, not every conceivable alternative must be included. The government biology report satisfies these requirements. Plaintiff argues that the government did not consider the no-action alternative. The court finds that the biological report did consider the no-action alternative because it discussed the impact of no action in its conclusion that "long-term operation jeopardizes . . . ."

Further, the government appears to have gone beyond its procedural requirements. While under NEPA, a conceptual list of mitigation possibilities need only be included in the report. The government has gone one step further to include a substantive mitigation plan, *i.e.*, to maintain the minimum lake level. This should be commended. Thus the government fully addressed the primary alternatives in considering plans which are different from the proposal itself.

From the record, it appears that the government followed the relevant procedure in making its decision under the ESA and NEPA.

## SAMPLE ANSWER TO QUESTION 5:

MEMORANDUM

**TO:** Client "WOW" We Ogle Whales
**FR:** Attorney's Desk
**RE:** The likelihood of a successful claim challenging the validity of the regulatory definition of harass

The merits of a claim contesting the validity of the regulatory meaning assigned to "harass" is appropriately assessed by contrasting it to the challenge to the statutory definition of "harm" in *Babbitt v. Sweet Home*. Based on the statutory construction analysis used in *Sweet Home*, including Justice Stevens' majority opinion, Justice Scalia's dissent and Justice O'Connor's concurrence, this suit challenging "harass" has a good chance of success on the substantive merits of the claim.

In applying Justice Stevens' statutory construction analysis, "harass" could be found to be a valid interpretation. Reasonableness is the appropriate standard to which the DOI's interpretation must comply as dictated by the *Chevron* court. The *Chevron* court held that Congress delegates broad interpretative power to government agencies by expressly authorizing the agency to regulate a specific statute such as the Endangered Species Act (ESA). With this Congressional grant of authority, an agency's interpretation of a statute and its terms is entitled to deference when the statute is silent or ambiguous. An agency is given deference because of the agency's presumed expertise and technological knowledge. The DOI's interpretation of "harass" (50 C.F.R. §17.3) is entitled to deference and must meet the reasonableness standard because Congress provided the DOT the authority to regulate the ESA in 16 U.S.C. §1533 and throughout the Act.

The DOI's interpretation of "harass" meets the standard of reasonableness. Applying the *Chevron* standard, the ESA does not define "harass"; therefore, the DOI has leave to interpret it. The DOI's definition comports with the general meaning of the other terms used in ESA §3(19) to define "take." The definition does not contradict the purpose of the statute, which is to preserve the ecosystem of endangered species delineated in ESA §2. As defined, "harass" will prevent the intentional or unintentional disruption of an endangered species ability to breed, eat, or seek shelter, without which a species' well-being is threatened. This line of reasoning also supports the construct that the DOI's interpretation is consistent with the broad purpose of the statute.

The congressional intent of the statute is an underlying factor in determining the validity of the ''harass'' interpretation. As stated, the DOI's interpretation advances the broad purpose of the ESA by extending protection to animals against activities that cause the precise harms Congress enacted the statute to avoid. Therefore, Congress necessarily intended to give the term ''take'' an expansive meaning and the use of ''harass'' as defined extends the meaning of ''take'' to include indirect takings.

Next, Stevens looks to the ordinary meaning of the term to weigh the appropriateness of the interpretation. If the contested word's ordinary meaning is how the word is understood to apply to the statute, then the agency interpretation is reasonable. The ordinary meaning is found in dictionaries or is the commonly understood meaning of a word. The ordinary meaning of ''harass'' is to annoy persistently or to worry something or someone. The ordinary meaning of ''harass'' is a reasonable approximation as to how ''harass'' is defined in 50 C.F.R. §17.3 and employed in §3(19). The ordinary meaning implies that both direct or indirect actions may constitute harassment and that is how the DOI interprets the term.

Under the construct of no surplusage, ''harass'' as used to define ''take'' can be validated. No surplusage holds that a word in a list of words serves no purpose unless it has an independent meaning and is not duplicative. The DOI's use of ''harass'' maintains an independent meaning because it endorses indirect and nonphysical injuries and actions, whereas the remainder of the words all have direct, physical qualities. Conversely, the no surplusage construct could also invalidate ''harass.'' The term ''harass'' as defined in §17.3 holds no independent meaning from harm. Annoying to the point of ''significantly disrupting normal behavior patterns'' is harming. Further, any harm that befalls an animal surely must be annoying or harassing. Thus, the §17.3 interpretation could be deemed invalid because it bears no independent meaning and consequently does not serve a purpose in the act.

Stevens would use the stated purpose of the ESA to uphold the DOI's interpretation of ''harass.'' ESA §2 states the purpose of the act by indicating that the preservation of endangered species is of paramount interest over economic growth and development. Moreover, the legislative history of the ESA shows that Congress, by enacting ESA amendments, has increasingly strengthened the ESA, thus demonstrating Congress' dedication to its declared purpose. The DOI's term ''harass,'' by incorporating indirect takings furthers Congress' purpose by enlarging the term ''take.'' Justice Stevens endorsed this view of the ESA's legislative history in *TVA v. Hill.*

The court also could validate ''harass'' by exercising the Congressional Ratification Theory. This theory carries an implied presumption that the Congress is aware of the Court's decisions and implicitly accepts the Court's interpretation of a statute by not enacting contradictory amendments. In *Babbitt v. Sweet Home,* the Court determined that the DOI's definition of ''harm,'' which included direct and indirect effects (for example a harm to the habitat), was a reasonable interpretation. If Congress opposed taking to include indirect takings or effects such as by omissions and annoyances, it would then have passed legislature to correct the Court's decision. Congress did not do so, thus, ''harass,'' which includes indirect effects, is implicitly accepted as an appropriate interpretation.

Last, in support of the validity of ''harass,'' the court will look to statutory context and the interplay of different sections of the ESA statute. ESA §10 authorizes the government to grant incidental takings permits to allow citizens, government, and business to legally act in a manner that would otherwise constitute a prohibited taking under ESA §9(a)(l)(B). This demonstrates that Congress understood that ESA §9 prohibited all takings, both direct and indirect. Otherwise, the incidental takings permits for indirect takings would be unnecessary. Therefore, to give effect to ESA §10, ''take'' must include indirect takings like ''harass,'' again validating the DOI's interpretation.

''Harass'' as set out in ESA §3, serves to define ''take.'' The term ''take'' is used in ESA §9 to delineate expressly prohibited acts by any person or government in order to protect endangered species. The DOI's definitional interpretation is consistent with ESA §9. Section 9 applies to private persons as well as public entities. Even with a broad definition of "harass" being applied to §9, ESA §5 and §7 still have independent purposes. ESA §5 is the land acquisition authorization allowing the federal government to protect habitats before any damage can occur, whereas under §9 the government may not enforce protection until after the harm has occurred. ESA §7 provides for habitat protection for which §9 does not expressly provide. Because "harass" is interpreted as broadening "take," §9 then serves to strengthen and support §§5 and 7. Overall, if the court, in considering WOW's claim objecting to "harass," applies a strict Stevens analysis of statutory construction, the court will uphold the DOI's interpretation of "harass."

Conversely, an evaluation of "harass" using Justice Scalia's approach in his *Sweet Home* dissent will invalidate the DOI interpretation. Through statutory construction, Scalia finds that "take" as defined in ESA §9 applies to direct or purposeful takings, not indirect takings, thus the DOI's definition necessarily is erroneous.

Scalia applies the concept of *noscitur a sociis* ("known by the company it keeps") which means that all the other words set out surrounding "harass" in ESA §3 must have a shade of meaning in common. The other terms, such as hunt, kill, trap, etc., are direct actions that result in an immediate injury to the endangered species. The concept presumes that statutes are repetitive to ensure clarity, thus, every word does not need to have a separate meaning. The rest of the words in §1532(19) all indicate an overt action: To shoot, to wound, to kill, to trap or to harm are direct physical harms which cannot be performed by omission or failure to act. Harass must be interpreted in a similar fashion so as to include the same definitional shade of meaning. Because all the other words in ESA §3 constitute direct takings, a reasonable definition of "harass" is "a direct injurious action." The definition in §17.3 gives "harass" a meaning that is contradictory to the rest of the words in the context. Section 17.3 describes "harass" as an omission. Further, "harass" as meaning "to annoy" is not a physical overt action, again a glaring inconsistency.

Further, the plain language of "take" connotes a physical act of capturing or taking possession of, not an indirect action. Its synonyms are to seize, grasp, clutch, or capture. The definition provided by the DOI of "harass" would lend an entirely different meaning not suggested by the plain meaning of "take." Courts always consider the plain language of a statute to determine the reasonableness of an agency interpretation. The plain language of "take" contradicts the DOI's definition of harass and thus invalidates it.

Scalia applies a textual approach to statutory interpretation. Textualism deems legislative history to be unimportant because of societal changes and because legislative history can be easily manipulated. A textualist approach does not consider a statute's legislative history in interpreting a statute.

Scalia considers the structure of the statute to determine the validity of an interpretation. Scalia's approach holds that one section of a statute should not be interpreted in such a way as to negate another section, nor should any section be redundant. If "harass" is defined as to include indirect takings through unintentional omissions that may affect the animal's habitat, then ESA §7's habitat protection language would be superfluous and redundant. Thus, "harass" must define "take" in a manner that does not include habitat protection language to avoid negating the purpose of that section's existence. Another example is if indirect takings through habitat modification is construed as part of ESA §9, then ESA §5 also becomes meaningless, because §9 would then adequately provide for the prevention of damage to endangered animals.

Lastly, "harass" as defined in §17.3 leads to a patently absurd result. Interpretations that lead to patently absurd results are disfavored. If any disruption or annoyance of an animal, even through disruption to its habitat, was prohibited, people would be afraid to leave their homes for fear of committing an unlawful activity with each step they took. The DOI is attempting to regulate acts that do not constitute actual injuries. This is a strong argument in favor of invalidating §17.3.

Justice O'Connor's analysis of agency interpretations would also lead to the invalidation of the ''harass'' definition. Based on her opinion in *Sweet Home*, O'Connor would hold that the acts or omissions that constitute ''harassing'' as defined by the DOI would have to lead to real harm to real animals with an obvious proximate cause to be a valid interpretation. While O'Connor finds an actual injury in any action or omission which could disturb breeding patterns, actual injury is contingent upon finding a resulting reduction in the animal population. The definition of ''harass'' states that the acts or omission must annoy to the point of significant disruption to the animal that would limit the animal's ability to breed, feed, or shelter. O'Connor would dismiss this definition as inappropriate because it does not provide for the final link to a proximate cause which results in an actual injury to the animal. The indirect meaning lent to ''harass'' does not constitute an actual injury, but only constitutes a potential injury. Furthermore, harassing through omission is not a physically demonstrative act. An omission leads to a future or potential effect on the animal, not an actual present injury as required. Therefore ''harass'' in §17.3 becomes too tenuous and overly broad.

In balancing the two arguments, most likely harass as defined in §17.3 will not be upheld. Justice O'Connor's analysis tips the balance in favor of rejecting the agency interpretation of ''harass.'' Obviously, ''harass'' as a term that incorporates indirect acts will lead to patently absurd results and appears inconsistent with the remainder of the statute. The recommendation to We Ogle Whales (WOW) is to proceed with the claim against the DOI's regulatory definition.

# Table of Cases

Principal discussion of a case is indicated by page numbers in *italics*.

# Table of Statutory Sections and Restatement References

**Code of Federal Regulations**

# Table of Conventions and Declarations

# Table of Acts

# Subject Matter Index